Illustrated History of Hymns and Their Authors

You are holding a reproduction of an original work that is in the public domain in the United States of America, and possibly other countries. You may freely copy and distribute this work as no entity (individual or corporate) has a copyright on the body of the work. This book may contain prior copyright references, and library stamps (as most of these works were scanned from library copies). These have been scanned and retained as part of the historical artifact.

This book may have occasional imperfections such as missing or blurred pages, poor pictures, errant marks, etc. that were either part of the original artifact, or were introduced by the scanning process. We believe this work is culturally important, and despite the imperfections, have elected to bring it back into print as part of our continuing commitment to the preservation of printed works worldwide. We appreciate your understanding of the imperfections in the preservation process, and hope you enjoy this valuable book.

Ab: Ken.

Illustrated History

OF

Hymns and their Authors.

FACTS AND INCIDENTS OF THE ORIGIN, AUTHORS,
SENTIMENTS AND SINGING OF HYMNS, WHICH,
WITH A SYNOPSIS, EMBRACE INTERESTING
ITEMS RELATING TO OVER EIGHT
HUNDRED HYMN-WRITERS.

With many portraits and other illustrations.

SECOND EDITION.

By Rev. Edwin M. Long,

Author of "Precious Hymns of Jesus," "Talks to Children," "Good News,"
"Work of Grace in the Hearts of the Young," etc.

PHILADELPHIA:
PUBLISHED BY P. W. ZIEGLER & CO.
518 ARCH STREET.

Entered, according to act of Congress, in the year 1876, by
EDWIN M. LONG,
In the Office of the Librarian of Congress, at Washington.

Music
Library

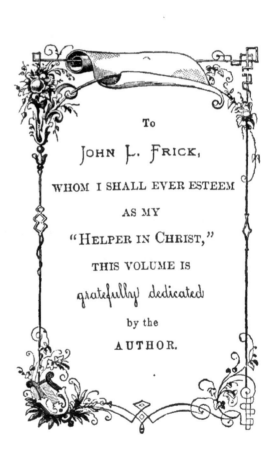

To
JOHN L. FRICK,
WHOM I SHALL EVER ESTEEM
AS MY
"HELPER IN CHRIST,"
THIS VOLUME IS
gratefully dedicated
by the
AUTHOR.

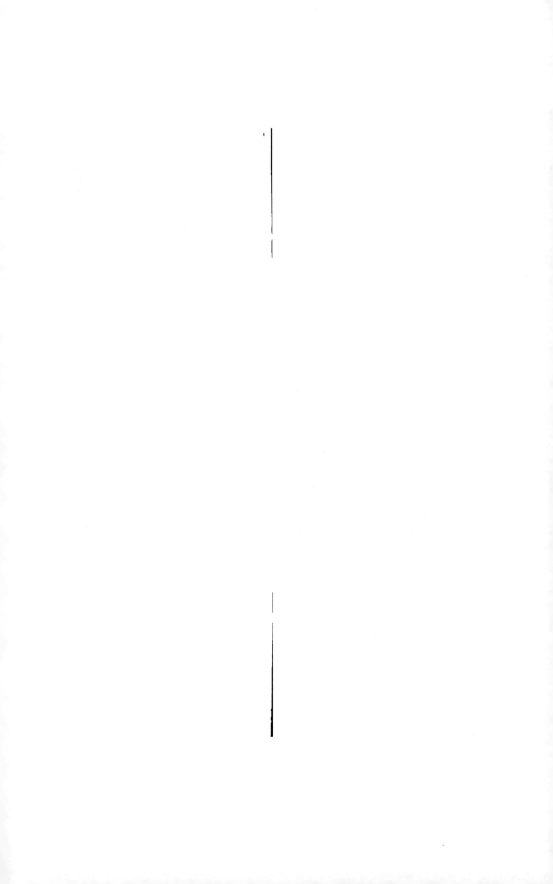

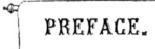

PREFACE.

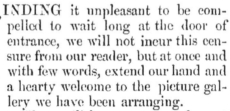

FINDING it unpleasant to be compelled to wait long at the door of entrance, we will not incur this censure from our reader, but at once and with few words, extend our hand and a hearty welcome to the picture gallery we have been arranging.

There will be seen many pleasant faces of old friends, whose hymns have become enshrined in our hearts' affections, and have so often sounded forth in our songs of praise.

At the entrance you will meet one whose face beams with a sweet meekness, and you will be glad to recognize in him, Bishop Ken, who, for nearly two centuries, has been teaching the world to

"Praise God, from whom all blessings flow."

Take a few steps along our gallery and the reader will meet the pensive face of one, whose ready pen sketched the immortal hymn:—

"There is a fountain filled with blood."

Near by will be perceived the noble and expressive

features of Doddridge, who, among his three hundred hymns, inserted the gem:—

"Grace, 'tis a charming sound."

If our reader loves

"———— to steal awhile away
From every cumbering care,"

the sight of Mrs. Phœbe H. Brown will surely be welcome, as well as Montgomery, who wrote that

"Prayer is the soul's sincere desire,
Uttered or unexpressed."

Those who for a life time have been wont to hear the oft-repeated words,—

"Come, thou Fount of every blessing,
Tune my heart to sing thy grace,"

will be glad to form the acquaintance of its author, Robert Robinson.

Those whose heavenly home-sickness has caused them oft to sing the hymn,—

"On Jordan's stormy banks I stand,
And cast a wishful eye,"

will not be reluctant to be introduced to its writer.

Then we meet the full German face of Gerhardt, who has banished many a mourner's tear by the solace afforded in his precious hymn:—

"Commit thou all thy griefs
And ways into his hands."

Passing along we meet one whose cheerful and intelligent expression of countenance at once finds way into our hearts, one whose grand missionary hymn has been sung

"From Greenland's icy mountains,
To India's coral strand."

If our reader can say with the psalmist, "a day in thy courts is better than a thousand," he will gladly welcome Dr. Dwight, the author of "I Love thy kingdom, Lord."

Near by his side sits one who has helped many a hesitating sinner into the kingdom, by teaching him to say,

"Just as I am, without one plea,
But that thy blood was shed for me."

Farther along is one whose lips were wont to say, and whose pen has taught the world to sing:—

"How sweet the name of Jesus sounds."

The early forests of America gave birth to one whose Indian face will be seen among the group. One who was

"Awaked by Sinai's awful sound,"

and then told the story in a hymn that God's children have ever since loved to repeat, as expressive of their own experience.

"India's coral strand" has darkened the face of another, who has united with the blood bought throng in saying,

"O Thou, my soul forget no more
The friend who all thy sorrows bore."

Passing thus along in alphabetical order, we meet the revered countenance of the "Father of Modern Hymnology," and gazing upon his pleasant features, we wonder why the object of his affection should have marred the serenity of that face, by saying, that while she loved the "jewel, she did not admire the casket." Certainly those who love to linger on Calvary's mount, will ever cherish the name of him, who in our devotions enables us to exclaim:—

"Alas! and did my Saviour bleed?
And did my Sovereign die?"

and then to add:—

"When I survey the wondrous cross,
On which the Prince of glory died,
My richest gain I count but loss,
And pour contempt on all my pride."

Near to Watts will be seen the cheerful face of one

who ranks with him in hymnic honor, one to whom the world is indebted for—

"Jesus, lover of my soul,
Let me to thy bosom fly."

Next to Charles Wesley comes the beaming countenance of his brother, John, whose voice is still echoing in his hymn to perishing sinners:—

"Ho! every one that thirsts, draw nigh."

While passing thus around the circle, the reader will not fail to pause long enough to gaze upon the youthful face of Henry Kirk White, who rode "once upon the raging seas" of doubt and fear, and then when "safely moored" sang so sweetly of his rescue in

"The Star—the Star of Bethlehem."

The reader will no doubt be gratified to find Lady Huntingdon among the group; one who has gained a world-wide reputation by her gifts and graces, and as the author of that heart searching hymn that propounds the solemn question:—

"When thou, my righteous Judge, shalt come
To take thy ransomed people home,
Shall I among them stand?"

The interest that clusters around the romantic history of Madame Guyon will invite attention to her countenance, so meek and mild, and awaken desires to become better acquainted with her hymns, that still form a part of the songs of the sanctuary.

It will be needless to accompany the reader any further in words of introduction to such hymn-writers as the noble hearted Zinzendorf, the saintly Baxter, the eccentric Berridge and the heroic Luther, with many others whose portraits beautify our gallery; as they are "old enough to speak for themselves."

In the preparation of this work, we have been aided, in the synopsis and in other particulars, by our friend, Mr. Francis Jennings, who may be fitly denominated, a walking encyclopedia of hymnology. He is a native of British soil, around which cluster the most interesting associations of hymn history. Having devoted half a century in treasuring up dates and facts, it is no wonder, that, while his locks are becoming silvered with the frosts of many winters, his life-long zeal in this department remains unabated.

We have also received favors, which we would gratefully acknowledge, from Rev. F. M. Bird, Rev. Dr. E. F. Hatfield, Rev. H. Sheeleigh, David Creamer, Esq., and Mr. Philip Cressman.

To Mr. Asa Hull, author of "The Golden Sheaf," and other choice music books, we are also indebted for services rendered in harmonizing some of the music contained in this volume.

Of English publications on hymnology, that we have found serviceable, we may mention the following: "Singers and Songs of the Church," by Josiah Miller, M. A.; "Hymn-writers and their Hymns," by Rev. S. W. Christophers; "The Methodist Hymn Book and its Associations," by G. J. Stevenson; "Historical Notes to the Lyra Germanica," by Theodore Kubler. Of American issues: "Historical Sketches of Hymns," by Joseph Belcher, D. D.; "Evenings with the Sacred Poets," by Frederick Saunders; and "Trophies of Song," by Rev. W. F. Crafts.

We have been highly favored in opportunities for gathering material for a book of this kind, as we have been brought into contact with so many pastors and others, who have furnished facts and incidents, fresh from their observation and experiences. During the past fifteen years, in the delivery of courses of Illustrated Sermons, and in other evangelistic labors, it has been our privilege to preach in over six hundred churches, in nineteen states of the Union, among twelve different denominations, and in the German as well as the English language.

With the abundance of matter on hand, for which we cannot find room in the present volume, we have arranged, Providence permitting, to go on immediately in the preparation of a second work to embrace mainly historical sketches of the hymns and hymn-writers of the present century, as well as the origin, singing, and authors of children's hymns and Sunday school songs. It will be of the same size, and illustrated with as many portraits and other engravings, as this book. Many of the portraits are already engraved, while others are in course of preparation.

As there are constantly new facts and incidents transpiring, connected with the singing of hymns, we have occasionally introduced floral letters, and in other ways have arranged our material in order to have all articles end with the bottom of the page, so that other pages can easily be inserted in other editions of this work. We shall be very grateful to any of our readers, if they can furnish us with any additional material for this book, or with any incidents or facts suited to our second volume. Communications to be sent to 1859 N. 12th Street Philadelphia Pa.

June 1875.   E. M. L.

Engravings.

(THE STEEL ENGRAVINGS ARE INDICATED BY AN ASTERISK. *)

PORTRAIT OF THOMAS KEN. *...................................FRONTISPIECE.
    Author of "Praise God, from whom all blessings flow."
PORTRAIT OF HENRY ALFORD..35
    Author of "Come, ye thankful people, come."
PORTRAIT OF RICHARD BAXTER. *.......................................43
    Author of "Lord, it belongs not to my care."
BAXTER BEFORE JEFFRIES..49
PORTRAIT OF JOHN BERRIDGE...59
    Author of "O happy saints who dwell in light."
PORTRAIT OF HORATIUS BONAR..67
    Author of "I heard the voice of Jesus say."
POTRAIT OF PHŒBE H. BROWN...75
    Author of "I love to steal a while away."
PORTRAIT OF PHŒBE CARY.*..85
    Author of "One sweetly solemn thought."
PORTRAIT OF WILLIAM COWPER..93
    Author of "There is a fountain filled with blood."
THE OLNEY COTTAGE PRAYER MEETING...................................103
COWPER AND HIS HARES...117
DODDRIDGE'S MOTHER TEACHING HIM FROM DUTCH TILES...................129
PORTRAIT OF PHIL'P DODDRIDGE. *....................................133
    Author of "Grace 'tis a charming sound."

PORTRAIT OF TIMOTHY DWIGHT*..151
    Author of "I love thy kingdom, Lord."
PORTRAIT OF CHARLOTTE ELLIOTT...157
    Author of "Just as I am, without one plea."
PORTRAIT OF JOHN FAWCETT...167
    Author of "Blest be the tie that binds."
PORTRAIT OF PAUL GERHARDT..173
    Author of "Commit thou all thy griefs."
PORTRAIT OF MADAME GUYON...185
    Author of "I would love thee, God and Father."
PORTRAIT OF HENRY HARBAUGH..191
    Author of "Jesus, I live to thee."
PORTRAIT OF REGINALD HEBER*...203
    Author of "From Greenland's icy mountains."
VIEW OF GREENLAND'S ICY MOUNTAINS....................................209
PORTRAIT OF ROWLAND HILL...213
    Author of "Cast thy burden on the Lord."
ROWLAND HILL'S SURREY CHAPEL...217
PORTRAIT OF LADY HUNTINGDON*...221
    Author of "When thou, my righteous Judge, shalt come."
HUSS SINGING IN THE FLAMES OF MARTYRDOM........................231
PORTRAIT OF ADONIRAM JUDSON*...235
    Author of "Our Father God, who art in heaven."
PORTRAIT OF JOHN KEBLE..241
    Author of "Sun of my soul, thou Saviour dear."
PORTRAIT OF THOMAS KEN...245
    Author of "Praise God, from whom all blessings flow."
CHURCH ALONG SIDE OF AND THE TOMB IN WHICH KEN WAS BURIED 249
PORTRAIT OF MARTIN LUTHER*..263
    Author of "All praise to thee, eternal Lord."
LUTHER SINGING IN THE STREETS..267
THE CASTLE OF COBURG...271
PORTRAIT OF SAMUEL MEDLEY...281
    Author of "Awake my soul in joyful lays."
PORTRAIT OF JAMES MONTGOMERY*..291
    Author of "O where shall rest be found."
MONTGOMERY'S RESIDENCE*...295

PORTRAIT OF JOHN NEWTON..307
    Author of "How sweet the name of Jesus sounds."
MONICA WATCHING AUGUSTINE'S DEPARTURE.........................314
PORTRAIT OF SAMSON OCCOM..324
    Author of "Awaked by Sinai's awful sound."
PORTRAIT OF KRISHNA PAL..331
    Author of "O thou my soul forget no more."
PORTRAIT OF ROBERT ROBINSON..345
    Author of "Come, thou Fount of every blessing."
PORTRAIT OF JOHN RYLAND...351
    Author of "O Lord, I would delight in Thee."
PORTRAIT OF HANS SACHS..355
    Author of "Why vail thy self in gloom, my heart?"
RESIDENCE OF ANNE STEEL...360
PORTRAIT OF SAMUEL STENNETT.......................................367
    Author of "On Jordan's stormy banks I stand."
PORTRAIT OF AUGUSTUS TOPLADY......................................381
    Author of "Rock of ages! cleft for me."
ABNEY HOUSE WHERE WATTS LIVED AND DIED........................388
PORTRAIT OF ISAAC WATTS *...401
    Author of "Alas! and did my Saviour bleed."
MONUMENT TO WATTS...405
A SCENE IN AN ILLUSTRATED SERMON..................................427
PORTRAIT OF CHARLES WESLEY *.......................................435
    Author of "Jesus, lover of my soul."
SINGING ON A SINKING VESSEL..443
"THE SEA"..450
A YOUNG MAN SUNG TO CHRIST..457
PORTRAIT OF JOHN WESLEY *..479
    Author of "How happy is the pilgrim's lot."
PORTRAIT OF HENRY KIRK WHITE......................................487
    Author of "When marshaled on the nightly plain."
THE CLOUDY PILLAR LEADING THE HOSTS OF ISRAEL.................490
PORTRAIT OF NICHOLAS ZINZENDORF...................................499
    Author of "Jesus, thy blood and righteousness."
CHURCH SINGING IN OLDEN TIMES.....................................509

CONTENTS.

Addison and his hymns..25
"Sing and pray, eternity dawns"..................................28
Sarah F. Adams, and "Nearer, my God, to thee"..........29
A blind girl's application of "Nearer, my God, to thee"..........30
Draw me Saviour nearer..32
Alford and his hymns..34
King Alfred and his hymns..40
Baxter and his hymns..42
Baxter's hymns illustrated before an Indian Massacre..................52
Beddome, author of "Did Christ o'er sinners weep"..................54
Bernard's hymn 700 years old..56
Berridge and his hymns..58
Bonar and his hymns..66
Bonar's hymn, "As meant for me"..71
   " " "I was a wandering sheep"..72
   " " Sung to a weary teacher..73
Origin of "I love to steal awhile away"..74
Phœbe H. Brown and her hymns..77
A little girl stealing away to Jesus..81
A captive girl recovered by a hymn..82
Phœbe Cary, author of "One sweetly solemn thought"..................84
Gamblers reclaimed by Miss Cary's hymn..86
Cennick, author of "Jesus my all to heaven is gone"..................90
"Now will I tell to sinners round"..91
Cowper and his hymns..92

Cowper's conversion and hymns relating thereto......96
Origin of Cowper's second hymn......98
Cowper's Olney hymns......100
Birth-place of "There is a fountain filled with blood"......102
Illustrations of Cowper's hymns......108
Diversions of Cowper......116
Origin of "God moves in a mysterious way"......120
Davies and his hymns......122
Singing in time of peril......123
Midnight echo of "Home, sweet home"......125
Singing the heart open......126
Conquered by song......127
Doddridge and his hymns......128
Singing of "O happy day"......143
A hymn of one word......145
A revival started by singing a hymn......146
Heaven as represented in song......147
Origin of "Stand up! stand up for Jesus"......148
Dr. Dwight author of "I love thy kingdom, Lord"......150
Singing in a forsaken church......153
      "   heard in the wilderness......154
A prisoner singing himself into liberty......155
Miss Elliott and her hymns......156
"O sir, I've come, I've come"......161
"Just as I am" uttered with a dying breath......162
The young chorister's last hymn......164
Fawcett and his hymns......166
Origin of "Blest be the tie that binds"......170
A sweet hymn born in sorrow......172
Paul Gerhardt and his hymns......175
Relief brought while singing......178
"Relief in Jesus illustrated"......179
A popular hymn written by a boy ten years old......180
Grigg and "Behold a stranger at the door"......181
Gustavus's battle-hymn......182
Hymns upon the battle field......183
Madame Guyon and her hymns......184

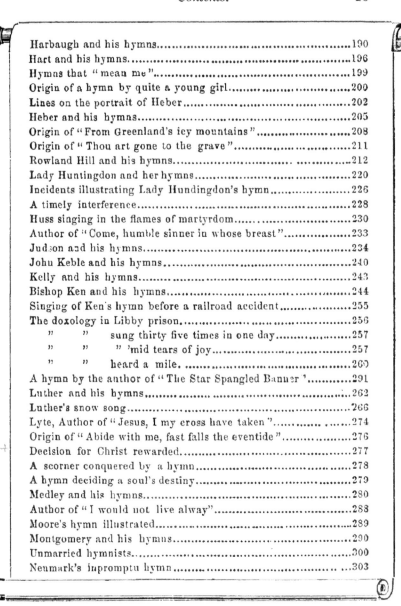

Harbaugh and his hymns	190
Hart and his hymns	196
Hymns that "mean me"	199
Origin of a hymn by quite a young girl	200
Lines on the portrait of Heber	202
Heber and his hymns	205
Origin of "From Greenland's icy mountains"	208
Origin of "Thou art gone to the grave"	211
Rowland Hill and his hymns	212
Lady Huntingdon and her hymns	220
Incidents illustrating Lady Hundingdon's hymn	226
A timely interference	228
Huss singing in the flames of martyrdom	230
Author of "Come, humble sinner in whose breast"	233
Judson and his hymns	234
John Keble and his hymns	240
Kelly and his hymns	243
Bishop Ken and his hymns	244
Singing of Ken's hymn before a railroad accident	255
The doxology in Libby prison	256
" " sung thirty five times in one day	257
" " " 'mid tears of joy	257
" " heard a mile	260
A hymn by the author of "The Star Spangled Banner"	291
Luther and his hymns	262
Luther's snow song	266
Lyte, Author of "Jesus, I my cross have taken"	274
Origin of "Abide with me, fast falls the eventide"	276
Decision for Christ rewarded	277
A scorner conquered by a hymn	278
A hymn deciding a soul's destiny	279
Medley and his hymns	280
Author of "I would not live alway"	288
Moore's hymn illustrated	289
Montgomery and his hymns	290
Unmarried hymnists	300
Neumark's inpromptu hymn	303

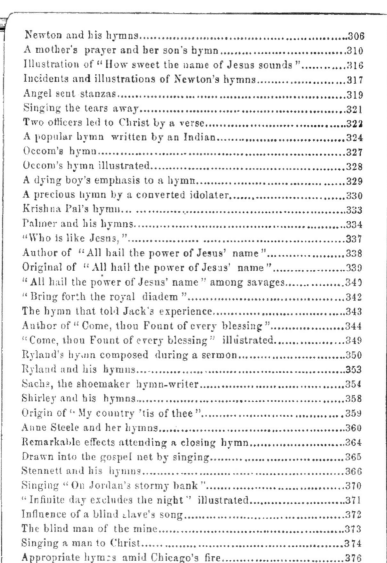

Newton and his hymns	306
A mother's prayer and her son's hymn	310
Illustration of "How sweet the name of Jesus sounds"	316
Incidents and illustrations of Newton's hymns	317
Angel sent stanzas	319
Singing the tears away	321
Two officers led to Christ by a verse	322
A popular hymn written by an Indian	324
Occom's hymn	327
Occom's hymn illustrated	328
A dying boy's emphasis to a hymn	329
A precious hymn by a converted idolater	330
Krishna Pal's hymn	333
Palmer and his hymns	334
"Who is like Jesus,"	337
Author of "All hail the power of Jesus' name"	338
Original of "All hail the power of Jesus' name"	339
"All hail the power of Jesus' name" among savages	340
"Bring forth the royal diadem"	342
The hymn that told Jack's experience	343
Author of "Come, thou Fount of every blessing"	344
"Come, thou Fount of every blessing" illustrated	349
Ryland's hymn composed during a sermon	350
Ryland and his hymns	353
Sachs, the shoemaker hymn-writer	354
Shirley and his hymns	358
Origin of "My country 'tis of thee"	359
Anne Steele and her hymns	360
Remarkable effects attending a closing hymn	364
Drawn into the gospel net by singing	365
Stennett and his hymns	366
Singing "On Jordan's stormy bank"	370
"Infinite day excludes the night" illustrated	371
Influence of a blind slave's song	372
The blind man of the mine	373
Singing a man to Christ	374
Appropriate hymns amid Chicago's fire	376

Contents.

"That sweet music"	377
Tennent, and the music he heard while in a trance	378
Toplady, author of "Rock of Ages"	380
Alterations in "Rock of Ages"	384
A babe hid in the cleft of a rock	386
A man saved by a cleft in a rock	387
"Rock of ages" uttered with Prince Albert's dying breath	388
Singing of "Rock of Ages" by fifty operatives	389
"Rock of ages" floating over a field of death	390
"Rock of ages" drowning rowdy songs	391
Clinging close to the rock	392
The clefts in the rock	393
"Rock of ages" illustrated	394
A new version of "Rock of ages" by Ray Palmer	395
Isaac Watts	396
Abney house where Watts lived and died	399
The monument of Watts	404
Origin of "How vain are all things here below"	407
Origin of Watt's first hymn	408
Origin of "There is a land of pure delight"	408
Effects of singing "Give me the wings of faith to rise"	409
A heart broken by a hymn	410
Hymns upon the battle field	412
Hymns making a bloody impression	413
Illustrations of "Not all the blood of beasts."	414
Conversion through the illustration of a hymn	415
"My faith would lay her hand" illustrated	416
A pirate vessel driven away by the singing of Watts' hymn	417
The closed lips	418
A singular coincidence	419
Illustrations of "Alas! and did my Saviour bleed"	420
Watts' hymn illustrated	421
"Here, Lord, I give myself away" illustrated	422
"A guilty, weak and helpless worm" illustrated	423
"Love so amazing, so divine" illustrated	424
Singing lies	425
A hymn illustrated while it was being sung	426

Illustrations of "Come, Holy Spirit heavenly dove" 429
A hymn that a church refused to sing 430
A hymn that woke up the sleepers 431
Different illustrations of Watts' hymns 432
Xerxes illustrating "And must this body die" 433
Charles Wesley and his hymns 434
Charles Wesley's last hymn 437
Origin of "O for a thousand tongues to sing" 438
"A charge to keep I have" illustrated by its author 439
Origin of "Jesus lover of my soul" 440
"Jesus lover of my soul" sung on a sinking vessel 442
Dr. Cuyler's use of "Jesus lover of my soul" 445
A mother floating out at sea singing "Jesus lover of soul" 446
Singing an enemy away 447
"Jesus lover of my soul" in a hurricane 448
The last hymn on a wrecked vessel 449
"Like the sea" 450
Singing as death's "billows near me roll" 452
The drummer boy's last hymn 454
Effects of singing "Jesus lover of my soul" 456
Dr. Beecher's last utterance of "Jesus lover of my soul" 460
An accident the occasion of a hymn 461
Cross bearing in song 462
An actress and "Depth of mercy" 464
Origin of "Come, thou all victorious Lord" 465
Wesley's hymn in an alley 466
The death song of a murdered Christian 468
A mob occasioning a hymn 469
Origin of "Lo! on a narrow neck of land" 470
Illustration of "Lo! on a narrow neck of land" 471
Passing away 472
A man dropping dead after the singing of a hymn 473
Eternal things impress 474
Illustration of "Give me the enlarged desire" 475
An evening funeral song 476
"Why I shall sing forever" 477
John Wesley and his hymns 478

Hymn sung by Wesley when dying	482
Wesley's hymn Illustrated by "Foolish Dick"	483
Wesley singing at the table	484
Singing around Mrs. Wesley's body the moment after death	485
Henry Kirk White and his hymns	486
William Williams and his hymns	490
Illustrations of "Guide me, O thou great Jehovah"	492
Singing Satan away	494
The name that makes "devils fear and fly"	495
Walford, author of "Sweet hour of prayer"	496
Xavier and his hymn	497
Zinzendorf and his hymns	498
Department of church singing and music	503
Churches opposed to singing	504
Singing in America two centuries ago	506
Old style hymnology	507
Church singing in olden times	508
A hymn illustrated by a choir leader	511
Expressive epitaph of a chorister	512
A hymn illustrated by a thunder storm	513
Incidents of the tune of Old Hundred	514
Hymns disjointed by fugue tunes	516
Massacre of church music	518
Choir difficulties	519
Solemn mockery in singing	520
Old Adam manifested in song	521
A clergyman in a fix	523
Inappropriate hymns	520
Roman Catholic hymns	526
The braying of an ass imitated in church song	527
A maniac subdued by the singing of a hymn	528
A life saved by singing	530
Saved by the attraction of music	531
Solomon's song	532
A ruffian charmed	533
The singing of Ira D. Sankey	534
Synopsis of hymn-writers	537-558

ILLUSTRATED HISTORY

OF

Hymns and their Authors.

Addison and his Hymns.

FIVE hymns have floated down the stream of time, during the past one hundred and sixty years, that have become so endeared to the people of God that scarcely any church hymn-book can be found without them. They are the production of the polished and refined pen of Addison. He was born at Milston, England, in 1672, and was the son of an Episcopal clergyman.

In early life he gave many evidences of a precocious intellect. A poem to King William, in 1695, and one in 1695, on the "Peace of Ryswick," procured him a pension of 300*l*. a year. With this pecuniary aid he was enabled in early manhood to extend his knowledge of the world by travel. While in this pursuit he met with many narrow escapes from death on sea and land. It is supposed, when in after years he glanced over these many dangers, he felt inspired to say, in the language of his well-known hymn,—

"When all thy mercies, O my God,
My rising soul surveys,
Transported with the view, I'm lost
In wonder, love and praise."

After publishing his travels and other works, he rose in popular favor till in 1717 he obtained the responsible position of Secretary of State.

His hymns were attached to articles written for *The Spectator*. The first of the immortal five appeared July 26, 1712, at the end of an essay on "Trust in God," in which he says: "The person who has a firm trust in the Supreme Being is powerful in His power, wise by His wisdom, happy by His happiness. He reaps the benefit of every Divine attribute, and loses his own insufficiency in the fulness of infinite perfection," which beautiful truths he sets forth in poetic form in his hymn:—

"The Lord my pasture shall prepare,
And feed me with a Shepherd's care,
His presence shall my wants supply,
And guard me with a watchful eye;
My noon-day walks he shall attend,
And all my midnight hours defend."

The following month, August 23, he sent forth his next hymn, attached to an article on "The right means to strengthen faith," in which he would lead us up to

"The spacious firmament on high,
With all the blue ethereal sky,"

and show us how the spangled heavens

"——utter forth a glorious voice;
For ever singing as they shine,—
The hand that made us is divine."

A month later, September 20, appeared a paper on

"The Sea," to which he afterwards added the hymn:—

"How are thy servants blessed, O Lord!
How sure is their defence."

It had originally ten verses. In one he beautifully says,

"The storm is laid, the winds retire,
Obedient to thy will;
The sea, that roars at thy command,
At thy command is still."

The last hymn appeared the month following, October 18, 1716. In the prose article that preceded, it is said, "Among all the reflections which usually arise in the mind of a sick man, who has time and inclination to consider his approaching end, there is none more natural than that of his going to appear naked and unbodied before Him, who made him."

"When, rising from the bed of death,
O'erwhelmed with guilt and fear,
I see my Maker face to face —
Oh! how shall I appear?"

When his dying hour drew near, it was with such calm composure that he could look ahead to the time when he should meet his "Maker face to face," that he sent for his step-son, the Earl of Warwick, saying with all the solemnity of death's surroundings, those ever memorable words:—"I have sent for you, that you may see how a Christian can die."

To this a poet thus refers:—

"He taught us how to live; and Oh! too high
The price of knowlege! taught us how to die."

He died at the Holland House, June 17, 1719. Although unable to finish his intended version of the Psalms, yet he can now fulfil his heart's desire as thus expressed in one of his hymns:—

"Through all eternity to thee
A joyful song I'll raise;
But oh! eternity's too short
To utter all thy praise."

"Sing and Pray, Eternity Dawns."

WHEN the Rev. Dr. Eddy was suddenly confronted with the idea, contained in Addison's hymn, of meeting his "Maker face to face," he could joyously answer the question:—

"Oh! how shall I appear?"

When, by medical advice, the unexpected news was first communicated to him, he welcomed it with great calmness. After adjusting his worldly affairs, "he marched rapidly to his end, a shouting victor all the way."

To Bishop Janes he remarked, "I am resting in Jesus, O *so* sweetly! A poor sinner saved by grace, but *saved*."

"Beyond the parting and the meeting,
I shall be soon.
Beyond the farewell and the greeting,
Beyond the pulse's fever beating,
I shall be soon."

As his weeping family gathered around his death-bed, he extended his hands over them, and pronounced the apostolic benediction.

His joyous countenance seemed to be lit up as with light streaming through the gates of the celestial city. In his ecstacy of joy he raised his trembling hands trying to clasp them, but unable to guide them in his weakness, they would pass each other while, with clear voice, he would sing out, "Hallelujah! Hallelujah!" His last words were, "Sing and pray, eternity dawns."

Thus amid the songs of earth, he passed to the hallelujahs above. Well may we say with Watts:—

"My willing soul would stay
In such a frame as this,
And sit and sing herself away
To everlasting bliss."

Author of "Nearer, my God, to Thee."

THIS language was the heart-utterance of Mrs. Sarah Flower Adams, daughter of Benjamin Flower, editor of *The Cambridge Intelligencer*, and wife of William B. Adams, an eminent engineer, and also a contributor to some of the principal newspapers and reviews.

She was born February 22, 1805.

Her mother is described as a lady of talent, as was her elder sister Eliza, who was also an authoress.

She was noted in early life for the taste she manifested for literature, and in maturer years, for great zeal and earnestness in her religious life, which is said to have produced a deep impression on those who met with her. Mr. Miller says: "The prayer of her own hymn, 'Nearer, my God, to Thee,' had been answered in her own experience. Her literary tastes extended in various directions. She contributed prose and poetry to the periodicals, and her art-criticisms were valued. She also wrote a Catechism for children, entitled 'The Flock at the Fountain' (1845). It is Unitarian in its sentiment, and is interspersed with hymns. She also wrote a dramatic poem, in five acts, on the martyrdom of 'Vivia Perpetua.' This was dedicated to her sister, in some touching verses. Her sister died of a pulmonary complaint in 1847, and attention to her in her affliction enfeebled her own health, and she also gradually wore away, 'almost her last breath bursting into unconscious song.'" Thus illustrating the last stanza:—

> "Sun, moon, and stars forgot,
> Upward I fly,
> Still all my song shall be,
> Nearer, my God, to Thee."

She died August 13, 1849, eight years after the issue of her popular hymn, and was buried in Essex, England.

A Blind Girl's Utterance of "Nearer my God."

WE condense a touching narrative as given by an anonymous writer. Ethel Bent had been for weeks stretched upon a sick bed, where she was brought nigh unto death. The disease had so affected her eyes that she had to be kept in a dark room, and it was feared that if she did get well she might still lose her eyesight.

Ethel could not believe it possible that so dread a calamity could overtake her. While alone, one Sabbath morning, she said to herself in her darkened chamber, "The Bible says we are not tried above that we are able to bear, and I could not endure that. Oh! no, I shall not be blind." While musing thus a low sweet voice near her said: "Sister Ethel, may I come in?"

"Why yes, Ruthie, if you want to."

"I wanted to recite my hymn to you; it is some new verses to 'Nearer my God, to thee,' and I like them so much."

"Well dear say them; I dont mind."

> "If where they lead my Lord,
> I, too, be borne,
> Planting my steps in his,
> Weary and worn—
> May the path carry me
> Nearer, my God, to Thee,
> Nearer to Thee!"

"That's not for me," thought Ethel, "it means the old-time martyrs." She tried to shake off the feeling. How could the dark path bring her nearer to God!

But the childish voice continued,—

> "If Thou the cup of pain
> Givest to drink,
> Let not my trembling lips
> From the draught shrink;
> So by my woes to be
> Nearer, my God, Thee,
> Nearer to Thee!"

"Never mind finishing it Ruthie; my head aches, and I want to be alone."

Once the thin, white hand was raised as if to dash "the cup of pain" from her lips.

Days passed. As her strength came back the inflammation in her eyes decreased. She no longer spoke of her hopes and fears. She looked more and more calmly at her cross. The path, though dark, had one ray of light, which, if followed, must bring her to her Saviour, for it came from him.

One day she cried, "O mamma! I cannot wait; let the light in now;" but her mother said, "Have patience darling; the noon-day is too bright; I will promise you to let the morning sun into your room."

All day long she waited, her lips moving in prayer. The morning dawned.

"Open the blinds wide mamma; let in all the light you can before I take off the bandage."

She turned toward the window; on her bare arms she felt the warm sun and morning breese, but no light came to her eyes.

"Mamma, mamma, why are you so silent? Is the room light?"

Her mother's low pained voice answered "My darling, the sun shines in your face."

She sank upon her knees; the clasped hands where uplifted, as if reaching for something unattainable; the face quivered with inward anguish; but the expression of her sightless eyes was more beautiful than in their days of undenied beauty they had ever been.

As her mother bent over her she heard the pale lips whisper—

> "So by my woes to be
> Nearer, my God, to Thee,
> Nearer to Thee."

As the eagles soaring,
 Higher and higher ascend,
Thus, while Thee adoring,
 Upward I would tend.
Further from earth and sin away,
Nearer heaven's perfect day;
Even now, oh, may I be
Drawn still closer, closer to thee.
Closer, closer, closer to thee.

As the river flowing,
 Ever draws nearer the sea,
Thus would I keep going,
 Till I'm lost in thee.
Daily advance and grow in grace,
Till I see thee face to face,
Then I'll sing eternally,
Drawn still closer, closer to thee.
Closer, closer, closer to thee.

SAYS Jesus, "And I, if I be lifted up from the earth, will draw all men unto me."

The sainted Alfred Cookman remarked on his death-bed, "Jesus is drawing me closer and closer to his great heart of infinite love." To his wife he said, "I am Christ's little infant. Just as you fold your little babe to your bosom, so I am nestled close to the heart of Jesus."

Albert Barnes, commenting on Christians mounting "up with wings as eagles," says: "The image is derived from the fact that the eagle rises on the most vigorous wing of any bird, and ascends apparently farther towards the sun. The figure denotes strength and vigor of purpose; strong and manly piety; an elevation above the world; communion with God, and a nearness to his throne—as the eagle ascends towards the sun."

"Ah," said a dying soldier, "tell my mother that last night there was not one cloud between my soul and Jesus."

Alford and his Hymns.

DEAN HENRY ALFORD was a son of an Episcopal clergyman of the same name. He was born in 1810, and closed his earthly career in 1871. He is widely known through his great work, "The Greek Testament with Notes."

He began very early in life to "make his mark,"—at least his pencil marks. For in his memoir it is stated that when only six years of age he wrote and illustrated a book of fourteen pages, three inches by two in size. "The travels of St Paul from his Conversion to his Death, with a book of Plates."

When ten years old he made a more durable mark with ink, in a work that he wrote entitled: "Looking unto Jesus, or the Believers Support under Trials and Afflictions. By Henry Alford Jun. 1st edition."

At this time he began to court the Muses, and in his eleventh year composed "A Collection of Hymns for Sundry Occasions." Among the number is one that begins —

"Life is a journey, heaven is our home,"

and ends with this verse:—

"Just as the school-boy longing for his home,
Leaps forth for gladness when the hour is come;
So true believers, eager for the skies,
Released by death on wings of triumph rise."

The figure drawn from a school-boy's experience, came readily to him at this period; for at this time he was attending a new school he did not like, and had some symptons of that old complaint, called home-sickness.

In his sixteenth year he wrote in his Bible, "I do this day, as in the presence of God, and my own soul, renew my covenant with God, and solemnly determine henceforth to become His, and do His work as far as in me lies."

HENRY ALFORD.

"Saying grace" he did not simply reserve for meal time. But also as he obtained food for the mind. And so habituated did he become in this that as he closed his books after a hard day's study, he would "stand up as at the end of a meal, and thank God for what he had received."

This early habit of acknowledging God in all his ways, of constantly looking for divine guidance was afterwards richly rewarded in his eventful life. It also found a natural expression in the beautiful hymn that he wrote when but sixteen years of age. A hymn well worthy to stand by the side of Williams' grand invocation:—

"Guide me, O thou great Jehovah."

We are glad to meet with it in some American hymnals, lately issued. We give it herewith:—

"Forth to the land of promise bound,
Our desert path we tread;
God's fiery pillar for our guide,
His Captain at our head.

"E'en now we faintly trace the hills,
And catch their distant blue;
And the bright city's gleaming spires
Rise dimly on our view.

"Soon, when the desert shall be crossed,
The flood of death past o'er,
Our pilgrim host shall safely land
On Canaan's peaceful shore.

"There love shall have its perfect work,
And prayer be lost in praise;
And all the servants of our God
Their endless anthems raise."

His "Poetical Works" reached a fourth edition in 1865. In 1867 he issued a collection of hymns entitled, "The Year of Praise," of which 55 were of his own composition. One is found in nearly all collections, commencing,

"Come, ye thankful people, come."

While once waiting for some bishops he wrote:—

"I'm glad I'm not a bishop,
To have to walk in gaiters,
And get my conduct pulled about
By democrat dictators."

Alford manifested wonderful powers of versatility. It is said, "He was a painter, a mechanic, a musician. He was a poet, a preacher, a scholar, and a critic."

He loved to contemplate the

"———————— raptured greeting
On Canaan's happy shore."

Say he, "Our thoughts have been much turned of late to the eternal state. Half of our children are there, and where the treasure is there will the heart be also." One of his most popular hymns vividly pictures the glories of the redeemed. The singing of it formed part of his own funeral service. In it he says;——

"Ten thousand times ten thousand,
In sparkling raiment bright,
The armies of the ransomed saints
Throng up the steeps of light.
'Tis finished—all is finished—
Their fight with Death and Sin:
Fling open wide the golden gates,
And let the victors in.

"What rush of hallelujahs
Fills all the earth and sky!
What ringing of a thousand harps
Bespeaks the triumph nigh!
O day for which creation,
And all its tribes were made;
O joy, for all its former woes
A thousand fold repaid.

"O then what raptured greetings
On Canaan's happy shore;
What knitting severed friendships up
Where partings are no more,
Then eyes with joy shall sparkle,
That brimmed with tears of late;
Orphans no longer fatherless,
Nor widows desolate."

As a member of the Evangelical Alliance, and in many other ways, Alford evinced a catholic spirit that endeared him to many outside of his own branch of the church. Asking a neighboring clergyman to help him find a curate, he said, "I want him to teach and preach Jesus Christ and not the church, and to be fully prepared to recognize the pious Dissenter as a brother in Christ, and as much a member of the church as ourselves."

In his sixtieth year he was compelled by failing health to heed his physician's advice and "do nothing," and soon after entered into the rest that remaineth to the people of God.

On his tomb was carved, by his request, the expressive words:—

THE INN OF A TRAVELLER ON HIS WAY TO JERUSALEM.

In his dying moments he sweetly realized the desire of his heart as expressed in the following hymn, which was sung in the great cathedral on the day of his funeral:—

"Jesus, when I fainting lie,
And the world is flitting by,
Hold up my head.
When the cry is 'Thou must die,'
And the dread hour draweth nigh,
Stand by my bed.

'Jesus, when the worst is o'er,
And they bear me from the door,
Meet the sorrowing throng.
'Weep not,' let the mourner hear,
Widow's woe and orphans' tear
Turn into song.

"Jesus, in the last great day,
Come thou down and touch my clay,
Speak the word 'Arise;'
Friend to gladsome friend restore,
Living, praying evermore
Above the skies."

King Alfred's Hymn.

ONE thousand years ago there lived a Christian King who ascended the English throne in 871, and was justly distinguished as "Alfred the Great." Although he was twelve years old before he was taught the alphabet, yet he afterwards applied himself with such diligence to his studies that he became celebrated as the author of numerous works, the founder of seminaries and of the University of Oxford.

Though burdened with the cares of a kingdom, he could find time and pleasure in greeting the morning light with songs of praise, and saying with King David, "Yea, I will sing aloud of thy mercy in the morning." This is evident from his sweet morning hymn, which was translated by Earl Nelson, and which still finds a place in different church hymn-books. It begins thus:—

> "As the sun doth daily rise
> Bright'ning all the morning skies,
> So to thee with one accord
> Lift we up our hearts, O Lord!

After many conflicts with the Danes, who invaded his land, he was at last compelled for a time to abandon his throne, and conceal himself in disguise in a cottage of one of his herdsmen. While performing menial service in his hiding-place his hostess gave him a severe repremand for permitting some oatmeal cakes to be burned, which, while baking, she had directed him to watch; saying, "No wonder thou art a poor houseless vagrant with such neglect of business, I shall set by all the burnt cakes for thy portion of the week's bread, and thou shalt have no other till they are all eaten." Dependent thus on others for his daily bread, although a King, he could in after years feel the import of his words addressed to the King of Kings in the second verse of his hymn,—

> "Day by day provide us food,
> For from thee come all things good;
> Strength unto our souls afford
> From thy living Bread, O Lord!

In the defence of his country he was compelled to fight no less than fifty six battles by sea or land, in which he exposed himself to innumerable dangers, and no doubt often uttered the prayer contained in the third verse,—

> "Be our Guard in sin and strife;
> Be the Leader of our life;
> Lest like sheep we stray abroad,
> Stay our wayward feet, O Lord!

Having translated the Psalms into English, and constantly carried a copy in his bosom, the fourth verse was certainly the language of his heart:—

> "Quickened by the Spirit's grace,
> All thy holy will to trace,
> While we daily search thy Word
> Wisdom true impart, O Lord!

The hordes that stole around at night and rendered life insecure, gave emphasis to his figure of the fifth verse,

> "When hours are dark and drear,
> When the Tempter lurketh near,
> By thy strength'ning grace outpoured,
> Save the tempted ones, O Lord!

Before a critical battle with the pagans, Alford managed to get into the ranks of the enemy disguised as a travelling minstrel, and with his harp and enrapturing song, was enabled so to win their applause that they detained him three days and nights.

The knowledge he thus obtained of the position and forces of the foe, was the means of saving his country. After he became victor, many of the pagans remained in England, renounced their idolatry, and were baptized on profession of their Christian faith.

Author of "Lord, it belongs not to my care."

THE name of Richard Baxter is endeared to many through the reading of his two widely known books, *The Call to the Unconverted*, and the *Saints' Everlasting Rest*. He was born at Rowton, in Shropshire, England, on the 12th of November, 1615.

His conversion took place when about the age of fifteen, by reading "an old torn book, lent by a poor man to his father, entitled 'Bunny's Resolutions.'" "Sibb's Bruised Reed,'" was also of great assistance. Thus says he: "Without any means but books, was God pleased to resolve me for Himself."

Montgomery gives Baxter a place among the poets of England. Of his hymns and poems, contained in the volume, entitled, "*Poetical Fragments*," he says that they are "far above mediocrity in many passages of poetry."

As tunes were not numerous in those days, Baxter prepared some of his hymns so that they could be sung either as long or common metre, by using or omitting the words contained in brackets. He claimed to be the inventor of this plan. We herewith give a specimen of a part of his version of the twenty-third Psalm:—

"The Lord himself my Sheperd is,
    Who doth me feed and [safely] keep;
What can I want that's truly good,
    While I am [one of] his own sheep?

"He makes me to lie down and rest
    In [pleasant] pastures, tender grass;
He keeps, and gently leadeth me
    Near [the sweet] stream of quietness.

"My failing soul he doth restore,
    And lead [in safe] and righteous ways,
And all this freely that his grace,
    And [holy] name may have the praise."

Baxter prepared a metrical version of the Psalms which was issued the year after his death. One of his hymns is almost universally found in hymn books. It is one among the many influences that he set in motion two centuries ago, that still lives. In the original it consists of eight eight-line stanzas, and begins:—

"My whole, though broken heart, O Lord!
From henceforth shall be thine."

It was entitled, "The Covenant and Confidence of Faith." At the end he adds the following note:—"This convenant my dear wife, in her former sickness, subscribed with a cheerful will."

We will embody it among some of the many incidents of his life that illustrate its sentiments. The first verse as now in use commences,—

"Lord, it belongs not to my care
Whether I die or live."

Baxter had a bodily frame so frail that it seemed ready at any time to fall to pieces.

His studious habits he explained on this wise, "Weakness and pain helped me to study how to die; that set me to study how to live." When on his death bed the intensity of pain constrained him to pray to God for his release by death, he would check himself by saying, "It is not for me to prescribe: *when* thou wilt, *what* thou wilt, *how* thou wilt."

To this language a half century later Dr. Watts refered in his dying moments, "it is good to say as did Mr Baxter, 'What, when, and where God pleases.'"

When Baxter first went to Kidderminster the people were "ignorant, coarse and of loose manners; superstitious, sensual and easily roused to deeds of violence and brutal outrage;" and yet that wilderness became as the garden of the Lord through the faithful labors of this man of God.

He toiled and prayed until it could be said "from every house within his pastorate there was daily the all but ceaseless voice of psalms and hymns. He was literally compassed about with songs of deliverance."

Family worship was generally practiced among his people. He says that as one passed along the street on a Sabbath evening, "one might hear a hundred families singing psalms and repeating sermons."

Although he observed great strictness in the admission to the church yet his membership increased to six hundred communicants; he says there were not twelve of whom he had not a good hope.

A hundred years later, Dr. Fawcett, one of his successors says, "the religious spirit thus happily introduced by Baxter is yet to be traced in the town and neighborhood."

He spoke of Kidderminster as a "place which had the chiefest of my labors, and yielded me the greatest fruits and comfort." He told the people that he came with his heart stirred up "to speak to sinners with some compassion, as a dying man to dying men." Here it was he uttered his loud "Call to the Unconverted," and in his earnest preaching exemplified his couplet:—

"I'd preach as though I ne'er should preach again,
And as a dying man to dying men."

This was indeed characteristic of Baxter throughout a long life; even when near four score years of age he still staggered up the pulpit steps to proclaim the gospel.

An old gentleman, who heard him preach, related that when he ascended the pulpit, with a man following him to prevent his falling backward, and to support him, if needful in the pulpit, many persons would be ready to say he was more fit for the coffin, than for the pulpit.

It was feared the last time he preached that he would

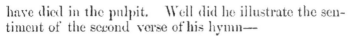

have died in the pulpit. Well did he illustrate the sentiment of the second verse of his hymn—

> "If life be long I will be glad,
> That I may long obey:
> If short yet why should I be sad
> To soar to endless day?"

May 1662, the king set his seal of approval to the famous "Act of Conformity," by which every clergyman of the Church of England must, on the 24th of August following, "openly and publickly, before the congregation there assembled, declare his unfeigned assent and consent to the use of all things" in the "Book of Common Prayer."

Baxter was among the two thousand godly ministers who were willing to leave their weeping flocks, and their pecuniary support, to face poverty and persecution for conscience's sake. As many were not silenced by this, the "Conventical Act" was passed in 1664, by which "the meeting of more than four persons in any other manner than allowed by the liturgy and practice of the Church of England is forbidden," under a penalty of a fine or imprisonment. To prevent the Non-conformist ministers being even among their flocks, the "Five Mile Act" followed, which prevented them from coming or being within five miles of any city or town corporate, or any place where they had at any time exercised their ministry.

Although Baxter yielded obedience to the law so far as to abstain from public preaching, yet he kept up family worship, and as some, of their own accord, would drop in and swell the number beyond the legal limit of "four," a warrant was issued for his arrest, and he was incarcerated for six months in Clerkenwell prison.

Some years later having dared to deliver five sermons, and to live in a corporate town, his enemies seized him again. His goods were taken from him and sold, "even to the bed that he lay sick on." "When they had taken and sold all" he says, "and I had borrowed some bedding and necessaries of the buyer, I was never the quieter."

At length when unable to find any other fault, they discovered a comment in his "Paraphrase on the New Testament" in which he had written some censures on persecuting prelates, and on closing the mouths of godly ministers who sought to preach in the name of their Master. This, as they thought, justified the charge of sedition which they now brought against him. He was summoned to appear for his trial before the notorious Jeffries. This furnished the Judge an opportunity to give vent to his coarse, vulgar spleen. To empty the vials of his wrath upon the head of an innocent old man.

After calling him a rogue, rascal, an old blockhead, an unthankful villain, and other vile epithets, Baxter ventured to put in a word of explanation. "Richard, Richard," roared the judge, "dost thou think we will hear thee poison the court?

"Richard, thou art an old fellow, an old knave; thou hast written books enough to load a cart, every one as full of sedition, I might say treason, as an egg is full of meat. Hadst thou been whipped out of the trade forty years ago, it had been happy..... Come, what do you say for yourself, you old knave?—come speak up. What doth he say? I am not afraid of you, for all the sniveling calves you have got about you," (alluding to some persons near Baxter who were in tears).

To this shameful tirade Baxter meekly replied, "These things will be understood some day, and lifting up his eyes to heaven he added; "I am not concerned to answer such stuff; but am ready to produce my writings for refutation of all this; and my life and conversation are known to many in this nation."

BAXTER BEFORE JEFFRIES.

As neither justice nor mercy could be obtained before this tribunal, Baxter was pronounced guilty.

While afterwards confined for two years in the dark cells of a prison, and comparing his mock trial with the one through which his Saviour passed, he could draw comfort from the third stanza of his hymn:—

> "Christ leads me through no darker rooms
> Than He went through before;
> He that into God's kingdom comes,
> Must enter by this door."

Notwithstanding his life-long weakness and pains—the bitter persecution and cruel imprisonments, Baxter did a marvelous amount of labor. His works number one hundred and sixty-eight, which, it is said would make a library themselves, of sixty volumes of five hundred octavo pages each. And yet when reminded on his deathbed of his good deeds, he replied: "I was but a pen in God's hand, and what praise is due to a pen." In triumphant peace and joy, he ended his days December 8, 1691.

"I have pains" said he, "there is no arguing against sense: but I have *peace*, I *have* peace." When asked, "How are you?" his answer was, "*Almost well.*" This thought is brought out in a verse of his hymn:—

> "My knowledge of that life is small,
> The eye of faith is dim;
> But 'tis enough that Christ knows all,
> And I shall be with Him."

While contemplating "the innumerable company" in heaven spoken of in Heb. xii. 22, of which he was soon to form a part he said, "It deserves a thousand—thousand thoughts. Oh how comfortable the promise that eye hath not seen, nor ear heard, neither have entered into the heart of man, the things which God hath prepared for them that love Him." To a friend he said these, his last words, "The Lord teach you how to die."

A Hymn Sung before an Indian Massacre.

STIRRING scenes were witnessed in the early history of our country.

The following fact given in the *Hallean Annals*, contains an exclamation in time of danger, that was almost the literal language of the first verse of Baxter's hymn:—

"Lord, it belongs not to my care
Whether I die or live."

In the early settlement of our country about the year 1750, there were frequent scenes of sudden death through the sudden invasion of the Indian savage.

Among the catechumens of the Lutheran pioneer missionary, the Rev. H. M. Muhlenburg, at New Holland, Pa., were two grown daughters, who, after their reception into the church, removed with their father to a farm near the Blue Mountains. At this period the Indian war was raging, rendering life very insecure in those forests.

One Friday evening, in the fall of the year, they told their father that they felt as though they had not long to live, and proposed singing the following appropriate German hymn, in which their voices all united:—

"Wer weiss wie nahe mir mein ende?"

which has been translated into English thus:—

"Who knows how near my life's expended?
Time flies, and death is hasting on;
How soon, my term of trial ended,
May heave my last expiring groan!
For Jesus' sake, when flesh shall fail,
With me, O God, may all be well!

> "My many sins!—oh, vail them over
> With merits of thy dying Son!
> I here thy richest grace discover,—
> Here find I peace, and here alone:
> And for his sake, when flesh shall fail,
> With me, O God, may it be well!
>
> "His bleeding wounds give me assurance
> That thy free mercy will abide;
> Here strength I find for death's endurance,
> And hope for all I need beside:
> For Jesus' sake, when flesh shall fail,
> With me, O God, may it be well!"

After singing they united in prayer and retired to rest. Next morning while the father was in his fields looking for his horses, he saw two Indians swiftly approaching with deadly weapons. He was so terrified that he knew not what to do, and seemed unable to move.

As they came near, he cried out, *"O Lord Jesus, to thee I live! O Lord Jesus, to thee I die."* This exclamation seemed to have paralized the Indians, while he at once was inspired with new strength, with which he was enabled to outrun the Indians, and thus escaped to a distant woods. From thence he hastened to some neighbors to procure help, so as to defend his children and property. But alas! as he drew near, the terrible noise and crying of old and young, revealed the fact that the Indians were there also, doing their deadly work. Hastening homewards to see after his children, he saw the flames of his own house and barn rising over the tree-tops, and heard the terrible bellowing of his cattle that were burning up alive.

By the time he reached his former home it was in ashes; his eldest daughter was also consumed that nothing but a few fragments of her body were left; the second was yet alive, but scalped, cut and gashed from head to foot with the tomahawk. As she was still able to speak she bade her father stoop down and give her a parting kiss, as she was passing away to the home above.

Author of "Did Christ o'er Sinners weep."

THE hymns of Rev. Benjamin Beddome have maintained a prominent position in church psalmody for nearly a century. He was the son of a Baptist minister, born in 1717, and brought to Christ in 1737.

He early heeded the Bible injunction to "acknowledge the Lord in all thy ways," and so he had the sweet experience of finding out in after years that the Lord "shall direct thy paths," and "give thee the desires of thine heart." This is very evident from some lines which he penned in his early Christian life, entitled, "The Wish," commencing,

> "Lord, in my soul implant thy fear:
> Let faith, and hope, and love be there.
> Preserve me from prevailing vice
> When Satan tempts or lusts entice."

Seven years afterward he was married to a help-meet, that was truly from the Lord, as an answer to this part of his prayer:—

> "Let the companion of my youth
> Be one of innocence and truth:
> Let modest charms adorn her face;
> And give her thy superior grace:
> By heavenly art first make her thine,
> Then make her willing to be mine.

Such an one he found when a pastor, in the daughter of one of his deacons, with whom he was happily wedded for thirty four years of his life. In contemplating the ministry, he further expressed his heart's wish about settlement:—

> "My dwelling place let Bourton be
> And let me live, and live to thee."

And so it proved to be, and here he also fully realized

> "Of friendship's sweet may I partake,
> Nor be forsaken, or forsake.
> Let moderate plenty crown my board,
> And God for all be still adored."

At Bourton the people became so attached to him and he to them, that he spent his entire ministerial life of fifty-two years among them. At one time a church in London was so bent on endeavoring to get him to become their pastor that they sent "call after call," and when this failed, delegated one of their number to press the suit. While on this visit, a poor man discovered his mission and having the visitor's horse in charge, became so excited that when he brought the horse to Mr. Beddome's door, he exclaimed in the presence of the Londoner, "Robbers of churches are the worst of robbers," and at once he set the horse free to take his own course.

Beddome sent, as his final answer, "I would rather honor God in a station, even much inferior to that in which he has placed me, than intrude myself into a higher without his direction."

His earnest ministry won many trophies for his Master, and so anxious was he to die with his harness on that when unable through age and infirmites to walk, his attached people carried him to church, and listened to his sermons while he preached sitting. Even one hour before his death his busy pen was still at work composing a hymn, when he was suddenly caught up to the skies in the seventy-ninth year of his age. His departure took place, September 3, 1795. A volume of his hymns was issued in 1818. Of his many hymns that are still in frequent use and much beloved, we may mention the following, commencing,

"Come, Holy Spirit, come."
"And must I part with all I have,"
"Jesus, my Lord, my chief delight,"
"If Christ is mine, then all is mine,"
"Did Christ o'er sinners weep?"
"Witness, ye men and angels! now,"
"Let party names no more."

A Hymn Seven Hundred Years Old.

BERNARD, the celebrated Abbot of Clair Vaux, wrote a Latin hymn to "the sweet memory of Jesus," which has been, and still is highly prized by those who love that precious name. Translated by E. Caswell the first verse reads,—

> "Jesus, the very thought of Thee,
> With sweetness fills my breast;
> But sweeter far Thy face to see,
> And in Thy glory rest."

He was born in Burgundy, A. D. 1091, and was consecrated to God from the first, by Aletta, his devotedly pious mother, who could say with Hannah, "for this child I prayed." Her death chamber was his spiritual birth-place. She died responding to a chant.

He was selected with twelve others to build a monastery, which they accomplished in a "pathless forest haunted with robbers." There they toiled with songs of praise till at length it became *Clair Vaux* "the bright valley."

By his learning, eloquence, and piety, he obtained great influence. Kings and Popes consulted him, and were subject to him. Peter the Venerable said he "had rather pass his life with Bernard than enjoy all the kingdoms of the world." Luther held him in high esteem, and said he was "the best monk that ever lived."

Among his other sacred lyrics that are still held in high estimation, we may mention,—

> "Hail, thou Head! so bruised and wounded"

The missionary Schwartz found great comfort in his dying hours by hearing the native Christians in India singing this hymn in their own Tamil language. After he had died, as was supposed, he was roused to life again by this favorite hymn, and his resuscitation was made known to them by his joining with them in the song.

Bernard died in 1153, being sixty-two years of age.

Like Andrew, he at "first findeth his own brother" and "brought him to Jesus." His father as well as his five brothers were among his first followers that he led in the narrow way.

Of his brother Gerard's death, he touchingly says, "Who could ever have loved me as he did? He was a brother by blood, but far more by religion........ God grant, Girard, I may not have lost thee, but that thou hast preceded me; for of a surety thou hast joined those whom in thy last night below thou didst invite to praise God; when suddenly to the great surprise of all, thou, with a serene countenance and a cheerful voice, didst commence chanting, 'Praise ye the Lord, from the heaven; praise Him, all ye angels'"

Bernard has been designated the *honeyed teacher*, and his writings a *stream from Paradise*. His heart seemed to overflow with love to Christ, of which in the first mentioned hymn, he says,—

> .... "Ah! this
> Nor tongue nor pen can show:
> The love of Jesus what it is,
> None but his loved ones know."

The thoughts expressed by Bernard in this verse, were also forcibly brought out in a striking figure by one partially insane at Cirencester, in 1779.

> "Could we with ink the ocean fill,
> Were the whole earth of parchment made,
> Were every single stick a quill,
> Were every man a scribe by trade;
> To write the love of God alone,
> Would drain the ocean dry;
> Nor would the scroll contain the whole,
> Though stretched from sky to sky."

Author of "O happy saints, who dwell in light."

PROMINENT among the workers that brought about the great revival of the eighteenth century was the Rev. John Berridge. He is described as "the salt of the church of England, and an instrument in God's hand of working revivals of religion within her pale, worthy of record with those that his compeers, Whitefield and Wesley, wrought without her."

At nineteen he entered college at Cambridge, and became quite celebrated for his attainments, wit and humor. Though awakened in early life to a sense of his sinfulness, he entered the work of the ministry, without knowing the way of salvation.

As six years passed around in his first charge at Stapleford, England, without any souls being brought to Christ, he says, "God would have shown me, that *I* was wrong by not owning my ministry, but I paid no regard to this for a long time, imputing my want of success to the naughty hearts of my hearers, and not to my own naughty doctrine; that we are to be justified partly by our faith and partly by our works."

In 1755 he removed to Everton, where there was a similar want of success. Until, as he says, "I began to be discouraged and now some secret misgivings arose in my mind that I was not right myself. Those misgivings grew stronger, and at last very painful. Being then under great doubts, I cried unto the Lord very earnestly. The constant language of my heart was this: 'Lord, if I am right, keep me so; if I am not right, make me so. Lead me to the knowledge of the truth as it is in Jesus.' After about ten days' crying unto the Lord, he was pleased to return an answer to my prayers, and in the following wonderful manner. As I was sitting in my house one morning, and musing upon a text of Scripture

JOHN BERRIDGE.

these words were darted into my mind with wonderful power, and seemed indeed like a voice from heaven, "Cease from thy works." Before I heard these words my mind was in a very unusual calm; but as soon as I heard them my soul was in a tempest directly, and the tears flowed from my eyes, like a torrent. The scales fell from my eyes immediately, and I now saw the rock I had been splitting on for nearly thirty years. Do you ask what this rock was? Some secret reliance on my own works for salvation."

After his conversion, he says in relation to his preaching, "I dealt with my hearers in a very different manner from what I used to." The effect was manifest at once. Soon one with a broken heart called upon him.

"Why, what is the matter, Sarah?" he asked.

"Matter! I dont know what's the matter. Those *new* sermons. I find we are all to be lost now. I can neither eat, drink, nor sleep. I don't know what's to become of me."

The same week came two or three more on a like errand. This sank him into the dust of self-abasement, to see what a blind leader of the blind he had been before. Immediately he burnt all his old sermons, and with tears of joy witnessed their destruction. The secret of his previous failures he expresses on this wise:—

> "No wonder sinners weary grow
> Of praying to an unknown God,
> Such heartless prayer is all dumb show,
> And makes them listless, yawn, and nod."

His warm heart now overflowed with emotion for perishing sinners. The church was awakened from its long sleep; some of his parishioners became angry; some opened their eyes with astonishment; while one and another began to come secretly, and revealing a broken heart, would tell him their lost condition.

Soon others came with the same story. His church became crowded. It is said: "The windows being filled within and without, and even the outside of the pulpit to the very top, so that Mr. Berridge seemed almost stifled." Within a year as many as a thousand persons visited him, inquiring the way of life.

He now began to visit and stir up the neighboring towns and villages. Being threatened with imprisonment, if he kept on preaching out of his parish, he replied that he would rather go to jail "with a good conscience, than be at liberty without one; adding there is one canon, my lord, which I dare not disobey, and that says, 'Go, preach my gospel to every creature.'"

As churches could not always contain the great multitudes that flocked to hear him, he would resort to the open fields, as did his eloquent co-laborers, Whitefield and Wesley. The effect that often followed his preaching is described as truly remarkable.

He had a tall and commanding figure, deep voice, a bold and impressive manner of speech, and a vivid fancy, that would often play around his utterances, as lightning about a cloud. Ten to fifteen thousand persons would often hang with breathless attention upon his weighty words as he portrayed the interests of time and eternity. His eccentricity no doubt helped to swell the number of his hearers. It is said that sometimes the curl of his lips and "the very point of his peaked nose" would seem to add to the effectiveness of his spicy sayings. But his quaint speech was always used as the diamond point on the arrow of truth, that helped to make it pierce far into the citadel of the heart. The slain of the Lord would be many after his use of the sword of the Spirit. Strong men would sink to the earth in great agony, and in a single year of "campaigning" as many as four thousand would thus become "pricked in heart."

An amusing story is told of Berridge while on a visit in the North of England. Stopping at a village where he must needs stay over the Sabbath, he requested the proprietor of the inn to let the "parson of the parish" know that there was a clergyman stopping with him who would gladly assist at the service on the morrow.

In reply to this statement the cautious shepherd remarked to the landlord, "We must be careful, for you know there are many of those wandering Methodist preachers about. What sort of man is he?" "Oh, it is all right sir," was the answer, "just see his nose, sir, that will tell you he is no Methodist." "Well, ask him to call on me in the morning," said the rector, "and I shall judge for myself." At the morning call it is said, "the waggish and somewhat rubecund nose" disarmed prejudices, and opened the way to the pulpit, where he delivered a memorable discourse.

"And fools, who came to scoff, remained to pray."

In 1785 he issued his "Sion's Songs, or Hymns composed for the use of them that love and follow the Lord Jesus Christ in sincerity," of which he says in the preface; "Many years ago, these hymns were composed in a six months' illness, and have since lain neglected by me, often threatened with fire, but have escaped that martyrdom." Of the singing in his day, he says, "It has become a vulgar business in our churches. This tax of praise is collected, chiefly from an organ, or a clerk, or some bawling voice in a singing loft. The congregation may listen if they please, or talk in whispers, or take a quiet nap."

His hymns number three hundred and forty-two. We give five of the six verses of the one on "pleasures for evermore." This is thought to be his best, and is found in nearly all the church hymn-books of the present day:—

"O happy saints, who dwell in light
And walk with Jesus clothed in white,
Safe landed on that peaceful shore
Where pilgrims meet to part no more.

"Released from sin and toil and grief,
Death was their gate to endless life:
An opened cage to let them fly
And build their happy nests on high.

"And now they range the heavenly plains,
And sing their hymns in melting strains:
And now their souls begin to prove
The heights and depths of Jesus' love."

"He cheers them with eternal smile;
They sing hosannas all the while;
Or, overwhelmed with rapture sweet,
Sink down adoring at his feet.

"Ah, Lord! with tardy steps I creep,
And sometimes sing and sometimes weep;
Yet strip me of this house of clay,
And I will sing as loud as they."

As a specimen of some quaint verses that spice his collection, we give the following:—

"But when thy simple sheep
  For form and shadows fight,
I sit me down and weep
  To see their shallow wit,
Who leave their bread to gnaw the stones,
And fondly break their teeth with bones.

Hymn number seven commences thus:—

"With solemn weekly state
  The worldling treads thy court,
Content to see thy gate,
  And such as there resort,
But, ah, what is the house to me,
Unless the master I can see.

Another contrasts the law and grace on this wise:—

"Run, John, and work, the law commands,
Yet finds me neither feet nor hands;
But sweeter news the gospel brings,
It bids me fly, and lends me wings.

Although Berridge was never married, he has furnished a good marriage hymn, that is about the only one on that subject in most hymn-books. It commences,

> "Since Jesus freely did appear
> To grace a marriage feast,
> Dear Lord, we ask thy presence here,
> To make a wedding guest."

His purse was as open as his heart, so that during his lifetime he gave away a fortune and all his patrimony.

For four and twenty years he preached on an average ten or twelve sermons a week, and travelled a hundred miles. In a characteristic epitaph he thus epitomizes the events of his life. This, in accordance with his wish, was placed on his tomb-stone after death, with the date of the last line added:—

"Here lie the earthly remains of John Berridge, late Vicar of Everton, and an itinerant servant of Jesus Christ, who loved his Master and his work, and after running his errands many years, was called up to wait on him above.

"Reader, art thou born again?

"No salvation without a new birth.

"I was born in sin, February, 1716.

"Remained ignorant of my fallen state till 1730.

"Lived proudly on faith and works for salvation till 1751.

"Admitted to Everton vicarage, 1755.

"Fled to Jesus alone for refuge, 1756.

"Fell asleep in Christ Jesus, January 22, 1793."

He was in his seventy-sixth year when the summons of death suddenly arrived. A clergyman remarked, "Jesus will soon call you up higher." He replied, "Ay, ay, ay, higher, higher, higher." Once he exclaimed, "Yes, and my children, too, will shout and sing, '*Here comes our father!*'"

Bonar and his Hymns.

WHEN the feet of the psalmist were taken "out of an horrible pit and the miry clay," he says that there was also "put a new song in my mouth, even praise to our God." After the escape from Egyptian bondage, and from the waters of the Red Sea, what was more natural to God's Israel than the spontaneous outburst of praise upon the banks of deliverance.

How often the redeemed soul, while surveying the great salvation, has found the language of Bonar's three well-known hymns exactly suited to tell the story. While sweetly led through "green pastures" how easy to sing along the banks of "the still waters" the hymn commencing,

> "I was a wandering sheep,
> I did not love the fold;
> I did not love my Shepherd's voice,
> I would not be controlled."

Or when nestled near the loving heart of Jesus, to recount his wondrous love in the hymn:—

> "I heard the voice of Jesus say,—
> 'Come unto me and rest;
> Lay down, thou weary one! lay down
> Thy head upon my breast.'
>
> "I came to Jesus as I was,
> Weary, and worn, and sad;
> I found in him a resting-place
> And he has made me glad."

Even the smallest babe in Christ can tell the plan of redemption in the simple verse that makes up the hymn commencing,

> "I lay my sins on Jesus,
> The spotless Lamb of God."

Our readers will surely need no invitation to gaze upon the pleasant features of Bonar's likeness that ac-

HORATIUS BONAR.

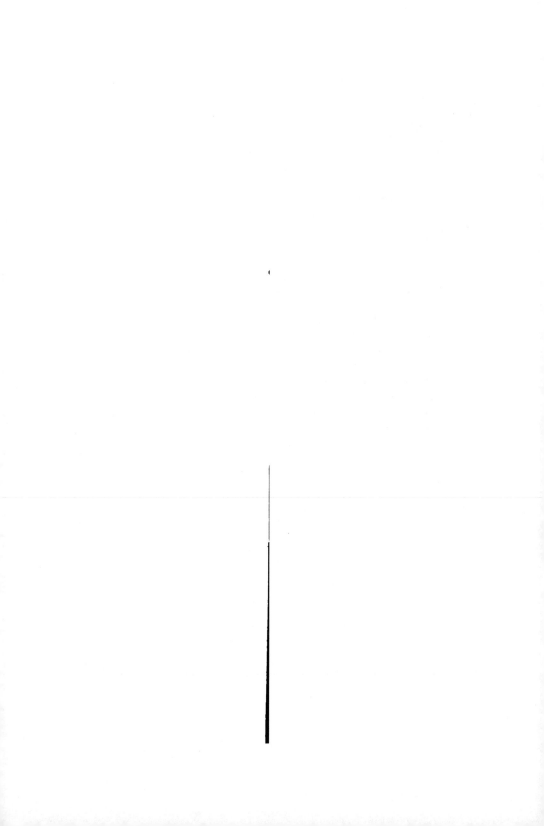

company these remarks, and see in them that goodness of heart that is indelibly stamped upon all that he has written.

The Rev. Horatius Bonar D. D. was born in Edinburgh Scotland in 1808. He was set apart to the work of the ministry at Kelso, in 1837, and has continued his pastoral work at Edinburgh, since 1867. In 1843 he united with the Free Church of Scotland.

His pen has been not only busy and fruitful, but far-reaching in its influence.

His "Night of Weeping; or Words for the Suffering Family of God," reached its forty-fifth thousand already in 1853. A sequel, "The Morning of Joy," was issued in 1850. His precious work called "The Blood of Christ," has also gained a world-wide reputation. His hymns and poems issued in 1857, entitled "Hymns of Faith and Hope," reached an eighth edition in 1862, and were followed by a second series in 1861, and a third in 1866. A second series was published in 1861.

His earnest life has been in keeping with the heart-wish so well expressed in his lines entitled, "Use Me:"—

"Make use of me my God!
 Let me not be forgot;
A broken vessel cast aside,
 One whom thou needest not.

"I am thy creature Lord;
 And made by hands divine;
And I am part, however mean,
 Of this great world of thine.

"Thou usest all thy works,
 The weakest things that be;
Each has a service of its own
 For all things wait on thee.

"Thou usest the high stars,
 The tiny drops of dew,
The giant peak and little hill;—
 My God, Oh use me too."

"I was a Wandering Sheep."

DURING a revival in a female seminary in Massachusetts, many of the pupils had shown the natural "enmity" of the "carnal mind" to spiritual things. Helen B—— was among those who noticed the Spirit's work only by a curling lip and a scornful laugh.

It seemed in vain to talk with her, or seek to induce her to attend a prayer meeting. Christians could do nothing more than to pray for her.

One evening, however, as a praying band had gathered, the door opened, and Helen B—— entered. Her eyes were downcast, and her face was calm and very pale. There was something in her look which told of an inward struggle. She took her seat silently, and the exercises of the meeting proceeded. A few lines were sung, two or three prayers offered, and then as was their custom, each repeated a few verses of some favorite hymn. One followed another in succession, until it came to the turn of the new-comer. There was a pause, and a perfect silence, and then, without lifting her eyes from the floor, she commenced,

"I was a wandering sheep,
I did not love the fold."

Her voice was low, but distinct, and every word, as she uttered it, thrilled the hearts of the listeners. She repeated one stanza after another of that beautiful hymn of Bonar, and not an eye save her own was dry, as, with sweet emphasis, she pronounced the last lines:

"No more a wayward child,
I seek no more to roam;
I love my heavenly Father's voice—
I love, I love his home."

That single hymn told all. The wandering sheep, the proud and wayward child had returned.

Comfort Sung to a Weary Teacher.

AN infant school teacher thus describes her experience: "I was not very well, and all my nerves seemed to be in a quiver. It was washing-day, with extra cares and labors. There was company in the house which must be entertained. There was fruit to be attended to—a duty that cannot be put off a single day. In fact there seemed to be everything to do, and the most of it must be done by my own tired hands. My head ached, too.

"I went into the garden for a breath of fresh air, and behold, the long rains had brought out the weeds in unprecedented luxuriance. It would never do to leave those weeds. I went to work with a will—with more will than strength, indeed—and worked till I was utterly exhausted. Then I went into the house to resume my labors there, but I was weary and worn, and the complaining thought uppermost in my mind was, 'Must it be so always? Can I never, anywhere, find rest?'

"As if in answer to my question, a little voice, clear and sweet, came from under the clustering vines in the next yard. It was the voice of one of my own little scholars, and she was singing to herself, one line of a favorite song she had learned in my class:—

'I lay my head on Jesus—I lay my head on Jesus.'

She repeated it over and over again. But it was enough.

"When they were learning that song, I had told them they should go to Jesus whenever they were tired or sick or sorry, and they should lean their heads on him, and there they would find rest and peace.

"It all came back to me. I tried then and there, weary and depressed as I was, to "lean my head on Jesus." I seemed to feel on my hot forehead the touch of his own hand in benediction, and the promised rest entered into my spirit."

The Leafy Closet of Prayer.

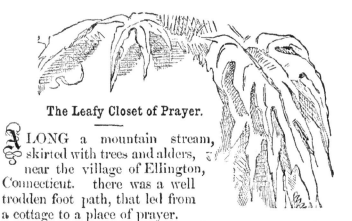

ALONG a mountain stream, skirted with trees and alders, near the village of Ellington, Connecticut, there was a well trodden foot path, that led from a cottage to a place of prayer.

At the close of the day, a mother was wont to leave the cares of her family, and, in the quiet of this secluded spot, to hold sweet communion with God.

One summer evening she was criticised by a neighbor for the seeming neglect of her family, and for this habit of stealing thus "a while away."

When she returned home her heart was much pained at what had been said. So she at once took her pen and wrote an answer to the criticism. She headed it, "An apology for my twilight rambles addressed to a Lady."

This mother was Mrs. Phœbe H. Brown.

In 1824 she gave Dr. Nettleton permission to issue it in his "Village Hymns." The first verses of the original hymn commenced thus:—

"Yes, when the toilsome day is gone,
   And night with banners gray
Steals silently the glade along,
   In twilight's soft array—

"I love to steal awhile away
   From little ones and care,
And spend the hours of setting day
   In gratitude and prayer."

PHŒBE H. BROWN.

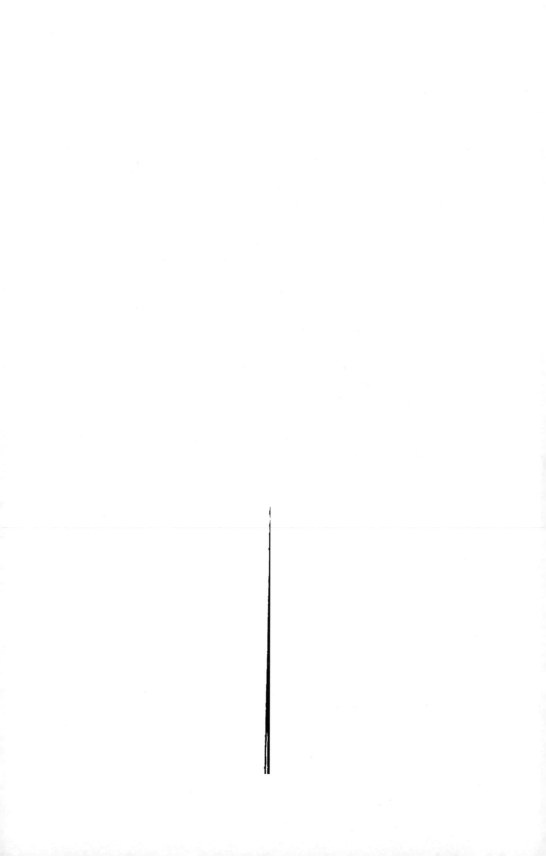

One of the "little ones" for whom she was thus accustomed to pray is now the Rev Samuel R. Brown. D. D. who has been a most efficient missionary in Japan since 1859. What an example to praying mothers, and what an apt illustration of God's promises showing that those who resort to "the secret place of the most high shall abide under the shadow of the Almighty"—that when we pray to him in secret he shall reward us openly.

When it is known how true the language of this hymn was, as the heart utterance of its author, and how truthfully it expresses the inward emotion of every prayerful soul, it is no wonder that it finds a place in nearly all the standard hymn-books of Christendom.

As long as Christians are like their Master, of whom it is said: "Rising up a great while before day he went out, and departed into a solitary place and prayed," they will also love to sing:—

"I love to steal awhile away
  From every cumbering care,
And spend the hours of setting day
  In humble, grateful prayer.

"I love in solitude to shed
  The penitential tear,
And all his promises to plead,
  Where none but God can hear.

"I love to think on mercies past,
  And future good implore,
And all my cares and sorrows cast
  On Him whom I adore.

"I love by faith to take a view
  Of brighter scenes in heaven;
The prospect doth my strength renew,
  While here by tempest driven.

"Thus when life's toilsome day is o'er,
  May its departing ray
Be calm as this impressive hour
  And lead to endless day"

The tune called "Monson" was composed for this hymn by her son, the Rev. Dr. Brown, who is "a lover of song and an admirable singer." William B. Bradbury also wrote a tune expressly for this hymn, and named it "Brown," as a compliment to its gifted authoress." One of the omitted verses of her hymn reads;—

> "I love to meditate on death,
> When will its summons come,
> With gentle power to steal my breath.
> And waft an exile home?"

We are indebted to Rev. Charles Hammond for the following particulars. He is in possession of her autobiography, a manuscript volume of four hundred and twelve pages quarto, and a volume of her poems, nearly as large, besides many unpublished papers of equal value.

Mrs. Brown was the wife of Timothy H. Brown of Monson, Mass. She was born at Canaan, N. Y., May 1st, 1783. Her father, George Hinsdale, having died suddenly of small-pox when she was but ten months old, she was placed in the care of her grandmother.

In her autobiography written in her old age, Mrs Brown pays a tribute to the deathless impressions of her grandmother's instructions, in which she says, "the bright and sunny period of my first nine years has never been forgotten, nor can be undervalued while memory and reason retain their empire." Being placed in other hands from the age of nine until eighteen her life was one of bondage, hardly less severe and hopeless than that of slavery itself. She lived in poverty, never went to school a day, and for years did not get to church, and was compelled through all the plastic period of youth to spend her time in unrequited toil, and in the most menial service. At the age of eighteen she left the abode of her sorrows and managed to go to school, where, with little children, she learned to write for the first time, and to sew, and some of the primary studies in a common-school education.

Returning to Canaan, the residence of her childhood, she was most kindly cared for by the Whiting family, and with them shared in the results of a revival, which, near the beginning of the century, visited that region. No sooner had she learned to write with the pen mechanically, than she began to write as the composer of verses, and essays in prose. Her pen was never laid aside until extreme age and disease prevented its further use.

Next to her "twilight hymn" in popularity was the one of which she left the following record: "Prayer for a Revival." This hymn was written from the impulse of a full heart, incidentally shown to a friend, that friend begged a copy for his own private use, but it soon found its way to the public in "The Spiritual Songs." The hymn is familiar to all commencing:—

> "O Lord! thy work revive
> In Zion's gloomy hour,
> And let our dying graces live
> By thy restoring power."

We need not wonder that to a *full* heart, overflowing in such earnest cries, a speedy answer should be witnessed. For this verily followed the same year in the neighborhood from which her earnest petition ascended to the skies.

The children growing up under the influence of so many prayers, did not disappoint a mother's wishes for positions of usefulness. The eldest daughter, Julia, was married to the Rev. Daniel Lord; the second to the Rev. Joseph Winn; the remaining daughter, Hannah, first to Mr. Lord of Connecticut, and after his death to Deacon Elijah Smith, now of Illinois. All her children are numbered with the departed, except the son in Japan.

Not only at the close, but also at the dawn of day did

she love to "steal a while away." Even when bending under the weight of old age, she wrote to a friend, saying, "I have risen before the light, that I may have a quiet hour for communion with my God and Saviour." In 1819, she wrote the following Morning Hymn for a sunrise prayer meeting, held in Monson, during a season of revival:—

> "How sweet the melting lay,
>   Which breaks upon the ear,
> When at the hour of rising day,
>   Christians unite in prayer.
>
> "The breezes waft their cries
>   Up to Jehovah's throne,
> He listens to their heaving sighs
>   And sends his blessings down.
>
> "So Jesus rose to pray
>   Before the morning light,
> Once on the chilling mount did stay
>   To wrestle all the night.
>
> "Glory to God on high,
>   Who sends his Spirit down
> To rescue souls condemned to die,
>   And make his people one."

By special request, she added a Mid-day Hymn, for the Fulton street prayer meeting, where it is often sung. It commences,

> "Jesus this mid-day hour
>   We consecrate to Thee;
> Forgetful of each earthly care,
>   We would Thy glory see."

Some writers mention Monson, as the place where she wrote her twilight hymn. This is a mistake. On the original manuscript, in the hands of Mr. Hammond, she says; "Written at Ellington, Connecticut, in reply to a censure for Twilight Rambles, August 1818." Near the close of her pilgrimage, she penned these lines: "As to my history, it is soon told; a sinner saved by grace and sanctified by trials."

Stealing Away to Jesus.

A brief circular, announcing the preaching of my Illustrated Sermons, attracted the attention of little Minnie whose parents would not permit her to go to any church or Sunday school, as they did not believe in Christ. Through her pleadings permission was given her to attend our services in the "Union Tabernacle" at Broad St. and Girard Ave., Philadelphia.

Minnie made herself a little book in which to put down every wrong word and action during the day. Said she to her mother, "It seems as if my little page gets *so* full every day, that it makes me feel very bad. I am *so* naughty. It seems every thing I do, is sinful."

Our meetings continued six weeks. Daily would Minnie come, long before the time of service, and putting her hand in mine would look up so imploringly, asking the way to Jesus.

We gave her a little hymn book, which, with her little Bible, she kept in a little garret store-room, where she would go after service, saying, that she wished to be left alone. Her mother supposed it was in order to play, or read some favorite book, and never interrupted her; but after her death, her Bible and hymn-book were found lying there, having been evidently much read. Thus it became evident that this little disciple had been stealing away to this garret, to enjoy quiet and sweet communion with her Saviour.

Two verses in Isaiah, she had emphasized, and then referred to them especially on the fly leaf of her Bible as expressive of her experience, "Behold, God is my Salvation: I will trust and not be afraid; for the Lord JEHOVAH is my STRENGTH and SONG; he also is become my salvation; Therefore with joy shall ye draw water out of the wells of salvation."

A Mother Recognized by a Hymn.

WAR was raging in Canada in 1754 between the French and English. The Indians took part with the French and came as far as Pennsylvania, where they burned the houses, and murdered the people.

In 1755 they reached the dwelling of a poor Christian family. The father and son were instantly killed. A little daughter, Regina, was taken, with many other children, into captivity.

They were led many miles through woods and thorny bushes, that nobody could follow them.

Regina and a little girl two years old were given to an old Indian widow. The poor children were forced to go into the forest to gather roots and other provisions for the old woman; and when they would not bring her enough, she would beat them in so cruel a manner that they were nearly killed.

Regina continually repeated the verses from the Bible, as well as the hymns which she had learned at home, and taught them to the little girl. And often would they retire to a tree and kneel down, when Regina would pray, and teach her little companion the way to Jesus.

Often they cheered each other by the hymn,

> "Alone, yet not alone am I,
> Though in the solitude so drear."

In this sad state they remained nine long years, till Regina reached the age of nineteen, and her little companion eleven years.

In 1764 the providence of God brought the English Colonel Boquet to the place where they were in captivity. He conquered the Indians and forced them to ask for peace. The first condition he made was that they should restore all the prisoners they had taken.

Thus the two girls were released. More than four hundred captives were brought to Col. Boquet.

It was an affecting sight. The soldiers gave them food and clothing, took them to Carlisle, and published in the newspapers that all parents who had lost their children might come and get them.

Regina's mother came; but, alas! her child had become a stranger to her. Regina had acquired the appearance and manners of the natives, and by no means could the mother discover her daughter. Seeing her weep in bitter disappointment, the colonel asked her if she could recollect nothing by which her poor girl might be known. She at length thought of, and began to sing, the hymn,

> "Alone, yet not alone am I,
> Though in this wilderness so drear;
> I feel my Saviour always nigh,—
> He comes the weary hours to cheer.
> I am with him, and he with me;
> Even here alone I cannot be."

Scarcely had the mother sung two lines of it when Regina rushed from the crowd, began to sing it also, and threw herself into her mother's arms. They both wept for joy; and with her young companion, whose friends had not sought her, she went to her mother's house. Happily for herself, though Regina had not seen a book for nine years, she at once remembered how to read the Bible.

This narrative was recorded by Pastor Rone of Elsinore.

Author of "One sweetly solemn thought."

THIS hymn, so precious to those whose affection is set on things above, was penned by Miss Phœbe Cary.

She was born in the Miami Valley, Ohio, September 4, 1824. Early in life she and her sister Alice became so busy with their poetic pens, that by the year 1849 they had a volume ready for the press of which Phœbe made the following record: "Alice and I have been collecting and revising all our published poems to send to New York for publication. We are to receive for them one hundred dollars." After the issue of this volume they were tempted to visit their unknown friends in the East, who had written kind words of approbation.

Mr Whittier commemorates their visit by a poem published after the death of Alice, which commences thus:—

> "Years since (but names to me before,)
> Two sisters sought at eve my door;
> Two song-birds wandering from their nest
> A gray old farm house in the West."

Speaking of the welcome he gave, he says:—

> "What could I other than I did?
> Could I a singing bird forbid?
> Deny the wind-stirred leaf? Rebuke
> The music of the forest brook?"

The wind that stirred their forest nest was some unpropitious gales that made home uncomfortable after the death of a mother, and unsuited to that intellectual advancement they so much coveted. So with much courage and but little money, the sisters bade adieu to the home of their childhood, and sought to make to themselves one in the city of New York. Having rented two or three rooms in an unfashionable neighborhood they began to do with their might, whatsoever their hands could do with the pen, to make a living. Success attended their efforts till they were enabled to purchase a home on

Twentieth street, from which they ascended in after years to their home above.

The two sisters were united by the warmest affection. Phœbe said, "It seems to me that a cord stretches from Alice's heart to mine." When this cord was severed by the rude hand of death it left a bleeding wound which time could not heal. A shadow seemed to linger upon the hearthstone after the loved form of Alice was removed to the Greenwood cemetery that became the shadow of death to the surviving sister. How keenly she felt the departure of Alice can be judged from the last sweet hymn she penned, in which she says;—

"O mine eyes be not so tearful;
Drooping spirit, rise, be cheerful;
Heavy soul why art thou fearful?

"Nature's sepulchre is breaking,
And the earth, her gloom forsaking,
Into life and light is waking!

"O the weakness and the madness
Of the heart that holdeth sadness
When all else is light and gladness!

"Though thy treasure death hath taken,
They that sleep are not forsaken,
They shall hear the trump and waken.

"Shall not he who life supplieth
To the dead seed where it lieth
Quicken also man who dieth?

"Yea the power of death was ended
When He who to hell descended,
Rose, and up to heaven ascended.

"Rise, my soul, then, from dejection,
See in nature the reflection
Of the dear Lord's resurrection.

"Let his promise leave thee never:
'If the night of death I sever
Ye shall also live forever.'"

During the heat of the summer of 1871 she went to Newport hoping to revive her sinking frame but suddenly and unexpectedly the summons came that called her to that home of which she wrote in her popular hymn:—

> "One sweetly solemn thought
> Comes to me o'er and o'er,
> I am nearer home to day
> Than I have been before."

In the last year of her life she was much cheered by the incident, given on the opposite page. Writing to an aged friend, she says: "I enclose the hymn, and the story for you, not because I am vain of the notice, but because I thought you would feel a peculiar interest in them, when you know the hymn was written eighteen years ago, (1852,) in your house. I composed it in the little back third story bed-room, one Sunday morning, after coming from church; and it makes me happy to think that any word I could say, has done a little good in the world." After her death, Mr. Conwell received a letter from the old man referred to, of whom he says, that he "has become a *hard working Christian*, while 'Harry' has renounced gambling and all attendant vices, and thus the hymn has saved from ruin, at least two, who seldom or never entered a house of worship."

The thought of the following verse was exemplified in her death. Mary C. Ames, her biographer, says, "Without an instant's warning, her death throe came. She knew it. Throwing up her arms in instinctive fright, this loving, believing, but timid soul, who had never stood alone in all her mortal life, as she felt herself drifting out into the unknown, the eternal, starting on the awful passage, from whence there is no return, cried, in a low, piercing voice: 'O God, have mercy on my soul!' and died."

> "O, if my mortal feet
> Have almost gained the brink;
> If it be I am nearer home
> Even to-day than I think," etc.

Gamblers Reclaimed by a Hymn.

ECHOES of hymns reverberate a long while.

Col. Russel H. Conwell while on a visit to China, was an eye-witness to the following scene:—

"Two Americans, one a young man, the other over forty, were drinking and playing at cards in a gambling house in China. While the older one was shuffling the cards, the younger began to hum, and finally sung in a low tone, but quite unconsciously, the hymn:—

"'One sweetly solemn thought
Comes to me o'er and o'er,
I am nearer home to-day
Than I have been before.'

The older one threw down the cards on the floor and said;

"'Harry, where did you learn that tune?'

"'What tune?'

"'Why, that one you have been singing.'

"The young man said he did not know what he had been singing. But when the older one repeated some of the lines, he said they were learned in the Sunday School.

"'Come, Harry,' said the older one, 'come, here's what I've won from you. As for me, as God sees me, I have played my last game, and drank my last bottle. I have misled you, Harry, and I am sorry for it. Give me your hand, my boy, and say that, for old America's sake, if no other, you will quit the infernal business.'"

Mr. Conwell says that both of the gamblers were permanently reclaimed by the influence of this hymn.

"Jesus, my all to Heaven is gone."

THIS sweet hymn is said to have been a description of the author's experience. It was written by John Cennick, who was born at Reading in 1717.

"As a youth he delighted in attending dances, playing at cards, and going to the theatre." In 1735, while pacing the streets of London, he suddenly felt great convictions of sin. At first he yielded to despair, was "weary of life, and often prayed for death."

He fled to and fro, seeking rest in infidelity and open sin. At length he tried to rid himself of sin by penance. Says he, "I even ate acorns, leaves of trees, crabs, and grass." For three long years he groaned under the burdens of a guilty conscience. This thought he expresses in the verses:—

> "This is the way I long have sought,
>   And mourned because I found it not;
> My grief a burden long has been,
>   Because I was not saved from sin.
>
> The more I strove against its power,
>   I felt its weight and guilt the more;
> Till late I heard my Saviour say,
>   Come hither, soul, I am the way."

While reading Whitfield's journal light dawned upon his soul.

In 1739 he commenced work for Christ, in teaching and preaching among the colliers at Kingswood.

Eventually he went along with Wesley and Whitfield in their preaching tours. In 1745 he cast his lot with the Moravians. In 1755 he was taken ill of fever and died in London.

He is the author of the well known hymn,

"Children of the Heavenly King."

"Now, I will tell to sinners 'round
What a dear Saviour I have found."

BEING much exhausted during the delivery of a course of "Illustrated Sermons" at Cleveland, Ohio, we proposed to meet any in a social gathering, on Saturday evening in the parlor of a friend. After spending the evening in general conversation, the group of young friends were about bidding each other "good night," when a little orphan, about ten years of age, of her own accord, arose at the sofa and said: "Mr. Long, before we separate, I would like to say something." Breathless silence following, she added: "I have been seeking Jesus all day at home in my closet, and I have found Him, and I want my playmates to seek and find Him too. Let us pray." As we sank in that parlor, many tears attested the effect of that little pleading voice that was leading us at a throne of grace, and of the interest awakened by the unexpected testimony of one so young, whose heart was so full that she could not go home without telling "'round what a dear Saviour" she "had found."

The next week she met a little ragged boy on the street, and was overheard saying to him, as she caught him by the hand, "Are you interested in Jesus?" "I guess I would be if I had anybody to tell me about Him. But I've got no mother." "Neither have I," said the little Mary, "but come to Jesus and he will take care of you."

At the close of an "Illustrated Sermon" in the Lutheran church at Ashland, Pa., on going down the aisle, I saw a little girl getting up on the bench, that she might speak to me. As I drew near she wished me to bend over my head, that she might whisper a precious secret. As I did so, she said softly: "I've found Jesus." It came so joyously and sweetly from her lips that it left an echo that shall never cease from my memory.

Cowper and his Hymns.

WILLIAM COWPER is a name that will linger upon the page of hymnology, as long as there are sinners upon the earth to sing of the "fountain filled with blood." He was the son of the rector of Berkhampstead England, the Rev. John Cowper. The poet was born November 15, 1731. One of the greatest misfortunes that ever befell him was the loss of an affectionate mother, when he was but six years of age.

His father seemed ill adapted for the training of a child whose "shyness, nervousness and sensitiveness were greatly aggravated by feeble health, and weak eyes. We may infer his injudiciousness from the fact that when his boy was eleven, he made him read a treatise on suicide and give him his opinion upon it."

At 18 he began the study of law for which he did not seem to be naturally inclined, as he says he was "constantly employed from morning to night, in giggling and making giggle." A cousin having procured for him the "Clerkship of the Journals," he was notified to stand an examination at the bar of the House of Lords. The time appointed was to him such an approaching "day of terror" that its prospect weighed so heavily upon his frail tenement that at length it unsettled his reason.

The dark November night preceding he made several attempts to commit suicide, first by taking poison. Twenty times he put the black phial to his mouth. His courage failing him he next tried to drown himself, then with a knife tried to stab himself, and at last with a cord tried to hang himself at the top of his door. But the cord breaking and other means failing the half-dead man now began to turn his eyes away from the bar of the House of Lords, to the bar of the King of Kings.

At length his brother found him in his terrible agony,

his knees smiting together, and his quivering lips uttering the piercing cry, "Oh, brother, I am damned! Think of *eternity*, and then think what it must be to be damned."

While in this condition he penned those piteous lines:—

> "Man disavows and Deity disowns me
> Hell might afford my miseries a shelter;
> Therefore hell keeps her ever-hungry mouths all
>   Bolted against me."

It is sad to think how one, who has since poured into so many broken hearts the balm of Gilead, should have had his own wrung with what he called "unutterable anguish," and yet this bitter experience may have taught him afterwards to say with more emphasis of that fountain the "thief rejoiced to see,"

> "And there have I, as vile as he,
> Washed all my sins away."

The Rev. Martin Madan, a cousin whom he had hitherto avoided came to him in this time of need, and told him of Jesus. As they were seated on the bedside Cowper burst into a flood of tears, as a ray of hope flit across the dark horizon, but shortly afterwards actual brain disease came on that resulted in insanity, and poor Cowper was taken to St Alban's.

Here it was that in less than two years he was restored mentally and saved spiritually, and in a double sense was found "sitting at the feet of Jesus, clothed, and in his right mind." In after years how exquisitely he described this experience in poetic form:—

> "I was a stricken deer that left the herd
> Long since: with many an arrow deep infixed
> My panting side was charged, when I withdrew
> To seek a tranquil death in distant shades.
> There was I found by One who had Himself
> Been hurt by archers. In his side He bore
> And in his hands and feet the cruel scars.
> With gentle force soliciting the darts,
> He drew them forth, and healed and bade me live."

Cowper's Conversion and Hymns relating Thereto.

COWPER'S hymns were types of his varied experiences. This was especially true of those referring to his new birth.

July, 1764, after being an inmate of the Insane Asylum at St. Albans for six months, he seated himself near the window, and seeing a Bible, took it up, and as he opened it, his eyes lit on Romans III. 25. The scales fell at once from his eyes. Says he,—

"Immediately I received strength to believe, and the full beams of the Sun of Righteousness shone upon me. I saw the sufficiency of the atonement He had made, my pardon sealed in his blood, and all the fullness and completeness of his justification. In a moment I believed and received the Gospel."

These words he had doubtless said before, but only now he could say, "I saw;" thus illustrating the sentiments of his exquisitely beautiful hymn beginning,—

"The Spirit breathes upon the word,
And brings the truth to sight."

To this he refers, as he continues:—

"Whatever my friend Madan had said to me so long before revived in all its clearness 'with demonstration of the Spirit and with power.' Unless the Almighty arm had been under me, I think I should have died of gratitude and joy. My eyes filled with tears and my voice choked with transport; I could only look up to heaven in silence, overwhelmed with love and wonder.

After this blissful experience, he composed his first hymn, which he entitled, "The happy change,"—

"How blest thy creature is, O God,
When, with a single eye,
He views the lustre of thy word,
The day-spring from on high!"

"But the work of the Holy Spirit is best described in his own words; it was 'joy unspeakable and full of glory.' Thus was my heavenly Father in Christ Jesus pleased to give me the full assurance of faith, and out of a stony, unbelieving heart to raise up a child unto Abraham. How glad I should have been to have spent every moment in prayer and thanksgiving! I lost no opportunity of repairing to a throne of grace, but flew to it with an eagerness irresistible and never to be satisfied. Could I help it? Could I do otherwise than to love and rejoice in my reconciled Father in Jesus Christ? The Lord had enlarged my heart, and I ran in the ways of His commandments."

This last thought he beautifully expressed in this—

"My soul rejoices to pursue
The steps of him I love,
Till glory breaks upon my view
In brighter worlds above."

"I should have been glad to have spent every moment in prayer and thanksgiving! For many succeeding weeks tears were ready to flow if I did but speak of the Gospel, or mention the name of Jesus. To rejoice day and night was my employment. O, that the ardor of my first love had continued!"

This thought he embodies in the well-known hymn,—

"Oh, for a closer walk with God."

In which he says in the second and third stanza,—

"Where is the blessedness I knew
When first I saw the Lord?
Where is the soul-refreshing view
Of Jesus and his word?

"What peaceful hours I then enjoyed!
How sweet their memory still!
But now I find an aching void
The world can never fill."

Origin of Cowper's Second Hymn.

IN June 1765, Cowper, being restored to health, left the asylum at St. Alban's. Of his tour to Huntingdon, he says, "It is impossible to tell with how delightful a sense of his protection and fatherly care of me, it pleased the Almighty to favor me during the whole of my journey."

Feeling his loneliness in his new home, and his heart at the same time yearning for communion with his newly found Saviour, he, at eventide, wandered forth in the fields, where he found a closet among the green shrubbery and bushes. While in this "calm retreat," and "silent shade," the gate of heaven seemed opened to his view, and the Lord gave him a glorious manifestation of his presence.

The next day being the Sabbath his feet turned to the sanctuary. This was the first time he met with God's people in their Sabbath home, since his conversion.

The story of the Prodigal Son was the lesson of the day. Cowper's heart was so full that he found it difficult to restrain his emotions. Of one, devoutly engaged in worship in the same pew, he says: "While he was singing the Psalms I looked at him; and observing him intent upon his holy employment, I could not help saying in my heart, with much emotion, 'The Lord bless you for praising Him, whom my soul loveth!'"

After the church services were over, he hastened at once to the secluded spot that had become so hallowed with the associations of the day before. "How," he exclaims, "shall I express what the Lord did for me, except by saying that he made all his goodness to pass before me? I seemed to speak to him face to face, as a man converseth with his friend, except that my speech was only in tears of joy, and groanings which cannot be uttered. I could say indeed with Jacob, not how *dreadful*, but how *lovely* is this place!—this is none other than the house of God."

This foretaste of heaven, in the "secret place of the Most High" gave rise to Cowper's second hymn, that has become incorporated in all the standard hymn books of Christendom.

How precious and memorable the stanzas of the following hymn when we thus take into account the surrounding circumstances that gave them birth:—

"Far from the world O Lord, I flee,
  From strife and tumult far;
From scenes where Satan wages still
  His most successful war.

"The calm retreat, the silent shade,
  With prayer and praise agree;
And seem, by thy sweet bounty made
  For those who follow thee.

"There, if thy Spirit touch the soul,
  And grace her mean abode,
Oh with what peace, and joy, and love,
  She communes with her God!

"There like the nightingale, she pours
  Her solitary lays,
Nor ask a witness of her song,
  Nor thirsts for human praise."

Speaking of Cowper at this period, Montgomery says:—

"The first fruits of his muse, after he had been baptized with the Holy Ghost and with fire, will ever be precious (independent of their other merits) as the transcript of his happiest feelings, the memorials of his walk with God, and his daily experience amidst conflicts and discouragements of the consoling power of that religion in which he had *found* peace, and often enjoyed peace to a degree that passed understanding."

Cowper was a man of prayer, and Newton said of him, "No one walked with God more closely."

Cowper's Olney Hymns.

COWPER had gone to Huntingdon to be near his brother, who was then studying at Cambridge.

Here he made the acquaintance of the Unwins, who kindly received him as a member of their family, and became his warmest friends for life.

After the death of Mr. Unwin in 1767, Rev. John Newton invited Cowper and Mrs. Unwin to move to Olney and secured a residence for them near his own dwelling. The twelve succeeding years became the happiest period of Cowper's life.

Newton's estimate of Cowper's worth he in after years expressed in this strong language:—

"In humility, simplicity, and devotedness to God, in the clearness of his views of evangelical truth, the strength and the comforts he obtained from them, and the uniform and beautiful example by which he adorned them, I thought he had but few equals. He was eminently a blessing, both to me and to my people, by his advice, his conduct, and his prayers. The Lord who had brought us together, so knit our hearts and affections, that for nearly twelve years we were seldom separated for twelve hours at a time, when we were awake and at home. The first six I passed in daily admiring and trying to imitate him; during the second six I walked pensively with him in the valley of the shadow of death."

Newton had a thousand parishioners. In the cultivation of this extensive field of usefulness, he employed every available instrumentality. He says: "We had meetings two or three times in a week for prayer. These Cowper constantly attended with me. For a time his natural constitutional unwillingness to be noticed in public kept him in silence. But it was not very long before the ardency of his love to his Saviour, and his desire of being useful to others, broke through every restraint. He frequently felt a difficulty and trepidation in the attempt; but, when he had once begun, all difficulty vanished, and he seemed to speak, though with self-abasement and humiliation of spirit, yet with that freedom and fervency as if he saw the Lord, whom he addressed, face to face."

Newton felt the need of hymns specially adapted to these prayer-meetings and the heart experiences of the common people, and so in 1770 he induced Cowper to undertake their preparation. Six years later, by their united efforts, these hymns formed a volume, and were sent forth to the world under the title of the "Olney Hymn Book."

Among the first was the following one, so often repeated since, in similar circles of prayer.

When we remember that at this time such prayer-meetings in private houses, not specially dedicated to God was something new, and quite an innovation on old customs, we see great force and beauty, in the wording of this hymn:—

"Jesus, where'er thy people meet,
There they behold thy mercy-seat;
Where'er they seek thee, thou art found,
And every place is hallowed ground.

"For thou, within no walls confined,
Inhabitest the humble mind;
Such ever bring thee where they come,
And going take thee to their home.

"Dear Shepherd of thy chosen few,
Thy former mercies here renew:
Here to our waiting hearts proclaim
The sweetness of thy saving name.

"Here may we prove the power of prayer
To strengthen faith, and sweeten care,
To teach our faint desires to rise,
And bring all heaven before our eyes."

Birth place of "There is a fountain filled with blood."

AS it is interesting to trace the origin of our great rivers, that carry with them so many and such varied blessings in their meandering course, so the child of God finds it a pleasing and profitable exercise to go back in the streams of hymn-history to their humble starting point. As Christianity was cradled in a manger, so "Rock of Ages," one of its most famous hymns is traceable to the conversion of its author amid the enclosure of an Irish barn. What a mighty stream of influence has swept through the world through the channel opened up by the singing of

"Jesus, lover of my soul,"

yet it was born in a lowly spring-house, to which Wesley had fled for shelter from the infuriated mob. It was thus by the side of a little bubbling spring, he taught the world to sing of Christ,

"Thou of life the fountain art,
Freely let me take of thee."

In the secluded shelter of some over-hanging trees and rocks that shaded a little brook, Mrs. Phœbe H. Brown was accustomed to resort in the summer of 1818, and co-mingle her voice in prayer and praise, with the soft murmurs of the silver streamlet. That quiet nook gave birth to a hymn that has since been repeated the world over by the hosts of God's Israel, who with her can say,

"I love to steal a while away."

The childrens' hymn, known and loved as far as the English language extends,

"I think when I read that sweet story of old,"

first echoed forth from an humble stage-coach in England, where it was written by a young lady in 1841.

On the opposite page will be seen the little group in the Olney prayer-meeting, for which Cowper wrote his

Olney Cottage Prayer-Meeting, Led by Newton and Cowper.

immortal hymn, that has encircled the world with its hallowed influences. The Great House is especially designated as the place where the Olney prayer-circle was accustomed to gather for addresses, singing, and prayer.

Little did Cowper imagine, when he first heard Newton announce, and this small praying band unite in singing, that

> "There is a fountain filled with blood,"

that there was starting a song that would afterwards be caught up by unnumbered millions, and that a century later, while his

> "—— poor lisping, stammering tongue
> Lies silent in the grave,"

would still be repeated from the rising to the setting of the sun—and continue to echo round the globe

> "Till all the ransomed church of God
> Be saved, to sin no more."

We give the last of the seven verses of this precious hymn, as they are generally omitted:—

> "Lord, I believe Thou hast prepared,
> Unworthy though I be,
> For me a blood-bought free reward,
> A golden harp for me.
>
> "'T is strung, and tuned for endless years,
> And formed by power divine,
> To sound in God the Father's ears
> No other name but Thine."

These were days of sunshine in Cowper's spiritual firmament. Newton tells us how their voices came to blend, while singing of "the Lamb once slain."

> "I heard him and admired, for he could bring
> From his soft harp such strains as angels sing:
> Could tell of free salvation, grace, and love,
> Till angels listened from their home above;
> I woke my lyre to join his rapturous strain,
> We sang together of the lamb once slain."

A Visit to Cowper's Grave.

"I went alone. 'Twas summer time;
And, standing there before the shrine
   Of that illustrious bard,
I read his own familiar name,
And thought of his extensive fame,
And felt devotion's sacred flame,
   Which we do well to guard.

"'Far from the world, O Lord, I flee.'
How sweet the words appeared to me,
   Like voices in a dream!
'The calm retreat, the silent shade,'
Describe the spot where he was laid,
And where surviving friendships paid
   Their tribute of esteem.

"'There is a fountain.' As I stood
I thought I saw the crimson 'flood,'
   And some 'beneath' the wave;
I thought the stream still rolled along,
And that I saw the 'ransomed' throng,
And that I heard the 'nobler song'
   Of Jesus' 'power to save.'

"'When darkness long has veiled my mind,'
And from these words I felt inclined
   In sympathy, to weep;
But 'smiling day' has dawned at last,
And all his sorrows now are past;
No tempter now, no midnight blast,
   To spoil the poet's sleep.

"'O for a closer'"—even so,
For we who journey here below
   Have lived too far from God.
Oh, for that holy life I said,
Which Enoch, Noah, Cowper, led!
Oh, for that 'purer light' to shed
   Its brightness on 'the road!'

"'God moves in a mysterious way;'
But now the poet seemed to say,
   'No mysteries remain.
On earth I was a sufferer,
In heaven I am a conquerer;
God is his own interpreter,
   And he has made it plain.'"

The Hymn on which a Heart "Rose to God."

WHILE Mr. Ralph Wells was hurrying to meet the cars, a Sunday school teacher hailed him, saying:

I have just come from the hospital, where I found on one of the beds, one of my scholars, a lad who sent for me. I found that he had met with a terrible accident, that had nearly severed both his limbs from his body.

"O teacher!" he said, "I have sent for you. I am glad you have come before I die. I have something to ask of you. I want you to tell me a little more about Jesus."

"Well, my dear boy, have you a hope in Him?"

"Yes, teacher, thank God, I have had it for six months."

"Why, you never said anything to me about it."

"No, I did not, teacher, but I have had it, and I find it sustains me in this hour. I have only a few minutes to live, and I would like you to sing for me."

"What shall I sing?"

"O sing:—

"There is a fountain filled with blood,
Drawn from Immanuel's veins,
And sinners plunged beneath that flood
Lose all their guilty stains.'"

The teacher began to sing. The dying lad joining in the song with a sweet smile on his countenance.

"It was that hymn," said he, "among other things, on which my heart rose to Christ."

He then put his arms up and said, "Teacher, bend your head." He bent it down. The dying boy kissed him. "That is all I have to give you," said he. "Good bye," and he was gone.

"There is a fountain filled with blood" Illustrated.

MONTGOMERY thought the figure of a "*fountain filled*" was faulty and ought to be represented as "*springing up;*" but the Christian world has not seen fit to adopt the substitute he proposed, which reads thus:—

> "From Calvary's cross a fountain flows
> Of water and of blood,
> More healing than Bethesda's pool,
> Or famed Siloa's flood."

A traveller, going over a mountainous region, through an accident, fell into a deep chasm, from which there seemed to be no way of escape. The sides were so steep that he could not climb up, and being so far away from the reach of human ears, he felt as if his cries were also in vain. While overwhelmed with the thought of impending ruin, he heard the murmur of a stream, that was stealing its way under the overhanging rocks. It seemed to be his only way of escape. As it was a matter of life and death, it did not take him long to decide to venture upon the stream of life. So he

> "————plunged beneath that flood,"

and by its waters was carried out of "the horrible pit," into a place of safety. His life was thus saved; his fears were gone, and in the clear sunlight of freedom, he went on his way rejoicing.

> "Lose all their guilty stains."

A little girl expressed this thought very forcibly. She was asked: "Are you a sinner?" to which she promptly replied, "No, sir!" "Have you never done anything wrong?" "Oh, yes," she replied; "a great many times." "How then can you say you are not a sinner?" "It is *tooken away*," said she, "I have trusted in Christ."

Illustrated by a Death Scene.

IT was our privilege to preach in the Tenth Baptist Church, Philadelphia, during a season of revival in January, 1874. At the close of one of the evening meetings, Captain Timothy Rogers, long a member of the church, and one of the noblest and most faithful followers of Jesus, rose, and plead with sinners to come to the "fountain filled with blood." At the conclusion of his earnest address, the pastor, Rev. A. J. Rowland, announced a hymn. Captain Rogers requested that this might be changed to "There is a fountain filled with blood." "Yes," said the pastor, "let us sing Captain Rogers' favorite hymn, and while we sing, let us all rise. If there be any who would be cleansed in this precious "fountain," let them come forward to the front seats as we sing, and be remembered in a closing prayer."

All arose; among them Captain Rogers, who stood taller than all the rest, looking anxiously and tenderly over the room, to see who would accept the invitation. While the words of the second verse were being sung:—

"And there have I, as vile as he,
Washed all my sins away,"

the captain suddenly sank, and fell on the floor.

A number of the brethren, among them Dr. S. Brown, hastened to his side, and carried him into an adjoining room. Thinking he had fallen in a fit, that would soon subside, the audience kept on singing the hymn. As they were singing the last verse,

"Then, in a nobler, sweeter song,
I'll sing thy power to save,
When this poor lisping, stammering tongue
Lies silent in the grave,"

the pastor returned to the audience-room, and said: "Captain Rogers is *dead*." The scene that followed baffles description. A wail of sorrow burst from every lip, and, while some fainted, the sound of weeping was heard everywhere. In the subsequent meetings a number referred to the death-scene, as the means of their awakening and conversion.

It is a singular fact that Captain Rogers had frequently said to the chorister of the church: "When I lie on my death-bed, I want you to come and sing over me the hymn, "There is a fountain filled with blood."

Although at the time, he asked for the singing of the hymn at this meeting, he had no idea of his death being at hand, yet it so happened, that under the sound of the singing of this hymn, *led by this chorister*, he passed away to mingle his praises with the singing hosts on high.

Captain Rodgers was converted on his ship, while out at sea, and so anxious was he to confess Christ at once, that, a Baptist minister being at hand, he had his yawl-boat lowered in the China sea, and using it as a baptistery, he was baptised in the presence of his crew, and of the British fleet that was anchored near by.

He was truly a veteran of the cross, and died with the full armor on. How literally he illustrated the sentiment of the lines of the hymn on which he had been speaking, and to which he had referred as his last utterance on earth:—

> "E'er since by faith, I saw the stream
> Thy flowing wounds supply,
> Redeeming love has been my theme,
> And shall be till I die."

A like occurrence took place with Rev. Dr. Beaumont. He had just announced with quivering lips the verse:—

> "The lowest step above thy seat
> Rises too high for Gabriel's feet
> In vain, the tall archangel tries,
> To reach thine height with wondering eyes."

While it was being sung, he sank to the floor and died.

> "The dying thief rejoiced to see
> That fountain in his day;
> And there have I, as vile as he,
> Washed all my sins away."

WHILE preaching in Maryland, I was told of a thief who was then and there rejoicing that the "fountain" was still open "in his day."

The evening before the execution of a murderer, a devoted Christian lady felt herself constrained to prolong her devotions on behalf of the culprit, before retiring.

In her importunate prayer she mentioned thieves and similar characters as those for whom the atoning blood had been efficacious in apostolic times. Her soul was so stirred with sympathy, that she could not get asleep for a long time after going to bed.

Toward midnight she thought she heard a noise beneath her bed. At length she saw the head of a thief appearing at the foot. Being alone and not near any of the family to whom she could call for help, she closed her eyes in silent prayer, and calmly trusted in divine aid for protection.

The thief trod softly along the bed-side. To see if she was asleep, he bent over her pillow, coming so near that she felt his breath upon her face.

He then quietly descended the stairway and endeavored to get out, but he could not find the key to the door, as that was kept in a secret place.

While he was engaged in trying to escape, this Christian heroine awoke a brother, and told him that there was a thief in the house who was striving to get out.

Getting a lamp, they descended the stair-steps, when the light fell upon the face of the intruder, who was a man from the village whom they knew. He confessed that he came there to steal. Being unable to meet a note, due the next day, of three hundred dollars, he knew that this lady had that amount. Supposing she kept it in her bed-chamber, he concealed himself under her bed, intending to search for it when she was asleep. But her prayer for thieves so completely disarmed him, and so convicted him of sin, that he resolved to seek pardon in the blood of the Lamb.

After hearing his confession, the sister was so impressed with the genuineness of his contrition, that she told her brother to get the money and loan him the amount needed. He afterward not only repaid the money, but became an earnest Christian, and at the time of my visit was superintendent of the Sunday school of the village.

REV. JOHN WESLEY was once stopped by a highwayman, who demanded his money. After he had given it to him, he called him back, and said: "Let me speak one word to you; the time may come when you may regret the course of life in which you are engaged. Remember this: *The blood of Jesus Christ cleanseth from all sin.*" He said no more, and they parted. Many years afterwards, when he was leaving a church in which he had been preaching, a person came up and asked if he remembered being waylaid at such a time, referring to the above circumstances. Mr. Wesley replied that he recollected it. "I," said the individual, "was that man; that single verse on that occasion was the means of a total change in my life and habits. I have long since been attending the house of God and the Word of God, and I hope I am a Christian."

AFTER giving a black catalogue of criminals, among whom were thieves, drunkards, &c., the apostle adds: "such were some of you, but ye are washed, but ye are sanctified, but ye are justified in the name of the Lord Jesus Christ, and by the Spirit of God."

Calling upon a home missionary, a man remarked: "Sir, I hope you will excuse me, but I have been leading a very bad life, and I want to give it up. I want to work for my living in future. I was put in jail for stealing. A Bible reader used to visit and talk to us. While I was there I thought over what he said, and determined that when I got out I would try and get a living honestly." While the missionary assured him of his aid, he also taught him that as long as he was Christless he was helpless in his good resolutions.

The thief afterward attended upon the preaching of the Word, became deeply penitent, and soon realized the "peace of God which passeth all understanding."

He wished to state publicly what grace had done for him, but it was thought best for him to wait awhile, and was so advised. Being absent from public worship on the next Sunday, it was ascertained that he was dangerously ill. The missionary found him lying on a miserable bed in a garret in great pain, expressed sympathy for him, and then alluded to the sufferings of Jesus. "Yes," said he, "that's the wonder when I think that he suffered for such as I—for such a wretch as I."

Being removed to a hospital to undergo an operation, he soon afterwards sank away. As the hymn—

"There is a fountain filled with blood,"

was repeated to him, he was greatly moved by the second verse:—

"The dying thief rejoiced to see
That fountain in his day,
And there have I, though vile as he,
Washed all my sins away."

"Yes," he exclaimed, "*I* am that thief,—it meant *me*,—it was written for *me*,—that's just *me*."

The Diversions of Cowper.

IN the shattered condition of Cowper's nervous system, he found it necessary to seek some recreations with which to occupy his active mind, and to turn it out of the channels of gloom and despondency into which it was so apt to run. He says: "It is no easy matter for the owner of a mind like mine to divert it from sad subjects, and fix it upon such as may administer to its amusement."

Some friends in hearty sympathy with him on account of his mental depression, presented him with some tame hares, to which he became greatly attached. They grew up under his oversight and became objects of great interest for eleven years. He has written beautifully of them, both in poetry and prose, in Latin and English. Of the two, he named Bess and Puss, he says:—

"I always admitted them into the parlor after supper, when, the carpet affording their feet a firm hold, they would frisk, and bound, and play a thousand gambols, in which Bess, being remarkably strong and fearless, was always superior to the rest, and proved himself the Vestris of the party. One evening, the cat, being in the room, had the hardiness to pat Bess upon the cheek, an indignity which he resented by drumming upon her back with such violence that the cat was happy to escape from under his paws, and hide herself.

"Puss grew presently familiar, would leap into my lap, raise himself upon his hinder feet, and bite the hair from my temples. He would suffer me to take him up, and to carry him about in my arms; and has more than once fallen fast asleep upon my knee. He was ill three days, during which time I nursed him, kept him apart from his fellows, that they might not molest him, (for, like many other wild animals, they persecute one of their own

COWPER AND HIS HARES.

species that is sick,) and, by constant care, and trying him with a variety of herbs, restored him to perfect health. No creature could be more grateful than my patient after his recovery; a sentiment which he most significantly expressed by licking my hand, first the back of it, then the palm, then every finger separately, then between all the fingers, as if anxious to leave no part of it unsaluted: a ceremony which he never performed but once again, upon a similar occasion."

Rabbits, guinea-pigs, dogs, canaries, goldfinches, a magpie, a jay, and a starling were added to his household treasures. In addition to these means of recreation he tried his hand at sketching, and "drew mountains, valleys, woods, streams, ducks, and dabchicks." "I admire them," he wrote, "and Mrs. Unwin admires them, and her praise and my praise are fame enough for me."

But notwithstanding these various efforts to allure his mind away from the return of that midnight of mental gloom, its shadows began again to deepen around him.

In January 1773, soon after Cowper had penned his last Olney Hymn, his sad depression culminated in an attack of insanity. He afterwards in a measure recovered his health, but while he became sane on every other subject, yet, as long as life lasted, suffered under the monomania that he was rejected of God.

His judicious friend, Mrs. Unwin, sought now to occupy his attention by writing poetry. He says: "When I can find no other occupation, I think; and when I think, I am apt to do it in rhyme." To this attempted diversion the world is indebted for those unrivalled poems that followed each other in such rapid succession and that have encircled his name with so much fame and honor.

Southey describes him as "the most popular poet of his generation, and the best English letter-writer."

Origin of "God moves in a mysterious way."

MONTGOMERY describes this hymn of Cowper's, as a "lyric of high tone and character, and rendered awfully interesting by the circumstances under which it was written,—in the light of departing reason."

Its original title, "Light shining out of Darkness," is supposed to have had reference to its singular origin.

It is said, "When under the influence of the fits of mental derangement to which he was subject, he most unhappily, but firmly believed that the divine will was that he should drown himself in a particular part of the river Ouse, some two or three miles from his residence at Olney. One evening he called for a post-chaise from one of the hotels in the town, and ordered the driver to take him to that spot, which he readily undertook to do as he well knew the place.

"On this occasion, however, several hours were consumed in seeking it, and utterly in vain. The man was at length most reluctantly compelled to admit that he had entirely lost his road. The snare was thus broken; Cowper escaped the temptation; returned to his home, and immediately sat down and wrote the hymn," so descriptive of God's wonder-working providence, and that has proved a beacon light to many who have wandered in darkness.

A somewhat similar providence is reported in the life of Augustine of whom it is said that having occasion to preach at a distant town, he took with him a guide to direct him in the way. This man by some unaccountable means, mistook the road, and fell into a by-path. It afterwards proved that in this way the preacher's life was saved, as his enemies, aware of his journey, had placed themselves in the proper road with a design to kill him.

> "Can a woman's tender care
> Cease towards the child she bare?"

COWPER knew of a "mother's tender care" by sweet experience. These lines are in his hymn:—

> "Hark, my soul! it is the Lord,"

Though he lost his mother when only six years of age, yet forty years after, he wrote, "that not a week passes, (perhaps I might with equal veracity, say a day,) in which I do not think of her; such was the impression her tenderness made upon me, though the opportunity she had for showing it was so short."

In 1790, he received the gift of his mother's picture, on which he wrote a touching poem. The extract we give will show the impress of a mother's love,—

> "My mother! when I learned that thou wast dead,
> Say, wast thou conscious of the tears I shed?
> Hover'd thy spirit o'er thy sorrowing son,
> Wretch even then, life's journey jus' begun?
> Perhaps thou gavest me, though unfelt, a kiss;
> Perhaps a tear, if souls can weep in bliss—
> Ah, that maternal smile! it answers—Yes.
> I heard the bell toll'd on thy burial day,
> I saw the hearse that bore thee slow away,
> And, turning from my nursury window, drew
> A long, long sigh, and wept a last adieu!
> But was it such? It was. Where thou art gone
> Adieus and farewells are a sound unknown.
> May I but meet thee on that peaceful shore,
> The parting word shall pass my lips no more!
> Thy maidens, grieved themselves at my concern,
> Oft gave me promise of thy quick return.
> What ardently I wish'd, I long believed,
> And, disappointed still, was still deceived.
> By expectation every day beguiled,
> Dupe of to-morrow even from a child.
> Thus many a sad to-morrow came and went,
> Till, all my stock of infant sorrows spent,
> I learned at last submission to my lot,
> But, though I less deplored thee ne'er forgot."

Author of "Lord! I am thine, entirely thine."

REV. SAMUEL DAVIES, D. D. was the author of a number of choice hymns. He was born in Delaware, November, 3, 1724. His devoted Christian mother, believing that he had been given in answer to her earnest prayers, named him Samuel.

At fifteen he became an earnest Christian, and began his preparation for the work of the ministry. At twenty-two he was licensed to preach, and soon after entered upon a field of labor in Virginia, which extended over several counties.. Great success attended his arduous and self-denying labors, so that in three years time one of his feeblest churches increased to a membership of three hundred.

He was described as a "model of the most impressive oratory. As his personal appearance was venerable, yet benevolent and mild, he could address his auditory, either with the most commanding authority, or with the most melting tenderness. He seldom preached without creating some visible emotion in great numbers present."

In 1759, he was chosen president of the college at Princeton, New Jersey, as successor to the celebrated Jonathan Edwards. Six years previously, he had visited England, and received large benefactions on behalf of this institution. His sermons abound in striking thoughts and richest imagery. They were issued in three volumes, to which was appended his poems."

At the beginning of the year 1761, he preached on the words, "This year thou shalt die." A month latter, he himself was a corpse. He was but thirty-six when he was laid in his coffin. As his venerable mother gazed upon him, lying there, she said: "There is the son of my prayers, and my hopes—my only son—my only earthly support. But there is the will of God, and I am satisfied."

Singing in Time of Peril.

HOW impressive was the singing of one of the hymns of Davies, as narrated in the *Trophies of Song*:—

"A Christian captain, who had a Christian crew, was caught near a rocky shore in a driving storm. They were being driven rapidly toward the rocks, when he ordered them to 'cast anchor.'

"They did so, but it broke. He ordered them to cast the second. They did so, but it dragged. He then ordered them to cast the third and *last*.

"They cast it while the captain went down to his room to pray. He fell on his knees and said, 'O Lord, this vessel is thine, these noble men on deck are thine. If it be more for thy glory that our vessel be wrecked on the rocks, and we go down in the sea, 'thy will be done.' But if it be more for thy glory that we live to work for thee, then hold the anchor.' Calmly he rose to return to the deck, and as he went, he heard a chorus of voices singing:—

"'Lord, I am thine!'

It seemed like an angel song. Reaching the deck, he found his brave men standing with their hands on the cable, that they might feel the first giving of the anchor, on which hung their lives, and looking calmly on the raging of the elements, as they sung 'with the spirit and with the understanding also:—'

"'Lord, I am thine!'

"The anchor held till the storm was past, and they anchored safe within the bay."

"Home, sweet, sweet home."

REV. DAVID DENHAM a Baptist minister in England issued in 1837, the well known hymn of "Sweet Home," commencing,

"Mid scenes of confusion and creature complaints."

He wrote this and much of his poetry for the religious magazines. His field of ministerial labor was Margate, London, and Cheltenham. Having in early life been called to his "sweet home" above he need no longer sing in the language of his hymn:—

"I sigh from this body of sin to be free,
Which hinders my joy and communion with thee;
Though now my temptation like billows may foam,
All, all will be peace, when I'm with thee at home.
Home, home, sweet, sweet home:
Prepare me dear Saviour, for glory, my home."

The tune of "Sweet Home" was written by Sir Henry Rowley Bishop in 1829, and the song of "Sweet Home" by J. Howard Payne in 1825. He sold it to Charles Kemble for 30 pounds. When it was first sung in public by Miss Tree it so fascinated a wealthy gentleman of London that he made her the offer of his hand and fortune, which were accepted. Paine was a homeless wanderer.

"How often," said he, "have I been in the heart of Paris, Berlin and London, or some other city, and heard persons playing 'Sweet Home,' without a shilling to buy the next meal, or a place to lay my head. The world has literally sung my song until every heart is familiar with its melody. Yet I have been a poor wanderer from my boyhood. My country has turned me ruthlessly from office, and in my old age I have to submit to humiliation for my daily bread."

He died at Tunis while acting as U. S. Consul.

Midnight Echo of "Home, sweet, sweet home."

IT was our privilege to hear, from the lips of one who is now a popular pastor of one of the largest churches in Philadelphia, the following interesting statement, relating to the echo of a hymn that proved to be the means of his salvation. Having run away as a prodigal from his father's home in Virginia when a young man, he had had little regard for the broken hearted parents that he had forsaken, until one Christmas night, when in the fourth story bed-room of a hotel on Chestnut street Philadelphia, he was awakened by the chimes of bells of an Episcopal church near by. The tune of "Home, sweet, sweet home," was being played. As in the quiet of the midnight hour the sound of this hymn floated over the city, thoughts of his forsaken home began to echo through the chambers of his soul. A father's plaintive voice, and a mother's streaming eyes seemed to beckon him home again. His pillow soon became wet with tears of penitence. At the repetition of the tune he could no longer remain in bed. His heart was now yearning for "Home, sweet, sweet home," and soon his hands were packing up to start for home, and not long after his feet were hastening down the flight of stairs, up Chestnut street, down Broad street, and at the Baltimore depot he took the first train of cars for home.

How many similar prodigals would start for the heavenly land, if they would wake from their slumbers long enough to listen to some of those sweet echoes that tell us of the soul's "sweet, sweet home."

> "My Father's house on high,—
> Home of my soul,—how near,
> At times, to faith's farseeing eye,
> Thy golden gates appear!"

Singing The Heart Open.

A Presbyterian minister, an American by birth, but of Scottish parentage, happening to be in New Orleans, was asked to visit an old Scottish soldier who had sickened, and was conveyed to the hospital.

On entering and announcing his errand, the Scotchman told him, in a surly tone, that he desired none of his visits—that he knew how to die without the aid of a priest. In vain he informed him that he was no priest, but a Presbyterian minister, come to read him a portion of the Word of God, and to speak to him about eternity. The Scotchman doggedly refused to hold any conversation with him, and he was obliged to take his leave.

Next day, however, he called again, thinking that the reflection of the man on his own rudeness, would prepare the way for a better reception. But his manner and tone were equally rude and repulsive; and at length he turned himself in bed, with his face to the wall, as if determined to hear nothing, and relent nothing.

The minister bethought himself, as a last resourse, of the hymn well known in Scotland, the composition of David Dickson, minister of Irvine, beginning, "O mother dear, Jerusalem, when shall I come to thee?" which his Scottish mother had taught him to sing to the tune of Dundee. He began to sing his mother's hymn.

The soldier listened for a few moments in silence, but gradually turning himself round, with a relaxed countenance, and a tear in his eye; inquired, "Who taught you that?" "My mother," replied the minister. "And so did mine," rejoined the now softened soldier, whose heart was opened by the recollections of infancy and of country; and he now gave a willing ear to the man that found the key to his heart.

Conquered By Song.

IN Louisiana, over a century ago, itinerant Methodist preachers fared roughly. A travelling minister was one evening reduced to the very verge of starvation.

He had spent the preceding night in a swamp, and had taken no food for thirty-six hours, when he reached a plantation. He entered the house and asked for food and lodging. The mistress of the house, a widow with several daughters and negroes, refused him.

He stood warming himself by the fire, a few minutes, and began singing a hymn commencing,—

"Peace my soul, thou needest not fear;
The Great Provider still is near."

He sang the whole hymn, and when he looked around they were all in tears. He was forthwith invited to stay not a single night, but a whole week, with them.

Mr. Bushnell of Utica, N. Y. had occasion to stop at a hotel in a neighboring town. Some twenty men were in the bar room in which temperance was being denounced as the work of priests and politicians.

Mr. Bushnell, finding it impossible to stem the current of abuse by an appeal to their reason, proposed singing a temperance song, and accordingly commenced the "Stanch Teetotaller." On glancing around the room after he had concluded, he observed the tear trickling down the cheek of almost every man.

The song carried their thoughts back to their families and firesides, surrounded as they once were with plenty but now with poverty and disgrace. Those hardened men could but acknowledge its truth by tears.

Soon after the landlord came in, and he repeated it for his special benefit. After Mr. Bushnell had concluded, he grasped him by the hand, and exclaimed, "*I will never sell another glass of liquor as long as I live.*"

Author of "Grace, 'tis a charming sound."

THIS is one among the three hundred hymns penned by Philip Doddridge, D. D., widely known by his commentary on the Scriptures, the "Family Expositor," and as the author of "The Rise and Progress of Religion in the Soul." This has been so widely circulated and translated into so many languages, that it has been designated as the most useful book of the eighteenth century. It was written at the suggestion of Dr. Watts, whom he regarded as one of his warmest friends.

Doddridge was born in London, June 26, 1702. Of his early life his biographer says: "At his birth he shewed so little sign of life that he was laid aside as dead. But one of the attendants, thinking she perceived some motion, or breath, took that necessary care of him, on which, in those tender circumstances, the feeble frame of life depended, which was so near expiring as soon as it was kindled." He was the twentieth child of a mother, who was the daughter of an exiled Bohemian clergyman, the Rev. John Bauman. The mother had imbibed the devoted Christian spirit of her father, of whom, it is said, that for conscience's and Christ's sake, he left Prague in Bohemia about 1626. Giving up a large estate and friends at the age of twenty-one, he withdrew on foot from his country, clad as a peasant, "carrying with him nothing but a hundred broad pieces of gold, plaited in a leathern girdle, and a Bible of Luther's translation."

Doddridge counted it a great honor to have descended from these suffering saints of Christ.

His mother taught him the history of the Old and New Testaments before he could read, by the assistance of some Dutch tiles in the room where they commonly met. As these early impressions shaped his destiny, and were so valuable to him in after life, he frequently rec-

commended to parents to imitate her example. With such a mother's training, it is no wonder that it is said that while attending grammar school at Kingston, the one previously taught by his grandfather Bauman, from his tenth to his thirteenth year "he was remarkable for his piety and diligent application to learning." His parents dying while he was young he could afterwards say, when pleading for orphans, "I know the heart of an orphan, having been deprived of both of my parents at an age in which it might reasonably be supposed I should be most sensible of such a loss."

In his orphanage he found it difficult to pursue his studies for the ministry. A tempting offer was made of assistance in the study of law. He was to return an answer at a certain time. As the period drew near he devoted one morning to seek divine direction, and while in the *act of prayer* the post-man called at the door with a letter from the Rev. Samuel Clark, a Presbyterian minister, in which he said that he had heard of his difficulties, and offered to give him the needed aid to fit him for the ministry. This he looked upon as an answer from heaven, "and" says he, "while I live I shall always adore so seasonable an interposition of divine Providence."

When just twenty years old he entered the ministry. His first sermon was greatly honored of God in the conversion of two souls. It was delivered at Hinckley, on the text, "If any man love not the Lord Jesus Christ, let him be Anathema, Maran atha."

His first charge was at Kibworth. In 1730 he took charge of a church, and started an academy at Northampton. This was designed for the training of young men for the ministry. About one hundred and twenty of his students entered the sacred office. Here he spent the rest of his life, attending to his collegiate and church duties, and writing his numerous and voluminous works.

Doddridge is described as a man "above the middle stature, extremely thin, and slender. His sprightliness and vivacity of countenance and manner commanded general attention in the pulpit and private circles. Mr. Hervey, speaking of spending a night with him at Northampton, says: "I never spent a more delightful evening, or saw one that seemed to make nearer approaches to heaven. A gentleman of great worth and rank in the town, invited us to his house, and gave us an elegant treat; but how mean was his provision, how coarse his delicacies, compared with the fruit of my friend's lips!—they dropped as the honey-comb, and were a well of life."

Doddridge possessed a vein of humor that would sometimes reveal itself through his pen. His daughter having had a thorn pierce her foot one day, he sent her these lines:—

"Oft I have heard the ancient sages say
The path of virtue is a thorny way:
If so, dear Celia, we may surely know
Which path it is you tread, which way it is you go."

This was the little daughter who was asked, how it was that everybody loved her, when she answered: "I know not," "unless it be that I love every body."

To one of his pupils, whose weak imagination had led him to think that he had invented a machine by which he could fly to the moon, he sent these lines:—

"And will Volatio leave this world so soon
To fly to his own native seat, the moon?
'Twill stand, however, in some little stead
That he sets out with such an empty head."

Dr. Johnson, who had been styled "the Old King of Critics," said that the following lines, written by Doddridge on his family arms, *Dum vivimus vivamus*, was the finest epigram in the English language:—

DODDRIDGE'S MOTHER TEACHING HIM.

> "'Live while you live,' the epicure would say,
> 'And seize the pleasures of the present day.'
> 'Live while you live,' the sacred preacher cries,
> 'And give to God each moment as it flies.'
> Lord, in my view let both united be:
> I live in pleasure when I live to thee.'

Of this "pleasure," he made frequent mention in his diary, and letters. After a season of sickness, he wrote:—

"It is impossible to express the support and comfort, which God gave me on my sick-bed. His promises were my continual feast. They seemed, as it were, to be all united in one stream of glory, and poured into my breast. When I thought of dying, it sometimes made my very heart to leap within me."

> "Awake, my soul, to meet the day,"

was written by Doddridge, who arose every morning at 5 o'clock. It was entitled, "A Morning Hymn, to be Sung at Awaking and Rising." His custom was to spring out of bed, while using the words of the sixth verse, commencing, "As rising now," &c. His Communion Hymn, is much used; the first stanza reads:—

> 'My God! and is thy table spread?
> And does thy cup with love overflow?
> Thither be all thy children led,
> And let them all its sweetness know."

Of this "sweetness" he speaks on this wise, after drinking from the cup of affliction, occasioned by the death of a much-loved daughter:—

"I recollected this day, at the Lord's table, that I had some time ago, taken the cup at that ordinance with these words, 'Lord, I take this cup as a public solemn token, that, having received so inestimable a blessing as this, I will refuse no other cup which thou shalt put into my hands.' *God hath taken me at my word*, but I will not retract it; I repeat it again with regard to every future cup, much *sweetness* is mingled with this potion."

When, through excessive labor, a deep seated consumption so enfeebled him, that he was hardly able to speak or move his dying body, the following incident occurred that illustrates the verse of one of his best hymns:—

> "When death o'er nature shall prevail,
> And all its power of language fail,
> Joy through my swimming eyes shall break,
> And mean the thanks I cannot speak."

"What, in tears again, my dear doctor," said Lady Huntingdon, as she entered his room and found him weeping over the Bible lying before him. "I am weeping, madam," he faintly replied, "but they are tears of joy and comfort. I can give up my country, my friends, my relatives, into the hands of God; and as to myself, I can as well go to heaven from Lisbon, as from my own study at Northampton." This calm resignation he had beautifully expressed in his hymn:—

> "While on the verge of life I stand,
> And view the scene on either hand,
> My spirit struggles with its clay,
> And longs to wing its flight away.
>
> Where Jesus dwells my soul would be;
> It faints my much-loved Lord to see;
> Earth! twine no more about my heart,
> For 'tis far better to depart."

"My profuse night-sweats" says he, "are weakening to my frame; but the most distressing nights to this frail body have been as the *beginning of heaven* to my soul. God hath, as it were, let heaven down upon me in those nights of weakness and waking. Blessed be his name."

It was thus, from blissful experience, he could say, in the language of his hymn:—

> "When, at this distance, Lord! we trace
> The various glories of thy face,
> What transport pours o'er all our breast,
> And charms our cares and woes to rest!"

Doddridge yielded to the advice of his friends to go to the warmer climate of Lisbon, for the winter of 1751. "I see indeed no prospect of recovery," said the dying man, "yet my heart rejoiceth in my God and my Saviour, and I can call him, under this failure of every thing else, its strength and everlasting portion."

"On the 30th of September," writes one of him, "accompanied by his anxious wife and servant, he sailed from Falmouth; and, revived by the soft breezes and the ship's stormless progress, he sat in his chair in the cabin enjoying the brightest thoughts of all his life. 'Such transporting views of the heavenly world is my Father now indulging me with, as no words can express,' was his frequent exclamation to the tender partner of his voyage."

When the ship was gliding up the Tagus, and Lisbon, with its groves and gardens and sunny towers, loomed up in the distance before him, the enchanting scene brought vividly before his mind that city which hath foundations, of which he so sweetly wrote in one of his hymns:—

> "See!—Salem's golden spires,
> In beauteous prospect, rise,
> And brighter crowns than mortals wear,
> Which sparkle through the skies."

Two weeks after the vessel landed at Lisbon, he exchanged the shores of time for the sunny plains of the Canaan above. The "peace of God which passeth all understanding" smoothed his dying pillow and spread such a halo of glory around his death-couch, that his afflicted wife could sit down afterwards and write to her children, saying: "Oh, my dear children, help me to praise Him. Such supports, such consolations, such comforts has he granted, that my mind at times is astonished and is ready to burst into songs of praise under its most exquisite distress."

Origin of Doddridge's Hymns.

DODDRIDGE possessed great versatility of talent. As, in his day, there was not a great variety of hymns adapted to the different subjects of discourse, he was accustomed, while his heart was aglow with the composition of his sermon, to arrange the leading thoughts in a hymn. This was sung at the close of his preaching, and served to give emphasis to his utterances, and to fix the truth more indelibly in the minds and upon the hearts of his hearers. For instance, after a sermon on the words, "Unto you therefore which believe, he is precious," he gave out the sweet hymn he had prepared:—

> "Jesus, I love thy charming name;
> 'Tis music to mine ear:
> Fain would I sound it out so loud,
> That earth and heaven could hear."

After preaching on the text, "There remaineth therefore a rest to the people of God," he announced the favorite Sunday hymn, beginning,

> "Lord of the Sabbath hear our vows."

As now in use, the hymn is often made to commence with the second verse:—

> "Thine earthly Sabbaths, Lord, we love,
> But there's a nobler rest above;
> To that our laboring souls aspire
> With ardent hope and strong desire."

The Rev. Dr. James Hamilton, referring to these hymns thus originated, says:—

"If amber is the gum of fossil trees, fetched up and floated off by the ocean, hymns like these are a spiritual amber. Most of the sermons to which they originally pertained have disappeared forever; but, at once beautiful and buoyant, these sacred strains are destined to carry the devout emotions of Doddridge to every shore where his Master is loved and where his mother-tongue is spoken."

Doddrige led by a Special Providence.

GREAT events often turn on a small pivot. The field of Doddridge's great usefulness was Northampton, yet he felt quite reluctant to go there, when the call was first extended, because of his sense of weakness and unfitness.

Among the means, which Providence used to decide the question, he mentions the following:—

On the last Sunday in November, 1729, he went to Northampton to decline the call, and, as he says, "to dispose them to submit to the will of God in events, which might be most contrary to their views and inclinations." To this end, he had arranged a sermon on the text, "And when he would not be persuaded, we ceased, saying, 'The will of the Lord be done.'" But he adds:—

"On the morning of that day, an incident happened, which affected me greatly. Having been much urged on Saturday evening, and much impressed with the tender entreaties of my friends, I had, in my secret devotion, been spreading the affair before God, though as a thing almost determined in the negative; appealing to Him, that my chief reason for declining the call, was the apprehension of engaging in more business than I was capable of performing, considering my age, the largeness of the congregation, and that I had no prospect of an assistant. As soon as ever this address ended, I passed through a room of the house in which I lodged, where a child was reading to his mother, and the only words I heard distinctly were these, '*And as thy days, so shall thy strength be.*'" This seemed a voice from heaven, he afterwards accepted the call and wrote of his charge:—

"'T is not a cause of small import
The pastor's care demands!
But what might fill an angel's heart,
And filled a Saviour's hands."

Doddridge's Hymn Sung with Dying Breath.

MRS. SARAH L. SMITH left Boston in 1833, for a foreign missionary field, where, two years later she sank into the grave, in the thirty-fourth year of her age. "Tell my friends," said she, "I would not for all the world lay my remains anywhere but here, on missionary ground." Of her triumphant death, an eye-witness wrote:—

"We sung the first verse of that beautiful hymn of Doddridge, on the eternal Sabbath:—

> "'Thine earthly Sabbaths, Lord, we love,
> But there's a nobler rest above;
> To that our laboring souls aspire
> With ardent hope and strong desire.'

"To my surprise, her voice, which she had so long been unable to use for singing, was occasionally heard mingling with ours. Her face beamed with a smile of ecstacy; and so intense was the feeling, expressed in her whole aspect, that we stopped after the first verse, lest she should even expire while drinking the cup of joy, we had presented to her. But she said to us 'Go on;' and, though all were bathed in tears, and hardly able to articulate, we proceeded to sing:—

> "'No more fatigue, no more distress,
> Nor sin, nor hell shall reach the place;
> No groans to mingle with the songs,
> Which warble from immortal tongues,'

"I was sitting with her hand in mine. While singing this second verse, she pressed it, and turned to me at the same time such a heavenly smile as stopped my utterance. Before we reached the end, she raised both her hands above her head, and gave vent to her feelings, in tears of pleasure, and almost in shouting. Afterwards she said, 'I have had a little glimpse of what I am going to see. . . . . It seemed a glorious sight.'"

The Hymn-prayer at the Gate.

AT the close of an "Illustrated Sermon" inquirers and others were invited to retire to an adjoining room for prayer. As many filled the room and were disposed to take the prodigal's first step homeward, for the encouragement of such, a stranger, an old gentleman from the South, arose and said: "Over forty years ago, during a season of similar awakening in Virginia, a young prodigal felt it was time for him to start home. He had never been accustomed to pray and felt afraid to venture near the Majestic Ruler of the universe. He was then attending an academy, a mile distant from his father's house. Taking a short cut through the fields to his home, he thought he could possibly find some suitable place to unburden his heavily-laden heart in prayer.

"As he beheld a retired spot in the fence-corner, he concluded to open his lips there. But his courage failed him, and he said to himself, 'In the distance is a big, white oak tree; that will shield me.' But when under the tree his stubborn will would still not yield. A fork in the road and nearly a dozen other places he tried, but when he drew near to them, the tempter also drew near, and caused postponement, until at length he got to the gate at the head of the lane leading to the house. This was the last resort where he could pray unseen. It seemed to him as the turning point. As he sank at Jesus' feet, a hymn came to his lips as the language of his heart, and so he cried out:—

> "'Show pity, Lord! O Lord, forgive;
> Let a repenting sinner live.'

The six verses of that hymn-prayer decided his destiny. He became a minister, has been preaching many years, and is now the old man you see before you."

"O happy day that fixed my choice."

JOINING the church is often attended with the singing of this expressive hymn, written by Philip Doddridge.

The fourth verse was once the means of bringing peace to an anxious soul, as thus described by an English writer:—

"It was my happiness some time since to be a guest in a family. One morning I saw one of the servants in the deepest exercise of soul about her salvation. She had been singing that hymn,—

> "'Now rest my long divided heart,
> Fixed on this blissful centre rest;
> With ashes, who would grudge to part,
> When called on angels' food to feast.'"

"I saw her troubled. She felt she had not loved God enough, or prayed enough, or wept enough. I knew she was occupying her mind about herself, and that she did not see what *Christ was*. I remarked that self was mere 'ashes.' I asked why not part with the condemned doomed ashes of self, and believe in Jesus? It was during the family service I saw her countenance so change from its old sadness into happiness and joy; and I thought—What a revulsion is taking place in that mind! and, wishing to know for myself, I called her aside into the drawing-room. I said, 'You seem happy now.' 'I am happy,' was the reply. 'What has made you happy?' 'Oh, I did just what you told me to do. I put myself down to the third chapter of John.' 'What do you mean?' 'Why there where it says, 'God so loved the world.' 'Yes, but was that a world of saints or of angels?' 'No.' 'What was it then?' 'A world of sinners. Then I put myself down into that world and I found God loved *me*, and had given his Son for me.'"

THIS hymn is often used as fitly describing the birthday into the kingdom, and is in this respect like the one Wesley wrote:—

"O for a thousand tongues to sing,"

which he styled, "*For the anniversary of one's conversion.*"

In 1871, there was an extensive revival in Wisconsin, and in one church they adopted the plan, whenever on an evening, a sinner decided to be Christ's, the audience united in singing:—

"Oh, happy day that fixed my choice
On Thee, my Saviour and my God."

"After the third night, there was the blessed privilege of singing it every evening for fifty days, for one or more, in whom this purpose was newly formed: and many were led to make the choice while it was sung."

The chorus and tune of "Happy day," became wedded to this hymn, and was everywhere and frequently sung during the great revival in 1858. A Maine physician was requested to certify to what is said in the second verse,—

"'Tis done, the great transaction's done;
I am my Lord's, and He is mine,"

when he answered, "I can certify to all but the the last words. I can say 'I am the Lord's,' but cannot say 'He is mine.' I have no consciousness of his acceptance of me." And yet his experience verified the Scripture statement, "With the heart man believeth unto righteousness, and with the mouth confession is made unto salvation." For the moment he opened his mouth and made this confession, he realized the sweet assurance, and afterwards could say, "HE IS MINE."

> "Awake, my soul, stretch every nerve,
> And press with vigor on:
> A heavenly race demands thy zeal,
> And an immortal crown."

A MINISTERIAL brother says that when a child he heard a sermon on the text, "So run that ye obtain," and hearing the members so urgently exhorted to engage in a race, he thought it was going to take place right after the service. Greatly did he feel disappointed, when, having hastened out of church to get a good position on the fence, from which he could get a good view of the racers, he found that they did not "run a bit."

In Cunningham valley, Pa., we had literally such a race at the close of preaching. The church consisted of but one audience-room, and that was wedged so full of hearers, that it was impossible in a prayer-meeting service to speak to those who desired to make known their anxieties, and to seek special advice. So we secured three rooms at a hotel a few squares distant. But these, proving inadequate to hold all, there was a regular race at the close of each service to gain admittance.

As there was a thaw in mid-winter, and the roads unpaved, it was an amusing sight to see the audience splashing through the mud on a regular trot,—men, women and children running as for their lives.

What still added to the impressiveness of the scene was the fact that the tavern sign, swinging on its rusty pivots over our heads as we entered the tavern, screeched most piteously, as if it were uttering the death groans of King Alcohol, and so they proved to be.

Most of the inmates of the landlord's family becoming subjects of grace, the sign-post was cut down after the close of our meeting, and the building was afterwards used for other purposes.

A Hymn of One Word.

IN an article concerning the Bedouin Arabs, in the *Christian Standard*, Dr. Stephen Fish gives the origin of a hymn made up of one word. Says he: "Many Bedouin Arabs have embraced the Christian religion. Mr. M. Roysce, of Jerusalem, gave me a very interesting account of the conversion of an Arab whom he knew to be a poet. Soon after he was converted Mr. Roysce was anxious to see if he would write religious poetry. He requested Suleiman to court the Muses, and compose for him a poem on the duties of the Christian missionary, and he did so, and wrote the following:—

"Taiyib, taiyib, taiyib, taiyib,
Taiyib, taiyib, taiyib,
Taiyib, taiyib. taiyib, taiyib,
Taiyib, taiyib, taiyib."

"Any trivial sentiment would not bear repeating quite so many times, but the translation of '*Taiyib*' is '*Go on,*' and the Arab, zealous in his new life, could think of nothing but going ahead in it and growing better and better."

TO a discouraged Christian who was about to give up some good work because he saw no results, a fellow laborer remarked, "I'll give out a hymn and you sing it. It is common metre." The verse above translated in English was the one announced:—

"Go on, go on, go on, go on,
Go on, go on, go on,
Go on, go on, go on, go on,
Go on, go on, go on."

The advice thus given was heeded. The weary one did "go on," and glorious results followed.

A Revival Started by Singing a Hymn.

A prayer-meeting of a country village was attended by but few during a season of coldness. The pastor was absent, his place being supplied by one of his deacons, who, for months past, had been deeply mourning in secret the sad decline.

Dr. Belcher says: "The hymn he selected with which to commence the service was the one:—

"'Hear, gracious Saviour, from thy throne,
And send thy various blessings down.'

Two or three verses were sung to an old tune, till the good deacon came to the last, which thus reads. The reader will observe especially the last two lines:—

"'In answer to our fervent cries,
Give us to see thy church arise;
Or, if that blessing seem too great,
Give us to mourn its low estate.'

While reading this verse, the good man paused: it evidently did not exactly accord with the feelings of his soul: it was not the expression of *his* prayer. He indulged a moment's thought,—swift and excellent: an alteration suggested itself,—his eye sparkled with joy, —and out it came:—

"'In answer to our fervent cries,
Give us to see thy church arise;
That blessing, Lord, is not too great,
Though now we mourn its low estate.'

Every heart was arrested, and sudden emotion so overpowered all in the little assembly that they could scarcely sing the words; but each in silence gave to the sentiment his own earnest amen. They happily proved it to be true. From that evening a revival began: the church arose from its slumber to new faith and works; and very soon the windows of heaven were opened and a plenitude of blessings was showered down, which continued for several years."

Heaven as Represented in Song.

A WRITER says in the *Ladies' Repository*: "Mr. Editor, in your notes on Sunday school songs you quote from one of our hymn-writers the lines—

> "'O Golden Hereafter!
> Thine ever bright rafter
> Will shake in the thunder of sanctified song.'

"Can you kindly refer me to the author and his place of residence, that I may write to him?

"He seems to possess information which I have been unable to get from my pocket Bible, and it is possible that he can relieve my anxiety about the 'Golden Hereafter.'

"What I want to know is, whether there is any danger of the plastering or timbers tumbling down when the rafters shake. Yours in affliction."

After a thirty years' residence in Jamaica, a missionary remarks, "One who knows what it is to be exposed to the sun of the torrid zone, shudders to read the lines of Doddridge, describing Heaven:—

> "'No midnight shade, no clouded sun,
> But sacred, high, eternal noon.'

"The idea is intolerable. It terrifies one to think of it. The man who wrote the lines must have lived far north, where the glimpse of the sun was a rare favor, and his highest enjoyment to bask in its rays a live-long summer day.

"I met once in Jamaica with a black boy, under the shade of a cocoa-nut tree, where we both had taken shelter from the glare of the meridian sun, and the dazzling sea-side sandy road. I said, 'Well, my lad, did you ever hear of heaven? 'Me hear, Massa.' 'And what sort of a place do you think it will be?' 'Massa, it must be a very *cool* place.'"

Origin of "Stand up! stand up for Jesus."

DURING the revival period of 1858, the watchword of Christ's army seemed to be the message of one of her fallen heroes, the Rev. Dudley A. Tyng, who, when suddenly, in the vigor of early manhood, was stretched out upon a death-bed, said, as his parting words to his brethren, *Stand up for Jesus.* Under their inspiration the Rev. George Duffield composed the popular hymn:—

"Stand up! stand up for Jesus,"

to be sung after his sermon on the Sabbath morning following the sudden death of Mr. Tyng in the spring of 1858.

Shortly before his departure he delivered a memorable sermon in Jayne's Hall, Philadelphia, on the text, " Ye that are men now serve Him," in which the slain of the Lord were many.

Mr. Duffield has embraced these words in quotation marks in the verse:—

"Stand up! stand up for Jesus!
  The trumpet call obey."
Forth to the mighty conflict
  In this his glorious day:
'Ye that are men, now serve him'
  Against unnumbered foes;
Your courage rise with danger,
  And strength to strength oppose."

During our meetings in the Union Tabernacle at Quakertown, in the fall of that year, we sang and often referred to those words. One morning the parents of a little girl were awakened by the repeated call of their little girl in the cradle, whose pleading voice kept saying, "Papa! mama! Pa-pa! ma-ma! Mis-ser Long say 'Tan up—tan up for Y-e-s-u-s."

This little stammering voice went so deep down in the hearts of the parents that in the evening of the same day they did "Stand up for Jesus," and after soliciting an interest in the prayers of God's people, became at length earnest and decided soldiers of the cross.

A gentleman gave a card to a little girl, one day, in a railroad car. Supposing that she could not read, he said: "This card says, 'Stand up for Jesus.'" "Does it?" said she. And as if acting under heavenly impulses, she went along the row of seats, saying to each one, "Stand up for Jesus! Stand up for Jesus!" When she got down one side, she turned around, and coming up the other side, repeated the same words, "Stand up for Jesus! Stand up for Jesus!" The unusual sound of such words, in such a place, and their frequent repetition, produced a deep impression on many. Her mother leaned over and wept as a child, and thereby was induced to seek the pardon of her sins. Two weeks later, she united with the church, and afterward did "Stand up for Jesus."

Another little one took a noble stand for Jesus, in the overflowings of her heart. A man, given to profanity, called at her father's house, one day, and in his conversation, dropped an oath. It fell like a hot coal of fire upon the tender conscience of the child, and so she burst out crying, as if severely hurt, and left the room. When the cause was inquired into, she sobbed out, "He cursed my Jesus." When the swearer heard the reproof, it pierced his heart, and was the means of his reformation.

Some commentators say that the verse in Exodus, XVII. 9, should be translated to read, "To-morrow I will *take my stand* on the top of the hill, and the staff of God in my hand."

Would that on all the hilltops of Zion, there were Moseses who would unfurl the banner of the cross, and take a stand for Jesus.

"Stand up, stand up for Jesus,
Ye soldiers of the cross."

Author of "I love Thy kingdom, Lord."

THIS hymn was issued in 1800 by Timothy Dwight, D. D., who was also the author of another hymn:—

> "While life prolongs its precious light,
> Mercy is found and peace is given."

He was born in Massachusetts in 1752. His father was a merchant, his mother a daughter of the celebrated Jonathan Edwards. She began in early infancy to enlighten his conscience and make him afraid of sin. These impressions became permanent. Such was his eagerness and capacity, that he learned the alphabet at a single lesson, and already "at the age of four could read the Bible with ease and correctness."

At eight he was so far advanced in his studies that he would have been ready for admission into Yale college, and when he actually did enter at thirteen, he was already master of history, geography and the classics. At seventeen he graduated. Devoting fourteen hours daily to close study, his sight was irreparably impaired, and he was compelled to employ an amanuensis. At nineteen he was appointed tutor.

At twenty he issued a work on the "History, Eloquence, and Poetry of the Bible," which procured him great honor. In 1777 he was chosen chaplain of the army, and in 1795, President of Yale college. In 1809 he issued his "Theology" in five volumes. After the severe studies of the day he would write poetry at night. Well could he say of the church:—

> "For her my tears shall fall;
> For her my prayers ascend;
> To her my cares and toils be given,
> Till toils and cares shall end."

He expired in 1817, saying of some Bible promises that were being read to him, "O what triumphant truths!"

REV. TIMOTHY DWIGHT, S.T.D. LL.D.
PRESIDENT OF YALE COLLEGE
FROM 1795 TO 1817.

Singing in a Forsaken Church.

IN the "Holland Purchase" a log church was built by Methodist pioneers. It flourished well for years, but eventually some of the old members died, and others moved away, till only one was left, when preaching also ceased.

This mother in Israel sighed over the desolations in Zion. She loved the old forsaken sanctuary, and still kept going there on the Sabbath to worship God and plead the promises.

At length it was noised abroad that she was a witch, that the old church was haunted with evil spirits, and that she went there to commune with them.

Two young men to satisfy their curiosity, secreted themselves in the loft to watch her. On her arrival she took her seat by the altar. After reading the Scriptures, she announced the hymn,

"Jesus, I my cross have taken,"

and sang it with a sweet but trembling voice, then kneeled down and poured out her heart in fervent prayer and supplication.

She recounted the happy seasons of the past, plead for a revival, and for the many who had forgotten Zion.

Her pleadings broke the hearts of the young men. They began to weep and cry for mercy.

As the Saviour called Zaccheus to come down, so did she invite them down from their hiding-place.

They obeyed, and there at the altar, where in other days she had seen many conversions, they too knelt, confessed their sins, sought and found the Saviour.

From that hour the work of God revived, the meetings were resumed, a flourishing church grew up, and the old meeting house was made to resound with the happy voices of God's children. *Dr. Strickland.*

Singing heard in the Wilderness.

ONE hundred years ago Georgia was a wild wilderness. Preaching places were "few and far between." In one of the settlements, six miles distant from each other, lived two pious women.

They felt lost when moving there, away from their accustomed places of worship in Maryland, and especially as the people in these settlements spent their Sundays in frolicking and hunting.

These two women agreed to meet half way between their homes, and hold a prayer-meeting by themselves. Sabbath after Sabbath they walked to their appointment, and there in the depth of that southern forest engaged in prayer and praise.

The singing, echoing through the wild woods, attracted the attention of a hunter.

As he drew near to a hiding place, he was overwhelmed by what he heard. Sabbath after Sabbath he would hide near enough to hear, till, at the close of one of their meetings, he could not conceal himself or his feelings any longer. He then invited them to meet at his cabin the next Sabbath, promising to collect in his neighbors.

The call seemed providential. They accepted it. It was soon noised abroad. The whole neighborhood turned out. Their husbands went along to see these strange women. When lo! their own wives took charge of the meeting. The Holy Spirit moved and melted first the heart of the hunter, then of the two husbands. They broke out in cries of mercy. The meeting continued night and day for some two weeks. After some forty were converted, Rev. B. Maxey heard of it. He took charge of the revival which continued to spread over a vast region of country, till many churches sprang up where preaching had never been heard before.

A Prisoner Singing Himself into Liberty.

THIS was the case with Deacon Epa Norris during the war between Great Britain and the United States, in 1812. He lived in the Northern Neck, Va. Being captured and taken to a British vessel, they in vain sought to obtain from him the position and numbers of the American Army.

Dr. Belcher says: "The commandant of the ship gave a dinner to the officers of the fleet, and did Mr. Norris the honor to select him from the American prisoners of war to be a guest. The deacon, in his homespun attire, took his seat at the table with the aristocracy of the British navy. The company sat long at the feast: they drank toasts, told stories, laughed and sang songs. At length Mr. Norris was called on for a song. He desired to excuse himself, but in vain: he must sing. He possessed a fine, strong, musical voice. In an appropriate and beautiful air, he commenced singing:—

"'Sweet is the work, my God, my King,
To praise thy name, give thanks, and sing.'

"Thoughts of home and of lost religious privileges, and of his captivity, imparted an unusual pathos and power to his singing. One stanza of the excellent psalm must have seemed peculiarly pertinent to the occasion:—

"'Fools never raise their thoughts so high:
Like brutes they live, like brutes they die;
Like grass they flourish, till thy breath
Blast them in everlasting death.'

"When the singing ceased, a solemn silence ensued. At length the commandant broke it by saying: 'Mr. Norris, you are a good man, and shall return immediately to your family.' The commodore kept his word; for in a few days Mr. Norris was sent ashore in a barge, with a handsome present of salt,—then more valuable in the country than gold."

Author of "Just as I am, without one plea."

THIS world-renowned hymn, issued in 1836 by Charlotte Elliott, is spoken of as "the divinest of heart-utterances in song that modern times have bestowed upon us." It is one of those hymns that are suited to all ages, characters, and conditions in life.

Mr. Saunders says: "The plaintive melody of the refrain cannot but awaken a responsive echo in every devout soul, as the sad notes of some lone bird are caught up and repeated amid the stillness of the silvan solitude."

Rev. R. S. Cook, of New York, sent to Miss Elliott a companion and counterpart to her hymn, commencing:

"Just as thou art, without one trace."

Miss Elliott is grand-daughter of the Rev. John Venn, and sister of Rev. E. B. Elliott, author of the "Horæ Apocalypticæ," and of Rev. Henry Venn Elliott, himself a writer of hymns.

Mr. Miller says (1869) "that she formerly resided at Torquay, where the neighborhood was greatly benefited by her piety and benefactions, and is now residing at an advanced age and infirm health at Brighton."

She is represented as "a lover of nature, a lover of souls, and a lover of Christ."

Her heart and pen are kept so busy with writing for her Master, that it is said that even in her old age, she seldom appears at the breakfast table without more or less of poetical composition in manuscript.

She has issued the following publications: In 1842, "Morning and Evening Hymns for a Week, by a Lady; in 1836, "Hours of Sorrow Cheered and Comforted;" in 1863, "Poems by E. C.;" yearly she has issued "The Christian Remembrance;" besides contributing one hundred hymns to the Invalids' Hymn-Book.

CHARLOTTE ELLIOTT.

"Just as I am" was an epitome of Miss Elliott's experience. Her sister says that in 1821 "she became deeply conscious of the evil in her own heart, and having not yet fully realized the fulness and freeness of the grace of God in the Lord Jesus Christ, she suffered much mental distress under the painful uncertainty whether it were possible that such a one as she felt herself to be could be saved."

After groping her way through darkness for a year, Dr. Malan of Geneva paid her a visit at her father's house on the ninth of May, 1822. Seeing how she was held back from the Saviour by her own self-saving efforts, he said: "Dear Charlotte, cut the cable, it will take too long to unloose it; cut it, it is a small loss," and then bidding her give "one look, silent but continuous at the cross of Jesus," she was enabled at once freely to say;—

> "Just as I am—without one plea
> But that thy blood was shed for me,
> And that thou bid'st me come to thee,
> O Lamb of God, I come!"

"From that time," says her sister, "for forty years his constant correspondence was justly esteemed the greatest blessing of her life. The anniversary of that memorable date was always kept as a festal day; and on that day, so long as Dr. Malan lived, commemorative letters passed from the one to the other, as upon the birthday of her soul to true spiritual life and peace." Dr. Malan as a skilful spiritual physician had carefully probed the wound, and led her to the true remedy for all her anxiety,—namely, simple faith in God's own word. It was thus from her own experience she could write:—

> "Just as I am —thou wilt receive,
> Wilt welcome, pardon, cleanse, relieve;
> Because thy promise I believe,
> O Lamb of God, I come!"

"From that ever memorable day," it is said her "spiritual horizon was for the most part cloudless," until, in the bright vision that attended her dying moments, she could say in the language of her last verse;—

> "Just as I am—of that free love,
> The breadth, length, depth, and height to prove,
> Here, for a season, then above,
> O Lamb of God, I come."

Calmly she closed her eyes in death, September 22, 1871.

A POOR little boy once came to a New York city missionary, and holding up a dirty and worn-out bit of printed paper, said, "Please, sir, father sent me to get a *clean* paper like that." Taking it from his hand, the missionary unfolded it, and found that it was a page containing the precious hymn:—

> "Just as I am—without one plea."

He looked down with deep interest into the face so earnestly upturned towards him, and asked the little boy where he got it, and why he wanted a clean one. "We found it, sir," said he, "in sister's pocket, after she died, and she used to sing it all the time she was sick, and she loved it so much that father wanted to get a clean one, and put it in a frame to hang it up. Wont you please to give us a clean one, sir?"

The son-in-law of the poet Wordsworth sent to Miss Elliott a letter, telling of the great comfort afforded his wife when on her dying bed, by the hymn. Said he, when "I first read it, I had no sooner finished than she said very earnestly, 'that is the very thing for me.' At least ten times that day she asked me to repeat it, and every morning from that day till her decease, nearly two months later, the first thing she asked me for was her hymn.

"Now *my* hymn," she would say—and she would often repeat it after me, line for line, in the day and night."

"O Sir! I've come, I've come."

THE Rev. Dr. McCook, while in his pastorate at St. Louis, was sent for to see a young lady who was dying of consumption. He soon found that she had imbibed infidelity through the influence of her teacher in the Normal School, and with her keen intellect was enabled to ward off all the claims of the gospel.

After exhausting all the arguments he could think of during his visits, he was exceedingly puzzled to know what more to do, as she seemed unshaken in her doubts. She at length seemed so averse to the subject of religion that when calling one day, she turned her face to the wall and seemed to take no notice of him. Mr. McCook said: "Lucy, I have not called to argue with you another word, but before leaving you to meet the issues of eternity I wish to recite a hymn." He then repeated with much emphasis the hymn:—

"Just as I am, without one plea,"

and then bade her adieu. She made no response. He was debating for some time whether, after so much repugnance, he should call again. But realizing her nearness to the eternal world he concluded to make one more visit. Taking his seat by her bedside she slowly turned around in bed. Her sunken eyes shone with unwonted lustre, as she placed her thin, emaciated hands in his and said slowly, and with much emotion:—

"'Just as I am, without one plea,
But that thy blood was shed for me,
And that thou bidst me come to thee,
O Lamb of God, I come, I come.'

"O Sir! *I've come. I've come.*" That hymn told the story. It had decided her eternal destiny. It had done what all the logical arguments had failed to do.

She soon afterwards peacefully crossed the river.

"Just as I am" Uttered with a Dying Breath.

JESSIE, a young lady of eighteen, whose home is in Vermont, while attending seminary was taken very ill. It seemed only a slight illness, but to the surprise of all, when the doctor was summoned, he said: "You can have but a few hours to live." A correspondent says: "Not one who was present will forget that look of awe and terror that covered Jessie's face. '*O pray for me*,' was her agonized request of all her friends. To her schoolmates she sent the message, 'Tell them to be Christians, for they know not at what moment they may be surprised as I have been.' She then began to say:—

> "'Just as I am, without one plea,
> But that Thy blood was shed for me,
> And that Thou bidst me come to Thee,
> O Lamb of God, I come.'

"The second verse was begun in a faint whisper:—

> "'Just as I am, and waiting not,
> To rid my soul of one dark blot,
> To Thee—'

With the word, '*Thee*' upon her lips, she breathed her last breath and passed away to the spirit-land."

FAR out on the Western prairies dwelt a father who had not been to church for fifteen years. After death laid some of his family in the grave, God's "still small voice" came to him. "All alone," said he, "out there on the prairie, with no religious teacher, no Christian friend, God spoke to me. I then gladly went to hear a missionary preach in a school-house. Was this salvation for me? Could I, so long a wanderer, come and be forgiven? While agitated with these thoughts, they sang:

> "'Just as I am, without one plea.'

It told my story, and before it was ended, I could say:—

> "'O Lamb of God, I come.'"

"To thee, whose blood can cleanse each spot."

A MISSIONARY in his travels, found a heathen expiring by the wayside. Inquiring of his hopes for the life to come, the dying man whispered: "The blood of Jesus Christ cleanseth us from all sin;" and with this utterance he breathed his last breath. The missionary, perceiving a bit of paper in his closed hand, took it from his grasp, when, to his great joy, he found it to be a leaf of the Bible, containing the First chapter of 1st John, on which was printed the text that gave him his hold on eternal life. Ascending thus to the skies, he could truthfully say, in the language of Miss Elliott's hymn:—

> "To thee, whose blood can cleanse each spot,
> O Lamb of God, I come."

ONE day, a dying girl, twelve years old, rousing from her slumbers, said: "Aunty, how do you know you are a Christian?" To which the answer was given: "Darling, we love Jesus, and try to do what he tells us. Do you want to be a Christian?" "Oh, yes aunty!"

The lines of the hymn were then quoted:—

> "Just as I am, without one plea.
> But that thy blood was shed for me,
> And that thou bidst me come to thee,
> O Lamb of God, I come! I come!" etc.

when she continued, "Oh, aunty, isn't that lovely?" During the convulsions that followed, and closed her earthly career, she could be heard saying: "Abba, Father, Thou knowest that I love thee. Aunty will teach me."

When her baby brother was brought in to see her in her coffin, he truthfully said: "TATIE SEEPIN." This seemed to the weeping parents but the echo of the Master's words: "She is not dead, but sleepeth."

The Young Chorister's Last Hymn.

EVERYBODY knew Claude Davenel was dying; he knew it himself, and his mother knew it as she sat there watching him. All the villagers knew it, and many an eye was wet as the name of little Claude was whispered among them.

Claude had taken his illness on a chilly autumn evening, when the choir was practising in church. One of his companions, Willie Dalton, complained of a sore throat, so that he could not sing, and he sat down cold and sick in his own place. Claude took off his comforter and wrapped it around his friend's neck, and when the practising was over he ran home with him, and then put on his comforter again as he went back to his own home.

Willie was sickening for the scarlet fever; and poor Claude caught it too. Willie recovered; but Claude had taken the disease in its worst form, and though the fever had left him, he had never been able to recover his strength, and he had grown weaker and wasted away.

And so it was on this calm Sunday evening. He had been drawn up close to the window, to listen to the church bells slowly ringing out and calling people in.

The bell stopped, and Claude's eyes grew more wistful as the sound of the organ fell upon his ear. That stopped too, and then all was still. He closed his eyes until he heard it again; and then he opened them, listening intently.

"They are coming out now, mother," he said, after a minute's pause. "Lift me up a little, mother dear; I want to see them. I can hear the boys' foot steps on the gravel—lift me up a little higher, mother—they are coming this way. I can't see them, but I can hear them—they are coming down our street. Mother, put your hand out, and wave my handkerchief to them."

The trampling of feet had stopped under his window, and there was a low murmur of voices. Another moment and there was a gentle tap at the door, and Willie Dalton slipped in.

"Mrs. Davenel, we want to sing to Claude."

The question had been whispered, but Claude heard and caught at it eagerly.

"Oh, do! do! Mother, let me hear them—just once more."

The poor mother nodded her head sadly.

"It can't hurt him, Willie, and he likes it."

The boy cast a loving glance upon his friend, and then went quietly out of the room.

There were a few minutes of silence below, and then the choir-boys sang Claude's favorite hymn:—

> "My God, my Father, while I stray
> Far from my home in life's rough way,
> Oh, teach me from my heart to say,
>   'Thy will be done!'"

He clasped his hands together and gently began to join in when they sang the fourth verse:—

> "If thou should'st call me to resign
> What most I prize, it ne'er was mine,
> I only yield Thee what is Thine:
>   'Thy will be done!'"

When the hymn was ended his mother bent down over her son. His head had fallen back upon the pillow and the color had fled from his cheeks.

"Mother," he said, "write 'Thy will be done' over my grave when I am gone."

So the little chorister died. He is buried in a spot near the path to the choir vestry; and till those choir-boys had given place to others, they used to sing each year the same hymn, at Claude Davenel's grave, on the evening of the day on which he died. *Children's Prize.*

Fawcett and his Hymns.

ALTHOUGH Whitefield did not perpetuate his influence through the composition of any hymns, yet he was the means of the conversion of some hymn-writers, who are, after the march of a century, still shaping the eternal destiny of precious souls. Who can measure the circle of influence that has widened out through the singing of that oft-repeated hymn:—

"Come, thou Fount of every blessing!"

Its author, Robert Robinson, was among the thousands of Whitefield's converts. So was also the Rev. John Fawcett, D. D. Both, when lads of about sixteen years of age, were drawn into the stream of salvation by the tide of Whitefield's popularity.

Fawcett was born at Lidget Green, England, January 6, 1739. His father having died when he was twelve years of age, he was apprenticed for six years at Bradford.

While at this place he was tempted to follow the crowds that everywhere surrounded the eloquent Whitefield.

The sermon, that was made effective to his conversion, was from the words, "And as Moses lifted up the serpent in the wilderness, even so must the Son of Man be lifted up." "As long as life remains," he says, "I shall remember both the text and the sermon."

In 1758, he united with the newly-formed Baptist church at Bradford. After using his talents in exhortation for some time, he was urged by the church to prepare for the regular work of the ministry. To this advice he yielded. In May, 1765, he was ordained as pastor of the Baptist church at Wainsgate. Two years later, he issued his "Poetic Essays," and in 1782, he gathered together his hymns, one hundred and sixty-six in number, in a volume, entitled, "Hymns adapted to the circumstances of Public Worship and Private Devotion."

JOHN FAWCETT.

In 1788, he published an invaluable little volume on "Anger." George III. having been presented with a copy, was so much pleased, that he sent word to the author, that he would confer any favor upon him that he might desire. Fawcett, however, modestly declined availing himself of the royal munificence.

Some time afterwards, however, the son of one of his most intimate friends committed forgery in an unguarded moment, and was sentenced to death. Fawcett interceded on his behalf, the king remembered his former offer, and granted the pardon. The young man afterwards became a devoted Christian, and was thus saved for time and eternity.

Fawcett often said, "If the Lord has given to man the ability to raise such melodious sounds and voices on earth, what delightful harmony will there be in heaven?"

One of his sweet hymns is entitled, "Praise on Earth and in Heaven," of which the first and fourth stanzas, are,

"Joyfully on earth adore him
Till in heaven our song we raise;
There enraptured fall before him,
Lost in wonder, love, and praise.

"Praise to thee, thou great Creator,
Praise be thine from every tongue;
Join, my soul, with every creature,
Join the universal song."

"Among his other hymns that are still frequently sung, we may mention those commencing,

"Religion is the chief concern
Of mortals here below."

"Sinners, the voice of God regard."

"Thy presence, gracious God, affords."

"How precious is the book divine."

"Thy way, O God, is in the sea."

"Blest be the Tie that Binds."

THIS sweet hymn was written by Rev. John Fawcett D. D. in 1772. The following are given as the interesting facts that occasioned it.

After he had been a few years in the ministry, his family increasing far more rapidly than his income, he thought it was his duty to accept a call to settle as pastor of a Baptist church in London, to succeed the celebrated Dr. Gill. He preached his farewell sermon to his church in Yorkshire, and loaded six or seven wagons with his furniture, books, etc., to be carried to his new residence. All this time the members of his poor church were almost broken hearted, fervently did they pray that even now he might not leave them; and, as the time for departure arrived, men, women, and children clung around him and his family in perfect agony of soul.

The last wagon was being loaded, when the good man and his wife sat down on one of his packing-cases to weep. Looking into his tearful face, while tears like rain fell down her own cheeks, his devoted wife said, "Oh, John, John, I cannot bear this! I know not how to go!" "Nor I, either," said the good man; "nor will we go. Unload the wagons and put everything in the place where it was before." The people cried for joy. A letter was sent to the church in London to tell them that his coming to them was impossible; and the good man buckled on his armor for renewed labors on a salary of less than three hundred dollars a year.

He then took his pen and wrote the words,

"Blest be the tie that binds
Our hearts in Christian love,"

as expressive of the golden bond of union that knit pastor and people so closely and tenderly together.

Dr. Belcher.

Singing of "Blest be the tie that binds."

MANY have been the occasions when this hymn has just suited to give expression to the outgushings of that brotherly affection that unites the hearts of God's dear children. It was sung with great emphasis and significance at the reunion of the Old and New School divisions of the Presbyterian Church, in 1859. The two bodies having met in two churches, at Pittsburg, Pa., they afterwards formed on opposite sides of the street, and then moved along one block, when a halt was made. The two moderators, who headed their respective columns, then approached and grasped each other's hands, which example was followed by the two opposite ranks, until "amidst welcomes, thanksgivings, and tears, they locked arms," and thus marched, as one united host, to the temple of God, where they sang:—

>"All hail the power of Jesus' name,"

and then blended their voices in the grand old doxology:—

>"Praise God, from whom all blessings flow."

The tide of feeling gradually rose till it reached its culmination, when Dr. Fowler, the moderator of the New School body, turned to Dr. Jacobus, the moderator of the Old School body, saying: "My dear brother moderator, may we not, before I take my seat, perform a single act, symbolical of the union which has taken place between the two branches of the church. Let us clasp hands." This challenge was immediately responded to, "amid prolonged and deafening applause." After which, the thousands present, amid flowing tears and swelling hearts, joined in singing:—

>"Blest be the tie that binds,
> Our hearts in Christian love;
> The fellowship of kindred minds,
> Is like to that above."

A Sweet Hymn Born In Sorrow.

PAUL Gerhardt was born in Saxony, in the year 1606. He is the author of many choice hymns. It was in a dark day he wrote the hymn—

"Give to the winds thy fears,
Hope and be undismayed.—"

On account of some conflict with the king in his religious sentiments, he was ordered to leave the Nicholas church at Berlin, where he had preached for ten years, and quit the country. With his helpless wife and little ones he turned his steps towards Saxony, his native land.

The journey, taken on foot, was long and weary. As they turned aside to spend the night in a little village inn, his wife, overcome with sorrow, gave way to tears of anguish. Gerhardt, concealing his own sadness, quoted the beautiful promise—"Trust in the Lord; in all thy ways acknowledge Him, and He shall direct thy paths."

His own mind was so impressed by these words, that he turned aside and composed this hymn.

Late that evening, as Gerhardt and his wife sat in the little parlor, two gentlemen came in, and after some general conversation, said they were going to Berlin to Gerhardt, the deposed minister. Madam Gerhardt turned pale with alarm, fearing some new calamity. Her husband, however, with entire self-possession, told the strangers that he was the man. One of the gentlemen then gave him a letter from Duke Christian, of Meresburg, informing him that in view of his unjust deposition from the church in Berlin, he had settled a pension on him. Gerhardt in the joy of that moment, quietly turned to his wife and gave her the hymn he had composed in the early part of the evening, when all was so dark and seemingly hopeless. "See," said Gerhardt, as he handed his wife the hymn, "see how God provides!"

PAUL GERHARDT.

The hymn, which, according to tradition, had this interesting origin, was first published in 1659.* It was one, among many others, which was translated by John Wesley. In German, it commences, "Befiehl du deine Wege," and consists of twelve stanzas of eight lines each. It is now so arranged as to form two hymns. One,

> "Commit thou all thy griefs
>   And ways into his hands,
> To his sure truth and tender care,
>   Who earth and heaven commands.
>
> "Who points the clouds their course,
>   When wind and seas obey,
> He shall direct thy wandering feet,
>   He shall prepare thy way." &c.

The other,

> "Give to the winds thy fears;
>   Hope, and be undismayed:
> God hears thy sighs and counts thy tears;
>   God shall lift up thy head.
>
> "Through waves and clouds and storms,
>   He gently clears thy way;
> Wait thou his time, so shall this night
>   Soon end in joyous day." &c.

June, 1676, Gerhardt reached his three score years and ten, and also the end of life's journey. After uttering some sweet final words, parting with his only son on the banks of the river, he cheered and comforted himself in his dying moments, by repeating, over and over again, the eighth verse of his hymn, "Wherefore should I grieve and pine;" and while the words were still lingering upon his lips, he breathed his last. The words were these; of the Christian he says:—

> "Him no
> Death has power to kill,
> But, from many a dreaded ill
>   Bears his spirit safe away,
> Shuts the door of bitter woes,
> Opens yon bright path that glows
>   With the light of perfect day."

---

* The discrepancy of dates makes this tradition doubtful.

His devoted wife had preceded him, in 1668, and by her own request, one of her husband's hymns was read to her as she entered the dark valley. Gerhardt wrote one hundred and twenty-three hymns and ranks next to Luther, in the grandeur and force of his sacred poetry. He is described as a man of medium height, of quiet but firm and cheerful bearing. His portrait in the Lubben Church bears, in Latin, this inscription: "*A divine sifted in Satan's sieve.*"

Among his best hymns that are now in use in the English language, we may mention the following, commencing,

"O sacred head, once wounded,"
"Jesus, thy boundless love to me,"
"Holy Ghost! dispel our sadness."

One of his heroic songs found in many hymn books begins,

"Since Jesus is my Friend,
And I to him belong,
It matters not what foes intend,
However fierce and strong.

"He whispers in my breast
Sweet words of holy cheer,—
How they who seek in God their rest,
Shall ever find him near."

DIFFERENT writers corroborate the following touching story connected with one of Gerhardt's hymns:—
"What a dreadful day was the 14th of September, 1796, for the small Hessian town of Lisberg, built on the wooded heights of the Vogelberg. Between nine and ten o'clock at night, five hundred fugitives of the French army, which had just been defeated by the Archduke Charles, fled through the city, breathing vengeance; and after they had destroyed, murdered, and plundered for many hours, they set fire to the town at all points, so that fifty-eight dwellings were burned to the ground.

"On the slope of the hill stood a cottage, where a mother sat at the bed of her sick child. From fear of endangering the life of her darling, she would not, in the cold September day, flee with it to the woods, as most of the inhabitants had done. But now, when the firing and murdering began in the place, and the smoke of the burning houses came down from the hill into the valley, then the poor lone woman was fearful unto death; she bolted the door of the cottage, and threw herself on her knees in prayer beside the cradle of her child. Thus she remained a long time, trembling as she listened to the shouts of the soldiers and the shrieks of the victims; at last her door was struck by the butt-end of a musket; and it quickly flew open, and a Frenchman rushed in, pointing his bayonet at the horrified woman. The mother laid her hands over her child, and with a voice of despair she prayed aloud the verse of Gerhardt's hymn:—

> "'My Jesus, stay thou by me,
> And let no foe come nigh me,
>   Safe sheltered by thy wing;
> But should the foe alarm me,
> Oh! let him never harm me,
>   But still thine angels round me sing.'

Suddenly the soldier lowered his deadly weapon, stepped to the cradle, and laid his rough hand softly on the child's head, his lips moved as if in prayer, and tear-drops fell over his bearded face. Then he gave his hand to the mother and went away in silence. After some time, she arose from her knees, and looked out of the little window, and behold! there stood the Frenchman, his musket on his arm. He had made himself the sentinel to protect the house and its inmates from all insult or harm. At last, when the whole troop, laden with booty, marched off, he left his post, with a greater treasure in his *heart* than his comrades had in their *sacks*."

Relief Brought while Singing.

"DEAR Warsaw, there once lived a pious peasant of German extraction, by name Dobry. Without any fault of his own, he had fallen into arrears with his rent; and the landlord determined to turn him out; and it was winter. He went to him three times and besought him in vain. It was evening, and the next day he was to be turned out with all his family; when, as they sat there in their sorrow, Dobry kneeled down in their midst, and sang ——

> "'Commit thou all thy griefs
> And ways into His hands.'

And as they came to the last verse,

> "'When Thou wouldst all our need supply,
> Who shall stay Thy hand?'

there was a knock at the window. It was an old friend, a raven, that Dobry's grandfather had taken out of the nest, and tamed, and then set at liberty. Dobry opened the window: the raven hopped in, and in his bill was a ring set with precious stones. Dobry thought he would sell the ring: but he thought again that he would take and show it to his minister; and he, who saw at once by the crest that it belonged to King Stanislaus, took it to him, and related the story. The king sent for Dobry, and rewarded him, so that he was no more in need, and the next year built him a house, and gave him cattle from his own herd; and over the house-door there is an iron tablet, whereon is carved a raven with a ring in his beak, and underneath this verse:—

> "'Thou everywhere hast sway,
> And all things serve thy might:
> Thy every act pure blessing is;
> Thy path, unsullied light!'"

"Commit thou all thy griefs."

THIS hymn is expressive of the experience of the author. When a boy, I gave my heart to Jesus and felt called to become a minister. On the evening of the day of my conversion I told mother. Her tears of sympathy were all the help she could give. So we agreed to tell Jesus about the matter and then leave it in his hands. Staying with a friend, who lived twelve miles from college the call seemed to ring so loudly that I was unable to sleep one Saturday night. Before daylight I arose and, without money or friends, started off for college.

Through the rain and mud I tramped the hilly road cheered with the constant thought that Jesus was with me, and would care for me in some way.

It was church time when my weary feet reached their destination. Not knowing where to go, or what to do, I walked up and down the streets of the strange town till I met a man that I thought looked like a Christian. I told him my story. He took me along to church. An aged minister arose and read as his text, "Casting all your care upon Him, for He careth for you." The text and sermon seemed all for me, I wondered who had told the preacher about me. Standing outside the church door, I watched for the Lord to send some one to care for me. I did not wait long until a Christian man came out to whom I told my story—how my heart was burdened with the desire to become a preacher, and how I had walked the long road trusting for relief through some kind providence. He at once extended a helping hand. Took me the next day to a banker, who said "Come on, I'll see you through;" with nimble feet I hastened home to tell my mother the good news. And before that week was around, I was at the preparatory school connected with the college, preparing to preach.

A Popular Hymn written by a Boy ten Years Old.

THE well-known hymn found in nearly all the church hymn-books commencing,—

"Jesus, and shall it ever be,"

was written by Joseph Grigg when but a child. It had for its heading when first published: "*Shame of Jesus conquered by love, by a youth of ten years.*" It first appeared in the "Gospel Magazine" for April, 1774. The Rev. Benjamin Francis afterwards re-wrote the hymn for Rippon's Selection. This is the form in which it is now used. Originally the first verse read:—

"Jesus, and shall it ever be
A mortal man ashamed of Thee?
Scorned be the thought by rich and poor,
Oh, may I scorn it more and more."

In early life Mr. Grigg labored as a mechanic, and issued, when a young man, a pamphlet containing nineteen hymns written while at work.

He at length became a minister, and preached in Silver Street, London, and married a widow lady of considerable wealth. He was "a friend of the poor, the charm of the social circle, and an attractive and useful preacher."

After a fruitful life he died, in 1768, at Walthamstow near London.

In 1765, he sent forth, in tract form, "Four Hymns on Divine Subjects, wherein the Patience and Love of Our Divine Saviour is displayed." One of the four was the hymn now in such frequent use, beginning,—

"Behold! a stranger at the door,
He gently knocks, has knocked before;
Has waited long, is waiting still:
You treat no other friend so ill."

Forty of his hymns with his "Serious Poems" were issued in book form, by Mr. Daniel Sedgwick, in 1861.

"Behold a stranger at the door."

THE following poetical illustration of the sentiments of this hymn was penned by Lopede Vega, who was born at Madrid, in 1562. In *Evenings with the Sacred Poets* it is said that he read Latin at five years of age; and such was his passion for verses, that before he could use a pen, he bribed his elder schoolmates with a portion of his breakfast, to write to his dictation, and then exchanged his effusion with others for prints and hymns.

Thus truly he lisped in numbers; and as he was the most prolific and voluminous of poets, he kept himself diligently exercised in that line to the end of his life.

> "Lord, what am I, that, with unceasing care,
>   Thou didst seek after me? that thou didst wait,
>   Wet with unhealthy dews, before my gate,
> And pass the gloomy nights of winter there?
> Oh, strange delusion, that I did not greet
>   Thy blessed approach! and oh, to heaven how lost,
>   In my ingratitude's unkindly frost,
> Has chilled the bleeding wounds upon Thy feet:
> How oft my guardian angel gently cried,
>   'Soul from thy casement look, and thou shalt see
> How He persists to knock and wait for thee.'
>   And oh! how often to that voice of sorrow,
> 'To-morrow we will open' I replied;
>   And when to-morrow came, I answered still,
>   ['to-morrow.'"]

A LITTLE boy had listened very attentively while his father read at family worship the third chapter of Revelation. But when he repeated that beautiful verse, "Behold, I stand at the door and knock: if any man hear my voice, and open the door, I will come in to him, and will sup with him, and he with me," he could not wait until his father had finished, but ran up to him with the anxious inquiry: "*Pa, did he get in?*"

Gustavus' Battle-hymn.

GUSTAVUS ADOLPHUS, the great and good king of Sweden, hearing of the straits into which Protestantism was brought in its struggles against Papacy in Germany, marched to the relief of his Christian brethren in 1630. With a small but disciplined army he turned the tide, and helped to preserve that land in its faith.

After his victory at Leipzic he wrote down, in a rude form, a hymn to be sung by his army, which, as revised and arranged by his chaplain, Dr. Fabricus, has thus been translated:—

> "Fear not, O little flock! the foe
>   Who madly seeks your overthrow.
> Dread not his rage and power!
>   What though your courage sometimes faints,
>   His seeming triumph o'er God's saints
>   Lasts but an hour."

> "Amen, Lord Jesus grant our prayer:
>   Great Captain, now thine arm make bare,—
> Fight for us once again:
>   So shall Thy saints and martyrs raise
> A mighty chorus to Thy praise,
>   World without end,—Amen."

At the commencement of the battle at which the king was killed, he commanded this hymn to be sung, accompanied by the trumpets and drums of the whole army. Then Gustavus knelt beside his horse in face of the soldiers and repeated his usual battle-prayer: "O Lord Jesus, bless our armies and this day's battle, for the glory of Thy holy name." Then passing along the lines giving a few brief words of encouragement, he gave the battle cry, "*God with us.*"

When found wounded on the field of battle, amid a heap of dying men, he exultingly cried out, "I am the king of Sweden, and seal with my blood the liberty and religion of the whole German nation."

Hymns upon the Battle-field.

A CHRISTIAN soldier, about to die on the battle-field during our late war, knelt deep in the mud, and said imploringly to the chaplain, "Oh brother! let us sing once more before I die."

"What shall I sing?"

"Sing the song my mother sung when I was her darling boy; and that always thrilled my soul as no other earthly song ever did. Sing, 'Rock of Ages, cleft for me.' That hymn, more than anything else, led me to the Rock Christ Jesus." He expired while the song was yet faintly moving on his lips.

DURING the Crimean war a touching account was given of a soldier, who, while on guard as a picket, felt so forlorn by being night after night exposed to the mud, fog, and rain of the battle-field, that he resolved to end his misery by committing suicide.

While retiring to a secluded spot to execute his purpose, he heard some one in the dark tramping through the mud and rain, cheerfully singing a sweet hymn. As he listened he found it came from a Christian whose faith enabled him ever to sing amid surrounding gloom:—

> "Content with beholding His face,
> My all to His pleasure resigned,
> No changes of season or place
> Can make any change in my mind."

Well did Luther say of Christian song:—

> "The Devil's work it doth impede,
> And hinders many a deadly deed.
> So fared it with King Saul of old;
> When David struck his harp of gold,
> So sweet and clear its tones rang out,
> Saul's murderous thoughts were put to rout."

Madame Guyon and her Hymns.

WHEN the heavens are overcast at night, sometimes the thick clouds will open far enough to let the light of some hidden star appear amid the surrounding gloom. Such a lone star was Madame Guyon, shining through the midnight darkness, and among the thick clouds of papal error and superstition.

Jeanne Marie Bouviers de la Motte Guyon was born April 13, 1648, at Montargis, about fifty miles south of Paris. She grew up under influences which gave her free access to the circles of fashion and wealth. Tall and beautiful in person, refined and prepossessing in manners, fluent and ready in speech, she was the centre of attraction in whatever position she moved.

At sixteen, through parental manœuvering, she was made the victim of an uncongenial marriage with M. Guyon, a man of wealth. "It was then," said she, "I began to eat the bread of sorrow, and mingle my drink with tears." After twelve years of cruel treatment, received from her mother-in-law, her husband died, leaving her with a family. These trials led her to seek a refuge from sin and sorrow. After many self-saving efforts, Christ became to her the "all" of salvation. With a heart all aglow with a Saviour's love, she sought by all possible means to make him known to others, in all parts of France and Italy.

Her converts became so numerous, and her influence so great, that the papacy sought in every possible way to neutralize her power. They publicly burnt her books, set in motion the vilest calumny, and instigated a servant to give her poison. "But," said she, "the more persecution raged against me, the more attentively was the word of the Lord listened to, and the greater the number of spiritual children were given to me." In 1688, by

MADAME GUYON.

order of the king, she was imprisoned in the Convent of St. Marie. Her daughter and all her comforts were taken from her.

Though the air of the small room, in which she was imprisoned, was so confined and heated, that she says "it seemed like a stove," yet now she realized that

> "—— prisons would palaces prove,
> If Jesus were with me there."

It was in this cell, she wrote those memorable lines:—

> "A little bird I am
>   Shut from the fields of air,
> And in my cage I sit and sing
>   To Him who placed me there;
> Well pleased a prisoner to be,
>   Because, my God it pleases thee.
>
> "Nought have I else to do,
>   I sing the whole day long,
> And He whom most I love to please
>   Doth listen to my song:
> He caught and bound my wandering wing,
>   And still he bends to hear me sing.
>
> "Oh! it is good to soar,
>   These bolts and bars above,
> To Him whose purpose I adore,
>   Whose Providence I love;
> And in thy mighty will to find
>   The joy, the freedom of the mind."

The king's wife having interceded on her behalf, she was set free after eight months' imprisonment. But on the charge that she did not worship saints, and held meetings in private houses, she was, in 1695, again arrested, and confined in the Castle of Vincennes.

"There," she tells us, "I passed my time in great peace, content to pass the rest of my life there, if such were the will of God. I sang songs of joy, which the maid who served me learned by heart, as fast as I made them; and we together sang thy praises, O my God! The stones of my prison looked in my eyes like rubies. I esteemed them more than all the gaudy brilliancies of the world. My heart was full of that joy thou givest to them that love Thee in the midst of their greatest crosses."

This maid, La Gautiere, to whom she refers, was one of her spiritual children, who was willing to go into prison with her for Christ's sake. When her brother sought to allure her away, she wrote saying, "If your house, my dear brother, had been made of precious stones, and if I could have been treated and honored in it as a queen, yet I should have forsaken all to follow after God." To write this letter she had to "use soot instead of ink, and a bit of stick instead of a pen," and yet what pen and ink ever wrote more heroic words. From this prison she was removed, in 1696, to the prison of Vaugirard, from which she was removed in 1698, to the famous Bastile, that "abode of broken hearts."

When incarcerated in the Bastile, they were separated and each had to sing alone. Here the maid exchanged her dark cell for a bright home in heaven. But Madam Guyon was imprisoned four years, when she was banished for the remainder of her life to Blois. It was here she could appropriately use the language of her hymn:—

> "My Lord! how full of sweet content,
> I pass my years of banishment!
> Where'er I dwell, I dwell with thee,
> In heaven, in earth, or on the sea.
>
> "To me remains nor place nor time;
> My country is in every clime:
> I can be calm and free from care
> On any shore, since God is there."

After leaving the Bastile she says: "My body was from that time sick and borne down with all kinds of infirmities." She died June, 1717, in her seventieth year. Her peaceful end is pictured in these words, that she wrote to a friend: "If my work is done, I think I can say, I am ready to go. In the language of the proverb,

I have already 'one foot in the stirrup,' and am ready to mount and be gone, as soon as my heavenly Father pleases."

Most of her hymns in use are translations by Cowper, who said: "Her verse is the only French verse I find agreeable, there is a neatness in it, equal to that which we applaud in the compositions of Prior." He says the Rev. Mr. Bull "rode twenty miles to see her picture in the house of a stranger, which stranger politely insisted on his acceptance of it, and it now hangs over his chimney. It is a striking picture, and, were it encompassed with a glory, instead of being dressed in a nun's hood, might pass for the face of an angel."

She composed many hymns and poems, which, with her other writings, fill five octavo volumes.

Her heart seemed to be ascending to God in a continual flame of warmest love. Her frequent ejaculations were, "*O my God, let me be wholly thine! Let me love Thee purely for thyself, for thou art infinitely lovely. O my God, be Thou my all! Let everything be as nothing to me.*"

How much significance such heart longings give to the language of her hymn:—

> "I would love thee, God and Father!
> My Redeemer! and my King!
> I would love thee: and without thee,
> Life is but a bitter thing.
>
> "I would love thee: look upon me,
> Ever guide me with thine eye :
> I would love thee; if not nourished
> By thy love, my soul would die.
>
> "I would love thee; may thy brightness
> Dazzle my rejoicing eyes;
> I would love thee; may thy goodness
> Watch from heaven o'er all I prize.
>
> "I would love thee,—I have vowed it;
> On thy love my heart is set;
> While I love thee, I will never
> My Redeemer's blood forget."

Harbaugh and his Hymns.

REV. HENRY HARBAUGH, D. D. wrote some beautiful poetry, but is more widely known through his three popular works: "The Sainted Dead," "The Heavenly Recognition," and "The Heavenly Home."

He was born near Waynesboro' Penn., Oct. 28, 1817.

In Harbaugh's autobiographical poems, he has interwoven some pleasing sketches of his life. And as they will give a clearer and more satisfactory insight into his character, than any picturing our pen may be able to give, we will furnish a few extracts herewith. His school-boy days, he describes in "The Old School-House at the Creek:"—

"I've travelled long and travelled far,
 Till weary, worn, and sick;
How joyless all that I have found,
Compared with scenes that lie around
 This school-house at the creek.

"'Twas here I first attended school,
 When I was very small:
There was the master on his stool,
There was his whip and there his rule—
 I seem to see it all.

"Around the cosy stove, in rows,
 The little tribe appears;
What hummings make those busy bees—
They better like their A, B, C's,
 Than boxing at their ears!

"The long desks ranged along the walls,
 With books and inkstands crowned;
Here on this side the large girls sat,
And there the tricky boys on that—
 See! how they peep around!"

"The master eyes them closely now,
 They'd better have a care;
The one that writes a billet-doux—
The one that plays his antics, too—
 And that chap laughing there!"

HENRY HARBAUGH.

Harbaugh was early led into the path of piety, while growing up under the nurture of Christian parents, and united with the German Reformed Church of which the Rev. G. W. Glessner was pastor. How graphically, in after years, he depicts his heart-yearnings towards that Christian home, and the devoted mother, whose blessings he craved when going away to prepare himself for the work of the gospel ministry. In his poem on "Home-sickness," he says:—

> "Two spots on this old friendly porch
>   I love, nor can forget,
> Till dimly in the night of death
>   My life's last sun shall set!
> When first I left my father's house,
>   One summer morning bright,
> My mother at that railing wept
>   Till I was out of sight!
> Now like a holy star that spot
>   Shines in this world's dull night.
>
> "Stil', still I see her at that spot,
>   With handkerchief in hand;
> Her cheeks are red—her eyes are wet—
>   There, there I see her stand!
> 'Twas there I gave her my good-bye,
>   There, did her blessing crave,
> And oh, with what a mother's heart
>   She that sought blessing gave.
> It was the last—ere I returned
>   She rested in her grave!"

In 1843, after the completion of his studies at Mercersburg, Pa., he was licensed to preach, and soon afterwards was installed as pastor of the Reformed Church at Lewisburg, Pa. Here he wrote his "Sainted Dead." After six years of successful labor, he accepted a call from the First Reformed Church of Lancaster, Pa. While at this place he received the title of doctor of divinity, wrote his "Heavenly Recognition," "Heavenly Home," "Birds of the Bible," "Union with the Church," and

"The true Glory of Woman," with other valuable works.

In 1860, he became pastor of St. Luke's Reformed Church, Lebanon, Pa. Here he wrote his "Hymns and Chants." Three years later, he was elected to the chair of Didactic and Practical Theology, in the seminary of the Reformed Church at Mercersburg. This position he filled with great honor, and general acceptance till his death, which took place December, 28, 1867.

His earnest Christian life was but the utterance of his most popular hymn. Heartily he could say:—

> "Jesus! I live to thee,
> The loveliest and best;
> My life in thee is life to me,
> In thy blessed love I rest."

The sentiments of his second and third verses were sweetly realized in his peaceful death. Just before his departure, on waking from slumber, he uttered as his last intelligible words: "You have called me back from the golden gates, from the verge of my heavenly home." Thus he could say:—

> "Jesus! I die to thee,
> Whenever death shall come;
> To die in thee is life to me
> In my eternal home.
>
> "Whether to live or die,
> I know not which is best;
> To live in thee is bliss to me,
> To die is endless rest."

The last verse of this hymn is carved on the beautiful monument erected to his memory:—

> "Living or dying Lord!
> I ask but to be thine;
> My life in thee, thy life in me,
> Makes heaven for ever mine."

Another of his hymns, highly prized, commences,

> "Christ, by heavenly hosts adored."

"Heavenly Recognition" was a theme upon which he loved to dwell. Those of our readers, who love to cherish the memory of the sainted dead, will be pleased with the following from Harbaugh's poetic pen:—

"Oft weeping memory sits alone,
  Beside some grave at even,
And calls upon the spirit flown:
Oh say! shall those on earth our own
  Be ours again—in Heaven?

"Amid these lone sepulchral shades
  To quiet slumbers given,
Is not some lingering spirit near,
To tell if those divided here,
  Unite and know—in Heaven?

"Shall friends, who o'er the waste of life,
  By the same storms were driven—
Shall they recount in realms of bliss,
The fortunes and the tears of this,
  And love again—in Heaven?

"Of hearts which had on earth been one,
  By death asunder riven,
Why does the one that has been reft
Drag off in grief the mourner left,
  If not to meet—in Heaven?

"The warmest love on earth is still
  Imperfect when 'tis given;
But there's a purer clime above,
Where perfect hearts in perfect love
  Unite; and this—is Heaven.

"If love on earth is but "in part"
  As light and shade at even;
If sin doth plant a thorn between
The truest hearts there is I ween,
  A perfect love—in Heaven.

"O happy world! O glorious place!
  Where all who are forgiven,
Shall find their loved and lost below;
And hearts, like meeting streams, shall flow
  Forever one—in Heaven."

"Come, ye sinners, poor and needy."

UPON many occasions of deep religious awakening this hymn is announced as the one to call forth decision for Christ. It is associated in the memory of God's people with very many seasons of revival.

The author was the Rev. Joseph Hart, who was born of pious parents in London in 1712. In 1759, he published a volume of "Hymns on Various Subjects, with the Author's experience."

In his preface, he says, "The following hymns were composed partly from several passages of Scripture, laid on my heart, or opened to my understanding, from time to time, by the Spirit of God. * * I desire wholly to submit myself, to the all-wise disposal of that God, the sweet enlivening influences of whose Spirit I often felt while they were composing."

Of his hymns that have become especially endeared to the lovers of Zion, we may mention the following, commencing thus:—

"Come, Holy Spirit, come."
"Once more we come before our God."
"O for a glance of heavenly day."
"Prayer is appointed to convey."
"Dismiss us with thy blessing, Lord."
"Once more before we part."

Though he received a good education, and was occupied at first as a teacher of languages, and at times felt anxious about his soul, yet he says: "In this abominable state I continued a bold-faced rebel for nine years, not only committing acts of lewdness myself, but infecting others also with the poison of my delusions," and even went so far as to write a work on "the unreasonableness of religion." * * "After a time I fell into a deep despondency of mind, and, shunning all company, I went about alone bewailing my sad and dark condition.

"In this sad state I went moping about till Whit Sunday, 1757, when I happened to go in the afternoon to the Moravian Chapel in Fetter Lane. The minister preached from Rev. iii. 10. I was much impressed.

"I was hardly got home, when I felt myself melting away into a strange softness of affection which made me fling myself on my knees before God. My horrors were immediately expelled, and such comfort flowed into my heart as no words can paint. The Lord, by his Spirit of love, came, not in a visionary manner into my brain, but with such divine power and energy into my soul, that I was lost in blissful amazement. I cried out, 'What, me, Lord?' His Spirit answered in me, 'Yes, thee!' I objected, 'But I have been so unspeakably vile and wicked!' The answer was, 'I pardon thee freely and fully!' The alteration I then felt in my soul was as sudden and palpable as that which is experienced by a person staggering and almost sinking under a burden, when it is immediately taken from his shoulders. Tears ran in streams from my eyes for a considerable while, and I was so swallowed up in joy and thankfulness that I hardly knew where I was. I threw myself willingly into my Saviour's hands; lay weeping at his feet, wholly resigned to his will, and only begging that I might, if He were graciously pleased to permit it, be of service to his Church and people. Jesus Christ and him crucified is now the only thing I desire to know. All things to me are rich only when they are enriched with the blood of the Lamb.

"The week before Easter, 1757, I had such an amazing view of the agony of Christ in the garden, as I know not well how to describe. I was lost in wonder and adoration; and the impression was too deep, I believe, ever to be obliterated. It was then I made the first part of my hymn:—

> Come, all ye chosen saints of God
> That long to feel the cleansing blood,
> In pensive pleasures join with me
> To sing of sad Gethsemane."

Many of his hymns were but counterparts of his own experience. He had been among the

> "sinners poor and needy,
> Weak and wounded, sick and sore;"

and for many years had been

> "weary, heavy laden,
> Bruised and broken by the fall."

In 1760, he settled in London as pastor of the "Old Wooden Meeting-house in Jewin Street," built nearly a century before for William Jenkyn.

Here he ministered to a very large congregation, who looked upon him as an "earnest, eloquent and much beloved" minister of the Gospel.

Though laboring under great affliction, he continued his labors among this people till May 24th, 1768, when, at the age of fifty-six, he passed up to his reward.

In his funeral sermon it was said, "He was like the laborious ox that dies with the yoke on his neck; so died he with the yoke of Christ on his neck: neither would he suffer it to be taken off: for ye are his witnesses that he preached Christ to you, with the arrows of death sticking in him."

A great exhibition of affection, it is said, was shown in that over twenty thousand persons attended his funeral.

Hymns that "Mean Me."

A FEW days ago, says Mr. Ralph Wells, we admitted six mission children from our school into the church.

When the session came to examine the candidates, one of the elders asked a little girl of twelve years, "Maggie, what first interested your heart in the Saviour." "It was one of those large hymns, sir, one of the printed hymns that they use in the school. The hymn was that beautiful one:—

> "'From the cross uplifted high,
> Where the Saviour deigns to die,
> What melodious sounds we hear
> Bursting on the ravished ear;
> Love's redeeming work is done,
> Come and welcome, sinner, come.'

"Oh sir!" said this child fresh from her tenement home, "It was those kind words:—

> "'Come and welcome, sinner, come.'

I said to myself that means *me*; for, if it means 'sinner,' it is for poor Maggie."

MR. Wells says that whenever he hears the sweet hymn:—

> "Jesus loves me, this I know,
> For the Bible tells me so,"

it recalls an incident of a half-witted colored boy, of whom a Sunday school teacher said: "Mr. Wells, you needn't speak to him. He don't know anything." "But," says Mr. Wells, "I did. I said 'What is your name, my son?' He looked at me a moment, and slowly answered: 'J-i-m-m-y, sir.' 'Can you tell me what the Bible tells Jimmy.' He looked all around the room, as if trying to find something, and then looked me right in the eye, and said: 'The Bible says, *Jesus loves Jimmy.*'"

Origin of a Hymn by "Quite a Young Girl."

IN reply to a private letter sent from Brooklyn, concerning a hymn that is now being widely sung, Miss Frances Ridley Havergal writes as follows:—

"*My Dear Unknown Friend in Jesus*—Mrs. S. asked me to write and answer myself your question about the hymn, "I give My life for thee." Yes, it is mine, and perhaps it may interest you to hear how nearly it went into the fire, instead of nearly all over the world.

"It was, I think, the very first thing I ever wrote which could be called a hymn, written when I was quite a young girl (1859). I did not half realize what I was writing about. I was following very far off, always doubting and fearing. I think I *had* come to Jesus with a trembling, hem-touching faith, but it was a coming in the press, and behind, never seeing His face, or feeling sure that He loved me, though I was clear that I could not do without Him, and wanted to serve and follow Him.

"I don't know how I came to write it. I scribbled it in pencil on the back of a circular, in a few minutes, and then read it over and thought, "Well, this is not poetry, anyhow! I won't go to the trouble to copy *this*." So I reached out my hand to put it into the fire! a sudden impulse made me draw it back; I put it, crumpled and singed, into my pocket. Soon after I went out to see a dear old woman in an alms house. She began talking to me, as she always did, about her dear Saviour, and I thought I would see if she, a simple old woman, would care for these verses, which I felt sure nobody else would ever care to read. So I read them to her, and she was so delighted with them that, when I went back, I copied them out, and kept them, and now the Master has sent them out in all directions. I have seen tears while they have been sung at mission services, and have heard of them being really blessed to many."

The following is the hymn:—

"I gave my life for thee,
   My precious blood I shed,
That thou might st ransom'd be,
   And quickened from the dead.
I gave, I gave my life for thee:
What hast thou given for me?

"My Father's house of light,
   My glory circled throne,
I left for earthly night,
   For wanderings sad and lone;
I left, I left it all for thee:
Hast thou left aught for me?

"I suffered much for thee,
   More than thy tongue can tell,
Of bitt'rest agony,
   To rescue thee from hell;
I've borne, I've borne it all for thee:
What hast thou borne for me?

"And I have brought to thee,
   Down from my home above,
Salvation full and free,
   My pardon and my love;
I bring, I bring rich gifts to thee:
What hast thou brought to me?

"O, let thy life be given,
   Thy tears that yet remain,
World fetters all be riven,
   Give me thy joy and pain;
Give thou, give thou thyself to me,
And I will welcome thee!"

Miss Havergal is the youngest daughter of Rev. W. H. Havergal. She has written seventy-seven hymns and poems. Her father wrote about one hundred.

Southey's Lines on the Portrait of Heber.

"Yes,—such as these were Heber's lineaments;
    Such his capacious front,
    His comprehensive eye,
    His open brow serene.
Such was the gentle countenance which bore
Of generous feeling and of golden truth
Sure Nature's sterling impress; never there
    Unruly passion left
    Its ominous marks infixed,
Nor the worst die of evil habit set
    An inward stain engrained.
Such were the lips whose salient playfulness
Enlivened peaceful hours of private life;
    Whose eloquence
    Held congregations open eared,
As from the heart it flowed, a living stream
Of Christian wisdom, pure and undefiled."

    *   *   *   *   *   *

"Yes, to the Christian, to the Heathen world.
Heber, thou art not dead—thou canst not die!
    Nor can I think of thee as lost.
    A little portion of this little isle
At first divided us; then half the globe;
The same earth held us still; but when,
O Reginald, wert thou so near as now?
'Tis but the falling of the withered leaf,
    The breaking of a shell,
    The rending of a veil!
    O, when that leaf shall fall,
That shell be burst, that veil be rent, may then
    My spirit be with thine!"

Rev. Dr. Turner, who followed Heber to the same field of labor, wrote of him the following lines, in imitation of the bishop's hymn, "Thou art gone to the grave:"

"Thou art gone to the grave; and while nations bemoan thee
Who drank from thy lips the glad tidings of peace,
Yet, grateful, they still in their heart shall enthrone thee,
And ne'er shall thy name from their memory cease."

Author of "From Greenland's icy mountains."

EGINALD HEBER, D. D., was born April 21, 1783, at Malpas, England. His father had the same name, and was rector of the Episcopal church at that place. Like many other hymnists, he began to display piety and talent from early childhood. He could not only read his Bible with fluency when but five years of age, but was already so familiar with its contents, that when his father, with some friends, were discussing as to the book where a particular passage could be found, they turned to little Reginald for information, when he at once named both the book and chapter.

Hearing the conundrum asked one day: "Where was Moses when the candle went out?" he answered at once, "On Mount Nebo, for there he died, and it may be said that his lamp of life went out."

At seven years of age he was already so proficient in Latin that he translated Phœdrus into English verse.

While at grammar school in his eight year, he became so absorbed in his studies that, receiving a new book, he was so completely "abstracted in it that he was not in the least aware of a 'barring out,' which, with all its accompanying noise and confusion, had been going on for a couple of hours around him, and of which he became conscious as the increasing darkness forced him to lay down his book. Well did his brother say, "Reginald did more than read books, he devoured them."

His heart was naturally so benevolent that while on a journey to his boarding school, he became so affected by the story of a poor man, that he gave away all he had, so that afterwards they found it "necessary to sew the bank notes, given him for his half year's pocket money in school, in the lining of his pockets, that he might not give them away in charity on the road."

When about fourteen years old he begged permission of his mother to unite with her in partaking of the sacrament of the Lord's supper on the the following Sabbath, to which his happy mother consented with tears of joy and affection.

He entered college in 1800, and in the following year gained a prize for a poem on "The Commencement of the New Century." After this followed another prize poem on "Palestine." The reading of this called forth great applause.

Miss Jermyn refers thus to his father who, as an eye-witness, was greatly moved by the occasion:—

"What means that stifled sob, that groan of joy,
  Why fall those tears upon thy furrowed cheek?
The aged father hears his darling boy,
  And sobs and tears alone his feelings speak."

After witnessing the hearty applause of an enraptured audience, Heber withdrew from the scene, and for some time could not be found by his anxious mother. At length to her surprise and joy, she came across him in his private chamber, where he was seen upon bended knees, laying his trophies at Jesus' feet.

After entering the ministry of the Episcopal church, he became rector of Hodnet, in Shropshire in 1807.

Improvement in church singing was among his first efforts. Writing to his friend Thornton, he says, "My Psalm-singing continues bad. Can you tell me where I can purchase Cowper's Olney Hymns, to put in the seats? Some of them I admire much, and any novelty is likely to become a favorite, and draw more people to join in singing."

After sixteen years of pastoral labors, he accepted of an appointment to go to—

"———India's coral strand."

The diocese, committed to his hands as bishop, extended over more than the whole of India. His excessive labors sank him to the grave in three short years.

At the close of a busy day's work, he entered a bath, where his exhausted frame was soon afterwards found a corpse. This took place at Trichinopoly, April 2, 1826.

At his funeral the road was crowded by heathen and Christian natives, who, by many tears and sobs, attested their heart-felt appreciation of his services. His remains rest amid the "coral strand,"—

> "Till o'er our ransomed nature
> The Lamb for sinners slain,
> Redeemer, King, Creator,
> In bliss returns to reign."

A monument was erected by his friends in Ceylon, in memory of his labors in this island as on the peninsula. So that his name is also embalmed amid "the spicy breezes" that—

> "——blow soft o'er Ceylon's isle."

There was a time when he could say, as he listened to the "joyful sound" from a great multitude of Christianized heathen voices,—

> "——earth's remotest nation,
> Has learned Messiah's name."

At a Tamul service at Tangore, which was attended by *thirteen hundred* native Christians, the bishop was greatly moved as he heard so many but lately rescued from the pollution of their heathen idolatry, now joining in singing the sentiments of the 100th psalm:—

> "We'll crowd Thy gates with joyful songs,
> High as the heavens our voices raise;
> And earth, with her ten thousand tongues,
> Shall fill Thy courts with sounding praise."

Said he, "For the last ten years I have longed to witness a scene like this, but the reality exceeds all my expectation. Gladly would I exchange years of common life for one such day as this."

Origin of "From Greenland's icy mountains."

OF the fifty-nine elegant hymns written by Bishop Heber none are so widely known or so frequently sung as his missionary hymn.

In 1819, a royal letter authorized collections to be taken in every church and chapel in England connected with the establishment, in furtherance of the Society for Propagating the Gospel.

On the evening of Whitsunday, which was the day appointed for this purpose, Heber had engaged to deliver the first of a series of Sunday evening lectures, in the church at Wrexham, which was in charge of his father-in-law, the Rev. Dr. Shipley.

On the Saturday previous, as they were seated around the table in the parsonage, the Dean requested his son-in-law to write something for them to sing in the morning, that would be suitable to the missionary service. Heber at once retired from the circle of friends to a corner of the room.

After a while his father-in-law inquired, "What have you written?" Heber then read the first three verses, which he had already produced. "There, that will do very well," said the Dean. "No,—no," said Heber, "the sense is not complete." Accordingly he added the fourth verse, commencing:—

"Waft, waft, ye winds, His story."

Next morning it was sung in the church at Wrexham, and soon after was caught up as the grand missionary hymn of the church universal, reaching "from pole to pole." The Rev. Dr. Raffles was in possession of the original manuscript, from which it is seen that so accurately was it written at first that he had occasion to alter but one word.

GREENLAND'S ICY MOUNTAINS.

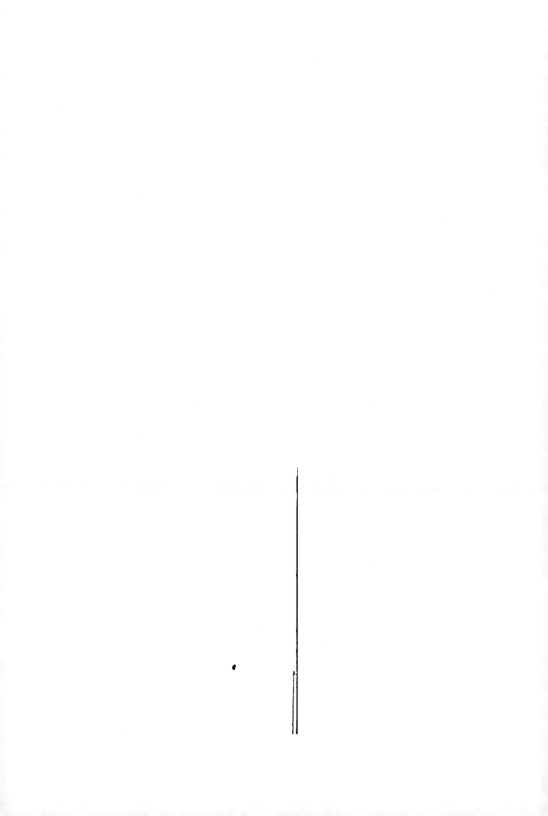

Origin of "Thou art gone to the grave."

IN the biography of Bishop Heber it is said: "The loss of their only child was long and severely felt by Mr. and Mrs. Heber; her father could never think of or name her without tears; and his private devotions generally concluded with an earnest prayer that he might, at his last hour, be found worthy to rejoin his departed child. To the feelings which this bereavement occasioned may be traced the production of the following lines:—

'Thou art gone to the grave, but we will not deplore thee,
Though sorrows and darkness encompass the tomb;
The Saviour has passed through the portals before thee,
And the lamp of his love is thy guide through the gloom.'"

Heber was characterized by great tenderness of heart. He says in a letter to a friend, that owing to his eyes being so blinded with tears, it took him two days to pen the lines that tell of the departure of his sainted father, of whose end he says: "A smile sat on the pale countenance, and his eyes sparkled brighter than I ever saw them. From this time he spoke but little; his lips moved, and his eyes were raised upwards. He blessed us again, we kissed him, and found his lips cold and breathless."

The vessel that took him to India had a detachment of invalid soldiers on board. For their salvation he labored so faithfully that they exclaimed, "Only think of such a great man as the bishop coming between decks to pray with such poor fellows as we are." Then again he opened his heart of sympathy to an afflicted mother, whose child had just been buried in an ocean-grave. "At intervals," says a witness, "I hear him weeping and praying for her in his own cabin. I have never seen such tenderness."

Rowland Hill and his Hymns.

ROWLAND HILL occupied a conspicuous place among the champions of the cross, during the last century. He was stimulated and encouraged by the advice and example of Berridge and Whitefield, in early life, and became, like them, distinguished for his ability to reach and move the masses. Not unfrequently would his audiences number from five to ten thousand, and sometimes even twenty thousand.

He was born at Hawkston, England, August 23, 1744. Dr. Watts's "Hymns for Children" produced a deep religious impression upon him in early childhood. But his conversion did not take place till he was seventeen. This was effected through the instrumentality of an earnest and faithful brother.

He became at once decided and whole-hearted in his Christianity. So much so that when he went to college at Cambridge he said, that, on account of his religion, "nobody ever gave me a cordial smile, except the old shoe-black at the gate, who had the love of Christ in his heart."

The report of his piety and zeal reaching the ears of Berridge and Whitefield, they frequently sent him words of encouragement. In one of Whitefield's letters he refers to his own student experience:—

"We never prospered so much at Oxford, as when we were hissed at and reproached as we walked along the street, as being called the dung and off-scouring of all things. That is a poor building that a little stinking breath of Satan's vassals can throw down. Your house I trust is better founded,—is it not built upon a rock? .... Lady Huntingdon is in town,—she will rejoice to hear that you are under the cross." Berridge wrote, "I feel my heart go out to you whilst I am writing, and can embrace you as my second self. How soft and

ROWLAND HILL.

sweet are those silken cords which the dear Redeemer twines and ties about the hearts of his children. . . . . . . I think your chief work for a season, will be to break up fallow ground." To this work Mr. Hill was inclined, and well fitted, both by nature and Providence.

That there was much "fallow ground" in those times, will appear from some of his own statements.

Two days after the receipt of Berridge's letter, he says in his diary, of one of his meetings:—

"There was such a noise with beating of pans, shovels, blowing of horns and ringing of bells, that I could scarce hear myself speak. Though we were pelted with much dirt, and eggs, I was enabled to preach out my sermon."

The irregularity of these student-efforts eventually caused six different bishops to refuse him orders as deacon. In 1773, however, he was enabled to write: "Through the kind and unexpected interposition of Providence, I was ordained without any condition, or compromise whatever." This took place through Dr. Wills, the aged bishop of Bath and Wells.

Believing that the "field is the world," he said, "Though I wander about, *I stick to my parish.*" Drawn by his flaming zeal, his apt illustrations, and his impressive oratory the people flocked around him in innumerable numbers, in churches, chapels, market-places, fields, and everywhere. "I like to go and hear Rowland Hill," said Sheridan, "because his ideas come red-hot from the heart." At one time, he said: "Because I am in earnest, men call me an enthusiast. But I am not; mine are the words of truth and soberness. When I first came into this part of the country, I was walking on yonder hill; I saw a gravel-pit fall in, and bury three human beings alive. I lifted up my voice for help so loud that I was heard in the town below, at a distance of a mile; help came, and rescued two of the poor sufferers. No one called me an enthusiast then; and when I see eternal destruction ready to fall upon poor sinners, and about to entomb them irrecoverably in an eternal mass of woe, and call aloud on them to escape, shall I be called an enthusiast now?"

In 1783, Rowland Hill's friends built for him the Surrey Chapel, that would hold three thousand persons. The site was upon what was called "one of the worst spots in London."

In 1783, Mr. Hill published a "Collection of Psalms and Hymns," which passed through many editions. In the preface, he says of the hymns, "Some of them are by no means the better for being entirely new." How many of them were his own is not certainly known. In 1790, he issued his "Divine Hymns for the Use of Children," which were corrected by Cowper. The following is a specimen of one of them:—

"Dear Jesus, let an infant claim
The favour to adore thy name;
Thou wast so meek that babes might be
Encouraged to draw near to thee.

"My gracious Saviour, I believe
Thou canst a little child receive;
Thy tender love for us is free,
And why not love poor sinful me?"

A number of his hymns were written to be sung at the close of his sermons. This was the case with "The Funeral of old Bigotry," beginning,

"Here lies old Bigotry, abhorr'd
By all that love our common Lord."

and closing with the verse:—

"Let names, and sects, and parties fall;
Let Jesus Christ be all in all.
Thus, like thy saints above, shall we
Be one with each other as one with thee."

After preaching on Psalm, xx, 7, 8, he introduced his

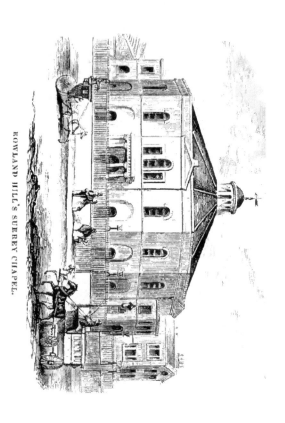

ROWLAND HILL'S SURREY CHAPEL.

popular hymn, that was sung with wonderful effect by an immense congregation, commencing,

"Come, thou incarnate word,
Gird on thy mighty sword."

As he lay upon his death-bed, watching his approaching end, he was heard repeating the language of the following beautiful hymn. He had written it for the comfort of a dying member of his congregation. It is found in many of the hymn-books now in use:—

"Gently, my Saviour, let me down
To slumber in the arms of death;
I rest my soul on thee alone,
E'en till my last expiring breath.

"Death's dreadful sting has lost its power;
A ransomed sinner, saved by grace,
Lives but to die, and die no more,
Unveiled to see thy blissful face.

"Soon will the storm of life be o'er,
And I shall enter endless rest:
There shall I live to sin no more,
And bless thy name forever blest."

The following lines, says his nephew, were perpetually on his lips for nearly a year before he died, and were the last words he tried to utter in the solemn hour of disssolution:—

"And when I'm to die,
Receive me, I'll cry,
For Jesus hath loved me, I cannot tell why."

On the 19th of April, 1833, in the eighty-ninth year of his pilgrimage, Mr. Hill calmly closed his eyes in death, without a sigh or groan, or any other evidence of a last struggle. "Those about him could scarcely believe he was gone, so peaceful was his end—so gently, in answer to his own hymn-prayer, was he let down to slumber in the arms of death."

He was buried under the pulpit in Surrey-chapel, from which he had proclaimed the gospel fifty years.

Author of "When thou, my righteous Judge shalt come."

LADY HUNTINGDON not only left to the world one of the brightest examples of a life wholly consecrated to Christ, but also the above hymn, that has been echoing in the praises of the sanctuary for over a century. Her soul was first awakened to realize its destiny and danger while attending the funeral of a playmate, when but nine years of age.

The sights and sounds of that day left an impress that the bright future, that gilded her girlhood days, could not dispel. Often would she visit that grassy mound of her departed friend, and then steal away to the little closet, to pour out her soul in earnest supplication, and ponder over the questions which, in later years, she so vividly expressed in her hymn:—

> "When thou, my righteous Judge, shalt come
> To take thy ransomed people home,
> Shall I among them stand?
> Shall such a worthless worm as I,
> Who sometimes am afraid to die,
> Be found at thy right hand?"

When twenty-one years of age, she was married to Theophilus Hastings, Earl of Huntingdon, and introduced to all the splendors and excitements of high English life.

This marriage brought her into contact with her sister-in-law, Lady Margaret Hastings, who, one day remarked that, since she had known and believed in the Lord Jesus Christ for life and salvation, she had been as happy as an angel."

This testimony stirred again the depths of her soul. Her early convictions and fear of death now returned, and so disturbed her bodily health, that she was thrown upon a sick bed, and for some time seemed fast tending towards the grave. At length, she was enabled to lift

Huntingdon

up her cry to God as afterwards repeated in her hymn,—
> "Thy pardoning voice, O let me hear,
> To still my unbelieving fear,"

when in a glad moment the sound of peace and pardon echoed through her soul, her bodily disease at the same time took a favorable turn, and she was in a double sense "a new creature."

Writing to Charles Wesley she says, "How solid is the peace, and how divine the joy that springs from an assurance that we are united to the Saviour by a living faith. Blessed be his name. I have an abiding sense of his presence with me, notwithstanding the weakness and unworthiness I feel, and an intense desire that he may be glorified in the salvation of souls." Among the many evidences of this " intense desire" we may mention the following. A workman who was repairing her garden wall she earnestly urged to take some thought concerning eternity and the state of his soul. Years afterwards speaking to another upon the same subject, she said, "Thomas, I fear you never pray, or look to Christ for salvation."

"Your ladyship is mistaken," replied the man; "I heard what passed between you and James at the garden wall, and the word you meant for him took effect on me."

"How did you hear it?" she asked.

"I heard it," Thomas answered, "on the other side of the garden, through a hole in the wall, and I shall never forget the impression I received."

One day at court, the then Prince of Wales asked, "where is my Lady Huntingdon, that she is so seldom here?" A Lady of fashion replied with a sneer, "I suppose praying with her beggars." The prince shook his head, saying, "When I am dying, I think I shall be happy to seize the skirt of Lady Huntingdon's mantle, to carry me up with her to heaven." Thus expressing the sentiment contained in her hymn,—

> "Among thy saints let me be found,
> Whene'er th'archangel's trump shall sound."

In her preface to her hymns she says, "And now, reader, it is neither your approbation of these hymns nor the objections you can make to them that is the material point; you are a creature of a day, and your heart, with trembling, often tells you this truth. Look well then, for a refuge from the sins of your life past, and from the just fears of death and judgment fast approaching. This is the grand point which lieth altogether between God and thy own soul. And be assured that nothing can bring comfort in life or death to thee, a sinner (and such thou now standest before God) but a Saviour so full and complete as Jesus is found to be."

Mr. Miller says, "Although the Countess was not much known as a hymn-writer, yet it is proved beyond doubt that she was the author of a few hymns of great excellence." Her collection for use in her chapels amounted to 317 hymns, in the fourth edition of which appeared the one referred to before, beginning,

> "Oh! when my righteous Judge shall come."

Originally it formed a second part of a piece on the Judgment Day, which is preceded by a first part, that commenced:— .

> "We soon shall hear the midnight cry."

"When I gave myself to the Lord," said she, "I likewise devoted to him all my fortune." This for most of her life amounted to an income of about sixty thousand dollars a year, and when these means did not reach all her demands she sold her jewelry which she laid aside, when she found the pearl of great price. For these she realized nearly thirty-five hundred dollars, with which she built a chapel near her residence.

This was the beginning of her life work of erecting chapels by means of which she sought to reach the perishing masses. She assisted, and associated with Watts, the Wesleys, Whitefield, Berridge, Romaine, Toplady, Doddridge and others whose names became so luminous in the history of the great awakening of the eighteenth century. At the time of her death her chapels numbered sixty-seven. To provide ministers for these she founded an Institution at her own expense, at Trevecca, South Wales, which was dedicated by Whitefield on the sixty-first anniversary of her birth day.

It was not her intention to leave the Established Church but found it neccessary after ecclesiastical proceedings were brought against her ministers. Shortly before her death the Connection was formed which continues to bear her name. In 1792 her college was removed to Cheshunt, where it has been flourishing ever since.

She knew by sweet experience what it was

"To see thy smiling face."

As she approached the end of life's journey there seemed to be sunset glories that gilded the horizon; coming from her chamber one morning, her countenance lit up with unusual joy she said, "the Lord hath been present with my spirit this morning in a remarkable manner, what he means to convey to my mind I know not; it may be my approaching departure, my soul is filled with glory—I am as in the element of heaven itself."

Soon after, the breaking of a blood vessel was the means of loosening life's silver cord that held her to earth, and thus in her eighty-fourth year she peacefully passed to those mansions, where, as she says in the closing verse of her hymn:—

" ——loudest of the throng I'll sing
While heaven's resounding mansions ring
With shouts of sovereign grace."

"What if my name should be left out
When Thou for them shalt call."

A SOLDIER, mortally wounded, was lying in a hospital dying. All was still; he had not spoken for some time. His last moment was just at hand. Suddenly the silence was broken, and the attending surgeon was startled by the voice of the dying man uttering, clear and strong, the single word, "Here!"

"What do you want?" asked the surgeon, hastening to his cot. A moment elapsed. There was a seeming struggle after recollection; then the lips of the dying soldier mumbled, "Nothing; but it was roll-call in heaven, and I was answering to my name."

These were his last words on earth.

SAID a pious father in writing to his friends, "On January last I dreamed that the day of judgment was come. I saw the Judge on his great white throne, and all nations were gathered before him. My wife and I were on the right hand; but I could not see my children. I said, I cannot bear this; I must go and seek them.

"I went to the left hand of the Judge, and there found them all standing in the utmost despair. As soon as they saw me, they caught hold of me and cried, "O! father we will never part." I said, "My dear children, I am come to try, if possible, to get you out of this awful situation." So I took them all with me, but when we came near the Judge I thought he cast an angry look, and said, "What do thy children with thee now? They would not take thy warning when on earth, and they shall not share with thee the crown in heaven; depart ye cursed."

At these words I awoke bathed in tears. A while after this, as we were all sitting together on a Sabbath evening, I related to them my dream. No sooner did I begin than first one, and then another, yea, all of them, burst into tears, and God fastened conviction on their hearts. Five of them now rejoice in God their Saviour."

N old lady, who was an inveterate smoker, had a dream one night, in which she thought, as she stood before the great white throne and the books were opened, her name could not be found in the book of life.

Feeling sure that it was there, she entreated that it might be searched for again. As the keen eye of the Judge went up and down the list, he said, to her amazement, "It cannot be found." With great agony she begged that he might but look through the book again; when, after a while, she was told, "Yes, here it is at the corner of a page, but it is hard to find, as it is covered over, and nearly blotted out with tobacco smoke."

This so alarmed her, that she awoke from the dream, and, as she feared that by persisting in sending up her smoke, it might entirely obscure her name, she threw away her pipe. Afterward she could calmly join in singing the second verse of Lady Huntingdon's hymn:—

> "I love to meet Thy people now,
> Before Thy feet with them to bow,
> Though vilest of them all;
> But—can I bear the piercing thought—
> What if my name should be left out,
> When Thou for them shalt call!"

A DISCONSOLATE believer dreamed one Sunday night that a hand was held before her, and for a long time she wondered what it meant. At length a finger pointed to the palm of the hand. With uplifted head and open eyes she traced the words: "Behold, I have graven *thee* upon the palm of my hand." Oh! her delight! her joy! as she saw her name thus engraved.

A Timely Interference.

DR. Lowell Mason relates a sad "fix" they were in while he was acting as organist and leader of the singing, at the Bowdoin St. Church, Boston.

He says, "The whole hymn was first read by the minister, and then, just before the singing-exercise commenced, the direction was given, 'Omit the second stanza.' The following are the first three stanzas, and the connection between the first and third stanzas will be seen:

'When thou, my righteous Judge shalt come
  To take thy ransomed people home,
    Shall I among them stand?
Shall such a worthless worm as I,
  Who sometimes am afraid to die,
    Be found at thy right hand?

'I love to meet thy people now,
  Before thy feet with them to bow,
    Though vilest of them all;
But—can I bear the piercing thought—
What if my name should be left out
    When thou for them shalt call?

'O Lord, prevent it by thy grace:
Be thou my only hiding-place
    In this the accepted day;
Thy pardoning voice, oh, let me hear,
To still my unbelieving fear,
    Nor let me fall, I pray.'

"The organist did not perceive the fearful connection between the first and third stanzas until a moment before it was time to commence the latter, when, startled and terrified, he cried out, 'Sing the second stanza!' just in time to avoid the utterance of the frightful petition."

"Warm were the thanks expressed by members of the congregation after the service for their deliverance from the terrible moral collision with which they were threatened."

Amusing Mistakes.

IN the parish church of Fettercairn a custom existed of the precentor, on communion Sabbaths, reading out each single line of the psalm before it was sung by the congregation. This practice gave rise to a somewhat unlucky introduction of a line from the first Psalm. In most churches in Scotland, the communion tables are placed in the centre of the church. After sermon and prayer, the seats round these tables are occupied by the communicants, while a psalm is being sung.

On one communion Sunday, the precentor observed the noble family of Eglantine approaching the tables, and likely to be kept out by those who pressed in before them. Being very zealous for their accommodation, he called out to an individual whom he considered to be the principal obstacle in clearing the passage, "Come back, Jock, and let in the noble family of Eglantine;" and then, turning to his psalm-book, he took up his duty, and went on to read the line,

"Nor stand in the sinners' way."

THE ORKNEY HERALD says that during the singing of the first Psalm in the parish church of Birsay, a goose entered and quietly waddled up the passage towards the pulpit.

The precentor got off the track with the music, and seemed unable to "go on."

The minister observing the goose, leaned over the side of the pulpit, and, addressing the officer of the church, said, "R———, put out the goose." The functionary, not observing the presence of the feathered parishioner, and supposing that he meant the music-blunderer, marched up and collared him, saying at the time, "Come out o' that, fallow."

Singing in the Flames of Martyrdom.

JOHN HUSS, the martyr, could truthfully say, that when shielded with Christ's blood and righteousness—

> "'Mid flaming worlds in these arrayed,
> With joy shall I lift up my head."

For his faithfulness in opposing the errors of Rome, and in bringing about a revival of primitive Christianity he was sentenced to be burned alive July, 1415.

A band of eight hundred soldiers, attended by an immense crowd of spectators, led him out of the city into a meadow as the place of execution. He was stripped of his priestly garments, and on his head was placed a mitre of paper, on which devils were painted, and the inscription, "*A ring-leader of Heretics.*"

When he came to the stake, he threw himself upon his knees, sung a psalm, and looking up to heaven, he prayed: "Into thy hands, O Lord, I commit my spirit. Thou hast redeemed me. Assist me that with a firm mind, by the most powerful grace, I may undergo this most awful death, to which I am condemned for preaching Thy most holy gospel, Amen."

Bundles of wood and straw were piled around his bare feet, and when the chain was placed on his neck, he exclaimed, "Welcome this chain for Christ's sake." As the faggots, at length, reached as high as his neck, he was called upon to recant, to which he replied, "No, no, what I taught I am willing to seal with my blood."

As the fire was kindled and blazed up around him, Huss *sang a hymn* with a *loud voice*, which was heard above the cracking, and roaring of the flames.

Jerome of Prague, an associate of Huss, also followed in his footsteps, and suffered martyrdom. As the faggots began to blaze around him he sang the hymn "Hail, Festal Day" in a loud voice until he was suffocated.

HUSS SINGING IN THE FLAMES OF MARTYRDOM.

Author of "Come, humble sinner, in whose breast."

MANY hymn writers have produced but one choice hymn by which their names are remembered and revered. It was thus with Rev. Edmund Jones.

Though he passed from earth over a century ago, his precious hymn still lives, and will doubtless live on as long as there are penitent sinners to whom the church would say:—

> "Come, humble sinner, in whose breast
> A thousand thoughts revolve,
> Come, with your guilt and fear oppress'd,
> And make this last resolve."

In some collection of hymns the first line reads—

> "Come, trembling sinner, in whose breast,"

and the first line of the last verse is altered to read—

> "I cannot perish if I go,

instead of—

> "I can but perish if I go."

He was born at Cheltenham, England, and born again early in life, as appears from the record given of him in the Baptist church at Upton-on-Severn. While young he was sent to Bristol to pursue his studies for the ministry, under the Rev. Bernard Fosket. In his nineteenth year he was called to serve the Baptist church at Exeter on trial. His probation proving satisfactory, he was ordained in 1743. His church originally had no singing in divine service. It was first introduced in 1759.

He spent the remaining twenty years of his life among this people, and added one hundred members to the church. He died April 15, 1765, aged forty-three years.

Judson and his Hymns.

ADONIRAM JUDSON is a name that is luminous in the history of early missions, and as he wrote a few hymns, he deserves a place in the list of hymn-writers. He was a son of a Congregational minister of the same name. His native place was Malden, Massachusetts, where he was born, August 9, 1788.

When but four years of age, he seemed to foreshadow his future career. Gathering the children of the neighborhood around him, he was wont to mount a chair, and go through a preaching service with marked earnestness. His favorite hymn upon these occasions was one of Watts's, commencing,

"'Go, preach my gospel,' saith the Lord."

During his course of studies at Providence college, a circumstance occurred that changed the whole future of his life. In his class was a young man named E——, to whom he was warmly attached, and by whose influence he was led into professed infidelity, to the great grief of his devoted parents.

Starting out on a travelling tour at the close of his school, Judson assumed another name and joined a theatrical company in New York. Whenever the thought of a mother's tears would occur, he tried to soothe his conscience, by saying, "I am in no danger, I am only seeing the world, the dark side of it, as well as the bright." After a while, pursuing his journey westward, he stopped at a country inn. As the landlord took him to his bedroom, he said: "I am obliged to place you next door to a young man, who is exceedingly ill, probably in a dying state, but I hope it will occasion you no uneasiness."

It proved, however, a very restless night; groans were frequently heard, and other sounds that made him think of Eternity. Alone, and in the dead of night, he felt the props of his infidelity give way. Then he would try to shame his fears, by thinking what his witty, clear-minded, intellectual E—— would say to such consummate boyishness.

At last, morning came, and the bright flood of light, which poured into his chamber, dispelled all his superstitious illusions. Going in search of the landlord, he made inquiry about his fellow-lodger.

"He is dead," was the reply. "Dead!" "Yes, he is gone, poor fellow!" "Do you know who it was?" "O yes, it was a young man from Providence College—a very fine fellow, his name was E——."

Judson was completely stunned. He knew not what to say or do. "Dead—Lost" were the two words that kept ringing in his head. He could go no further in his journey. This death-scene of his infidel companion, was the pivot on which turned his destiny, both for time and eternity.

Judson afterwards entered the Theological Seminary at Andover, became a decided Christian, and after reading the "Star in the East," resolved to become a Missionary.

After marrying Miss Ann H. Hasseltine, a young Christian lady as earnest and devoted, as she was accomplished and beautiful, the two set sail for the realms of heathen darkness, on the 19th of February, 1812.

Just as they were getting under way with their missionary work at Ava, the Capital of Burmah, war broke out and Mr. Judson and others were violently seized as English spies and cast into the death prison.

During nine months, he was stretched on the bare floor, bound by three pairs of iron fetters, and fastened to a long pole, to prevent his moving. This was during the hot season too, when he was shut up with a hundred prisoners in a room without any windows, or any appliances by which a breath of air could be admitted, except through the cracks in the boards. They were all obliged to lie in a row upon the floor, without a mattress, or even so much as a wooden block, which they begged might be granted them for a pillow. His whole period of indescribable suffering continued for one year and seven months. Yet from this dark prison issued a hymn of praise that is now echoing around this world in the psalmody of the church. Judson dates it, "Prison, Ava, March, 1825." It is a versification of the Lord's Prayer, and shows the thoughts and feelings that filled his heart during his long protracted agony. He says it is comprised in fewer words than the original Greek, and in only two more words than the common translation:—

> " Our Father, God, who art in heaven,
> All hallowed be thy name;
> Thy kingdom come; thy will be done
> In heaven and earth the same.
>
> " Give us this day our daily bread;
> And as we those forgive
> Who sin against us, so may we
> Forgiving grace receive.
>
> " Into temptation lead us not;
> From evil set us free;
> And thine the kingdom, thine the power,
> And glory, ever be."

Who can read or sing this hymn without a faltering voice, or a tearful eye, after knowing the surrounding circumstances under which it was written? Surely it was a marvelous faith that could mingle with the rattling of prison chains, the glad sound of praise.

We can easily imagine, how at one time, at least, it was with tremulous lips, that the author himself sang the words:

> " Give us, this day, our daily bread."

His loving wife, knowing what the "daily bread" meant in such a prison, arranged, by means of some buf-

falo meat and plantains, to get up a mince-pie, at least in appearance. But when it arrived in prison, its associations brought so vividly to mind the old comforts of home, that he bowed his head upon his knees, and wept till the tears flowed down to the chains about his ankles. Through his flowing tears he saw the home of his boyhood again,—his gentle mother, his revered father, his much loved sister and brother around the noonday meal. His heart was too full to partake of the delicious morsel, and so he thrust it into the hand of an associate.

In this time of trial he addressed thirty stanzas to his infant daughter, who, when twenty days old, was brought into prison to receive a father's kiss. The lines began,

"Sleep, darling infant, sleep,
Hushed on thy mother's breast;
Let no rude sound of clankering chains,
Disturb thy balmy rest."

And yet after passing through all these privations and painful experiences, he could brush away his tears, and write:—

"Sovereign love appoints the measure,
And the number of our pains,
And is pleased when we take pleasure
In the trials he ordains."

In 1850, Judson's health had so broken down, that his only hope for restoration was a protracted sea voyage. On the 3rd of April, he embarked on a vessel, bound to the Isle of France. Nine days later, while out at sea, he breathed his last, and all that was mortal of Dr. Judson, was committed to the ocean's deep, where his dust is rocked by the mighty billows, till, to sea and land, God's angel shall declare "that there should be time no longer."

Judson wrote two other hymns generally found in Baptist hymn books, commencing,

"Come, Holy Spirit, Dove divine,"
"Our Saviour bowed beneath the wave."

> "Sun of my Soul, Thou Saviour dear,
> It is not night if Thou be near."

DAILY at family worship, and often in the sanctuary, ascends the incense of praise in the language of this precious hymn.

It was penned by Rev. John Keble, who was born April 25, 1792, in Fairford, England. He received his early education from his father, who had, for fifty years, charge of the Episcopal church in this quiet village, that lies embedded among the celebrated Coteswold Hills.

At fourteen he entered the Corpus Christi College, where he obtained the highest honors ever attained before by one so young.

In 1815 he entered the ministry, in 1831 he was elected professor of poetry at Oxford, where he remained for ten years, and in 1835 became rector of the Hursley Church.

He wrote a poem on Mahomet when but sixteen years old. The two monuments on which rests his fame as a Christian poet are, "The Christian Year," and "Lyra Innocentium." Of the former, ninety-six editions were published during his lifetime,—a fact which is said to be "unprecedented in the annals of literature." Dr. Arnold, speaking of his hymns, says, "The wonderful knowledge of Scripture, the purity of heart, and the richness of poetry which they exhibit, I never saw paralleled." His church was open for daily morning and evening prayer. "Night and day he was unwearied in his ministrations to the sick, the poor, the afflicted. On many a dark evening he was seen, lantern in hand, wending his way to some distant cottage, with words of cheer. Though a man of fine scholarly tastes and culture, he was so meek and unassuming, that the poor looked up to him as their best friend." He died March, 1866.

JOHN KEBLE.

Kelley and his Hymns.

THE "Green Isle" has never furnished a greater or more prolific hymn-writer than Thomas Kelley. He was born in 1769, and was the son of Judge Kelley of Kelleyville, Ireland.

Thoughts of eternity impressed him early in life, but it was not till after he had completed his university studies at Dublin, that he found peace in believing. After being awakened through the perusal of Romaine's writings, he was in great distress, and, in various forms of self-punishment, sought to merit salvation. When at length he comprehended the new and living way, he became very zealous in proclaiming it to others. In 1793, he was ordained in the Established Church, but being restricted in his evangelistic efforts, he afterward united with the Independents. Crowds flocked around him wherever he lifted up the standard of the cross. Possessed of ample means, he built quite a number of churches. While he preached at many places, his main charge was in Dublin, where he broke the bread of life for sixty-three years.

Mr. Kelly was quite a scholar, and was well versed in the Oriental tongues. He was also a good musician, and prepared a book of music to accompany his hymn-book, which was entitled, "Hymns on Various Passages of Scripture." The first edition was issued in 1804, and contained but ninty-six hymns, but so prolific was his pen, that in the seventh edition, issued in 1853, the number of his hymns had increased to seven hundred and sixty-seven.

While in the act of preaching, he was stricken down with paralysis, and died the following year, 1855, eighty-six years of age. His last words were, "Not my will, but Thine be done."

"Praise God from whom All Blessings flow."

THIS doxology appeared as the last verse of the "Morning and Evening Hymns" added to the "Manuel of Prayers," by Bishop Ken in 1697. The morning hymn commences,

> "Awake my soul, and with the sun."

The evening hymn,

> "Glory to thee, my God, this night."

The "Morning Hymn" was very dear to its author, who used often to sing it in the early morning to the accompaniment of his lute.

Bishop Ken was born at Berkhampsted, England, in 1637. He was appointed chaplain to the Princes of Orange, 1669. In 1684, to King Charles II. In 1685, to James II.

When the king ordered him to read the well-known Declaration of Indulgence, he conscientiously refused to comply, for which he was imprisoned in the Tower.

Montgomery says of the doxology, "It is a masterpiece at once of amplification and compression: amplification, on the burden, 'Praise God,' repeated in each line; compression, by exhibiting God as the object of praise in every view in which we can imagine praise due to Him; praise for all His blessings, yea, for *all* blessings,' none coming from any other source,—praise, by every creature, specifically invoked, 'here below,' and in heaven 'above;' praise to Him in each of the characters wherein He has revealed Himself in His word, 'Father, Son, and Holy Ghost."

"Yet this comprehensive verse is sufficiently simple that, by it, 'out of the mouths of babes and sucklings,' God may 'perfect praise;' and it appears so easy that one is tempted to think hundreds of the sort might

BISHOP KEN.
A FAC SIMILE OF AN OLD WOOD ENGRAVING

be made without trouble. The reader has only to try, and he will be quickly undeceived: the longer he tries, the more difficult he will find the task to be."

This doxology daily echoes around the globe and probably has been more used than any other composition in the world with the exception of the Lord's Prayer, and it will, no doubt, continue to be till time shall be no more. "It has been said that Bishop Ken was accustomed to remark that it would enhance his joy in heaven to listen to his morning and evening hymns as sung by the faithful on earth." Whitfield says, that the hymns of Ken were of great benefit to his soul when ten years old.

An impressive scene occurred in 1858, at Andover, where they were having a great gathering at the collegiate dinner table. Unexpectedly it was announced that the telegraphic cable across the ocean was successful, when, it is said that "a thousand gentlemen spontaneously arose, and, in the majestic sounds of '*Old Hundred*' sang" the soul inspiring strain:—

"Praise God, from whom all blessings flow."

Ken died as he was on a journey to Bath, in March 1711, in the 74th year of his age. He had been in the habit of travelling for many years with his shroud in his port-manteau, which he always put on when attacked by sickness. Of this he gave notice the day before his death, in order to prevent his body from being stripped. He was never married.

In accordance with his own request, he was buried at sunrise. His morning hymn was sung as his body sank in the grave. His death was calm and peaceful, exemplifying his words:—

"Teach me to live, that I may dread,
The grave as little as my bed."

The Grave of Ken.

BISHOP KEN'S physician, Dr. Merewether, made the following entry in his diary for the year 1711:—

"March 16th,—I went to Longleate, to visit Bishop Ken.

"March 18th,—I waited on him again.

"March 19th,—All glory be to God. Between 5 and 6 in y⁰ morning. Thomas, late Bishop of Bath and Wells, died at Longleate."

Bishop Ken was buried aside of the eastern window in the parish church of Frome. The iron pales that fence the mound indicate in the picture opposite the resting-place of the dust of him who penned the immortal doxology.

"On yonder heap of earth forlorn,
  Where Ken his place of burial chose,
Peacefully shine, O Sabbath morn!
  And, eve, with gentlest hush, repose.

"To him is rear'd no marble tomb,
  Within the dim cathedral-fane,
But some faint flowers of summer, bloom,
  And silent falls the winter's rain.

"No village monumental stone
  Records a verse, a date, a name;
What boots it? When thy task is done,
  CHRISTIAN, how vain the sound of Fame!

"Oh, far more grateful to thy God
  The voices of poor children rise,
Who hasten o'er the dewy sod,
  'To pay their morning sacrifice.'

"And can we listen to their hymns,
  Heard, haply, when the evening knell
Sounds, where the village tower is dim,
  As if to bid the world farewell,

"Without a thought, that from the dust
  The morn shall wake the sleeping clay,
And bid the faithful and the just
  Up spring to heaven's eternal day!"

The Grave of Ken aside of the Church at Frome.

Ken was fond of children, and they of him. A pleasing fact is recorded, and adverted to in the preceding verses, that after his lips could no longer sing his morning hymn, the children took up the strain, and, at early morn, encircling his tomb, would re-echo it over his silent grave.

Rev. W. L. Bowles says, in his biography of Ken: "It is interesting to think, that when, to this day, (1831) the same words of Ken are sung to the same tune, every Sunday, by the parish church of Frome, they are sung over the grave of him, who composed the words, and who had sung them himself, to the same air, over one hundred and sixty years before, though he now lies in the church-yard without an inscription."

The following verses were originally wedded to the old tune of Talis, and were sung as a Morning Hymn, in the Winchester school that Ken attended.

To his poetic and musical ear, the sound of the uncouth poetry, and the want of harmony between the words and tune, suggested, it is supposed, the preparation of his Morning Hymn and the Doxology. These were to take the place of these crude stanzas, and were specially adapted, and for over a century afterwards, sung to the same tune of Talis.

Our readers will agree with us that some substitute was needed after reading the following:—

"Praise the Lord, ye Gentiles all,
  Which hath brought you into this light;
Oh praise him all people mortal,
  As is most worthy and right.

"For he is full determined
  On us to pour out his mercy;
And the Lord's truth, be ye assured
  Abideth perpetually.

"Glory be to God, the Father,
  And to Jesus Christ his true Son,
With the Holy Ghost, in like manner,
  Now, and at every season."

Ken's Morning Hymn.

HAWKINS informs us, that Ken "seemed to go to rest with no other purpose than the refreshing and enabling him with more vigour and cheerfulness to sing his Morning Hymn, as he used to do, to his lute, before he put on his clothes."

This fact adds additional interest to these words:—

> "Awake, my soul! and, with the sun,
> Thy daily stage of duty run;
> Shake off dull sloth, and joyful rise,
> To pay thy morning sacrifice."

One morning, Ken had special reason to praise God, in this language of his morning hymn:—

> "All praise to thee, who safe hast kept,
> And hast refreshed me while I slept."

This will appear from what he says in the following quaint letter, which we give in its original form:—

"ALL GLORY BE TO GOD."

"My Good L^d and B^r:

"The same post wch brought me your Lordshipp's, brought the news of ye Occasionall Bills being throwne out by ye Lords. I think I omitted to tell you ye full of my deliverance in y^e *late storme*, for the house being surveyed ye day following, ye workmen found y^t ye beame wch supported ye roof over my head was broken out to y^t degree, y^t it had but half an inch hold, so y^t it was a wonder it would hold together; for wch signall and particular preservation God's holy name be ever praised! I am sure I ought alwayes thankfully to remember it.

* * * * * *

"Your Lordshipp's most affec^e friend and B^r,
"*Bath, Nov.* 18." "Ken."

"For Mrs Hannah Lloyd, at Mr Hawling's,
a grocer, over against Sommersett-house,
London."

Ken's Imprisonment and Retirement.

IN 1684, Ken was appointed bishop of Bath and Wells. After four years of fruitful service, he was willing to go to prison, rather than read the famous "Declaration of indulgence," that was introduced by James II. to favor his Roman Catholic friends. In the course of two months, he was acquitted by a jury.

A cotemporary says: "When he and the other six bishops were released from their imprisonment, the universal joy was so great as to be heard many miles distant; and the shout given at their deliverance in Westminster-hall, had almost the effect upon the windows at Lambeth, as the discharge of a cannon gives. Bishop Ken came with the Arch Bishop of Canterbury in his coach to Lambeth, which took them up several hours, and the concourse of people was innumerable the whole way, hanging upon the coach, and insisting upon being blessed by these two prelates, who, with much difficulty and patience, at last got to Lambeth-house."

Again in 1691, having conscientiously refused to give in his allegiance to the new government, he was, as nonjuror, deprived of his Episcopal emoluments.

With his "lame horse," which is described as a "sorry one," his famous lute, his little Greek Testament, and his shroud, he bade adieu to the weeping friends of his diocese and retired to the hospitable home, extended to him at Longleat, the seat of Viscount Weymouth, and there spent the last twenty years of his earthly career.

> "Dead to all else, alive to God alone,
> Ken, the confessor meek, abandons power,
> Palace, and mitre, and cathedral throne,
> (A shroud alone reserved,) and in the bower
> Of meditation hallows every hour."

When, thirteen years later, Queen Ann granted him

a yearly pension of 200 l., and sent it to him through his successor in office, he acknowledged the receipt of it, in this letter:—

"ALL GLORY BE TO GOD."

"My Good Lord:

"Your Lordshipp gave me a wonderful surprise when you informed me y‍ᵗ y‍ᵉ Queen had been pleased to settle a very liberall pension on me. I beseech God to accumulate the blessings of both lives on her Majesty, for royall bounty to me, so perfectly free and unexpected; and I beseech God abundantly to reward my Lord Treasurer, who inclined her to be thus gracious to me, and to give him a plentiful measure of wisdom from above.

"My Lord, lett it not shock your native modesty, if I make this just acknowledgement, y‍ᵗ though y‍ᵉ sense I have of her Majesty's favour in y‍ᵉ pension is deservedly great, yet her choosing you for my successor gave me *much more satisfaction;* as my concerne for y‍ᵉ eternall welfare of y‍ᵉ flock, exceeded all regard for my owne temporall advantage.

* * * * * * *

"Your Lordshipp's most affectionate
"Friend and B‍ʳ.
"*June 7th*, 1704.   "Tho. Ken, L. B. & W."

The shaded groves surrounding his retreat were made vocal, with the echo of his morning and evening hymns, and with much emphasis he could say:—

"I, the small dolorous remnant of my days,
Devote to hymn my great Redeemer's praise;
Aye, nearer as I draw towards the heavenly rest,
The more I love the employment of the blest."

His evening hymn commenced originally, "All praise to thee, my God, this night," instead of "Glory to thee," &c., as now in use. Nearly all his letters were headed "All glory be to God." It is said, these were his last words.

"Glory to Thee, my God, this night."

THIS hymn of Bishop Ken, says Stevenson in his "Associations," was the dying song of Roger Miller, once a drunken copperplate printer of London, afterward a city missionary in Broadwall, Lambeth, where he labored long and usefully amongst the profligate and destitute. On the death of his mother, in 1847, Mr. Miller left London for Manchester, to attend her funeral. It was near midnight, when, as the train approached Wolverton, an accident occurred: the train ran off the lines, and several were killed. Mr. Miller had a few moments before united with the other passengers in singing the "Evening hymn," that they might close the day with a devotional song. The praises of the passengers arose amidst the noise of the rushing train, and most seemed heartly to join. How appropriate the words as contained in the third verse:—

> "Teach me to live, that I may dread
> The grave as little as my bed;
> Teach me to die, that so I may
> Rise glorious at the awful day."

The music of their voices became, with one, at least, in that company, blended with the hallelujahs of the redeemed, for Roger Miller was hurried in an instant to glory.

If all the impressive incidents thus associated with the hymns of Bishop Ken can be reported to him in Heaven, he certainly realizes in full, the joy anticipated, and expressed in the following stanza:—

> "And should the well-meant song I leave behind,
> With Jesus' lovers some acceptance find,
> 'Twill heighten even the joys of heaven to know
> That, in my verse, saints sing God's praise below."

The Doxology in Libby Prison.

REV. W. F. CRAFTS gives the following narrative as from the lips of Chaplain McCabe, in relation to the starving "boys in blue," while incarcerated in Libby Prison:—

"Day after day they saw comrades passing away, and their number increased by fresh, living recruits for the grave. One night about ten o'clock, through the stillness and the darkness, they heard the tramp of coming feet, that soon stopped before the prison door until arrangements could be made inside.

"In the company was a young Baptist minister, whose heart almost fainted as he looked on those cold walls and thought of the suffering inside. Tired and weary he sat down, put his face in his hands and wept. Just then a lone voice sung out from an upper window:—

"'Praise God from whom all blessings flow;'

and a dozen manly voices joined in the second line:—

"'Praise Him all creatures here below;'

and then by the time the third was reached, more than a score of hearts were full, and these joined to send the words on high:—

"'Praise Him above ye heavenly host;'

and by this time the prison was all alive, and seemed to quiver with the sacred song, as from every room and cell those brave men sang:—

"'Praise Father, Son, and Holy Ghost.'

As the song died out on the still night that enveloped in darkness the doomed city of Richmond, the young man arose and happily said:—

"'Prisons would palaces prove,
If Jesus would dwell with me there.'"

The Doxology Sung Thirty Five Times in one Day.

STEVENSON records the fact that during a season of revival in London, the church was accustomed to sing the doxology at each time the report was given of a new case of conversion. During one day they had occasion to repeat it thus thirty five different times, as one and another had been added as trophies of the cross.

He says that a twelve miles' walk after that day's service, during the snow of a cold February, did not dissipate the blessed memory of that memorable day.

The Doxology Sung 'Mid Tears of Joy.

REV. DR. TAYLOR states the following fact:—
"In the great cotton famine in England, which desolated Lancashire for long and weary months, the conduct of the operatives was the admiration of the world. There were no riots and no excess of crimes. The people, men and women, went into the Sunday school houses and prayed. They had been taught to do so, and they were upheld in the time of trial by the truths they had learned. When the first wagon load of cotton arrived, the people unhooked the horses and drew it themselves, and surrounding it began to sing. What do you think they sang? They sang the grand old doxology while the tears came flowing down their cheeks:—

"Praise God, from whom all blessings flow."

LETITIA OAKES, at the advanced age of eighty five, passed away, and with her dying breath, whispered the doxology:—

"Praise God from whom all blessings flow,"

and while the words were still on her lips she ceased to breathe.

Hymn by E. M. Long.

PRAISE TO THE TRINITY.

Words and Music by Rev. E. M. Long.

"Praise to the Trinity."

ELEVEN hundred years ago there ascended to the skies, the venerable Bede, whose last song on earth was "Praise to the Trinity." He was born about the year 672. Having become an orphan in early life he was trained in a monastery. He was justly distinguished for his piety and learning. Among the volumes that he wrote, was a "A Book of Hymns in Several Sorts of Metre or Rhyme," and a "Book of the Art of Poetry."

One of his pupils thus describes his last days: "He lived joyfully, giving thanks to God day and night; every day he gave lessons to us, his pupils, and the rest of the time he occupied in chanting psalms. He was awake almost the whole night, and spent it in joy and thanksgiving: and when he awoke from his short sleep, immediately he raised his hands on high, and began again to give thanks. . . . . . . And when he came to the words, 'leave us not orphaned behind Thee,' he burst into tears.

"Then in an hour he began to sing again. We wept with him; sometimes we read, sometimes we wept, but we could not read without tears."

His last effort was to translate the Gospel of John into Anglo-Saxon. He kept dictating to an amanuensis, bidding him write faster and faster, until death drew near.

At last his attendant said: "Dearest master, there is only one thought left to write." He answered, "Write quickly." Soon the answer was, that it was written, when he replied: "Raise my head in thy hand, for it will do me good to sit opposite my sanctuary, where I was wont to kneel down to pray, that sitting I may call upon my Father." While thus seated, with his eyes turned toward the courts of the Lord, he sang: "Glory to Thee, O God, Father, Son, and Holy Ghost;" and when he had named the Holy Ghost he breathed his last breath.

The Doxology Heard a Mile.

IN 1859, we had an extensive revival at Pottsville Pa., under the "Union Tabernacle."

We had four services daily for seven weeks. Hundreds had professed penitence, and as many had been received into the different churches, the pastors thought it would be pleasant to close this series of meetings with a grand union service. Twelve churches responded to the invitation representing ten different denominations.

Pottsville is surrounded by many smaller towns, two three, and four miles distant. From these came bands of Christians, singing the songs of Zion. So that as the setting sun was gilding the mountains, the hills overlooking the city were made to re-echo with the sentiments of hymns such as,

> Come we that love the Lord,
> And let our joys be known,"

and

> "Children of the Heavenly King,
> As we journey sweetly sing."

We had, by means of extra canvass, extended our Tabernacle, that ordinarily held several thousands, so that it covered an immense mass of human beings. One pastor estimated the number present at seven thousand.

Some fourteen hundred professed Christians took part in the exercises that were conducted in the English, German and Welsh languages. As we closed by singing the Doxology, the immense volume of sound arose so grandly in the calm evening air, that when the request was made that it be repeated, it was sung with hearts overflowing with gladness, eyes swimming in tears of joy, so that at a distance of a mile, a household distinctly heard the words :-

> "Praise God, from whom all blessings flow."

A Hymn by the Author of "Star-Spangled Banner."

IN some of the different church collections of hymns may be found one beginning,—

"If life's pleasures charm thee,
Give them not thy heart,
Lest the gift ensnare thee
From thy God to part.
His favors seek,
His praises speak,
Fix here thy hopes' foundation;
Serve Him, and He
Will ever be
The Rock of thy salvation."

It came from the pen of the author of the well-known "*Star-Spangled Banner;*" and, if the last-named composition shows the graceful patriot, the hymn certainly displays the Christian. This was still further manifested in a scene about the year 1835, as thus described by the clergyman officially engaged. He says, "I stood within the railing, at the side of the communion-table, and had administered the sacred elements to all, it seemed, who desired to partake of them. Just then, however, as though previously restrained by profound humility, a stranger approached the altar, knelt all alone, and so received the holy memorials of our Saviour's suffering and death.

"I trust that the service was one of true faith, and the result was one of great peace and comfort. That last communicant was the same person,—the distinguished poet, the accomplished lawyer and orator, the modest Christian, Francis S. Key."

Belcher's Historical Sketches.

Luther and his Hymns.

FIGURES can tell the immensity of space through which a rolling world makes its orbit, but who can decipher the circuit of that influence which encircles the centuries of time and the ages of eternity. The hymn-writing of Luther and his co-laborers, set in motion such a train of results, that no mortal pen can describe. It was the lever that moved the world of German mind. "The whole people," said a Catholic of that period, "is singing itself into this Lutheran doctrine." The Romanist had good reason for this assertion. Coleridge says: "Luther did as much for the Reformation by his hymns as by the translation of the Bible." During the time when Luther was most busy composing his hymns, four printers in Erfurt alone were kept at work in printing and publishing them. They seemed to fly all over the land, as if on the wings of the wind.

Writing to his friend Spalatin, he says: "It is my intention, after the example of the prophets and the ancient fathers, to make German psalms for the people; that is, spiritual songs, whereby the Word of God may be kept alive among them by singing. We seek, therefore, everywhere for poets. Now, as you are such a master of the German tongue, and are so mighty and eloquent therein, I entreat you to join hands with us in the work."

The second hymn that Luther wrote proved to be very popular in his day. A cotemporary says: "Who doubts not that many hundred Christians have been brought to the true faith by this one hymn alone, who before, perchance, could not so much as bear to hear Luther's name. But his sweet and noble words have so taken their hearts that they were constrained to come to the truth."

A singular use was made of this hymn in 1557. A number of princes, connected with the reformed religion,

having met at Frankford, arranged to have an evangelical service in the Church of St. Bartholomew. But a cunning Roman Catholic priest occupied the pulpit, and proceeded to preach in accordance with his own views. After enduring his remarks for a while, in "indignant silence," the whole congregation rose and drowned his voice by singing this hymn, and in this they persisted till they sang the affrighted priest out of church. We give herewith the first of the ten verses of this hymn, as translated by Catherine Winkworth:—

"Dear Christian people, now rejoice!
Our hearts within us leap,
While we, as with one soul and voice,
With love and gladness deep,
Tell how our God beheld our need,
And sing that sweet and wondrous deed,
That hath so dearly cost Him.

Luther calls hymns "a miniature Bible." He wrote thirty-seven, "which are to be weighed, not counted." He also composed music adapted to many of his hymns. After dinner, it is said, that whether at home or abroad, he was accustomed "to take a lute and sing and play for half an hour or more with his friends." It is therefore no wonder that he declared, "He who despises music, as all fanatics do, will never be my friend." In seeking to have all children taught to sing, he says: "I would fain see all arts, specially music, in the service of Him, who has given and created them." To so great an extent were the Reformers singers, that "psalm singer" and "heretic" became synonymous. Thus the great Reformer was also the great singer of the church, giving the hymn book, as well as the Bible to the people.

Luther was born at Eisleben, Nov. 10, 1483. He was the son of humble but pious parents. Even in early life his voice was tuned to hymn the Redeemer's praise, as will be seen from the following incident:—

Luther's Snow Song.

ON a cold, dark night, when the wind was blowing hard, Conrad, a worthy citizen of a little town in Germany, sat playing his flute, while Ursula, his wife was preparing supper. They heard a sweet voice singing outside:

"Foxes to their holes have gone,
 Every bird into its nest;
 But I wander here alone,
 And for me there is no rest."

Tears filled the good man's eyes, as he said, "What a pity it should be spoiled by being tried in such weather."

"I think it is the voice of a child. Let us open the door and see," said his wife, who had lost a little boy not long before, and whose heart was opened to take pity on the little wanderer.

Conrad opened the door, and saw a ragged child, who said:

"Charity, good sir, for Christ's sake."

"Come in, my little one," said he. "You shall rest with me for the night."

The boy said, "Thank God!" and entered. The heat of the room made him faint, but Ursula's kind care soon restored him. They gave him some supper, and then he told them that he was the son of a poor miner, and wanted to be a priest. He wandered about and sang, and lived on the money people gave him. His kind friends would not let him talk much, but sent him to bed.

When he was asleep they looked in upon him, and were so pleased with his pleasant countenance that they determined to keep him, if he was willing. In the morning they found that he was only too glad to remain. They sent him to school, and afterward he entered the

LUTHER'S STREET SONG.

monastery. There he found the Bible, which he read and from which he learned the way of life. The little voice of the little singer became the strong echo of the good news, "Justified by faith, we have peace with God through our Lord Jesus Christ." Conrad and Ursula when they took that little singer into their house, little thought that then they were nourishing the great champion of Reformation. The poor child was Martin Luther! "Be not forgetful to entertain strangers."

The following is the whole of the song which Luther sang on that memorable night:

Lord of heaven! lone and sad,
I would lift my soul to thee;
Pilgrim in a foreign land,
Gracious Father, look on me.
I shall neither faint nor die
While I walk beneath thine eye.

I will stay my faith on thee,
And will never fear to tread
Where the Savior-Master leads;
He will give me daily bread.
Christ was hungry, Christ was poor,
He will feed me from his store.

Foxes to their holes have gone,
Every bird into its nest;
But I wander here alone,
And for me there is no rest;
Yet I neither faint nor fear,
For the Savior-Christ is near.

If I live he'll be near me,
If I die to him I go;
He'll not leave me, I will trust him,
And my heart no fear shall know.
Sin and sorrow I defy,
For on Jesus I rely.

Coburg Castle and Luther's Hymn.

COBURG is a small city in Germany, and is one of the chief ducal residences. This old castle of the dukes stands on a height that rises more than five hundred feet above the town. It is still a place of strength, and contains a large collection of armor. But the chief attractions to visitors are the rooms and the bed which Luther occupied, and the pulpit from which he preached, nearly three and a half centuries ago.

The time of Luther's sojourn here was in the year 1530, during the meeting of the diet at Augsburg, when the great confession of the Protestant church was delivered. While Melanchthon and other theologians, together with the Elector, went to the diet, they left Luther on the way in the refuge afforded by the strong castle at Coburg, where he could easily be reached by letter.

As Luther had, nine years before called Wurtemburg Castle his Patmos, so he named this his Sinai; but in writing to Melancthon, he said he would make it a Zion. Here he remained nearly six months, laboring and praying for the kingdom of Christ; one of his principal occupations being the translation of the Bible into the German language.

It is said that during the diet, when great dangers threatened the church, he would daily go to the window of the castle, look up toward heaven and sing with great energy his celebrated hymn of faith:—

"A mighty fortress is our God."

Some writers have even maintained that this hymn was written at Coburg; but it is traceable to a date a year earlier. This hymn may well be associated with castles. It seems itself a grand tower of strength. It is founded on the forty-sixth Psalm, which opens with those words of power: "God is our refuge and strength."

The Castle at Coburg.

A Nobleman Brought in his Right Mind by Singing.

A HUNGARIAN nobleman lost a daughter whom he most tenderly loved. The circumstances of her death greatly aggravated his grief, and he became quite uncontrollable in his mental derangement. Every means was tried which wealth or influence could devise or secure to restore him, but without effect. Lying on his couch in a room draped with black, from which the light was excluded, he neither smiled or wept, and joy seemed forever to have fled from his breast.

At length it was proposed that Mara, who was noted for her vocal performances, should sing within hearing of the afflicted father, whose grief had now nearly worn him down to the grave. Handel's "Messiah" was chosen for the experiment, and in an adjoining room that sweet and marvellous voice began its almost more than human strains. At first it had no apparent effect on the nobleman. As she proceeded he slowly raised himself from his couch to listen, and the heart that had been dead to emotion began to swell with the rising tide. When she came to the passage, "Look and see if there be any sorrow like to my sorrow," that was rendered with a subdued pathos, which brought tears in the eyes of those present, sighs escaped the suffering father, and soon the tears followed, and then rising from his couch, he fell upon his knees, and by the time the full choir struck the hallelujah chorus, his voice united with theirs, and his spirit was free. This was a striking illustration of Luther's stanzas:—

> "Where friends and comrades sing in tune,
> All evil passions vanish soon;
> Hate, anger, envy cannot stay,
> All gloom and heartache melt away,
> The lust of wealth, the cares that cling,
> Are all forgotten while we sing."

Author of "Jesus, I my cross have taken."

THIS hymn of consecration was written by Rev. Henry Francis Lyte, and was first published in 1833, in a volume of "*Poems Chiefly Religious.*"

He was born at Kelso, Scotland, June 1, 1793.

While receiving a liberal education at Trinity college, Dublin, he struggled hard with poverty.

Lyte speaks of himself as having been worldly-minded, and a stranger to experimental religion, until 1818, three years after he had entered the ministry of the Church of England. His eyes were opened while at the death-bed of a neighboring clergyman, who had sent for him in great agony, because he was "unpardoned and unprepared to die." As they joined in the search of the Scriptures to find out the way of salvation, they both entered into the rest of faith while perusing the writings of St. Paul.

"I was greatly affected," says Lyte, "by the whole matter, and brought to look at life, and its issues with a different eye than before; and I began to study my Bible, and preach in another manner than I had previously done."

Of the departure of his friend, he says, "he died happy under the belief that, though he deeply erred, there was One whose death and sufferings would atone for all delinquencies, and He accepted for all that he had incurred." In 1823, he took charge of a church at Brixham, where he wrote most of his hymns.

Amongst this "busy, shrewd, somewhat rough, but warm-hearted population of a fishing coast, and seafaring district," he spent some twenty-four years of zealous, faithful labor. Here "he made hymns for his little ones, and hymns for his hardy fishermen, and hymns for sufferers like himself."

He gathered a Sunday school of several hundred scholars, and trained a band of some seventy teachers to teach them. In 1834, he published the "Spirit of the Psalms," a metrical version of the same; and in 1846, the "Poems of Henry Vaughan, with a Memoir."

His health failing, he was advised to journey to the South. Of this, said he: "They tell me that the sea is injurious to me. I hope not; for I know of no divorce I should more deprecate than from the ocean. From childhood it has been my friend and playmate, and never have I been weary of gazing on its glorious face. Besides, if I cannot live by the sea, adieu to poor Berry Head—adieu to the wild birds, and wild flowers, and all the objects that have made my old residence so attractive." After a little, he adds, "I am meditating flight again to the south. The little faithful robin is every morning at my window, sweetly warning me that autumnal hours are at hand. The swallows are preparing for flight, and inviting me to accompany them; and yet, alas! while I talk of flying, I am just able to crawl, and ask myself whether I shall be able to leave England at all."

In this time of trial and weakness, how appropriate and expressive the language of one of his hymns:—

> "Whate'er events betide,
>   Thy will they all perform;
> Safe in Thy breast my head I hide,
>   Nor fear the coming storm.
>
> "Let good or ill befal,
>   It must be good for me;
> Secure of having Thee in all,
>   Of having all in Thee."

In the autumn of 1847, before starting out on this, his last journey, he penned the lines of the following hymn, that an eminent writer regards as "almost perfect."

"Abide with me! Fast falls the eventide."

THIS hymn was the last poetic utterances of Lyte, written as the shadows of the dark valley were closing his labors on earth.

Though he was, as he says, scarcely "able to crawl," he made one more attempt to preach and to administer the holy communion. "O brethren," said he, "I can speak feelingly, experimentally, on this point; and I stand before you seasonably to-day, as alive from the dead, if I may hope to impress it upon you, and induce you to prepare for that solemn hour which must come to all, by a timely acquaintance with, appreciation of, and a dependence on the death of Christ."

Many tearful eyes witnessed the distribution of the sacred elements, as given out by one who was already standing with one foot in the grave.

Having given with his dying breath a last adieu to his surrounding flock, he retired to his chamber fully aware of his near approach to the end of time. As the evening of the sad day gathered its darkness, he handed to a near and dear relative this immortal hymn, with music accompanying, which he had prepared:—

> "Abide with me! Fast falls the eventide;
> The darkness deepens; Lord, with me abide!
> When other helpers fail, and comforts flee,
> Help of the helpless, oh, abide with me.
>
> "Swift to its close ebbs out life's little day;
> Earth's joys grow dim; its glories pass away;
> Change and decay all around I see;
> O Thou, who changest not, abide with me."

The Master did abide with him the few more days he spent on earth. His end is described as that of "the happy Christian poet, singing while strength lasted," and while entering the dark valley, pointing upwards, with smiling countenance, he whispered, "Peace, joy.'

"Jesus, I My Cross Have Taken."

ELIZA was the lovely daughter of a wealthy Infidel. During his absence as a member of the legislature, she stole away to a protracted meeting. As the loving heart of Jesus was unfolded in the sermon, she wept aloud. Going home she told her mother where she had been and how she felt. Her mother became very angry and said, "your father will banish you, if you persist."

The next evening found her at the same place of prayer, contrary to her mother's wishes. At the close of the sermon she cried for mercy, poured forth her heart in sobs and fervent prayers. Hymn after hymn was sung, and many prayers offered on her behalf. The last hymn was being sung. The last verse was reached.

> "Yet save a trembling sinner, Lord,
> Whose hope still hovering round thy word,
> Would light on some sweet promise there,
> Some sure support against despair."

As the last strain sounded in the ear of the penitent, she gently threw back her head and opened her calm blue eyes, yet sparkling with tears, but they were tears that told of sins forgiven.

Word reached Mr. P—— the father. Coming home on horse-back, Eliza ran to the gate to meet him with a kiss, but he rudely seized her by the arm, and with his horse-whip whipped her out of the gate, telling her to be gone, and with many curses forbade her return.

Sadly she went weeping down the lane. A poor widow took her into her house. There she spent the night in prayer. Her father, in great anguish, did the same, for he could not sleep. He sought and found mercy. Sent for his daughter, whom he met and embraced at the same gate, saying, "I give you my heart and hand to go with you to heaven." The mother followed and all were united in Christ, and are now with Christ above.

"I send the joys of earth away."

THE sentiments of this hymn are strikingly illustrated in the following narrative:—

A young gentleman, tenderly attached to a young lady, was obliged to take a journey. During his absence she became a follower of Jesus. He heard of the change, and wrote her a letter full of invectives against religion and its gloomy professors. Having a good voice, and playing well on the piano-forte, she had been accustomed to entertain him with her music, especially in performing one song, of which he was very fond, the burden of which was, "Ah, never! ah, no!" At their first interview after his return, he tauntingly said, "I suppose you cannot sing me a song now?" "Oh, yes," was her reply, "but I will;" and, proceeding to her piano, she sung a hymn she had composed to his favorite tune:—

"As I glad bid adieu to the world's fancied pleasure,
  You pity my weakness: alas! did you know
The joys of religion, that best hidden treasure,
  Would you bid me resign them? Ah, never! ah, no!

"You will surely rejoice when I say I've received
  The only true pleasure attained below.
I know by experience in whom I've believed:
  Shall I give up this treasure? Ah, never! ah, no!

"In the gay scenes of life I was happiness wooing;
  But ah! in her stead I encountered a woe,
And found I was only a phantom pursuing:
  Never once did I find her. Ah, never! ah, no!

"But in these bright paths which you call melancholy
  I've found those delights which the world does not know.
Oh, did you partake them, you'd then see your folly,
  Nor again bid me fly them! Ah, never! ah, no!"

By hearing these lines his prejudices gave way, his feet entered the narrow path, and they became a truly-happy pair.
Dr. Belcher.

A hymn Deciding a Soul's Destiny.

IN the *Christian at Work*, Henry P. Thompson gives the following statements:—

"I never could understand it. She was one of the brightest, sweetest, and most amiable young ladies I ever knew; and yet she and her mother, who was a widow, lived with her grand-parents, who, with the mother and an only uncle and an only brother, were the roughest people I ever knew. And it was not only the *exterior* that was rough. They would swear, and blackguard, and quarrel with each other in public or in private.

"At a certain time, when calling at the house, the young lady, at my request, sat at the instrument and played and sang. Presently she turned to a particular tune, and said: 'I think this is so beautiful,' and, as she played, sang the accompanying words:—

"'I am weary of my sin;
  O, I long for full release;
Saviour, come and take me in
  With thyself to dwell in peace.
I am weary of the earth,
  Where the wicked spurn thy love;
With thy sons of heavenly birth,
  Let me worship thee above.'

"Pointing to the words, 'I am weary of my sin; O, I long for full release;' I said, 'Is that true of you, Mary?' and while the quick tear trembled on the lid, she sweetly answered, 'Yes; I want to follow Jesus.' I said, 'For such He waits, and will receive and bless them.'

"At the next communion season she united with the church, and for four years, adorned her profession; till at the close of a Sabbath evening, she was called to join the church above."

"O could I speak the matchless worth."

THIS hymn was penned by Rev. Samuel Medley, who wrote two hundred and thirty hymns, which were gathered in a volume the year after his death.

He was engaged as midshipman in the British navy, and on various occasions engaged in battle, in which at length in a fearful conflict, he was severely wounded.

Taken to his grandfather's house for surgical treatment, he was brought under Christian influence and at length led to Christ by hearing read one of Dr. Watts' sermons. He left the sea, and became a faithful and successful preacher of that Saviour whose name in early life he often profaned. For twenty-seven years he faithfully served as pastor of the First Baptist Church at Liverpool, England, and also acted as one of the supplies of Lady Huntingdon's Tabernacle, and Tottenham-court Chapels in London.

In 1799, he closed his earthly career, being sixty-one years of age, joyfully exclaiming just before his departure, "I am now a poor shattered bark, just about to gain the blissful harbor; and O how sweet will be the port after the storm! Dying is sweet work, sweet work. I am looking to my dear Jesus, my God, my portion, my all in all; glory! glory! home! home!"

He also wrote the popular hymn—

"Awake my soul in joyful lays,
And sing thy great Redeemer's praise."

The sweet echo of this hymn still lingers in the memory of the writer as the one frequently used to give expression to his love and gratitude, when, as a child in years and grace, he passed from death unto life.

Some touching incidents connected with the singing of the first named hymn are given on the next page.

SAMUEL MEDLEY.

AN affecting circumstance was connected with the death of Rev. J. H. Kaufman, pastor of the Presbyterian Church at Matawan, N. J. On Sabbath afternoon, Oct. 26th, 1873 as he was reading these lines in the first hymn:—

> "Soon the delightful day will come,
> When my dear Lord will call me home,
> And I shall see his face,"

his strength gave out, and he sat down while the congregation sang the hymn through. Then he followed with a prayer in a feeble though earnest voice, and at the word "Amen," he fell over in a fit of apoplexy, from which he died in a few hours after being taken to his home. Mr. Kaufman's age was forty-seven. It is stated, as a very singular coincidence, that the Rev. Mr. Shafer, who was pastor of the same church about thirty-three years ago, fell dead in his pulpit from apoplexy, as he had concluded *the same line of the same hymn* which Mr. Kaufman read just before he was stricken.

A SIMILAR illustration of the sentiments of a hymn was also given in the death of Rev. Joseph Entwisle.

At ten years of age he became a Christian while at Kingswood School, Eng. He entered the ministry at twenty-five, and evinced fervent piety throughout a long and useful life.

On a Thursday evening in 1864, he was preaching at Moorside. He had just given out the hymn:—

> "God moves in a mysterious way,"

and whilst the congregation was singing the fourth line of the verse,—

> "And rides upon the storm,"

the preacher quietly sank down in the pulpit, and died.

Medley's Poetic Answers.

IN 1793 Rev. Samuel Medley gave the following answers to printed questions sent to him and others from London:

Ques.—In what town is your church?

> In one where sin makes many a fool,
> Known by the name of Liverpool.

Ques.—Is it a church, chapel or meeting?

> Why, my good sir,—'tis very true,
> 'Tis chapel, church and meeting too.

Ques.—By what denomination is your church known?

> By one that's most despised of all,
> Which folks in general, Baptists call.

Ques.—What is your Christian and surname, degree?

> My Christian name is called Saint,
> My surname rather odd and quaint,
>   But to explain the whole with ease,
> Saint Samuel Medley, if you please;
> And you from hence may plainly see,
>   That I have taken a degree.

Ques.—Have you an assistant?

> O yes! I've One of whom I boast,
> His name is call'd the Holy Ghost.

Ques.—What number of people attend?

> A many come, my worthy friend,
> I dare not say they all attend;
> But though so many, great and small,
> I never number them at all,
> For that was once poor David's fall.

Ques.—Is it encumbered with debt?

> Incumber'd with debt,
> It is certainly yet,
> Though I at the present don't state it;
>   But if ever from home,
>   I a begging should come,
> I'll readily to you relate it.

First Song of one who had been Speechless.

IN the institution for feeble minded children, formerly at Germantown, was placed a little child from Virginia, who had been speechless from her birth.

She was familiarly known as "Becca." Dr. Parrish, the superintendent, describes her as one afraid of every living thing. Blocks and sticks she would nurse, but if a nicely dressed doll were presented, she would scream with fear. She loved nobody, and seemed fond of hurting little children and destroying their playthings.

Little by little her antipathies and coldness of disposition gave way and she began to show affection for her matron. She soon began to love to sit in the School room with other children and listen to their little songs and hymns. In her eight year she would steal away and make sounds when alone in some hiding place.

One summer evening her nurse had put her in her little bed early. The birds were singing in the trees by her window; the sun had just gone away and left his golden shadows on the western sky; and in this sweet evening hour of twilight the imprisoned soul of the little child broke its bands, her tongue was loosend, and she lifted her voice, and sung.

The nurse, hearing the sound, hastened up the stairway, and, listening outside the bed-room door, was rejoiced to hear Becca comingling her voice with the bird choir without, and as her first utterance the appropriate language of Charles Wesley's hymn, she had heard other children sing:—

> "Gentle Jesus, meek and mild
> Look upon a little child!
> Pity my simplicity;
> Suffer me to come to thee."

"'Whosoever will'—O gracious word."

PRECIOUS is the gospel invitation given in the hymn by Medley, commencing:—

"O what amazing words of grace
Are in the gospel found."

The line at the head of this page is in the fourth verse, and tells us in Scripture language, who is invited.

This oft-repeated Bible word "whosoever" became the link of salvation to a wicked old man, who lay sick and dying.

He wanted to be saved, but he knew no Saviour; he wanted to get to heaven, but he did not know the way.

"Johnny" said he to his little boy one day, as the child sat by his bedside, "could you read to me a bit?"

"Yes, father," he said; "I'll read to you as much as I can; only I can't make out the hard words."

So the old man told his child to try; and as the little boy read from the Bible the father leant close to listen.

Johnny read on slowly until he came to the golden verse which says, "God so loved the world that He gave His only begotten Son, that——"

He stopped there. It was a long word, and poor little Johnny vainly tried to make it out. He spelt it over again and again; but at last he said:—

"I can't make it out, father; I'll just miss it, and go on reading."

So he began again. "God so loved the world, that He gave His only begotten Son, that——believeth in Him should not perish, but have everlasting life."

"O Johnny, lad," said the father, eagerly, "I do wish

you could make out that word. It's just what I'm wanting to know. I wonder what the word can be!"

The old man felt that he must know. It was such an intensely important question that his heart was asking now, "May I be saved—is heaven for me." Life and death depended upon it; an eternity of joy or sorrow hung on the word that Johnny could not read.

So he rose from his bed and came down into the little room below. He took the Bible in his hands, and sat at the street door with his fingers marking the word that he wanted so very much to know.

By and by a man came quickly down the street; the house door was open, and the old man heard the step, for he was sitting there waiting to ask any one who should pass if they would read to him Johnny's hard word.

Just as he was passing, the old man called to him, and asked him to come near and help him; and then they both bent close over the Bible to the place where the father's trembling finger still marked the word.

The other man looked at it, and then read, "Whosoever."

"Whosoever?" said the old man; "and could you tell us what that means?"

"Why it means anybody," said the man, as he turned away, and went down the street.

Quickly this aged sinner laid "hold of the hope set before him," as he now saw that he was included in the "whosoever." Gladly he took God at his word, believed, was saved, and was enabled with eyes beaming with joy to look forward to the time when he should exchange worlds and fully inherit eternal life.

Author of "I would not live alway."

THIS first appeared June 3, 1826, in the *Episcopal Recorder* of Philadelphia, as a part of a poetical composition of forty-eight lines, written by Rev. W. A. Muhlenburg, D. D., and was afterward revised by him in 1865.

As a committee of the General Convention of the Episcopal Church were collecting material for a new hymn-book, Bishop Onderdonk presented this as one of his selections. The author was then unknown. Dr. Muhlenburg was a member of the Convention, and argued against its admission. But though at first rejected, it was, by the importunity of Dr. Onderdonk, finally inserted in the "Hymns of the Protestant Episcopal Church."

Dr. Muhlenburg is descended "from a family of revolutionary fame."

In 1823, he was associate rector of St. James Church, Lancaster, Pa.; afterwards made Principal of St. Paul's College; then rector of St. Luke's Hospital, and of the church of the "Holy Communion," New York City.

In 1828, he issued a work consisting of "Church Poetry," and in 1858, "The People's Psalter."

We append the last verse of his hymn that is not found in the hymn-books:—

> "That heavenly music! hark sweet in the air
> The notes of the harpers, how clear ringing there!
> And see, soft unfolding those portals of gold,
> The king all arrayed in His beauty behold!
> Oh, give me, oh, give me the wings of a dove,
> To adore Him, be near Him, enwrapt with His love;
> I but wait for the summons, I list for the word,
> Allelujah, Amen, evermore with the Lord!"

Dr. Muhlenburg has given a new addition to this old hymn.

> "Earth has no sorrows that heaven cannot cure."

THUS ends each verse of the consoling hymn,—
> "Come, ye disconsolate, where'er ye languish."

As an illustration we give the following narrative sent to the *"Guide to Holiness."*

A physician in Illinois had been for fifteen years so afflicted with sore eyes, that at times he was compelled to shut himself up in a darkened room for weeks.

"Nov. 1. 1871 his eyes being worse, he went to the city for medical counsel, but all said 'Doctor, there is no hope for you, you will become quite blind in three months.' He returned to his home with a sad heart, and his wife and daughters deeply sympathized with him.

"A few evenings after his getting home, all, as was their custom, retired for their secret, or private prayers, and all felt deeply impressed to make the matter an object of special prayer. The doctor said, 'O blessed Jesus, I come to Thee for help: I want to both suffer and to do Thy will. If it is for my good, and Thy glory that I should go blind, Thy will be done. But if I can do more good, and glorify Thee more perfectly with sight, then let me see; but Thy will be done, and not mine.'

"Said he to me; 'It appeared as if Jesus touched my eyes, for in one moment I was perfectly cured. I rose to tell my family the good news, and my wife met me at the door, and said: 'Doctor, I do believe that Jesus will give you sight,' but before I had time to answer, my daughters came running to me, both saying, 'Pa, I know Jesus will hear us pray for your sight.' Said he, 'I told them that He had already cured my eyes. It was then too dark for them to see, but as soon as a light was struck, all saw that my eyes were perfectly cured, and they stay cured.'"

Montgomery and his hymns.

JAMES MONTGOMERY, who is sometimes called the Cowper of the nineteenth century, was the son of an earnest Moravian minister, the Rev. John Montgomery. He was born at Irvine, Scotland, on the 4th of November 1771. At the tender age of six he was placed under the paternal guardianship of the Brethren at Fulneck, England where he received his early schooling. Speaking of the Christian influence surrounding the school he says " Whatever we did, was done in the name and for the sake of Jesus Christ, whom we were taught to regard in the amiable and endearing light of a friend and brother. A change having been made in their ordinary beverage one day, a little fellow knelt down and said, " Oh Lord, bless us little children, and make us very good! We thank thee for what we have received, Oh, bless this good chocolate, and *give us more of it.*"

How beautifully in after years he thus describes his childhood experience at Fulneck.

> " Here while I roved a heedless boy
> Here while through paths of peace I ran,
> My feet were vexed with puny snares,
> My bosom stung with insect cares:
> But ah! what light and little things
> Are childhood's woes!—they break no rest!

After referring to the skylark's music he continues:—

> Like him, on these delightful plains,
> I taught, with fearless voice,
> The echoing woods to sound my strains,
> The mountains to rejoice.
> Hail! to the trees, beneath whose shade,
> Rapt into worlds unseen, I strayed:
> Hail! to the streams that purled along
> In hoarse accordance to my song—
> My song that poured uncensured lays
> Tuned to a dying Saviour's praise,
> In numbers simple, wild, and sweet,
> As were the flowers beneath my feet."

In his tenth year, Montgomery began to write poetry. So little inclination had he for his school studies, that, when fourteen, his friends placed him in a retail shop at Mirfield. Writing poetry engrossed his attention above every thing else. Speaking of this period, in later years, he says:—

"When I was a boy I wrote a great many hymns; indeed, the first fruits of my mind were all consecrated to Him, who never despises the day of small things, even to the poorest of His creatures."

The paraphrase of the 113th Psalm is the product of these boyhood days. The Archbishop of York was so pleased with it, that he gave it a place in a collection of hymns for the use of his diocese. The following lines, that form part of his hymn on "Praise for God's Condesension," was also written, it is said, while a youth at Mirfield:—

> "Servants of God! in joyful lays,
> Sing ye the Lord Jehovah's praise;
> His glorious name let all adore,
> From age to age, for evermore."

The parents of Montgomery having embarked for the missionary field, he resolved, when sixteen, to cut loose his moorings at Mirfield, and start out upon the sea of adventure. How or where to steer his course he did not know. On the second evening he landed at Wentworth Inn, with a little pack of clothing on his back, a little poetry in his pocket, and only three and sixpence in his money-purse. Hearing of a benevolent man, residing near by, he offered to sell some of his poetry. The kind hearted Earl Fitzwilliam read his little poem, and gave the young blushing poet a gold guinea, which seemed like a heaven-sent supply in this his time of need. On the fourth day, he secured a position with a grocer at Wath.

Here he remained a year, when he resolved to try to sell a volume of his manuscript poems at London. He first applied to Mr. Harrison, a bookseller. He declined the offer, but kindly tendered to him a position as clerk in his store. This he accepted, and during the following year made several other fruitless attempts to get into the market with his manuscripts. At length he read of an opening in the office of the editor of the *Sheffield Register*, a prominent weekly of some note in its day. This led to a visit to Sheffield, and a home in the family of its editor, Mr. Joseph Gales.

In 1794, for fear of prosecution for some articles of a political caste, Mr Gales left England, when Montgomery took his place, and changed the title of the paper to the "Iris," and of this he continued the editor for thirty-one years. Twice he was imprisoned. First for reprinting a song commemorating the fall of the Bastile, and again in 1795 for a description of the riot at Sheffield, articles that were too liberal for the government of that day. While in prison, he wrote short poems on "Prison Amusements."

In 1806, appeared his "Wanderer of Switzerland;" the following year, "The West Indies;" in 1813, "The World before the Flood;" in 1819, "Greenland;" and in 1828, the last of his longer poems, "The Pelican Island;" in 1833, he received a royal pension of 200*l*. a year.

In 1836, Montgomery, with Annie and Sarah Gales, his adopted sisters moved to the famous "Mount," at the west end of Sheffield a beautiful situation which he describes as "on the highest point, and overlooking all below, at a safe distance from the smoke, the smells, the bustle and all the goings on of human life in this strange place." Not long afterwards he had occasion to write, "We are one less at the Mount. Dear Anna departed

yesterday morning, and broke the threefold cord that bound herself, her sister, and me in domestic affection for more than five and forty years."

Here he remained eighteen years, till life's sunset began to tinge the summit of this hallowed Mount. As the evening shades of old age gathered around, none of his hymns were so expressive of his feelings as the one, "At Home in Heaven." Said he: "I received directly and indirectly more testimonials of approbation, in reference to these verses, than perhaps any other which I have written of the same class, with the exception of those on 'Prayer.'"

One day he placed in Mr. Holland's hands some transcripts of his original hymns, that he wished him to read aloud in his hearing. After listening for a while his full heart overflowed in many tears. As Mr. Holland desisted, he said:—

"Read on, I am glad to hear you. The words recall the feelings which first suggested them, and it is good for me to feel affected and humbled by the terms in which I have endeavored to provide for the expression of similar religious experience in others. As all my hymns embody some portions of the history of the joys or sorrows, the hopes and fears of this poor heart, so I cannot doubt but that they will be found an acceptable vehicle of expression of the experience of many of my fellow creatures who may be similarly exercised during the pilgrimage of their Christian life."

Hence at one period of his life his restless heart exclaims:—

"What can I do? I am tossed to an fro on the sea of doubts and perplexities; the further I am carried from that shore where once I was happily moored, the weaker grow my hopes of ever reaching another, where I may anchor in safety." And again:—

"My restless, and imaginative mind, and my wild and ungovernable imagination have long ago broken loose from the anchor of faith, and have been driven, the sport of winds and waves, over an ocean of doubts, round which every coast is defended by the rocks of despair that forbid me to enter the harbor in view." This was one of the "portions of the history," to which he refers, that afterwards enabled him to write from experience, when he penned that well-known hymn:—

> "O where shall rest be found,
> Rest for the weary soul?
> 'Twere vain the ocean depths to sound,
> Or pierce to either pole."

> "The world can never give
> The bliss for which we sigh;
> 'Tis not the whole of life to live,
> Nor all of death to die."

Montgomery did not become fully assured of his salvation till in his forty-third year, when he wrote to his brother, saying, "On my birth-day, after many delays, and misgivings, and repentings, I wrote to Fulneck for re-admission into the Brethren's congregation; and on Tuesday, December 6, the lot fell to me in that pleasant place, and on Sunday last I was publicly invested with my title to that goodly heritage." After referring to the Saviour he adds: "To him and to his people I have again devoted myself, and may he make me faithful to my covenant with him, as I know he will be faithful to his covenant with me! Rejoice with me, my dearest friends, for this unspeakable privilege bestowed on so unworthy and ungrateful a prodigal as I have been. Tell all the good brethren and sisters whom I knew at Bristol, this great thing which the Lord hath done unto me."

This experience he afterwards versified in his sweet hymn—

> "People of the living God,
>   I have sought the world around,
> Paths of sin and sorrow trod,
>   Peace and comfort nowhere found,
> Now to you my spirit turns,
>   Turns, a fugitive unblest;
> Brethren, where your altar burns,
>   O receive me into rest!
>
> "Lonely I no longer roam,
>   Like the cloud, the wind, the wave;
> Where you dwell shall be my home,
>   Where you die shall be my grave;
> Mine the God whom you adore,
>   Your Redeemer shall be mine;
> Earth can fill my heart no more,
>   Every idol I resign."

He issued, in 1825, "The Christian Psalmist," containing one hundred and three of his own hymns, and in 1833, "Original Hymns for Public, Social and Private Devotion."

The last day he spent on earth he seemed as well as usual. In the evening worship he led in prayer with an earnestness and pathos that excited special attention. Little was it thought to be an illustration of his hymn:—

> "Prayer is the Christian's vital breath,
>   The Christian's native air:
> His watchword at the gates of death—
>   He enters heaven with prayer."

Next morning there being no response to the knock at his door, it was opened, when he was found insensible on the floor. Consciousness returned for a while, and he lingered on till the afternoon, when, as Mrs. Gales sat by his bedside, he seemed to sink away in sleep. But

> "No—life had sweetly ceased to be:
> It lapsed in immortality."

It was thus on the 30th of April, 1854, that he fully realized the language expressed in his hymn:—

> "Forever with the Lord!—
> Amen! so let it be."

Unmarried Hymnists.

WE give in other articles the facts in relation to the disappointed love that caused Cowper, Watts, Anne Steele, and other hymn writers, to remain unmarried. The following, in relation to Montgomery, will be read with interest. The expressive stanzas are believed by his biographers to be autobiographical and "founded on fact." Says one:—

"Wath must be set down as the scene of an early and only love. The identity of the heroine, who gives name to the poem supposed to disclose the secrets of the heart, has sorely puzzled his friends. Of 'Hannah' the poet himself gave no clue. Village tradition points to Miss Turner, the young mistress of a fine old family mansion between Wath and Barnsley, where sometimes he visited."

The first verse of his little poem commences thus:—

> "At fond sixteen my roving heart
> Was pierced by Love's delightful dart;
> Keen transport throbbed through every vein,
> I never felt so sweet a pain."

The period at which he "felt so sweet a pain" was, it is supposed, about the year 1789, when he was acting as clerk at Wath, and spending his leisure hours in intellectual pursuits.

After an interval of changing hopes and fears he says:

> "When sick at heart with hope delayed,
> Oft the dear image of that maid
> Glanced like a rainbow o'er his mind
> And promised happiness behind.

Then

> "The storm blew o'er, and in my breast
> The Halcyon, Peace, rebuilt her nest;
> The storm blew o'er, and clear and mild
> The sea of youth and pleasure smiled.

"'Twas on the merry morn of May,
To Hannah's cot I took my way;
My eager hopes were on the wing,
Like swallows sporting in the spring.

"Then as I climbed the mountains o'er,
I lived my wooing days once more;
And fancy sketched my married lot,
My wife, my children, and my cot.

"I saw the village steeple rise,—
My soul sprang, sparkling, to my eyes;
The rural bells rang sweet and clear,—
My fond heart listened in mine ear.

"I reached the hamlet;—all was gay;
I love a rustic holiday;
I met a wedding—stept aside;
It passed—my Hannah was the bride!

"There is a grief that cannot feel;
It leaves a wound that will not heal;
My heart grew cold—it felt not then;
When shall it cease to feel again."

COWPER was ardently attached to his beautiful and accomplished cousin, Theodora Jane Cowper, but her father, Ashley Cowper, considered the relationship between them too close to admit of marriage. There was a long and painful struggle between love and filial obedience before they resigned all hope of being thus united. The following lines are supposed to depict Cowper's fading vision of happiness:—

"But now sole partner in my Delia's heart,
Yet doom'd far off in exile to complain,
Eternal absence cannot ease my smart,
And hope subsists but to prolong my pain.

"Oh then, kind Heaven! be this my latest breath;
Here end my life, or make it worth my care;
Absence from whom we love is worse than death,
And frustrate hope severer than despair."

Why Mr. Berridge Remained Unmarried.

REV. JOHN BERRIDGE, the author of a book of hymns, explains in a letter to the Countess of Huntingdon why he lived the life of a bachelor:—

"*To Lady Huntingdon, March 23rd,* 1770: Eight or nine years ago, having been grievously tormented with housekeepers, I truly had thoughts of looking out for a Jezebel myself. But it seemed highly needful to ask advice of the Lord. So, falling down on my knees before a table, with a Bible between my hands, I besought the Lord to give me a direction; then letting the Bible fall open of itself, I fixed my eyes immediately on these words, 'When my son was entered into his wedding chamber, he fell down and died.' (2 Esdras x. 1.) This frightened me heartily, you may easily think; but Satan, who stood peeping at my elbow, not liking the heavenly caution, presently suggested a scruple, that the book was apocryphal, and the words not to be heeded. Well, after a short pause, I fell on my knees again, and prayed the Lord not to be angry with me, whilst, like Gideon, I requested a second sign, and from the canonical Scripture; then letting my Bible fall open as before, I fixed my eyes directly on this passage, 'Thou shalt not take thee a wife, neither shalt thou have sons or daughters in this place.' I was now completely satisfied, and was thus made acquainted with my Lord's will."

A lady came to see him one day, in her carriage, to solicit his hand in marriage, assuring him that the Lord had revealed it to her that she was to become his wife. "Madam," said he in reply, "if the Lord has revealed it to you that you are to be my wife, surely he would also have revealed it to me that I was designed to be your husband; but as no such revelation has been made to me, I cannot comply with your wishes."

An Impromptu Hymn and Tune.

AT the close of the thirty years' war in Germany, George Neumark found himself in want, as did many others. He was born at Thurigen, March 16, 1621, just two years after the commencement of the long strife.

Having studied law in the University of which Simon Dach, the eminent poet and musician, was President, he became like him, also distinguished for his poetical and musical ability.

Having suffered many privations while seeking employment at Dantzic and Thorn, he tried to improve his fortune, by going to Hamburg, in 1651. There he obtained a precarious subsistence by the use of his violoncello, a six-stringed instrument, in use in those days, upon which he played most charmingly.

But after a while he was taken sick, and could not gain a support by his musical tours. Not wishing to reveal his abject poverty, and as his last resort, he took his violin to a Jew, who loaned him a small sum with the understanding that if it was not redeemed within two weeks, he was to forfeit it.

As he reluctantly gave it to the Jew with tearful eyes, it seemed like the sundering of heart-strings.

Said he; "You know not how hard it is to part from that violin. For ten years it has been my companion and comforter. If I have nothing else, I have had it; at the worst, it spoke to me, and sung back all my courage and hope. Of all the sad hearts that have left your door, there has been none so sad as mine. Were it possible, I would ten times rather pawn to you my very heart's blood than this sweetner of my poverty. Believe me, Nathan, among all the unfortunate whom stern necessity has compelled to pawn to you their little all, I am the most so." Here his emotions choked his utterance. Seizing the instrument again, he played a sweet melody, while he sang two stanzas of his hymn:

"I am weary, I am weary,
　Take me, dearest Lord, away;
In this world so bleak and dreary,
　I would fain no longer stay!
For my life is nought to me,
But one scene of misery!

Suddenly his melancholy and plaintive notes ceased, and he commenced in a cheerful strain to sing:—

"Yet who knows, but all this sadness,
　Will be made in joy to end;
And this heart be filled with gladness,
　Which is now with sorrow rent.
For the pleasures here we gain,
Often cause eternal pain!"

As he ceased, the tears were coursing down his cheeks and his voice trembled with the deep emotion within.

As he gave the instrument a sad adieu he meekly said, "As the Lord will I am still." Then, as with a heart swelling with sorrow, he rushed out of the door, he ran against some one who had been held spell-bound by his sweet music.

"Pardon me, Sir," said the stranger, "the hymn you have just sung has deeply affected me, where can I get a copy of it? I will amply pay you for it. It just meets my case."

"My good friend," said Neumark, "your wish shall be granted."

This listener was John Guteg, the servant of the Swedish ambassador, Baron Von Rosenkranz.

He gave the baron an account of this musical genius, of his poverty, of his pawning his favorite instrument as a last resort, and of the hymn he sang of which he had the copy. The story interested the ambassador, he sent for the sweet singer, and gave him at once a remunerative position as secretary.

Neumark was now enabled to reclaim his instrument.

Calling at the house of his landlady, who had sympathized with him in his misfortunes, he told her the good news. Soon the room was crowded with friends and neighbors to hear him sing and play again.

With a heart swelling with gratitude, in an impromptu manner, he sang, what has ever since been, one of the most popular German hymns:—

"Wer nur den lieben Gott læsst walten."

It has been translated as follows:—

"Leave God to order all thy ways,
And hope in Him, whate'er betide,
Thou'lt find him in the evil days,
Thine all-sufficient strength and guide.
Who trusts in God's unchanging love,
Builds on the rock that ne'er can move."

Thus he offered his thanksgiving to Him who had helped him in this his time of need. To the inquiry as to whether he had composed the hymn himself, he meekly answered: "Well, yes, I am the instrument, but God swept the strings. All I knew was that these words, 'Who trusts in God's unchanging love,' lay like a soft burden upon my heart. I went over them again and again, and so they shaped themselves into song, how I cannot tell. I began to sing, and to pray for joy, and my soul blessed the Lord; and word followed word like water from a fountain."

After being employed for two years as the secretary, the noble Lord Von Rosenkrantz obtained for him the more lucrative situation as Keeper of the Archives, and Librarian at Weimar, where he died in 1688.

> "Amazing grace! how sweet the sound,
> That saved a wretch like me."

> "In evil long I took delight,
> Unawed by shame or fear."

THESE two hymns of John Newton, issued in 1779, were photographs of his past experience.

He was born in London on the 24th of July, 1725. His father had charge of a ship engaged in the Mediterranean trade.

When a young man he gave himself up to a sea-faring life, and, being impressed, was put on board the Harwick man-of-war, where he gave vent to all his corrupt passions, and yielded himself to the influence of the baldest infidelity. While the boat lay at Plymouth he deserted, was caught, brought back and kept in irons, then publicly stripped and whipped, after which he was degraded from the office of midshipman, and his companions forbidden to show him the least favor or even to speak to him. He was thus brought down to a level with the lowest and exposed to the insults of all.

During the following five years he got leave to be exchanged and entered a vessel bound for the African coast. Here he became the servant of a slave trader, who with his wife treated him with savage cruelty. For fifteen months he lived in the most abject bondage.

Writing to his father, arrangements were made for a vessel to call for him and to bring him home.

While on the voyage home he found on the boat a copy of Stanhope's Thomas a Kempis, that he read to pass away the time. While perusing it, the thought flashed across his mind: "*What if these things should be true.*"

The following night a fearful storm arose. A friend, who took his place for a moment, was swept overboard.

JOHN NEWTON.

For a time it seemed as if the boat would be shivered to atoms. During the calm that followed, a tempest of sin arose within his bosom. His crimes, infidel scoffings, and many narrow escapes from sudden death, passed before his mind in dark array.

Then says he: "I began to pray; I could not utter the prayer of faith, I could not draw near to a reconciled God, and call him Father: my prayer was like the cry of the ravens, which yet the Lord does not disdain to hear. I now began to think of the Jesus whom I had so often offended. I recollected the particulars of his life and death; a death for sins not his own, but for those, who, in their distress, should put their trust in him. . . In perusing the New Testament, I was struck with several passages, particularly the prodigal—a case that had never been so nearly exemplified, as by myself—and then the goodness of the father in receiving, nay, in running to meet such a son, and this intended only to illustrate the Lord's goodness to returning sinners this gained upon me." Thus he became, as he says, "a new man."

In after years he brought out his experience in verse, on this wise:—

"I hear the tempest's awful sound,
I feel the vessel's quick rebound;
And fear might now my bosom fill,
But Jesus tells me, 'Peace! Be still!'

"In this dread hour I cling to Thee,
My Saviour crucified for me.
If that I perish be Thy will,
In death, Lord, whisper, 'Peace! Be still!'

"Hark! He has listened while I prayed,
Slowly the tempest's rage is stayed;
The yielding waves obey His will,
Jesus hath bid them, 'Peace! Be still!'"

A Mother's Prayer and Her Son's Hymn.

"Jesus, the Lord, will hear
His chosen when they cry,
Yea, though awhile he may forbear,
He'll help them from on high."

THIS verse, taken from Newton's oft-repeated hymn—

"Jesus, who knows full well
The heart of every saint,"

was illustrative of his own history. He was the child of many prayers. Says he: "I can sometimes feel a pleasure in repeating the grateful acknowledgment of David, 'O Lord, I am thy servant, the son of thy handmaid.' The tender mercies of God toward me were manifest in the first moment of my life, I was dedicated to him in my infancy."

When but four years old, his mother had already stored his memory with many valuable pieces, chapters and portions of Scripture, catechisms, hymns and poems. "My mother observed my early progress with peculiar pleasure, and intended from the first to bring me up with a view to the ministry."

When seven years of age, he lost his devotedly pious mother. His father and step-mother left him to mingle with careless and profane children, and to become like them. His subsequent life of prodigality seemed to neutralize and contradict the virtue of a Christian mother's prayers, yet nevertheless, the Lord does hear his—

"————chosen when they cry,"

and, as we see in Newton's case, though divine grace did—

"————awhile forbear,
He'll help them from above."

Though this faithful mother was dead and in the grave, her prayers and influence followed him in all his wanderings, as he says: "though, in process of time, I sinned away all the advantages of these early impressions, yet they were for a great while a restraint upon me; they returned again, and it was very long before I could wholly shake them off; and when the Lord at length opened my eyes, I found a great benefit from the recollection of them. Further, my dear mother, besides the pains she took with me, often commended me *with many prayers and tears to God.* I have no doubt but I reap the fruits of these prayers to this hour." How extensive and enduring the answer to those supplications of a mother's heart. Her son became not only a minister eminent in usefulness, and a writer of hymns, whose influence reaches as far as the English language extends, but the means of the conversion of others who have carried the light of gospel truth among the millions enveloped in the darkness of heathenism.

Newton was the means of the conversion of Claudius Buchanan, who afterwards went as a missionary to the East Indies. There he wrote a book, "The Star in the East," which was the first thing that attracted the attention of Adoniram Judson as a missionary to the East Indies, where he afterwards poured a flood of light on Burmah and its surrounding millions.

Thomas Scott, the renowned commentator, was also among Newton's trophies. In his autobiography, Scott honestly admits that he was unconverted when he received ordination, totally ignorant of the gospel and its saving power, till he was led to the truth by Mr. Newton.

Newton also, in connection with Doddridge, was instrumental in the spiritual change of Wilberforce, for whose conversion he is said to have prayed fourteen years. Wilberforce laid his princely fortune at the feet of Jesus, and also effected by his eloquence, after years of unceasing efforts, the abolition of the African Slave

Trade. He also wrote the useful book entitled, "A Practical View of Christianity," that has already passed through some fifty editions.

This book was the means of the conversion of Leigh Richmond, the author of the "Dairyman's daughter," whose eminently successful life and writings have resulted in the conversion of thousands.

Thus we see what a vast train of blessed results have followed the early training of John Newton, and how rich the eternal reward must be to such a faithful mother.

A SIMILAR case of a mother's prayers for a wayward son is given by Rev. J. T. Benedict.

A mother with several children, being left a widow, felt the heavy responsibility of her position.

She would arise at midnight, and, in the chamber where they were sleeping, would kneel and pray for them with wrestling importunity.

Her eldest son, becoming restive of religious restraints, forsook his home, and went to sea as a sailor.

During several years' absence, he became profligate, but at length was induced to re-visit the place of his nativity. His mother had died in the meantime and his relatives scattered. Not knowing where else to go to make inquiries concerning his departed mother, he went to the prayer-meeting she had been accustomed to attend.

Before the service was over, the echo of his dead mother's prayers so overcame him, that he exclaimed aloud, *"My mother's prayers haunt me like a ghost."*

After writhing for some weeks under the keenest conviction of sin he became truly penitent, and soon united with the church.

> "It shan't be said that praying breath
> Was ever spent in vain."

MONICA WATCHING AUGUSTINE'S DEPARTURE.

The Mother of Augustine.

NEWTON'S history, and the far-reaching influence of his mother's prayers and tears, bear a striking resemblance to that of Augustine and his prayerful mother, Monica. Augustine was born at Tagasta, Africa, in the year 354. In early life he evinced genius and great aptitude for learning. This induced his pious parents to send him away to the best schools.

Surrounded with the allurements of vice, he was led astray, until he became infamous in iniquity. But amid all his wanderings, his mother's importunate prayers surrounded him. On his departure from home, she would stand on the sea-shore, and send after him her warmest supplications, and, with tearful anxiety, watch the vessel as it would glide out of sight in the distant horizon.

Monica's tears left an impress upon the pages of church history, that the lapse of fifteen centuries has not yet erased. In his "Confessions," Augustine tells how the new song of praise escaped his lips after his feet were taken from the pit. "How," says he, "did I weep, through Thy hymns and canticles, touched to the quick by the voice of Thy sweet attuned church! The voices sank into mine ears, and the truth distilled into mine heart, whence the affections of my devotions overflowed; tears ran down and happy was I therein."

During a season of danger and persecution, when Christians fled to the church for shelter, he says: "The devout people kept watch in the church, ready to die with their bishop, Thy servant. There my mother, Thy handmaid, bearing a chief part in those anxieties and watchings, lived for prayer. . . . . . . Then it was instituted, that, after the manner of the Eastern churches, hymns and psalms should be sung, lest the people should wax faint through the tediousness of sorrow."

"How sweet the name of Jesus sounds."

NEWTON wished, one day, to sound out, with special emphasis, the precious name to which his hymn refers.

When he had passed his fourscore years, he could not desist from preaching. As it was with difficulty that he could see to read his manuscript, he took a servant with him in the pulpit, who stood behind him, and with a wooden pointer would trace out the lines.

One day, Newton came to the words in his sermon, "Jesus Christ is precious," and wishing to emphasize them, he repeated, *"Jesus Christ is precious."* His servant, thinking he was getting confused, whispered, "Go on, go on, you said that before;" when Newton, looking around, replied, "John, I said that twice, and I am going to say it again," when with redoubled force he sounded out the words again, "JESUS CHRIST IS PRECIOUS."

THE Rev. M. L. Hodge, D. D., an eminently devoted minister of the Presbyterian Church, near Petersburg, Va., when bidding adieu to the scenes of earth, requested his friends to sing. As they commenced with the words,

> "How sweet the name of Jesus sounds
> In a believer's ear!"

he could not remain silent. As he joined with a trembling voice, he seemed to summon all his departing strength, when they came to the words:—

> "Weak is the effort of my heart,
> And cold my warmest thought;
> But when I see thee as thou art,
> I'll praise thee as I ought."

His countenance lit up with unspeakable joy, as with much unction and emotion, he sang the last lines:—

> "And may the music of thy name
> Refresh my soul in death."

"What a friend we have above."

As illustrative of this line in the well known hymn of Newton, commencing,—

> "One there is above all others,
> Well deserves the name of Friend,"

we give the following touching account of "Little Peter," who realized that "every good gift and every perfect gift is from above, and cometh from the Father of lights." He was a poor orphan boy who sang so sweetly as he went begging his bread from door to door that he was seldom turned away empty-handed.

When his father was on his death bed, he said to his son, "My dear Peter, you will now be left alone, and many troubles you will have in the world. But always remember, that all comes from above; then you will find it easy to bear every thing with patience."

Ever after when alms were given him, he would acknowledge the gift by saying, "*It comes from above.*" When his knock at the door brought the response, "Who's there," he would often sing:—

> "Alms to little Peter give;
> Without shoes or hat I go
> To my home beyond the sky;
> I have nothing here below."

"Once, as he was passing through the town, a sudden wind blew off a roof-tile, which fell on his shoulder, and struck him to the ground. His first words were, '*It comes from above.*'

"The bystanders laughed, and thought he must be out of his wits, for of course the tile could not come from below; but they did not understand him. A moment after, the wind tore off an entire roof in the same street, which crushed three men to death. Had little Peter gone on, he would probably have been at that moment, just where the roof fell. Thus the tile did 'come from above.'

"At another time a distinguished gentleman employed him to carry a letter to a neighboring town, bidding him to make all haste. On the way he tried to spring over a ditch, but it was so wide that he fell in, and was nearly drowned. The letter was lost in the mud, and could not be recovered. When Peter got out again, he exclaimed, '*It comes from above.*' The gentleman was angry when Peter told him of his mishap, and drove him out of doors with a whip. '*It comes from above,*' said Peter, as he stood on the steps. The next day the gentleman sent for him. 'See here,' said he, 'there are two ducats for you, for tumbling into the ditch. Circumstances have so changed on a sudden, that it would have been a misfortune to me had the letter gone safely.'

"A rich Englishman who came into the town, having heard his story, sent for him in order to bestow on him some charity. When 'Little Peter' entered the room the Englishman said, 'What think you, Peter; why have I sent for you?' '*It comes from above,*' replied Peter. This answer greatly pleased the Englishman. After musing a while, he said, 'You are right; I will take you into my service and provide well for you. Will you agree to that?' '*It comes from above,*' answered Peter; why should I not?'

"So the rich Englishman took him away. We were all sorry that he came no more to sing his pretty verse under our windows. But he had become weary of begging, and as he had learned no trade we were glad that he was at length provided for. Long afterwards we learned that when the rich man died he bequeathed a large sum of money to 'Little Peter,' who was now a wealthy man in Birmingham. But he still said of every occurrence, '*It comes from above.*'"

"Angel Sent" Stanzas.

BY the manna which dropped from heaven, God's Israel was fed. Bread of life still drops from above, as seen in the following sketch :—

"An elderly gentleman came into our store one day, and asked for a book entitled 'The Changed Cross.' He said it contained a hymn which led him to the Saviour.

"Upon a little inquiry, he gave the following account :—

"'Twelve years ago, I was in a very agitated state of mind about my soul's welfare. I was working in a store on Federal Street one day, when I felt unusually distressed. I went up into the third story. The window was slightly lowered, — about a pane's length. While there, and in this state of mind, there came suddenly a little slip of paper floating in at the window. I picked it up, and found thereon these stanzas' (drawing a worn slip from his pocket) :—

"'In meek obedience to the heavenly Teacher,
Thy weary soul can find its only peace;
Seeking no aid from any human creature,
Looking to God alone for his release.

"'And he will come in his own time and power
To set his earnest-hearted children free:
Watch only through this dark and painful hour,
And the bright morning yet will break for thee.'

"'I cried, 'God be praised!' and I have been praising God ever since.' On being asked how that piece of paper came there, and why, he said, 'An angel sent it.'"

"We, alas! forget too often
What a friend we have above."

A LADY who had the charge of young persons not of kindred blood, became, on one occasion, perplexed with regard to her duty. She retired to her own room to meditate, and being grieved in spirit, laid down her head upon a table, and wept bitterly. She scarcely perceived her little daughter, seated quietly in the corner. Unable longer to bear sight of her mother's distress, she stole softly to her side, and taking her hand in both of her own, said, "Mamma once you taught me a pretty hymn:—

'If e'er you meet with trials,
Or troubles on the way,
Then cast your care on Jesus,
And don't forget to pray.'"

Mother did not "forget to pray" after that; but leaving her burden with Jesus, she went on her way rejoicing.

A SOMEWHAT similar circumstance was reported to me by a pastor in Pennsylvania. Said he:—

"Being under a cloud of difficulty, I sat in sadness in my study one Saturday night not knowing what to do.

"My little son seeing my tearful eyes, leaped up in my lap, and tried to wipe away my tears on this wise:— After inquiring the cause, he said, 'Papa, never mind; don't weep. When the birds sing early in the morning, I'll get out of bed and tell Jesus all about it.'"

And so he did, in his childlike way, while the father listened with deep emotion.

That very day, help came, and for many years since he has enjoyed the fruit of that answered prayer.

Singing the Tears Away.

WHEN words are fitly sung, they prove to be "apples of gold," as well as when fitly spoken.

A hymn I had often used while preaching to the young, sweetly reechoed as a "word in season," during the winter of "hard times" in 1857—58.

One morning I had occasion to be in a Christian family living at Norristown, Pa., who had keenly felt the pressure of the panic. They had gotten down to the scrapings of the empty barrel. They had nothing left for breakfast but the crumbs of other days. These were all gathered on one plate and place in the centre of the table.

All the family gathered around the scanty meal except two little boys, who were absorbed with their playthings in one corner of the room.

After the father had given thanks, tears rolled down the cheeks, as their eyes gazed upon the empty plates.

During the sad silence which followed, the two boys dropped their toys, arose to their feet, and, as if led by angel hands, marched forward to the table, and sang;

> "O do not be discouraged,
> For Jesus is your friend;
> He will give you grace to conquer,
> And keep you to the end."

Tears fled as dew-drops before the rising sun.

An unexpected Providence brought relief, and never since have tear drops fallen on empty dishes, as they joyfully continue to sing of Jesus as their "friend."

"Two Officers Led to Christ by a Verse."

THE great scholar, Dr. Valpy, who published an edition of Homer, and other learned works, became a Christian late in life, and shortly before he died, he wrote this beautiful hymn-prayer:—

> "In peace let me resign my breath,
> And thy salvation see;
> My sins deserve eternal death,
> But Jesus died for me."

The verses fell into the hands of Dr. March, who read them aloud once at a religious service in the family of Lord Roden. The nobleman was so much pleased with them that he had them nicely written out and framed, and hung over the mantle-piece in his study.

Gen. Taylor, a Waterloo veteran, while on a visit to Lord Roden some time afterwards, read the lines and was much impressed by them. He was a man who had thought little about religion, and never liked to talk about it. But now every time he came into the study, his eyes would rest upon that motto over the mantle-piece. At last, one day Lord Roden exclaimed:—

"General, you'll soon get that stanza by heart."

"I know it by heart now," said the general, with feeling. Gen. Taylor was a changed man ever after. At the end of two years he died, and his last words were:—

> "In peace let me resign my breath,
> And thy salvation see;
> My sins deserve eternal death,
> But Jesus died for me."

A good while after this Lord Roden told the above story in the hearing of a young officer lately returned from the Crimean War, and repeated the lines at the close. Apparently they made no impression upon the young man at the time, but a few months proved that he had them "by heart," too. Stricken down with a quick decline, and sensible that he was near his end, he sent for Lord Roden, saying that he wished to see him without delay. The nobleman hastened to the sick-room, and as soon as he entered, the dying man welcomed him with a smiling face. "I wanted to tell you what a blessing those lines have been to me," he said. "They have been God's message of comfort, brought to my memory after days of darkness here,—

> "In peace let me resign my breath,
> And thy salvation see;
> My sins deserve eternal death,
> But Jesus died for me."

And thus the sweet words of faith uttered in the simple rhyme of a dying scholar became the last consolation of two dying soldiers.

This interesting narrative is taken from *The Youth's Companion*.

"Stop, poor sinner, stop and think."

A YOUNG man met a gentleman who placed in his hand a slip of paper, on which was printed this hymn of John Newton:—

> "Stop, poor sinner, stop and think."

He was so much affected by it that he committed it to memory. Years afterward when a student at Brown University, during a season of revival, he entered a place where religious service was being held, just as the hymn was being commenced:—

> "Stop, poor sinner, stop and think."

His former impressions were at once revived. He did "stop and think," became an earnest Christian, and afterwards in the medical profession, a zealous worker in the vineyard of Christ.

A Popular Hymn Written by an Indian.

SAMSON Occom, an Indian preacher, wrote a hymn in 1760, which, though over a hundred years old, is still frequently sung. It originally contained seven verses. The first line of the first verse reads thus:—

"Awaked by Sinai's awful sound."

He is also accredited with the hymn:—

"O turn ye, O turn ye, for why will ye die."

He was born at Mohegan, near Norwich, Connecticut, about the year 1723. During a revival of 1740, under Whitfield, Tennent, and their co-laborers, several ministers visited the Indians. And among the number who professed conversion was Occom, then seventeen years of age. In a year or two after this, he learned to read, and went to the Indian school of Mr. Wheelock of Lebanon, where he remained four years.

He then taught a school, and preached among the Indians at Montauk, Long Island, and other places for some twenty years. His labors were blessed in a gracious revival among the Montauks.

In 1759, he was ordained by the Suffolk Presbytery.

In 1766, he was sent to England to advocate the cause of an Indian Charity School.

As he was the first Indian preacher who had visited England, he drew out immense audiences. In a little over a year, he preached four hundred sermons. During that time, he collected over forty-five thousand dollars for his school, which, at length, was merged into Dartmouth College.

His hymns have been much used in England and Wales.

After his return to this country, he was employed in general missionary labors among the Indians until in July, 1792, he died, aged sixty-nine years.

SAMSON OCCOM.

Occom's Hymn.

"Awaked by Sinai's awful sound,
My soul in bonds of guilt I found,
And knew not where to go;
Eternal truth did loud proclaim,
'The sinner must be born again,'
Or sink to endless woe.

"When to the law I trembling fled,
It poured its curses on my head,
I no relief could find;
This fearful truth increased my pain,
'The sinner must be born again,'
And whelmed my tortured mind.

"Again did Sinai's thunders roll,
And guilt lay heavy on my soul,
A vast oppressive load;
Alas! I read and saw it plain,
'The sinner must be born again,'
Or drink the wrath of God.

"The saints I heard with rapture tell
How Jesus conquered death and hell,
And broke the fowler's snare;
Yet when I found this truth remain,
'The sinner must be born again,'
I sunk in deep despair.

"But while I thus in anguish lay,
The gracious Saviour passed this way,
And felt his pity move;
The sinner, by his justice slain,
Now by his grace is born again,
And sings redeeming love."

MR. THORPE, with a group of scoffers tried to mimic Whitefield. One and another stood on a table to try their skill. Thorpe opened the Bible and read, "Except ye repent, ye shall all likewise perish. It was "Sinai's awful sound." He trembled, wept, ran from the room, was converted and became a useful preacher.

"Oh, turn ye, oh, turn ye, for why will ye die!"

"SISTER Mary requested me to write and tell you that she had gone to heaven." Thus wrote a brother from Elimsport, Pa.

At the close of a protracted meeting service on a snowy winter night, invitation was given for any that were anxious to attend a meeting for the special benefit of such, in an adjoining house. To induce decision for Christ, we remarked that all should act as they would wish they had acted when they thought of that night at the judgment day. The pastor and myself waited a long while at the appointed place for prayer, but it seemed in vain. At length the door slowly opened, and this weeping Mary entered. As she took her seat, said she, "Mr. Long, I went home; I could not summon courage to tear loose from my gay and giddy companions. But as I was about entering the gate, I thought of your remark about the judgment day. I at once turned around, and have walked back a mile through the snow to ask you to pray for me."

That turning point at the gate was the point on which hinged her eternal destiny. She became a devoted Christian, and was laid upon her death-bed the following summer.

We shall never forget the joy that flashed from her countenance as she pointed from that sick chamber to the wicket gate in the yard, where she took her first step in that narrow path that was now leading her to endless glory.

Before her departure she sent me the following lines: "I do not expect to arise from my bed again. During the last spell I had I was so weak that I could neither move hand nor foot, yet I could feel my Saviour's arm around and underneath me to hold me up."

A Dying Boy's Emphasis to a Hymn.

ON a Saturday night, during a Sunday school teachers' meeting, a sudden rap was heard at the lecture-room door of a Presbyterian church in St. Louis.

The pastor, Rev. Dr. McCook, was sent for in haste to see a little dying boy. He found it was at the house of a noted gambler. This man was on bended knees beside his child. Said he: "Pray for him. Do any thing you can." After prayer the boy's lips were observed to move. They found he was trying to say, "Sing! *sing!*" So Dr. McCook sang the words:—

> "Come to Jesus, come to Jesus,
> Come to Jesus, just now,
> Just now, come to Jesus
> Come to Jesus, just now.
>
> "He will save you, he will save you,
> He will save you, Just now,
> Just now, he will save you,
> He will save you, just now."

As the words, "Just now" were being repeated the boy would fix his dying eyes on his father and try to emphasize by saying as loudly as he could, "Now, *now, now,*" whenever the word occurred in the hymn.

Next morning as the father stood on one side of the corpse and Dr. McCook on the other, the latter reechoed in the ears of the father, that emphatic "Now" that so earnestly escaped from the pale lips that lay silent between them.

That gambler opened his heart to the sound, became a devoted Christian, renounced his life of sin, united with Dr. McCook's church and remained a consistent member till at length he followed his little boy to the skies.

A Precious Hymn by a Converted Idolator.

KRISNA PAL was among the first of the Hindoos who renounced caste and idolatry for Christ's sake. He was baptized at the close of the last century, in the river Ganges, near the missionary residence at Serampore.

Dr. Belcher says of him,—

"This man, then at the prime of life, being thirty-five years of age, became an eminent Christian, engaged in the ministry, which he pursued for many years, baptized many hundreds of converted idolators, and then died triumphant in the Lord Jesus. Joyfully did he bear witness that the service of Christ 'was the work of love,' and that in it 'he got nothing but joy and comfort.' He wrote two or three hymns, one of which continues to be sung in India in the Bengalee language, in which it was composed; and a part of it, translated into English, is printed in most of our books." The first verse reads:—

> "O thou, my soul, forget no more
> The friend who all thy sorrows bore;
> Let every idol be forgot;
> But, O my soul, forget him not."

The last verse was strikingly illustrated in his peaceful death.

> "Ah, no! till life itself depart,
> His name shall cheer and warm my heart;
> And lisping this, from earth I'll rise,
> And join the chorus of the skies."

KRISNA PAL.

Krishna Pal was brought in contact with the gospel through a broken limb, which the missionary was called in to set. This man of God, after administering surgical aid, spake to him of the more awful disease of sin, and of God's goodness in providing a great Physician.

Krishna was much affected by the story of the cross, and soon after professed faith in the crucified. During his baptism, Grigg's hymn was sung in Bengalee:—

> "Jesus, and shall it ever be,
> A mortal man ashamed of thee?"

He not only built himself a house for worship, but in 1804, was set apart for the work of the ministry. Dr. Cary described him as "a steady, zealous, well-informed, and I may add, eloquent minister of the gospel," averaging twelve to fourteen sermons a week.

In such self-denying labors he continued for twenty years at the small salary of six dollars a month.

We append the other verses of his hymn, referred to on another page:—

> "Jesus for thee a body takes,
> Thy guilt assumes, thy fetters breaks,
> Discharging all thy dreadful debt;—
> And canst thou e'er such love forget?
>
> "Renounce thy works and ways with grief,
> And fly to this most sure relief;
> Nor Him forget who left his throne,
> And for thy life gave up his own.
>
> "Infinite truth and mercy shine
> In Him, and he himself is thine;
> And canst thou then, with sin beset,
> Such charms, such matchless charms forget?
>
> "Ah! no—when all things else expire,
> And perish in the general fire,
> This name all others shall survive,
> And through eternity shall live."

Origin of "My faith looks up to Thee."

THIS universal favorite was written by Ray Palmer, D. D., an eminent Congregational minister of Albany, New York.* He was born in Rhode Island in 1808.

This hymn was written in New York in December 1830, just after he had left Yale College.

He says it was "written because it was born in his heart and demanded expression. 'I gave form to what I felt by writing, with little effort, the stanzas. I recollect I wrote them with very tender emotion, and ended the last line with tears.'"

The manuscript was laid away in his pocket-book and carried with him for some two years, until one day, while in Boston, he met on the street Dr. Lowell Mason, who told him of a new book he was about to issue, and asked him to furnish a few hymns for it. Palmer at once reached in his pocket and brought out the lines.

Soon after receiving the hymn, Dr. Mason said to young Palmer: "You may live many years, and do many good things, but I think you will be best known to posterity as the author of this hymn"—a prophecy that is already fulfilled. This hymn is now known, loved and sung as far as the English language extends, and has been translated in many foreign tongues.

One day during the insurrection in Syria, the students in a Protestant seminary were having their morning worship. When singing the third verse of this hymn,—

> "While life's dark maze I tread,
> And griefs around me spread,"

they were being surrounded by the savage Druzes, who were firing in the streets and were ready to enter the chapel.

As a little one was being put to bed she told her mother how bad she had felt during the day because of her sins, and how she had gone to "Frankie's room and prayed all by myself." Said she:

"I asked Jesus, and he helped me right away. Now, mamma, please sing,—

"'Take all my sins away.'"

"I have heard you sing it a good deal to-day, Lily."
"Oh, yes; but I don' know the whole, and I want you to sing it over and over until I go to sleep."

"My faith looks up to Thee,
Thou Lamb of Calvary,
Saviour divine!
Now hear me while I pray,
Take all my sins away;
Oh may I from this day
Be wholly thine!"

Gladly the mother responded to this touching request, and sang these words "over and over," until the little one sank asleep on the bosom of Him, who can—

"Take all my sins away."

While we were penning these lines it was our privilege to have an interview with Dr. Palmer, at his residence in Newark, N. J., at which he said that he had received, he supposed, a hundred testimonies in the form of letters, and others relating to the happy effect produced by this hymn. Of those that came under his own observation he related the following: While preaching at Albany, a young man, who had been accustomed to attend upon his ministry, came one Sunday morning to his church, some time before the hour of service; to pass away the time he opened a hymn-book that lay in the pew. His eyes lit at once upon the words:—

"My faith looks up to Thee,
Thou Lamb of Calvary,
Saviour divine!"

It was just the language suited to his sin-burdened

heart. While reading the hymn the Spirit applied the truth with divine power, so that he looked at once to Jesus and lived.

Calling afterwards at the residence of Dr. Palmer, to tell how he had found the Saviour, he learned to his great joy, for the first time, that the one to whom he was telling the story of his conversion had written the hymn.

At another time, a lady in the choir, who sometimes sang a solo at the close of service, chose this hymn as her anthem. To such an unusual degree did she throw her soul into it, and bring out each word with emphasis and power, that the audience seemed to listen with breathless silence. It was her last solo on earth. Next morning she was found dead in bed.

How appropriate, therefore, the last verse with which she ended her song:

"When ends life's transient dream,
When death's cold sullen stream,
　Shall o'er me roll,
Blest Saviour then in love,
Fear and distrust remove;
O bear me safe above,
　A ransomed soul!"

SAMUEL POTTER of Calmstock, England, on the last Sabbath he spent on earth sang with his family at the evening worship:—

"God moves in a mysterious way," etc.

Afterwards he sang this verse as a solo:—

"Oft as I lay me down to rest,
O may the reconciling word,
Sweetly compose my weary breast.
While on the bosom of my Lord,
I sink in blissful dreams away,
And visions of eternal day."

Rising from his bed in the morning he said: "Well, my work is almost done," and then sank down a corpse.

"Who is like Jesus."

IN nearly every revival there are certain hymns that become identified with it, and that seem especially adapted to give expression to existing feelings. We have found none better to put in the lips of the anxious than Palmer's

"My faith looks up to Thee."

At a meeting in Drums, Pa., where over two hundred became subjects of Divine grace, it became, night after night for nearly three months, the spontaneous utterance of the many who crowded around the gate of mercy.

During an extensive awakening in Shippensburg, Pa., in 1869, as one and another found Him who is the "fairest among ten thousand and the one altogether lovely," the natural and continued outburst of praise, seemed to be the chorus words, "O, who is like Jesus."

The multitude that crowded the streets on the way to church seemed to be, in number, like those who "fly as a cloud and as the doves to their windows."

The interest awakened by the first week's course of "Illustrated Sermons" spread so extensively, that the young men drew up a petition to their employers to close the stores at seven o'clock, that they might attend church, and the simultaneous closing of store shutters reverberating through the streets became our church bell.

Such crowds attended that they filled the seats and aisles, sat on each other's laps, and crowded the pulpit-steps and floors, that one church sank six inches in the centre through the weight of those packed within.

By my side is a little book filled with the autograph signatures of the many, who, having found a Saviour, so frequently and so heartily loved to sing:—

"Who is like Jesus."

Edward Perronet.

Author of "All hail the power of Jesus' name."

THIS widely known hymn first appeared in 1780 in *The Gospel Magazine*. It was written by Rev. Edward Perronet, a son of an Episcopal clergyman, who preached fifty years at Shoreham, England. Charles Wesley refers familiarly to him in his diary as "Ned," and as a companion and co-laborer. He had a brother Charles, who also entered the ministry, both of whom labored with Wesley for some time. Charles "desisted for want of health," and Edward "from some change in his opinions. Charles Perronet died at Canterbury in 1776, but his brother survived him many years, and possessed equal powers with him, to which was super-added a large fund of wit."

He labored in the employ of Lady Huntingdom, and preached with marked success at Canterbury, Norwich, and other parts of England.

In his last years he had charge of a congregation of dissenters at Canterbury, where he died, January, 1792. His dying words were: "Glory to God in the height of His divinity; glory to God in the depth of His humanity; glory to God in His all-sufficiency, and into His hands I commend my spirit." Thus with his dying breath he tried to

"—— crown him Lord of all."

This hymn had originally eight verses, and was entitled, "On the Resurrection."

Shrubsole, an organist at Spafield's Chapel, London, composed a tune called "Miles' Lane." This was generally sung to it, until it became wedded to "Coronation."

In 1785 his poems and hymns were collected in a volume entitled, "Occasional Verses, Moral and Sacred, published for the Instruction and Amusement of the Serious and Religious."

The Original of "All hail the power of Jesus' name."

"All hail the power of Jesus' name!
    Let angels prostrate fall;
Bring forth the royal diadem,
    To crown him Lord of all!

"Let high-born seraphs tune the lyre,
    And, as they tune it, fall
Before his face who tunes their choir,
    And crown him Lord of all!

"Crown him, ye morning stars of light,
    Who fixed this floating ball;
Now hail the Strength of Israel's might,
    And crown him Lord of all!

"Crown, him ye martyrs of your God,
    Who from his altar call;
Extol the stems of Jesse's rod,
    And crown him Lord of all!

"Ye seed of Israel's chosen race,
    Ye ransomed of the fall,
Hail him who saves you by his grace,
    And crown him Lord of all!

"Hail him, ye heirs of David's line,
    Whom David Lord did call,
The God incarnate, man divine!
    And crown him Lord of all!

"Sinners, whose love can ne'er forget
    The wormwood and the gall,
Go, spread your trophies at his feet,
    And crown him Lord of all!

"Let every kindred and every tongue
    That bound creation's call
Now shout in universal song,
    The crowned Lord of all."

"All hail the power of Jesus' name!" among Savages.

REV. E. P. Scott, while laboring as a missionary in India, saw on the street one of the strangest looking heathen his eyes had ever lit upon. On inquiry he found that he was a representative of one of the inland tribes that lived away in the mountain districts, and which came down once a year to trade.

Upon further investigation he found that the gospel had never been preached to them, and that it was very hazardous to venture among them because of their murderous propensities. He was stirred with earnest desires to break unto them the bread of life. He went to his lodging-place, fell on his knees, and plead for divine direction. Arising from his knees, he packed his valise, took his violin, with which he was accustomed to sing, and his pilgrim staff, and started in the direction of the Macedonian cry.

As he bade his fellow missionaries farewell, they said: "We will never see you again. It is madness for you to go." "But," said he, "I must carry Jesus to them."

For two days he travelled without scarcely meeting a human being, until at last he found himself in the mountains, and suddenly surrounded by a crowd of savages.

Every spear was instantly pointed at his heart. He expected that every moment would be his last. Not knowing of any other resource, he tried the power of singing the name of Jesus to them. Drawing forth his violin, he began with closed eyes to sing and play:—

> "All hail the power of Jesus' name!
> Let angels prostrate fall;
> Bring forth the royal diadem,
> And crown him Lord of all."

Being afraid to open his eyes, he sang on till the third verse, and while singing the stanza,—

> "Let every kindred, every tribe,
> On this terrestrial ball,
> To Him all majesty ascribe,
> And crown Him Lord of all,"

he opened his eyes to see what they were going to do, when lo! the spears had dropped from their hands, and the big tears were falling from their eyes.

They afterwards invited him to their homes. He spent two and a half years among them. His labors were so richly rewarded that when he was compelled to leave them because of impaired health and return to this country, they followed him between thirty and forty miles. "Oh! missionary," said they when parting, "come back to us again. There are tribes beyond us which never heard the glad tidings of salvation." He could not resist their entreaties. After visiting America he went back again to continue his labors, till he sank into the grave among them.

This interesting story of the happy effects of singing this good old hymn was related to William Reynolds Esq. of Peoria, Ill., by the missionary himself, while in this country trying to regain his health, and by Mr. Reynolds to the author of this volume.

"Crown Him Lord of all."

THE coronation of George III. was attended with great applause. Afterwards, when the two Archbishops came to him to hand him down from the throne, to receive the sacrament, he told them he could not approach the Lord's supper, with a crown upon his head, for he could not dare thus to appear before the King of kings. The Bishops replied, that, although there was no precedent for this, his request should be complied with. Having laid it aside, he requested that the same might be done with the crown of the queen.

"Bring forth the royal diadem."

A Sunday school teacher was dying. Just before he sank away he turned to his daughter, who was bending most lovingly over his bed, and said, "Bring—"

More he could not say, for the power of utterance failed him. His child looked with earnest gaze in his face and said:

"What shall I bring, my father?"

"Bring—"

His child was in an agony of desire to know that dying father's last request, and she said: "Dear precious father, do try to tell me what you want. I will do anything you wish me to do."

The dying teacher rallied all his strength and finally murmured:—

"Bring—forth—the royal diadem,
And crown him Lord of all."

"Crown him! crown him! crown him!"

A POOR child's funeral! A wagon for a hearse, and only a cart with three poor people in it to follow it! A very poor funeral indeed!

Yes, it was a poor funeral, but it was preceded by a glorious death. The child in that coffin had learned to pray and to trust in the Lord Jesus. He was therefore a prince in disguise. While he was dying his father sung these lines for him several times:—

"All hail the power of Jesus' name!
Let angels prostrate fall;
Bring forth the royal diadem,
And crown him Lord of all."

Whenever he came to the last line the dying boy would brighten up, and join in and sing, "*Crown* him! *Crown* him! *Crown* him!" leaving his father to finish the line.

The Hymn that Told Jack's Experience.

IN a parish in England, there was an old sailor, who went by the name of Jack. In going along the street one day he heard a number of women singing:—

"I'm a poor sinner,
And nothing at all;
But Jesus Christ
Is my all in all."

The man gave up his drunkenness, and very soon gave up his wickedness. At last Jack went to the minister and asked to be admitted to church membership. The minister asked, "What is your experience?" "I have none," said Jack. "Well then, John, I cannot admit you." "Well," says Jack, "I have no experience, but

"I'm a poor sinner,
And nothing at all;
But Jesus Christ
Is my all in all."

"Well," says the minister, "I will ask the deacons about your admission; but you will be expected to state your experience." The deacons were assembled, and Jack was called on to answer their questions, to which Jack always replied:—

"I'm a poor sinner,
And nothing at all;
But Jesus Christ
Is my all in all."

Says the old deacon, "That is not enough; tell us your doubts and fears, and why you seek admission." "Nay," says Jack, "I have no doubt whatever that

'I'm a poor sinner,
And nothing at all;

and I don't fear anything,

But Jesus Christ
Is my all in all."

Jack was admitted, and to the end led a Christian life.

AUTHOR OF "COME THOU FOUNT."

A HYMN almost as well known as "Rock of ages" is
"Come thou fount of every blessing,"

It was written by Robert Robinson, of Cambridge, England who was born 1735.

He was but a lad when he strolled into the Tabernacle to hear Whitfield preach. He was startled, arrested and determined then and there to give his life to God.

Gifted with extraordinary talent he entered upon the ministry, and in the Tabernacle moved his audience to enthusiasm with his powerful preaching.

But unstable as water, and as a wave of the sea, he went from one thing to another until at last he became an avowed Socinian.

In the darkness which encompassed him, sometimes a ray of the light of former years would fall across his path, and then would flash upon him

> "The blessedness I knew
> When first I saw the Lord."

One day he was travelling by coach with a lady, a stranger to him, she had been reading his hymn

> "Come thou fount of every blessing."

Turning to him she asked him if he knew it, and telling him of the comfort and happiness it had been to her.

He tried to parry her questions, but she returned to it again and again, until at length bursting into a flood of tears, he exclaimed passionately, "Madam. I am the poor, unhappy man who composed that hymn many years ago; and *I would give a thousand worlds if I had them, to enjoy the feelings I had then.*"

On Wednesday morning June 9th, 1790 he was found dead in bed, having expired, as he often expressed his wish to do, "softly, suddenly and alone."

ROBERT ROBINSON.

Robinson's father having died when he was young his widowed mother, while struggling with poverty found herself unable to give him that education he desired. Therefore at the age of fourteen he was apprenticed to a hairdresser in London.

But his thirst for knowledge caused his master to complain that he gave more attention to his books than to his business.

The means that led to his conversion were quite singular. Walking out one day with several companions their attention was called to an old woman who pretended to tell fortunes. Robinson was informed among other things that he would live to a very old age and see a long line of descendents.

"And so," said he when alone, "I am to see children, grandchildren, and great grand-children. I will then," thought he, "during my youth, endeavor to store my mind with all kinds of knowledge. I will see, and hear, and note down everything that is rare and wonderful, that I may sit, when incapable of other employments, and entertain my descendents. Thus shall my company be rendered pleasant, and I shall be respected, rather than neglected, in old age. Let me see, what can I acquire first? Oh, here is the famous Methodist preacher, Whitefield; he is to preach here, they say to-night; I will go and hear him."

From these strange motives, as he told the celebrated Rev. Andrew Fuller, he went to hear Whitefield preach. That evening his text was, "But when he saw many of the Pharisees and Sadducees come to his Baptism, he said unto them, O generation of vipers who hath warned you to flee from the wrath to come?" "Mr. Whitefield," said Robinson, "described the Sadducees' character; this did not touch me; I thought myself as good a Christian as any man in England. From this he went to that of the

Pharisees. He sketched their exterior decency, but observed, that the poison of the viper rankled in their hearts This rather shook me. At length, in the course of his sermon, he abruptly broke off; paused for a few moments; then burst into a flood of tears, lifted up his hand and eyes, and exclaimed, 'Oh, my hearers, *the wrath to come! the wrath to come!'* These words sunk into my heart like lead in the water: I wept, and when the sermon was ended retired alone. For days and weeks I could think of little else. Those awful words would follow me wherever I went: 'The wrath to come! The wrath to come?'"

After wandering for some time like a wounded deer, pierced with the arrows of conviction, he was found December 10th, 1755, of one, of whom he afterwards so sweetly wrote in the language of his hymn.—

> "Jesus sought me when a stranger,
>   Wandering from the fold of God;
> He, to rescue me from danger,
>   Interposed his precious blood."

Another grand hymn that displays the genius of Robinson, and that is often sung, originally commenced,—

> "Mighty God! while angels bless thee
> May an infant lisp thy name!"

The word "mortal," is often now taken for "infant." Dr. Belcher says that this was "composed for the use of the late excellent Benjamin Williams, Esq., for many years, senior deacon of the first Baptist church at Reading a man of great influence and usefulness. When a little boy, Benjamin sat on Robinson's knee while he wrote this hymn, who, after having read it to him, placed it in his hand.

"Well do we remember the deep feeling with which the venerable man described to us the scene as we sat with him at his own fireside."

"Tune my heart to sing thy grace."

MANY illustrations can be given of this line of "Come thou Fount." "Do you wish to sing as angels sing? Ask of God an heavenly mind. A harp must be tuned before it makes good music. And when the heart is put in tune, well warmed with the love of God, singing proves delightsome service, and a heavenly feast."

A pastor, who is now filling a Philadelphia pulpit, and has already added many jewels to the Saviour's crown, in giving his experience to the author, says that it was the marked contrast between heart service and lip service in singing, that led to his conversion.

When a young man he was attending the dedication of a new church in a dark corner of Pennsylvania, a section at that time bitterly opposed to vital godliness, and frozen over with a dead religious formalism.

A revival had brought together a little praying band who were consecrating their new building with a "living sacrifice" of praise. The fires of persecution, as well as the pentecostal flames from above had melted away all discord from the heart, so that the singing sounded forth upon the crowd of listeners with melting power. Among this group was our friend standing on a log under the trees, some distance away from the church. Hitherto he had prided himself upon his abilities as a choir-leader, but while under the sound of these heart-tuned voices he felt as if he had yet to learn the rudiment of Christian singing.

With trembling and tears he left that hallowed ground, and resolved to get his heart right before he would sing again. He at once resigned his position in the church of which he was a communicant member, and when the reason was asked, he replied that he was no longer going to mock his God with lip-service, while his heart was out of tune and far from him.

A Hymn Composed During a Sermon.

IN many books is found the hymn, commencing—

> "In all my Lord's appointed ways
> My journey I'll pursue;
> 'Hinder me not,' ye much-loved saints,
> For I must go with you."

It was written by Rev. John Ryland, D. D., an eminent Baptist minister, born in England in 1753. Blest with a pious mother, he was early taught, as Doddridge was, with Scripture lessons that adorned their fire-place.

When five years old he could read Hebrew, and at nine the entire New Testament in Greek. At fourteen he united with his father's church. At eighteen he preached his first sermon.

While pastor of the Baptist church at Northampton the hymn referred to above thus took its rise:—

"Several stage coaches daily passed through the town; and, as the good pastor lived at no great distance from the inn where they exchanged horses, he contrived to meet every evangelical minister who passed through the town, and not unfrequently almost compelled them to stay a day on the road, that they might give his people a sermon in the evening. On one occasion he had thus treated a brother in the ministry, who most reluctantly yielded and appeared in the pulpit with the text, 'Hinder me not,' Gen. XXIV. 56. Dr Ryland, as is still customary in England, sat in the desk below the pulpit to read the hymns; and, as his brother proceeded, every 'head of discourse' was 'turned into poetry,' which at the end of his sermon was duly read and a portion of it sung." In eight verses of the hymn the text was repeated. He is the author of ninety-nine hymns, the most popular being those commencing, "Sovereign 'Ruler of the skies,'" and "O Lord! I would delight in Thee."

JOHN RYLAND.

He received the degree of Doctor of Divinity, from Brown University of Rhode Island, America. In 1794, he accepted the presidency of the Baptist College at Bristol, together with the pastorate of Broadmead Chapel. In this twofold capacity, he continued to labor till his death, which took place in 1825, in the seventy-third year of his age. His last utterance was, "No more pain." His eminent successor, Robert Hall, passed a high eulogium upon him, as a pastor, preacher, tutor, and author.

The following is doubtless his best hymn, and is frequently sung:—

"O Lord, I would delight in thee,
And on thy care depend;
To thee in every trouble flee
My best, my only friend."

"When all created streams are dried,
Thy fulness is the same;
May I with this be satisfied,
And glory in thy name.

"No good in creatures can be found,
But may be found in thee;
I must have all things, and abound
While God is God to me.

"O! that I had a stronger faith,
To look within the veil,
To credit what my Saviour saith,
Whose word can never fail."

This hymn was issued in 1777, and consisted originally of seven verses. He makes the following note in relation to it, in the original manuscript: "I recollect deeper feelings of mind in composing this hymn, than perhaps I ever felt in making another."

His was a busy intellectual life, writing hymns even in his childhood, and gradually ascending the scale of honor, till he became one of the most eminent Hebrew scholars, and Theologians of his day.

The Shoemaker Hymn-Writer.

HANS SACHS was a remarkable man. Born of poor parents at Nuremberg in 1494, he was obliged in early life to leave his school for the bench of the shoemaker. At twenty he wrote his first poem, which was a hymn of praise to God. Afterwards he wrote many poems and hymns, which he would sing in the hearing of the people, and during five years visited many cities, working at his trade and singing wherever he went.

When the great Reformation under Luther commenced, Sachs was a young man of twenty-three. He at once joyfully embraced the good cause, and helped it along by writing and singing a great number of hymns and religious songs. These quickly followed one another and were scattered far and wide.

He is spoken of as "the best poet of his day; the one who linked the times that were passing to the new period that was coming in,

"'While dawn was piercing through the night;'

for he characteristically belonged to the Middle Ages, and yet was among the earliest and warmest adherents of the Reformation."

His pure and unostentatious life won for him great favor although he was represented in old doggrel rhyme as

"Hans Sachs, who was a shoe-
Maker, and a poet too."

Says one, "His poetry is distinguished by its heartiness, good sense, homely, genuine morality and freshness, its clear and healthy humor, and its skillful manipulations of material."

After writing poetry for fifty-two years, he took an account of his work, when he found that he had produced upwards of *six thousand and two hundred* pieces of various kind. In 1558 he had the pleasure of seeing the

HANS SACHS.

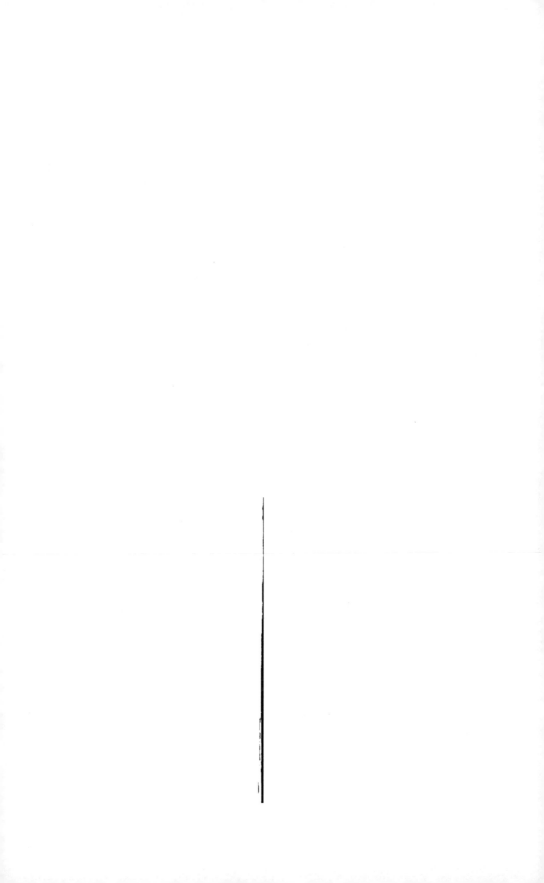

fruit of his poetic life gathered in five folio volumes.

In his old age he spent his time mostly at a table perusing the pages of his much-used Bible, of which he said in one of his hymns:—

> "'Twill make thee pure and holy,
> And teach thee that in Jesus lies
> Our hope and comfort solely."

He passed away, January 25, 1576, being in his eighty-second year. His well-cared-for grave is still to be seen in his native city. We give herewith the most famous of his German hymns, written during the seige of Nuremberg in 1561:—

> "Warum betruebst du dich mein Hertz?"

Entitled, "Reliance upon God in Trial." It has been thus translated by Rev. M. Sheeleigh:—

> "Why vail thyself in gloom, my heart,
> And grieve thyself with bitter smart
> Concerning earthly good?
> With humble trust do thou rely
> On God, who made the earth and sky.

> "He cannot, will not, turn from thee;
> Thy wants His eye full well doth see;
> Heaven and earth are His.
> My father and my God, indeed,
> Will keep me in each time of need.

> "While Thou my God and Father art,
> From me, Thy child, thou wilt not part
> O tenderest Father thou!
> A helpless one of dust my birth,
> No comfort do I find in earth.

> "When others to their riches cling,
> A trusting heart to God I bring;
> And though I be despised,
> This still my steadfast faith must be,—
> He shall not want who trusts in thee."

"Peace, troubled soul, whose plaintive moan."
"Lord, dismiss us with Thy blessing."

THE hymns commencing thus are often sung. They were written by Hon. and Rev. Walter Shirley, who was born of a noble family in England, 1725.

He was a first cousin of the devoted Countess of Huntingdon, and a frequent visitor to her London residence, where he became acquainted with Wesley and Whitefield.

After preaching in the chapels of Lady Huntingdon, and elsewhere with great success, he was called to fill the Episcopal pulpit at Loughrea, Ireland, where he spent the most of his life.

When the missionaries from Lady Huntingdon's College were about starting for America in 1772, he showed his interest in the work by writing the hymn:—

"Go, destined vessel, heavenly freighted, go,
For lo! the Lord's ambassadors are there."

He felt and manifested great sympathy for the great Methodist movement of his day, and was willing to bear bitter persecution in its behalf.

In 1760, he seemed much broken down by the execution of his brother, the Earl Ferrars, for shooting his servant. He wrote to Wesley, saying, "I have reason to bless God for the humbling lessons he has taught me through these awful visitations."

It is supposed that this sad occurrence gave rise to that well known hymn of his:—

"Peace, troubled soul, whose plaintive moan
Has taught these rocks the notes of woe."

As he grew in years he advanced in zeal and grace. When unable to leave the house because of a painful disease, he preached from his chair in his sick room to the many who flocked to hear him. The numbers frequently filling every available space in the house.

Origin of "My country, 'tis of thee."

REV. S. F. Smith D. D. an eminent New England Baptist minister, is the author of this and some thirty other hymns. In answer to some inquiries concerning the composition of this hymn, he says:

"One day, I think in the month of February, 1831 or '32, in turning over the leaves of music books, I fell in with the tune 'God save the King,' though I did not know it at that time to be the English national air. I at once wrote a patriotic hymn in the same measure and spirit, and soon after gave it to Mr. Lowell Mason, together with other pieces, and thought no more of it. On the next 4th of July, I found that the piece was brought out for the first time at a children's celebration of the day in Park street church, Boston. This was the beginning of its course. It gradually found its way into music books for children, and into public schools in various places; and thus I cannot but think, may have had an influence in infusing into many childish hearts a love of country, which prepared them to battle for the right, the true and the good, when the time of peril to our institutions and our country came.

"I have often remarked that if I had supposed the piece would have been so popular, I should have taken more pains to perfect it. 'Yes,' says some one, 'and thus, perhaps, you would have spoiled it.' It has won its way, most unexpectedly to myself, into the hearts of the people. I have heard most gratifying narratives of the places where the circumstances under which it has served as the expression of heart-felt love of country—in schools, in huts, on Western prairies, in churches, on the eve of battle, and in soldier's hospitals. I never designed it for a national hymn—I never supposed I was writing one."

Author of "The Saviour! O what endless charms."

A NAME that will linger long in the memory of those who love to sing the songs of Zion, is that of Anne Steele.

She was born in 1716, and was the eldest daughter of Rev. William Steele, pastor of the Baptist Church at Broughton, England. She united herself with the church when fourteen years of age, and remained in connection with her father's church till in her sixty second year she was transferred to the skies. When Rev. Henry Steele, her father's uncle and predecessor, had charge of the church, he was so popular that the neighboring Episcopal minister reported to his Bishop that his parish was sadly invaded by the dissenter. "How can I best oppose him?" said he. "Go home and preach better than Henry Steele, and the people will return," was the wise reply of Bishop Burnett.

She commenced writing poetry in early life, but withheld her name.

In her father's diary, dated Nov. 29. 1757, is made this entry concerning the issue of her first production:

"This day, Nanny sent part of her composition to London, to be printed. I entreat a gracious God, who enabled, and stirred her up to such a work, to direct in it and bless it for the good of many. * * * * I pray God to make it useful, and keep her humble."

Any one who traces the influences that her hymns have already wielded for over a century can see a bountiful answer to this father's prayer and solicitude.

Having consented, in early life, to be wedded to Mr. Elscourt, a young man of promise, the day of the wedding was fixed. But a short time before the appointed hour, he went down in the river to bathe, when getting beyond his depth, he was drowned.

ANNIE STEELE'S RESIDENCE.

Through an accident in her childhood, Miss Steele was made a sufferer, and an invalid all through life. In the retirement of her sick-chamber she was taught the lesson by experience, that she breathes out so sweetly in her hymn:—

> "Give me a calm, a thankful heart,
> From every murmur free;
> The blessings of Thy grace impart,
> And make me live to Thee."

The death of her father in 1769 was a great shock to her frail tenement, from which she never fully recovered. From this time, she was confined to her chamber, and "looked with sweet resignation to the time of her removal from earth, and when it happily arrived, she was, amidst great pain, full of peace and joy. She took the most affectionate leave of her friends who stood weeping around her, and uttering the triumphant words, 'I know that my Redeemer liveth,' closed her eyes, and fell asleep in Jesus." Thus she departed in 1778.

The one hundred and forty-four hymns, and thirty-four Psalms that issued from her pen, she lay upon the altar as an entire consecration to Him she so dearly loved, and would only permit them to be published with the understanding that all the profits should go to benevolent objects. It is supposed "that no woman, and but few men, ever wrote so many hymns that have been so generally acceptable in the church as did Miss Steele."

One secret of the success of her hymns, no doubt, is the warmth of her heart-breathings after Him, of whom she beautifully says:—

> "Jesus, my Lord, in Thy dear name unite
> All things my heart calls great or good or sweet;
> Divinest springs of wonder and delight.
> In Thee, Thou fairest of ten thousand, meet."

Remarkable Effects Attending a Closing Hymn.

REV. JAMES SHERMAN relates the following:—
"In the early part of the year 1837, I preached one Sabbath evening from Mark iv, 36, 'And there were also with him other little ships.' The subject was the earnestness with which men must seek for Christ, and the risk they must be willing to run to find him.

"As I proceeded in the illustrations and enforcement of the principles stated, there came from heaven a celestial breeze, and one little ship after another seemed to start in search of Christ, until they became a fleet.

"They were melted into penitance and tears. Never shall I forget the impression made when at the close of the sermon I gave out the hymn:—

> "Jesus, at thy command.
> I launch into the deep."

"When I descended from the pulpit, both vestries and the school-room were filled with persons anxious to converse with me. I began to talk with them one at a time, During my converse, and after he had waited more than an hour, a gentleman of some position knocked at my vestry door, and said, 'Sir here are enough to fill twenty boats; what will you do with us?' Exhausted beyond measure, I kneeled down and prayed with them. The place was literally a Bochim.

"After pronouncing the benediction, I begged for them to retire, and come and see me on the morrow or on Tuesday. But some begged, as for their life, that I would converse with them for a few minutes. I remained among them until eleven o'clock, listening to their repeated vows and anxious expressions of faith in Christ. Oh, it was worth dying for, to witness such a scene. After examination, many were admitted to the church, eight-four attributing their conversion to that sermon."

Drawn into the Gospel Net by Singing.

DURING the revolutionary war, shortly after the memorable 1776, there occurred a very interesting case of conversion in connection with the singing of the Rev. Caleb B. Pedicord amid the primitive forests of Maryland. He is described as "one of the saintliest men of his age. His voice, in both singing and preaching, had a dissolving power of tenderness."

While on his circuit in Dorcester county, Md., he was riding slowly along to his appointment at Mount Holly. As his eye of faith was looking ahead at the bright mansions of his Father's house, awaiting him at the end of life's journey, his overflowing heart began to sing aloud;—

> "I cannot, I cannot forbear
> These passionate longings for home;
> O when shall my spirit be there?
> O when will the messenger come?"

The echo of this song fell upon the ear of a young revolutionary soldier, who was wandering in an adjoining forest, as he listened his soul was stirred by the sweet melody of the voice, and the last two lines of the verse.

"After he ceased," writes the listening soldier, "I went out and followed him a great distance, hoping he would begin again. He however stopped at the house of a Methodist and dismounted. I then concluded he must be a Methodist preacher and would probably preach that evening."

That evening the young soldier was drawn out to hear the singer again. The sermon was the power of God to his salvation. He at once enlisted as a soldier for Jesus, and afterwards became a prominent preacher, and for many years a founder of many churches. He was the widely known and much beloved Rev. Thomas Ware.

Samuel Stennett and his Hymns.

THOUGH grace does not run like blood in the veins, from one generation to another, yet the virtue of the prayers, and godly example of Christians, does often descend, through the hearts of their children, to succeeding ages. A forcible illustration of this is given in the genealogy of the Stennetts.

The Rev. Edward Stennett was the father of the Rev. Joseph Stennett, born in 1663, who wrote the precious Sabbath Hymn, commencing,

> "Another six days' work is done,
> Another Sabbath is begun;
> Return my soul! enjoy thy rest,
> Improve the day thy God hath blessed."

To him was born a son, in 1692, who became the celebrated Rev. Joseph Stennett, D. D, a zealous Christian in early life, and afterwards a minister of high repute. He became the father of a son, whose likeness we give on the opposite page, the Rev. Samuel Stennett, D. D. A son of the latter, the Rev. Joseph Stennett, took his father's mantle, thus making the fifth link in the chain of ministers, descending through five generations.

Samuel Stennett was born at Exeter, England, in 1727. Ten years later, his father took charge of the Baptist church at Little Wild Street, London. There this son first became his assistant, and afterwards his successor. In this pastorate he continued for thirty-seven years, the remainder of his life.

He received the degree of Doctor of Divinity, from King's College, at Aberdeen, in 1763, and was highly esteemed by his sovereign, George III. High preferment was offered him in the Church of England, but faithful to his sense of duty, he declined, saying: "I dwell among mine own people."

SAMUEL STENNETT.

He was eminent in his literary attainments, and ranked with Addison in the style and force of his compositions, How beautiful the language of his hymn that commences in some books:—

> "Majestic sweetness sits enthroned
> Upon the Saviour's brow,"

During his last sickness, he gave expression to sentiments similar to those found in the third verse:—

> "He saw me plunged in deep distress,
> He flew to my relief;
> For me he bore the shameful cross,
> And carried all my grief."

Some vinegar, mixed with other ingredients had been given him as a throat gargle, when, with much emotion, he said: "'And in his thirst they gave him vinegar to drink,' Oh when I reflect upon the sufferings of Christ, I am ready to ask, What have I been thinking of all my life? What he did and suffered are now my only support."

In 1795, after the death of his wife, he had earnest longings to depart also, and could say in the language of his hymn:—

> "On Jordan's stormy banks I stand,
> And cast a wishful eye
> To Canaan's fair and happy land,
> Where my possessions lie."

He died in 1795, aged sixty-eight. His hymns number thirty-nine. In addition to the two popular ones, just referred to, we may mention the following as also frequently used:—

> "Come, every pious heart,"
> "How charming is the place,"
> "Here at thy table, Lord, we meet,"
> "Prostrate, dear Jesus, at thy feet,"
> "'Tis finished!' so the Saviour cried."

"On Jordan's stormy banks I stand."

MISS BARBARA JEWITT'S departure was illustrative of the sentiments of this well-known hymn, issued by Samuel Stennett, in 1750. Says the Wesleyan Magazine: "On the day of her death she was sitting in her chair, in which she had sat for three weeks, and broke out into singing in a loud tone the delightful hymn:—

"'On Jordan's stormy banks I stand,
And cast a wishful eye
To Canaan's fair and happy land,
Where my possessions lie.'

Her relatives were alarmed, for she had only been able to speak in a whisper for some weeks. After singing half-an-hour, she requested this hymn to be given out,—

"'Come on my partners in distress,'

in the singing of which she joined at intervals with earnestness. 'Sing on, sing on,' she frequently said to her friends. Then, as if talking to angelic spirits, she said, 'Stay, stay, I am not ready yet.' She requested this hymn to be sung,—

"'O glorious hope of perfect love.'

Her sight now failed her, and she asked her friends to come nearer and sing on. Whilst they were thus engaged she waved her hand round in triumph, and sang:—

"'And makes me for some moments feast
With Jesus's priests and king.'

She then fell back in her chair, and in a moment her spirit fled to the skies."

"Infinite day excludes the night."

A LITTLE child, trying to solve the mystery of the heavens above, gave expression to this pretty thought:

As, one evening, she was gazing upward with wondering eyes, she said: "Ma, don't you think the stars are gimlet-holes that God has bored through the floor of heaven, to let its light shine down on earth."

Heaven's light does reach earth, and often gilds the hilltops that overlook the valley of death.

As the Rev. Thomas Scott was exchanging worlds, he exclaimed as he got a glimpse of the glory-land, "This is heaven begun. I have done with *darkness* for *ever*—for *ever*."

A YOUNG girl, whose life's journey was just ending, made a feeble effort to speak. Mother, father, sister, and all came closer to her side. A joyous smile lit up her countenance, she laid her little hand within her mother's palm, then closed her eye-lids to the light of earth, and sank away. The cold damp of death's shadowy valley seemed circling over her. But see! the lips open again, and whisper the parting words: "Mother! mother! I see a *light!* I'm almost home!"

AS the shadows of death were gathering around the daughter of the Rev. Mr. Hughes of West Pennsylvania, she could no longer see the faces of loved ones that were bending over her couch, but still able to move the tongue, she whispered: "Papa, I cannot see you. I'm going to the *light-land* where it's dark no more."

THE father of the Rev. J. France of Baltimore, Md., when in the dark valley, cheered a weeping circle of friends by saying as his last words "*I see light ahead.*"

Influence of a blind Slave's Song.

A COLLEGE student in Virginia, proud of his intellectual attainments, thought if he ever became a Christian it would be through an eloquent sermon of some distinguished pulpit orator. While hunting deer during a vacation he was drawn to a gorge far away in the mountains, by the sound of a sweet female voice, engaged in singing. As he drew nearer he recognized the words of the hymn:—

"There is a happy land
Far far away."

At length he perceived a log cabin, and an old female slave, with hair as white as snow, standing without at her wash tub singing away as though her heart was overflowing with gladness. She was unusually tall and very straight. As the young student stood enchanted with the romantic scene, he found that she was also blind, and, as she kept on singing and washing, her happy soul would become so full of joy that she would stop washing, and, for a while straightening up, and turning her sightless eye-balls heavenward, would make the surrounding rocks and mountains ring as her joyful voice would sing:—

"There is a land of pure delight
Where saints immortal reign."

At length the student said to her, "Auntie," I see you are blind?" "No, massa," said she, "I is not blind." I can't see you, nor dese trees, nor dese rocks, nor dese mountains, but I can see into de kingdom. I can see de "happy land, far, far, away."

The young student was so impressed with what he saw and heard that, from that time on, he was deeply convicted of sin, and rested not till he found rest in Jesus.

He eventually became a minister, and told the author that the echo of that happy slave's song still follows him.

The Blind Man of the Mine.

I had descended one thousand feet beneath the earth's surface, in the coal pits of the Mid Lotian Mines in Virginia, and was wandering through their dark, subterranean passages, when the sound of music at a little distance broke upon my ear. It ceased upon our approach, and I caught only the concluding sentiment of the hymn,

"I shall be in Heaven in the morning."

On advancing with our lamps, we found the passage closed by a door, in order to give a different direction to the current of air for the purpose of ventilation, yet this door must be opened occasionally to let the rail cars pass, loaded with coal. And to accomplish this, we found sitting by that door an aged blind slave, whose eyes had been entirely destroyed by a blast of gunpowder many years before, in that mine. There he sat, on a seat cut in the coal, from sunrise to sunset, day after day; his sole business being to open and shut the door, when he heard the rail cars approaching. We requested him to sing again the hymn whose last line we had heard. It was one of those productions which we found the pious slaves were in the habit of singing, in part, at least, impromptu. But each stanza closed with the sentiment,

"I shall be in Heaven in the morning."

It was sung with a clear and pleasant voice, and I could see the shrivelled, sightless eyeballs of the old man roll in their sockets, as if his soul felt the inspiring sentiments.

There he stood, an old man, blind and enslaved—what could he hope for on earth? He was buried, too, a thousand feet beneath the solid rocks. There, from month to month, he sat in darkness. Oh, how utterly cheerless his condition! And yet that one pleasant hope of a resurrection morning was enough to infuse peace and joy in his soul.

Singing a Man to Christ.

"I'LL tell you what, I heard singin' to-night that made me wish I was in heaven, or good enough to go there," said an old backwoodsman to his wife, as, entering their log hut, he sat down to his evening meal.

"Where did you hear it? she asked.

"At our neighbor's up yonder. They must feel something I don't know about, or they couldn't sing so."

"When they first came here," said the wife, "I thought they were proud and stiff; but they were real good neighbors, and I heard after they were good church folks too."

"Well," said he, "I mean to go to church to-morrow, and see if I can't hear some singin' like that."

The singer knew that her neighbors were ignorant, rough, and unbelieving, nearing the decline of life, and unwilling to be approached on the subject of religion.

One glorious summer evening, as the sun was going down, the lady seated herself at the window, and involuntarily tuned her voice to sing. When near the close of the hymn, she cast her eyes to the field where her neighbor was at work, and saw that he was listening intently. Instantly the thought flashed into her mind, "Oh, if I could raise that poor man to think of heaven." She closed her refrain, and then commenced,

"On Jordan's stormy banks I stand,"

singing it "with the spirit and the understanding also." And as she sang, the old man listened, almost spellbound. The singer wished to glorify God by leading one of His creatures to think of Him. "I will sing God's praises whenever he can hear me, and perhaps he may be led to praise the Lord himself," was her resolve.

The next Lord's-day the old man was at church. This cheered the lady, and she said, "I will sing whenever he comes." Ere another week was closed he was at work again. This time she sang,

> "Just as I am, without one plea,
> But that thy blood was shed for me."

Slowly, but distinctly she sang, that he might take in the full meaning of the words, and feeling their sweet pathos in her inmost soul she sang the hymn. The listener shook his head, and rubbed his hand quickly over his eyes.

The next Lord's-day evening he was among the people of God, earnestly inquiring the way of salvation.

Being thus successful in bringing the husband in the way of life, the singer next tried to draw the wife, and so one day invited her into the parlor to hear her piano. She had never seen or heard such an instrument, and was wonderstruck. The lady called her daughters to her side, and all joined in singing, "All hail the power of Jesus' name," to the old tune, "Coronation."

"Do you like that?" said the lady.

"Oh, it's nice. I b'l'eve I heered that tune somewhere when I was a girl, but I've forgot."

"Probably you heard it at church. It is often sung there. We cannot sing the praises of Jesus too often, for He came to save us poor sinners." Then they all sang, "Come, humble sinner, in whose breast," etc. When the woman rose to go, she was invited to "Come again."

"Oh, I'll come often if I can hear you sing."

"Mother, you take a strange way to win souls?"

"Why not, my daughter? Has not God commanded that *whatsoever* we do, should be done to his glory? And if He has given us voices to sing, should we not use them in his service? There are many ears that will listen to a hymn for the sake of the tune, that will not hear a word from the Bible. Our voices and our musical instruments should all be employed in winning lost souls."

Appropriate Hymns amid Chicago's Fire.

WHEN the flames seized the great house of worship belonging to the First Baptist Church in Chicago, brethren, who had labored hard to save it, said, one to another, "Our house must go, but let us have one more prayer within its walls." And they bowed before God in face of the coming flames, while one who had been wont to lead in the fire and thunder of battle, led the cry of these faithful heroes before the mercy seat. Then, rising to their feet, they sang as they retreated:—

> "From every stormy wind that blows,
> From every swelling tide of woes,
> There is a calm, a sure retreat—
> 'Tis found beneath the mercy-seat."

The pastor of the New England Congregational church says that at the time when they were most afflicted by the loss of their beautiful edifice, a singular circumstance became known, which greatly cheered and encouraged them to put forth the most strenuous efforts to obtain the necessary means to rebuild. It seems that among the *debris* two bits of printed paper were found, one of which proved to be the only remaining fragment of a Bible, and the only legible portion was this verse, from 2nd Cor. v. 1: "For we know that if our earthly house of this tabernacle were dissolved, we have a building of God, an house not made with hands, eternal in the heavens." The other was a scrap from the hymn-book, upon which were these words of the hymn, No. 1180 from "Songs for the Sanctuary:"—

> "Daughter of Zion! from the dust
> Exalt thy fallen head;
> Again in thy Redeemer trust,
> He calls thee from the dead.
> Rebuild thy walls, thy bounds enlarge,
> And send thy heralds forth."

"That Sweet Music."

MARIA Sanders was an attentive Sabbath school scholar. She was thirteen years old when she lay upon her death-bed. She was very thoughtful about religious things for several weeks before she was taken sick, and some thought she had become a Christian.

During the first week of her sickness she was troubled in re-regard to her hope in Christ. But on Wednesday it became evident that she could not recover, and her father and mother, after a severe struggle alone with God, were able to say, "The Lord gave, and the Lord hath taken away; blessed be the name of the Lord."

When they returned to Maria's room, she greeted them with a happy smile; and then, as if talking to Jesus, said, "Jesus, I can trust thee; love thee, blessed Jesus."

A little later, looking upward, she said, "Oh, father, see those *golden stars.*" Upon this the family began to weep aloud. "Now you have driven them all away again." They hushed their crying, when she said, "There, I see them now."

It was the "Star in the East" that heralded the birth of Jesus, who is "the Bright and Morning Star;" and might not the bright angels, whom Jesus sends to take his little ones home, look like *golden stars?*

A few hours before she died, she said, "Oh, hear that *sweet music.* Don't you hear it? It is a comfort to know they will not get done singing until I get there." W. T. S.

Music Heard While in a Trance.

IN the days of the Revolution lived Rev. William Tennent, who was pastor of, and now lies buried in the Freehold Presbyterian Church of N. J. He was a most faithful and successful minister in his day.

His name is widely known in connection with his apparent death. For three days he remained in a trance. He had been ill in health, and emaciated in body until his life was despaired of.

One morning he seemed to expire. He was laid out and preparations were made for his funeral. The body was stiff and cold, but the physician thought he detected symptoms of life, and desired a postponement of the funeral. His brother and others thought there were no signs of life, and insisted on the funeral. The doctor begged again, until the funeral was postponed. The people were assembled to bury him. The doctor again, and again plead for a postponement.

At length Mr. Tennent opened his eyes, gave a dreadful groan, and relapsed again into apparent death. This movement was twice repeated after an interval of an hour, when life permanently remained, and the patient slowly recovered.

He was totally ignorant of every transaction of his life previous to his sickness. He had to be taught reading, writing, and all things as if he was a new born infant. At length he felt a sudden shock in his head, and from that moment his recollection was by degrees restored. These circumstances made a profound impression on the public mind.

Mr. Tennent has left on record the account of his feelings when in a state of catalepsy. He said, "While I was conversing with my brother on the state of my soul, and the fears I had entertained of my future welfare, I found myself in an instant, in another state of existence under the direction of a Superior being, who ordered me to follow him. I was accordingly wafted along, I knew not how, till I beheld at a distance an ineffable glory, the impression of which on my mind, it is impossible to communicate to mortal man. I immediately reflected on my happy change, and thought, 'Well, blessed be God! I am safe at last, notwithstanding all my fears.' I saw an innumerable host of happy beings surrounding the inexpressible glory, in acts of adoration, and joyous worship: but I did not see any bodily shape or representation in the glorious appearance. I heard things unutterable. I heard their songs and hallelujahs of thanksgiving and praise with unspeakable rapture. I felt joy unutterable and full of glory. I then applied to my conductor, and requested leave to join in the happy throng; on which he tapped me on the shoulder and said, 'you must return to the earth.' This sounded like a sword through my heart. In an instant I recollected to have seen my brother standing before me disputing with the doctor. The three days during which I appeared to be lifeless, seemed to me about ten or twenty minutes. The idea of returning to this world of sorrow and trouble, gave me such a shock that I fainted repeatedly."

Mr. Tennent said that *for three years, the ravishing sounds he had heard*, and the words that were uttered were not out of his ears. He was often importuned to tell what words were uttered, but declined, saying, "you will know them, with many other particulars, hereafter, as you will find the whole among my papers." But they were never found.

Tennent died on the 8th of March 1774, aged 71 years. Pastor of Freehold church, 43 years 6 months.

Elias Boudenott D. D.

Author of "Rock of Ages."

"ROCK of ages," was written by Augustus Toplady. It first appeared March 1776, in the "Gospel Magazine," which he edited.

It was entitled, "A Living and Dying Prayer for the Holiest Believer in the World."

When a lad of 16 years of age while on a visit to Ireland with his widowed mother, he strolled into a barn where an earnest uneducated layman was preaching on the text "ye who sometimes were afar off, are made nigh by the blood of Christ."

Says Mr. Toplady, "Under the ministry of Mr. Morris, that dear messenger of God, and under that sermon, I was, I trust, 'brought nigh by the blood of Christ,' in August 1756.

Strange that I, who had so long sat under the means of grace in England, should be brought nigh unto God in an obscure part of Ireland, amidst a handful of God's people, met together in a barn, and under the ministry of one, who could hardly spell his name."

The influence of that barn discourse has already been felt for a century, and is now echoing in all parts of the world, for through it was converted the lad who gave to the Church "Rock of ages." It has been translated and is now sung in almost every known tongue.

In 1768 he entered into his pastoral work at Broad Henbury, England. As a preacher he is thus described, "His voice was music. His vivacity would have caught the listeners eye; and his soul-filled looks and movements would have interpreted his language, had there not been

AUGUSTUS TOPLADY.
A FAC SIMILE OF THE LIKENESS IN THE MAGAZINE
FOR WHICH HE WROTE "ROCK OF AGES."

such commanding solemnity in his tones, as made apathy impossible, and such simplicity in his words that to hear was to understand.

From easy explanations, he advanced to rapid and conclusive arguments, and warmed into importune exhorations, till conscience began to burn, and feelings to take fire from his own kindled spirit, and himself and his hearers were together drowned in sympathetic tears."

He seemed to live in the clear sunshine of the Saviour's countenance. He frequently called himself " the happiest man in the world."

His death couch seemed to be flooded with the sunbeams of the glory-land. Said he with sparkling eye, "I cannot tell the comforts I feel in my soul: they are past expression. The consolations of God are so abundant, that he leaves me nothing to pray for; my prayers are all converted into praise. I enjoy a heaven already in my soul."

As he drew near his departure from earth finding his pulse getting weaker and weaker he said " why that is a good sign that my death is fast approaching; and blessed be God, I can add, that my heart beats everyday, stronger and stronger for glory." Just before his death, bursting into tears of joy he exclaimed, "It will not be long before God takes me; for no mortal can live after the *glories which God has manifested to my soul.*"

Thus he passed away in the thirty-eighth year of his age, realizing the import of his words,

> " When I rise to worlds unknown,
> And behold thee on thy throne,
> Rock of ages, cleft for me!
> Let me hide myself in thee."

Alterations in "Rock of Ages."

IT is unfortunate that a hymn so often used, should appear in so many various forms. The different versions we give herewith are taken from "Hymns and Choirs."

We will give first the lines of the original of Toplady, and then the different alterations made.

Rock of ages, cleft for me,
Altered thus:
    Rock of ages, shelter me.

From thy riven side which flowed
Altered thus:
    From thy wounded side which flowed.
    From thy side a healing flood.

Be of sin the double cure,
Cleanse me from its guilt and power,
Altered thus:
    Be of sin and fear the cure,
    Save from wrath and make me pure.

    Be of sin the perfect cure,
    Save me, Lord, and make me pure.

    Clease from guilt and grace ensure,

Could my zeal no respite know,
Could my tears forever flow,
All for sin could not atone,
Altered thus:
    Should my zeal no languor know
    Should my tears forever flow,
    This for sin could not atone.

    May my zeal no respite know;
    May my heart with love o'erflow.
    But can this for sin atone?

This for sin could ne'er atone.
This for sin could not atone.

Nothing in my hand I bring,
 Altered thus:
In my hand no price I bring.

Foul, I to thy fountain fly,
 Altered thus:
Vile I to the fountain fly.

When my eye-strings break in death,
 Altered thus:
When my heart-strings break in death.
When my eyelids sink in death.
When my eyelids close in death.

When I soar to worlds unknown,
See thee on thy judgment throne,
 Altered thus:
When I soar though tracks unknown.
When I rise to worlds unknown,
And behold thee on thy throne.

TOPLADY himself altered the hymns of others without always adding to their improvement.
The second verse of the hymn of Dr. Watts,—
 "When I survey the wondrous cross,"
was originally written thus:—

 "Forbid it, Lord, that I should boast,
  Save in the death of Christ, my God;
  All the vain things that charm me most
  I sacrifice them to His blood."

Toplady changed it to read thus:—

 "Forbid, O Lord, that I should boast
  Save in the death of Christ my God:
  I have, and wish to have, no trust
  But in his righteousness and blood."

A Babe Hid in the Cleft of a Rock.

A HIGHLAND mother was suddenly overtaken by a storm in the mountains of Switzerland.

"After attempting in vain for some time," says Dr. Macduff, "with her infant in her arms, to buffet the whirling eddies, she laid the child down among heather and ferns, in the deep cleft of a rock, with the brave resolve, if possible, to make her own way home through the driving sleet, and obtain succor for her little one. She was found by the anxious neighbors next morning stretched cold and stiff on a snowy shroud. But the cries of the babe directed them to the rock-crevice, where it lay, all unconscious of its danger, and from which it was rescued in safety.

"Many long years afterwards that child returned from distant lands a disabled soldier, covered with honorable wounds. The first Sabbath of his home-coming, on repairing to a city church, where he had the opportunity of worshipping God 'after the manner' and in the cherished language of his forefathers, he listened to an aged clergyman unfolding, in Celtic accents, the story of redeeming love. Strange to say, that clergyman happened to be from the same Highland glen where he himself had spent his youth. Stranger still, he was illustrating the divine tale with the anecdote, to him so familiar, of the widow and the saved child.

"A few days afterwards, that pastor was called to visit the death-bed of the old soldier. 'I am the son of the widow,' were the words which greeted the former as he stood by the couch of the dying man. 'Lay my bones besides hers in the churchyard among the hills. The prayers she offered for me have been answered. I have found deliverance in old age where I found it in childhood, in the cleft of the rock; but it is the Rock of Ages!'"

A Man Saved by a Cleft in a Rock.

ONE morning a village, along that part of the Pacific that forms one of the new boundaries of New South Wales, was thrown into consternation by tidings that fragments of a wreck were floating about the harbor, some with the name "Dunbar" upon them. A passenger-vessel of that name was due. Steamers were at once despatched to the Heads, and it soon became evident that an awful shipwreck had occurred, and that probably every one on board had perished. The excitement in the city was intense; only they who have been witnesses of a like calamity can understand what a thrill of anguish was sent through the nerves of a small community like that, by the loss of fifty well-known individuals. The day was spent in securing the cargo and collecting the mutilated remains of those who had been so suddenly snatched away, which lay scattered among the rocks in every direction. Not one, apparently, survived to tell the history of the disaster.

On the day following it was noised abroad that a voice had been heard in the rocks, and measures were at once taken to give them a thorough examination. From the vessels and boats near the spot, the rocks were scanned with eager eyes; men were let down by ropes, and one poor fellow was at last found, almost lifeless, half-way between the surface and the water, in a cleft of rock.

From his evidence at the inquest, it appeared that the vessel, unable to make the harbor, had drifted helplessly upon the rocks. The sea closed upon the ship and passengers, and in less than five minutes all was over. He had been lifted by a wave into his place of security.

The cleft of that rock illustrates the sentiments of

> "Rock of ages, cleft for me,
> Let me hide myself in Thee."

Singing of "Rock Of Ages."

"Dr. Pomeroy entered a church at Constantinople, where a company of Armenians were singing a hymn which caused the tears to stream from the eyes.

He inquired what they were singing! A man present translated the words and lo! they were the dear old lines of Rock of ages."

When Prince Albert, the husband of the Queen of England, was leaving this world his dying breath was heard whispering the sweet words of

"Rock of ages cleft for me."

"Thus" says Dr. Cuyler "it came to pass that the dying *prince* laid hold of those precious thoughts which had their root in the rude discourse of an obscure Christian layman in an Irish barn."

On how many hearts have the undying lines been impressed that have been chiseled in marble on a monument in Greenwood Cemetery. They are found under a statue representing faith kneeling before the cross.

"Nothing in my hands I bring
Simply to thy cross I cling."

The Rev. Stephen H. Tyng D. D. says, that when his son the Rev. Dudley Tyng. was approaching the Jordan of death just after he had spoken those ever memorable words "Stand up for Jesus—" he aroused from the sleep of death, and said to those in tears by his bed side, "*Sing, Can you not sing?*" "We hesitated. It was impossible. When he himself began to sing

"Rock of ages cleft for me."

And we sang together two verses of that hymn, he and his wife louder than any of us. He could sing no more—no more could we."

"Rock of Ages."

A. W., in the *American Messenger*, furnishes the following :—

"'T was a sultry day in June. The scorching beams of the noonday sun came slanting through the broad uncurtained windows, falling directly on the operators and sewing-girls ranged along the room, making their heads throb and ache almost to bursting. Wearily the machines turned, and the tired eyes of the girls glanced now and then at the clock noting the moments as they dragged heavily by.

"The calls on the ice-cooler had been frequent that morning, and now at one o'clock the water was spent. One after another had gone to it, expecting to get a cooling drink, but had turned away disappointed. The merry song was hushed, the laughing jests were dropped, and tired hands toiled on, longing for the close of the day, that they might find rest and water.

"Suddenly in the deep hush, came the sweet, low voice of an operator, singing,

"'Rock of ages, cleft for me,
Let me hide myself in thee.

One after another joined in, forgetting their burning thirst, until the whole fifty girls were singing. Grandly the closing stanza rang out,

"'While I draw this fleeting breath,
When my heartstrings break in death,
When I soar to worlds unknown,
See thee on thy judgment-throne,
Rock of ages, cleft for me,
Let me hide myself in thee.'

No more sadness, no more weary looks or anxious glances towards the clock. Hymn after hymn was sung, and almost too soon came the six o'clock bell."

"Rock of Ages" Floating over a Field of Death.

A MINISTER in Wales gave a friend the following account of his conversion after the battle of Alma, during the Crimean war, in which he was engaged as a soldier.

"I had," said he, "gone down a hill to get some water. In consequence of the number of my fellow-men lying dead on the field, the water there was not fit to drink, so I had to go a long way to get some.

"After getting all I required I retraced my steps to the camp. As I stepped over the bodies now stiff and cold in death, my thoughts wandered to those families in England, who were deprived of a father, husband or brother, when all at once the sound of singing floated in the air. I drew near to the place and found a company of soldiers singing in the Welsh language. In the midst of them was a soldier whose sands of life were nearly gone, and he had requested his comrades to sing:—

"'Rock of ages, cleft for me.'

"When they sang the last verse,

"'While I draw this fleeting breath,
When my eyelids close in death,'

he lifted his eyes to heaven and faintly exclaimed, "Sing it again." They did so. But before they had finished it, his soul left the tenement of clay for the home above.

"The solemn scene had such an effect on me that I began to seek the way of salvation, and am now what you see me, a minister of the gospel."

"Rock of Ages" Drowning Rowdy Songs.

AT the commencement of a two weeks' course of "Illustrated Sermons" in the Calvary Church, Cleveland, Ohio, January, 1870, we were much impressed by the prayer of a ministerial brother, who begged for two hundred souls, as the fruit of that special effort. We soon found in it an exemplification of the promise, "Open thy mouth wide, and I will fill it."

At the close of each sermon, a service was held for the special benefit of those who were penitent. Soon the number became so great, that sixteen of the front pews were reserved for such, and so great was the anxiety to press forward to occupy those seats, that men had to be stationed in each aisle, to prevent the rush from occasioning any accident. Never shall we forget the sound of that church echo, when about a hundred persons would rise simultaneously to their feet, and hasten to secure a place among those who were clustering around the cross.

The subject one evening being "The Prodigal Son," the illustrations served to draw in from the streets a wanderer, who, unable to secure one of the front seats, at the close of the sermon dropped down upon bended knees in the aisle. An evening or two later, as he arose to testify how he had been plucked as a brand from the burning, he remarked that he found great difficulty in *drowning* the echo of the rowdy songs he had been accustomed to sing. "But," says he, "I have succeeded by singing, 'Rock of ages,' and to-day I have been kept busy in singing 'Rock of ages,' from morning till night."

By the close of the two weeks, the pastor received the names of two hundred and eight souls, who were induced to seek salvation. The brother's prayer thus was more than answered, and we had a fresh illustration of the text, "According to your faith be it unto you."

Clinging Close to the Rock.

PASSING over the Alleghany Mountains was a long train of cars on its way eastward. It was crowded with passengers. As the iron horse snorted and rushed on, they began to feel that it had begun to descend, and needed no power but the invisible power of gravitation to send them down with terrific swiftness. Just as the passengers began to realize their situation they came to a short curve cut out of the solid rock—a wall of rock lying on each side. Suddenly the steam whistle screamed as if in agony, "Put on the brakes! put on the brakes!"

Up pressed the brakes, but with no apparent slacking of the cars. Every window flew open, and every head that could be was thrust out to see what the danger was, and every one rose up in his place, fearing sudden destruction. What was the trouble?

Just as the engine began to turn in the curve the engineer saw a little girl and her baby brother playing on the track. In a moment the cars would be on them; the shriek of the whistle startled the little girl, and every one looking over could see them. Close to the rail, in the upright rock, was a little niche, out of which a piece of rock had been blasted. In an instant the baby was thrust into this niche, and as the cars came thundering by, the passengers, holding their breath, heard the clear voice of the little sister on the other side of the cars, ring out, "*Cling close to the rock, Johnny! cling close to the rock!*" And the little creature snuggled in, and put his head as close to the corner of the rock as possible, while the heavy cars whirred past him.

And many were the moist eyes that gazed, a silent thanksgiving went up to him who is the

"Rock of ages cleft for me."

"That Is My Hope."

I was at the death-bed, not long ago, of a man who for many years had been living a life of profligacy.

For years his friends knew nothing of him, but at last the hand of disease was laid upon him, and then he sought for home. His friends received him, attended him with all kindness, and as he lay in that sick-bed Jesus came knocking again at the door of his heart, and he was received in. A few days before his death, I asked on what his hope was resting. He stretched forth his hand for a hymn book, and with his long, pale, wasted fingers, turned over its leaves, and then handing it to me, pointing to one of the hymns, he said, "*that* is my hope"— "*Rock of ages, cleft for me.*"

The Clefts in the Rock.

AN unbeliever was shown the clefts in the rock of Mount Calvary. Examining them critically, he turned in amazement to his fellow travellers and said, "I have long been a student of nature, and I am sure the clefts and rents in this rock were never done by nature, or an ordinary earthquake; for by such a concussion, the rock must have split according to the veins and where it was weakest in the adhesion of parts: for this, I have observed to have been done in other rocks when separated or broken after an earthquake, and reason tells me it must always be so.

But it is quite otherwise here; for the rock is rent athwart and across the veins, in a most strange and preternatural manner; and therefore, " said he, "I thank God that I came hither to see the *standing monument* of miraculous power by which God gives evidence to this day of the Divinity of Christ."

"Thou must save, and Thou alone."

THE following extracts, taken from children's letters, will illustrate this line in "Rock of Ages," and also how much a sinner needs a Saviour's help.

"Tuesday, in school.

Dear Mr. Long:—

How I wish I was good! I wish ---- but I suppose it's no use to wish. I am the worst girl ever was, almost.

I try to be good; and I pray, but then pretty soon I forget all about it, and be just as bad as before. Mr. Long won't you pray for me? I am afraid I like the world too much.

My teacher told the girls to sit up,—so I'll have to stop."

"I make good Resolutions every day, but in a little while they are all broken. Won't you pray for me?"

"If I say in the morning I will be good, to-day,—it seems I hardly get down-stairs before I say a cross word. I have tried so often to be good but always failed."

"I should like to be a good boy but I have so many temptations; Bad boys tempt me, and my bad heart. I dont get asleep any more in church. Pray for me."

"Dear Sir:—Sometimes I am good for about three weeks, then I get bad again; and I cannot help it. Will you pray for me?"

Rock of Ages, by Rev. Dr. Ray Palmer.

From "Evenings with the Sacred Poets."

O Rock of Ages! since on Thee
   By grace my feet are planted,
'Tis mine in tranquil faith, to see
   The rising storm, undaunted;
When angry billows round me rave,
   And tempests fierce assail me,
To thee I cling, the terrors brave,
   For Thou canst never fail me;
Though rends the globe with earthquake shock,
Unmoved Thou stand'st, Eternal Rock!

Within Thy clefts I love to hide,
   When darkness o'er me closes;
There peace and light serene abide,
   And my still heart reposes;
My soul exults to dwell secure
   Thy strong munitions round her;
She dares to count her triumph sure,
   Nor fears lest hell confound her;
Though tumults startle earth and sea,
Thou changeless Rock, they shake not Thee!

From Thee, O rock once smitten! flow
   Life-giving streams for ever;
And whoso doth their sweetness know,
   He henceforth thirsteth never;
My lips have touched the crystal tide,
   And feel no more returning
The fever, that so long I tried
   To cool, yet felt still burning;
Ah, wondrous Well-Spring! brimming o'er
With living waters evermore.

On that dread day when they that sleep
   Shall hear the trumpet sounding,
And wake to praise, or wake to weep,
   The judgment-throne surrounding;
When wrapt in all-devouring flame,
   The solid globe is wasting,
And what at first from nothing came
   Is back to nothing hasting;
E'en then, my soul shall calmly rest,
O Rock of Ages! on Thy breast.

Rev. Isaac Watts D. D.

WATTS, the author of many of the hymns contained in the Church hymn books of our day, was born in Southampton, England, on the 17th of July, 1674.

His father kept a flourishing boarding-school in that town, which was held in such high repute that students were sent to it from America and the West Indies. He was an earnest Christian, a deacon of the Independent or Congregational church. Soon after the birth of Isaac, their first born child, the father was imprisoned in the South-Castle Jail, because of his non-conformity.

The mother, in her affliction, is said to have often seated herself on a stone near the prison door, with the poet, then an infant "suckling at her breast," and at times, to have "lifted him up to the cell window to comfort the father in bonds."

His precocious intellect soon began to show itself. Before he could speak plainly, when money was given him he would say, "A book! a book! buy a book."

In his fourth year he began the study of Latin; in his ninth, the study of Greek; in his tenth, the study of French; and in his thirteenth, the study of Hebrew.

During the play-hours in his father's school, his mother promised a copper-medal to those of the pupils who would construct the best verses, when little Isaac, but some seven years of age produced the couplet:—

"I write not for your farthing, but to try
How I your farthing-writers can outvie."

His piety was very early manifested. Well could he adopt the beautiful language of Mrs. Rowe:—"My infant hands were early lifted up to Thee, and I soon learned to know and acknowledge the God of my fathers."

ABNEY HOUSE WHERE WATTS LIVED AND DIED.

In 1698, on his birthday, when just twenty-four years of age, he preached his first sermon, and in the same year was chosen assistant pastor of the Independent Church, Mark Lane, London, and in 1702, became its sole pastor.

On account of his feeble health his people provided him with an assistant, the Rev. Samuel Price. Though an invalid, Dr. Watts served his church for nearly fifty years. Often his exertions in the pulpit were followed by such weakness and pain that he was obliged to retire immediately to bed and have his room closed in darkness and silence.

Invited by Sir Thomas Abney in 1712 to visit his mansion at Theobalds, for a change of air, he gladly complied. It became his home for the rest of his life.

A lady calling to see him one day, Dr. Watts said: "Madam, your ladyship is come to see me on a very remarkable day. This very day, thirty years ago, I came to the house of my good friend, Sir Thomas Abney, intending to spend but one single week under his friendly roof, and I have extended my visit to his family to the length of exactly thirty years."

Lady Abney, who was present, immediately replied, "Sir, what you term a long thirty years' visit, I consider the shortest my family has ever received."

Soon after he had a dangerous illness, from which, after a long confinement, he but slowly recovered.

Dr. Gibbons says: "Here he dwelt in a family, which, for piety, order, harmony, and every virtue, was a house of God. Here he had the privilege of a country recess, the fragrant bower, the spreading lawn, the flowery garden, and other advantages to soothe his mind, and aid his restoration to health; to yield him, whenever he chose them, most grateful intervals from his laborious studies, and to return to them with redoubled vigor and delight."

His physical frame is thus described by his biographer: "He measured only about five feet in height, and was of a slender form. His complexion was pale and fair, his eyes small and gray, but when animated, became piercing and expressive; his forehead was low, his cheek bones rather prominent; but his countenance was, on the whole, by no means disagreeable. His voice was pleasant, but weak. A stranger would, probably, have been most attracted by his piercing eye, whose very glance was able to command attention and awe."

Being at a hotel with some friends, some one made the remark, rather contemptuously,— "What! is that the *great* Dr. Watts?" As this was unexpectedly overheard by Dr. Watts, he at once replied, as he turned towards the critic, and said:—

> "Were I so tall to reach the pole,
> Or grasp the ocean with my span,
> I must be measured by my soul,
> The mind's the standard of the man."

The apt reply is said to have produced silent admiration for the "great" little man.

Dr Gibbons speaks thus of his mental greatness:—

"Perhaps very few of the descendents of Adam have made nearer approaches to angels in intellectual powers and divine dispositions than Dr. Watts; and among the numerous stars which have adorned the hemisphere of the Christian Church he has shone and will shine an orb of the first magnitude."

Dr. Johnson, the eminent lexicographer, gives the following estimate of his capacity:—"Few men," says he, "have left behind such purity of character, or such monuments of laborious piety. He has provided instruction for all ages,—from those who are lisping their first lessons to the enlightened readers of Malebranche and Locke."

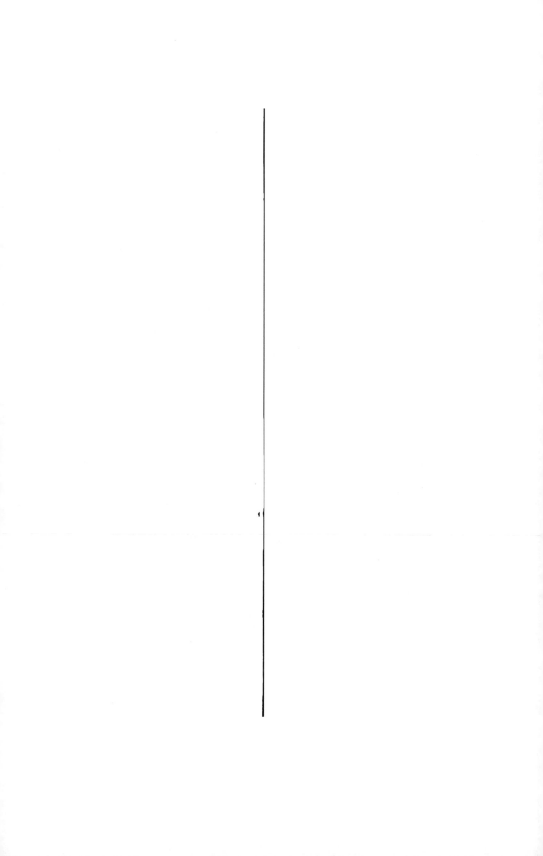

> "Not Jordan's stream, nor death's cold flood,
> Should fright us from the shore."

THIS language was typical of the experience of its author. It is said of Watts, "Calmly and peacefully did his weary, longing spirit leave its feeble earthly tenement and wing its way to God."

Often would he say; "I bless God I can lie down with comfort at night, not being solicitous whether I wake in this world or another." Before his departure, he said:

"It is good to say as Mr. Baxter, 'What, when, and where God pleases.' If God should raise me up again I may finish some more of my papers, or God can make use of me to save a soul, and that will be worth living for. . . . . It is a great mercy to me that I have no manner of fear or dread of death: I could if God please, lay my head back and die without terror, this afternoon or night."

Being "worn out by infirmities and labor," rather than by any particular disease, he simply ceased to breathe on the 25th of November, 1748, in the 75th year of his age.

In accordance with his catholic spirit, and his expressed wish, his body was conveyed to its resting-place by pall-bearers that consisted of two ministers from each of the three denominations.

The following description of his monument is given in the *Sabbath at Home*.

A MONUMENT in honor of Dr. Watts was erected some years ago in the town of his birth. It was the product of public subscription. On the inauguration-day, an address was delivered by the Earl of Shaftesbury; and the memorial was afterward formally delivered over to the mayor and corporation of Southampton. The monument, sculptured by Mr. R. T. Lucas, stands in the Western Park. It has an entire height of nineteen feet, with a base eight and a half feet square. The statue represents the minister of religion addressing his congregation, and is of the purest white Sicilian marble, about eight feet high, facing the south. It surmounts a pedestal of fine polished gray Aberdeen granite, which has three marble basso-rilievos on the sides. One on the front represents the teacher instructing a beautiful group of children, under which is the motto,—

"He gave to lisping infancy its earliest and purest lessons."

The youthful poet is sculptured on the west side, with upturned glance; and underneath is his own descriptive line:—

"To heaven I lift my waiting eyes."

On the east side, Dr. Watts is depicted as a philosopher with globe, telescope, hour-glass, and Dr. Johnson's delineation of him:—

"He taught the art of reasoning and the science of the stars."

On the north side is a marble tablet, with an inscription written by John Bullar, Esq:—

A. D. 1861.
Erected by Voluntary Subscriptions,
In memory of Isaac Watts, D. D.,
A native of Southampton.
Born 1674; died 1748.

An example of the talents of a large and liberal mind, wholly devoted to the promotion of piety, virtue, and literature.

A name honored for his sacred hymns wherever the English language extends.

Especially the friend of children and of youth, for whose best welfare he labored well and wisely, without thought of fame or gain.

"From all that dwell below the skies
Let the Creator's praise arise;
Let the Redeemer's name be sung,
Through every land by every tongue."
Watts.

MONUMENT OF WATTS.

"How Vain are All Things here Below."

REV. DR. WATTS is the author of this expressive hymn. Dr. Belcher narrates the following interesting facts as to its origin:—

It is well known that the worthy doctor lived and died a bachelor. The cause of this seems to have been that in early life he met with a severe disappointment. Attracted by the personal, the intellectual, and spiritual lovliness of Miss Elizabeth Singer, afterward the well-known Mrs. Rowe, Isaac Watts tendered to her his heart and his hand, and was unhappily repulsed,—the lady telling him that, though she loved the jewel, she could not admire the casket which contained it. Thus was poor Watts treated, as were others, by this excellent but surely somewhat capricious lady, whom Mrs. Barbauld in some degree taunted when she said to her, in the language of high compliment,—

> "Thynne, Carteret, Blackmore, Orrery approved,
> And Prior praised, and noble Hertford loved:
> Seraphic Ken and tuneful Watts were thine,
> And Virtue's noblest champions filled the line."

Though disappointed and grieved, the pious poet submitted to what he considered an arrangement of Divine Providence, and then wrote the hymn to which we have referred the beauty of which both the Christian and the poet will admire. Happy the man who could at such a time pray,

> "Dear Saviour, let thy beauties be
> My soul's eternal food."

Origin of Watts' First Hymn.

IT can be easily imagined how verses, like those given on another page (507) must have grated on the sensitive ears of Watts. It was to him like the sound of the file in sharpening the saw.

When giving vent to his wounded feelings, the answer was, "Give us something better, young man."

He complied with the request, and the church was invited to close its service in the evening with the following new hymn:—

> "Behold the glories of the Lamb
> Amidst His Father's throne;
> Prepare new honors for His name,
> And songs before unknown."

The hymn consisted of eight verses, and was the first of that long list which has wreathed his name with immortal glory.

Origin of "There is a land of pure delight."

WATTS, it is said, wrote this hymn in his native town, Southampton, "while sitting at the window of a parlor, which overlooked the river Itchen, and in full view of the Isle of Wight. It is indeed a beautiful type of that paradise of which the poet sung. It rises from the margin of the flood and swells into boundless prospect, all mantled in the richest verdure of summer, checkered with forest-growth and fruitful fields under the highest cultivation, and gardens, and villas, and every adornment which the hand of man, in a series of ages, could create on such susceptible grounds. As the poet looked upon the waters then before him, he thought of the final passage of the Christian:—

> "Death, like a narrow sea, divides
> This heavenly land from ours."

> "Give me the wings of faith to rise
> Within the vail, and see
> The saints above, how great their joys,
> How bright their glories be."

DODDRIDGE wrote in a letter to Watts an account of the effect produced by the singing of this, his hymn, soon after it was composed.

Says he: "I was preaching to a large assembly of plain country people at a village, when, after a sermon from Heb. vi. 12, we sung one of your hymns, * * * * and in that part of the worship, I had the satisfaction to observe tears in the eyes of several of the people. After the service was over, some of them told me that they were not able to sing, so deeply were their minds affected; and the clerk in particular said he could hardly utter the words as he gave them out." This hymn is said to be "one of the finest in the collection."

Toplady, the author of Rock of ages, longed for these—

> "———wings of faith, to rise
> Within the vail———."

Said he, "O how this soul of mine longs to be gone: like an imprisoned bird, it longs to take its flight. O that I had the wings of a dove, I should flee away to the realms of bliss, and be at rest for ever. I long to be absent from the body and present with the Lord." At another time he said, "O what a day of sunshine has this been to me. I have no words to express it; it is unutterable. O, my friends, how good our God is. Almost without interruption his presence has been with me." Being near his end, having awakened out of sleep, he said: "O what delights: who can fathom the joys of the third heavens!" And just before he expired, he said: "The sky is clear; there is no cloud: Lord Jesus, come quickly."

A Heart Broken by a Hymn.

DR. Belcher gives the following narrative as furnished by Rev. J. Parker.

I was seated at the table of a boarding house, kept by Mrs. F——, at which were some fifteen guests. One of these was a gentleman full of animation, and whose vivacity created the impression, that whoever else might be affected by the solemnities of the time, he was not.

On a sunday morning, Rev. Dr. Perrine preached an effective sermon on the consequences of a life of sin. Full of unction and tenderness, its vivid pictures of hell's torments produced a most solemn effect.

As we were sitting at the dinner table, and remarks were passing freely in regard to the morning service, the young man above mentioned expressed in strong terms his disapprobation of the sermon, and added, "Such preaching only hardens me and makes me worse." I replied, "It is possible that you think it makes you worse, when it only makes you conscious of sin that was before slumbering in your heart." "No," said he, "it hardens me. I am at this moment less susceptible to any thing like conviction for hearing that discourse. I feel more inclined to resist every thing like good impressions than usual." "Yet," I rejoined, "*good impressions* are those which are best adapted to secure the desired end; and I am greatly mistaken if an increase of the effect which you feel would not be greatly useful to you. If, for instance, you should read now the Fifty-First Psalm,-

"Show pity, Lord; O Lord, forgive."

it would take a deep hold on your heart."

"Not the least," said he, "I could read it without moving a muscle. I wish I had the book, I would read it to you."

"We have one," said Mrs. F——, who was fully aware of the excitement under which he was laboring; and the book was handed him, opened at the place. He commenced to read, with compressed lips and firm voice:

> "Show pity, Lord; O Lord, forgive;
> Let a repenting sinner live:
> Are not thy mercies large and free?
> May not a sinner trust in Thee?"

Toward the last part of this stanza a little tremulousness of voice was plainly discernible. He rallied again, however, and commenced the second verse with more firmness:

> "Oh, wash my soul from every sin,
> And make my guilty conscience clean:
> Here on my heart the burden lies,
> And past offences pain mine eyes."

At the last part of this stanza his voice faltered more manifestly. He commenced upon the third verse with great energy, and read in a loud, sonorous voice, the whole company looking on in breathless silence:

> "My lips with shame my sins confess."

As he read the second line,

> "Against thy law, against thy grace,"

his lips quivered, and his utterance became difficult. He paused a little, and entered upon the third line with an apparently new determination:

> "Lord, should thy judgment grow severe."

Yet before he came to the end his voice was almost totally choked; and when he began upon the fourth line,

> "I am condemned, but thou art clear,"

an aspect of utter discouragement marked his countenance, and he could only bring out, in broken sobs, "I am condemned," when his utterance changed to a heart-broken cry of grief, and he rising at the same time rushed from the room, as a deeply convicted sinner.

Hymns upon the Battle-Field.

IT is related of a Christian officer at the battle of Shiloh, that he lay all night on the field, wounded in both thighs. Said he, "The stars shone out clear over the dark battle-field, and I began to think about that God who had given His Son to die for me, and that He was up above those glorious stars. I felt that I ought to praise Him, even while wounded and on that battle-ground. I could not help singing that beautiful hymn:—

"'When I can read my title clear,
To mansions in the skies,
I'll bid farewell to every fear,
And wipe my weeping eyes.'

"There was a Christian brother in the brush near me. I could not see him; but I could hear him. He took up the strain. Another beyond him heard it, and joined in and still others too. We made the field of battle *ring* with the hymn of praise to God." To which one adds:

"What an exquisite touch that is in ancient Job, where a 'widow's heart is made to sing for joy.' So Paul and Silas felt such inward gratitude and joy that even at midnight, in their noxious and filthy dungeon, they pealed out God's praises. When a soul is filled with the love of Jesus, the voice of praise is irrepressible."

REV. MR. SPURGEON says: "At the battle of Dunbar, when Cromwell and his men fought up hill, and step by step achieved the victory, their watchword was the Lord of hosts, and they marched to the battle singing:—

"'O Lord, my God, arise, and let
Mine enemies scattered be;
And let all them that do thee hate,
Before thy presence flee.'

"When they had won the day, the grand old leader,

saint and soldier in one, bade his men halt and sing with him; and there they poured forth a psalm with such lusty music, that the old German ocean might well have clapped its hands in chorus, 'Sing unto the Lord, for he hath triumphed gloriously.'

"But what a song will that be when we, the followers of Christ against sin, shall at last see death and hell overcome, and with our Leader standing in our midst, shall raise the last great hallelujah to God and the Lamb, which hallelujah shall roll on forever and ever."

AFTER the battle of Agincourt was won, the king wanted to acknowledge the divine interposition. Ordering the chaplain to read a psalm, when he came to the words, "Not unto us, O Lord, not unto us, but unto Thy name give the glory," the king and the cavalry dismounted, and all the host, officers and men, prostrated themselves upon the ground.

Hymns Making a Bloody Impression.

AMONG the records of the revolution an incident is given of a party of British soldiers. Having fired into the parsonage of a Presbyterian minister, named Caldwell, in Connecticut, and shot his wife who was at prayers with her infant, the exasperated minister turned out and fought in the ranks of his townsmen.

The ammunition of the patriots, in the article of wadding, failing them at a critical moment, the minister rushed into the chapel, and soon reappeared bearing in his arms a pile of hymn books, which he scattered along the line of combatants, exclaiming: "Now my lads, put Watts (wads) into them."

The historian intimates that it is easy to guess, after this which party was victorious.

"Not all the Blood of Beasts."

PRECIOUS and oft-repeated is this hymn of Dr. Watts. We give herewith some interesting statements relating to it.

A Bible colporteur in London gives the following interview he had with a dying Jewess on the day of her death:

"She had been brought from affluence to abject poverty for the faith of Christ. She had at one time kept her own carriage. One day she cast her eye on the leaf of a hymn-book which had come into the house, covering some butter, and she read upon it these words:—

> 'Not all the blood of beasts
> On Jewish altars slain
> Could give the guilty conscience peace,
> Or wash away the stain.'

"The verse haunted her. She could not dismiss it nor forget it; and after a time she went to a box where she remembered she had a Bible, and, induced by that verse, began to read, and read on until she found Christ Jesus, 'the Lamb slain from the foundation of the world.'

"She became openly a convert to Christianity. This caused her husband to divorce her. He went to India, where he married again and died. She lived in much poverty with two of her nation, Jewish sisters, who had also become Christians.

"She died triumphing in Christ as her Rock, quoting and applying to him the Psalms of David, passing without a fear through the dark valley."

THE Rev. J. D. Reardon, in illustrating the "joys of salvation," said, that, like Zaccheus, he himself was led as a penitent to receive "Christ joyfully." Heavily laden with guilt and fear, and groping for a long while in darkness, he was in a moment brought into the light and liberty of God's people by the quoting of the third verse of this hymn.

His pastor had been unfolding the way of salvation to him and other inquirers, when, to impress the truth of the Bible contained in this verse, he reached out his hands just as the ancient priest was supposed to do when placing the sins of the people upon the scape goat, and said, "Sinner, it is just this, only this for you to do, and say:—

> "My faith would lay her hand
> On that dear head of Thine,
> While like a penitent I stand,
> And there confess my sin."

My eyes opened at once to see it. I burst out with laughter; I couldn't help it. My heart in a moment was filled with joy and has been ever since.

SOME military officers and other Christian friends in Montreal were singing the hymn—

> "Not all the blood of beasts,"

when Captain L—— remarked to Captain Hammond, "I have a curious fancy concerning that hymn: I should like it sung by six young men as they lower me into the grave." It was but a short time afterward when he died, and his body sank to rest in the grave amid the impressive singing of the hymn, as requested; and soon after this his friend Captain Hammond also followed him to the eternal world.

"My Faith would Lay her Hand."

VERY beautiful is the Scripture figure that underlies this, the third verse of the hymn:

"Not all the blood of beasts."

An English clergyman gives the following statement:

I knew of a little child in Kingston, who in her dreams seemed to remember what I had been preaching about, one morning particularly calling to mind these words of the hymn:

"My faith would lay her hand
On that dear head of thine."

You know, when Dr. Watts wrote these words, he referred to the Levitical custom of putting the hands on the head of the sacrifice, and confessing the sins of the people over it: thus laying the burden of their sins upon him, that when he went forth he took them far away—away to the land of forgetfulness, where they could never be found or remembered again.

This young disciple in her sleep thought, "Oh! how I should like to put *my* hand on his dear bleeding head." Then she thought she saw the blessed Saviour nailed to the cross, enduring such agony; His sacred head was bowed, weighed down with the awful load of sin; and as she gazed steadfastly, she thought she drew near, and by some means found herself putting one hand *on* that bleeding head, and the other *under* it, to support it and bear it up. "And oh!" she felt, "how happy am I to do this. Oh! this is bliss—this is life!"

"Before Jehovah's awful throne."

THIS is Watts' version of the hundredth Psalm. The first verse, which is now omitted, reads thus:—

> "Sing to the Lord with joyful voice;
> Let every land His name adore;
> The British isles shall send the noise
> Across the ocean to the shore."

The first two lines of the second verse,—

> "Nations attend before His throne,
> With solemn fear, with sacred joy,"

were altered and greatly improved by Wesley, and made the beginning of the hymn as now in use:—

> "Before Jehovah's awful throne,
> Ye nations, bow with sacred joy,"

Dr. Dempter, formerly the senior professor in the Garrett Biblical Institute, relates a happy effect produced while singing this hymn upon the sea. He was going to South America, accompanied with his wife and two other missionaries and their wives, when to their surprise, they found a pirate vessel in fast pursuit of them. As the disguised enemy refused to exchange salutations, and kept drawing nearer, they ascended to the deck and engaged in singing to the tune of "Old Hundred" this grand old hymn:—

> "Before Jehovah's awful throne,
> Ye nations, bow with sacred joy;
> Know that the Lord is God alone;
> He can create, and He destroy."

Dropping on their knees, they prepared to meet what seemed to be their doom, in earnest prayer. The echo of this hymn and prayer seemed to have had the desired effect, for soon after, the pirates were seen to turn away and disappear. Truthfully they sung in the hymn:—

> "We are His people, we His care."

The Closed Lips.

A daughter had grown up to maturity in a Christian family, who was always accustomed to hear a father's voice lead in prayer and praise before breakfast.

Although busily employed in secular engagements, he could always find time to worship Him, who was all the time caring for, and loving him.

He could not afford to travel on life's dangerous journey without daily renewing his spiritual, as well as his physical strength.

Placing his incense upon the family altar, he would blend his voice with the Psalmist in singing,

> "Lord, in the morning thou shalt hear
> My voice ascending high;
> To thee will I direct my prayer,
> To thee lift up mine eye."

The daughter, being so often prayed for, had become so accustomed to the familiar sound, that it seemed like a meaningless song.

During the silence of a midnight hour, a cry was heard "Behold the bridegroom cometh." The father, with his well filled and well trimmed lamp, entered the marriage feast of the Lamb.

The usual breakfast hour arrived for those who were left behind. The victuals were steaming on the table, ready to be eaten. But as the worship always preceded the meal, they were afraid to approach the table. There lay the old Bible and hymn book waiting for use. After a long, sad silence, the young lady stole away to a side room, in which lay her father on his cooling board. As the morning sun was peeping in, she drew down the white linen from his closed lips, and exclaimed with uplifted hands and streaming eyes, "O God who'll pray for us now."

A Singular Coincidence.

SOME few years ago, one of the Boston papers related a very beautiful coincidence. During the morning service at Christ's Church, Salem Street, an incident occurred which would have been interpreted by some of the ancients as a signal of divine approbation. The Rev. Mr. Marcus, of Nantucket, the officiating minister, read, in order to be sung, the Eighty-Fourth Psalm, in which may be found the verse,—

> "The birds, more happier far than I,
> Around thy temple throng:
> Securely there they build, and there
> Securely hatch their young."

While he was reading this psalm, a dove flew in at one of the windows and alighted on the capital of one of the pilasters near the altar, and almost over the head of the reader. A note of the psalm and hymn to be sung had been previously given, as is customary, to the choir, or it might have been supposed that there was design in the selection; for the second hymn commenced,—

> "Come, Holy Spirit, Heavenly Dove,
> With all thy quickening powers,
> Kindle a flame of sacred love
> In these cold hearts of ours!"

The preacher was unconscious of the presence of the bird until the close of the services, when the innocent visitor was suffered to depart in peace.

"Alas! and did my Saviour bleed,
And did my sovereign die."

AT Nashville cemetery Tenn., a stranger was seen planting a flower over a soldier's grave.

When asked: "Was your son buried there?" "No" "A brother?" "No." "A relative?" "No."

After a moment's pause the stranger laid down a small board which he had in his hand, and said: "Well, I will tell you. When the war broke out I lived in Illinois. I wanted to enlist, but was poor. I had a wife and seven children. I was drafted. I had no money to hire a substitute, so made up my mind that I must leave my poor, sickly children, and go.

After I had got all things ready to go, a young man whom I knew came to me and said: 'You have a large family, which your wife cannot take care of. I will go for you.' He did go in my place, and in the battle of Chickamauga was wounded, and taken to Nashville. Here he died, ever since I have wished to come to see his grave, so I have saved up all the spare money I could, and came on, and found my dear friend's grave."

With tears of gratitude running down his cheek, he took up a board and pressed it down into the ground as a tomb-stone.

Under the soldier's name were written only these words: "He died for me."

This was a touching exhibition of love and gratitude. But how much greater reason have we as sinners with grateful hearts, to inscribe on the uplifted cross; "JESUS DIED FOR ME."

> "Well might the sun in darkness hide,
> And shut his glories in."

A HISTORIAN gives us the following interesting facts:—

"The wonderful darkening of the sun at our Lord's death, and earthquake, are recorded by Phlegon, whom Eusebius calls an excellent computer of the Olympiads. He says: 'Then there was a great and wonderful eclipse beyond any that ever happened. The day, at the sixth hour, was so far turned into dark night that the stars appeared; and an earthquake in Bithynia did overthrow many houses in the city of Nice.

"'Now this darkening of the sun recorded by Phlegon and that in the holy evangelists at our Lord's death, are the one and the same; for both happened the same year, namely, the eighteenth of Tiberius; the same hour, viz, the sixth hour of the day; and a great earthquake made both more memorable.

"'Therefore, Tertulian, when pleading the cause of Christians against the heathen, appeals to their public tables and records as witnesses of the fact.

"'Lucianus of Antioch, the martyr, appeals to the archives of Nicomedia, before the president of the city: 'Consult,' said he, 'the annals, and you'll find that, in the time of Pilate, while Christ suffered, in the middle of the day, the sun did disappear, and chase away the day.' 'Tis also observable that it is reported in the history of China, written by Hadrianus Greslonius, that the Chinese remark: 'That at the same time we Christians compute Christ suffered, in the month of April, an extraordinary eclipse, beyond the laws and observation of the motions of the planets, then happened, at which event Quamvutius the emperor was very much moved.'

"Here, Lord, I give myself away."

MR. RALPH WELLS tells of a little girl who presented him with a small bouquet of dandelions—an ordinary flower, but early, and doubtless the only one she could well procure at that season. He inquired why she gave him the bouquet.

"Because I love you," the child answered.

"Do you bring little gifts to Jesus?" said Mr. Wells.

"Oh," said the little child, "*I give myself to Him.*"

ONE evening several newly-converted people were telling each other what God had done for their souls. Among them a little girl about seven years of age, with a face beaming with happiness, said, "I have given up *my heart* to Jesus, *every bit of it!*"

TWO days after a boy had found the Saviour he appeared at a meeting with a sad countenance. A tear was trickling down his cheeks. His pastor said to him, "What is the matter, John? I thought you had given your heart to Jesus."

"Yes," said John, "I did give him my heart, but I have taken it back again."

"I HAVE given my tongue to God," said a little boy, "so I must take care how I use it."

A YOUNG man, very poor, having no money to put on the plate at a missionary meeting, wrote on a slip of paper, "Myself," and dropped that in.

SAID a little girl, "Mother, I can't tell how happy I felt in prayer this morning! When I gave myself to God, it seemed as if there was a sun in my heart."

"Tis all that I can do."

THIS is the last line of the hymn noticed on the preceding pages.

In eastern Pennsylvania, during a season of revival, a lad solicited the prayers of the church for some two weeks, and on the last night of the protracted meeting, having found no relief, he proposed to two Christian friends, on leaving the church door, that if they would pray for him at their homes, he would spend the night in prayer.

Entering a barn he ascended the hay-mow and engaged in earnest pleadings for mercy. The dawn of day scattered the darkness of night but found him still shrouded in gloom. When at length the streaks of sunlight shot across the haymow, he arose from his knees in utter despair, saying in the deepest agony, "Well, its all of no use, I have done all *I can do.*" As he seated himself upon the beam which overhung the threshing-floor his eyes were opened to see his mistake in hiding behind what he and others were doing, rather than in what Christ had already done for him. So leaving go every human prop his heart utterance was,

> "A guilty, weak and helpless worm
> On thy kind arms I fall,
> Be Thou my strength and righteousness,
> My Jesus, and my all."

As he dropped from the haymow, he seemed to fall into the loving arms of his complete Saviour, fully realizing the import of the words,

> "Tis all that I can do."

and ran out of the barn with joyful haste to tell his friends the good news of his salvation.

"Love so amazing, so divine,
Demands my soul, my life, my all."

SOMETIMES these lines are sung when they do not give a true expression of the feelings of the heart. As these thoughts were brought out in a charity sermon, a stingy Christian, nearly deaf, unconsciously talked out the struggle that was going on within. As reported by the *Presbyterian*, "he sat under the pulpit with his ear trumpet directed upward toward the preacher. The sermon moved him considerably. At one time he said to himself—"I'll give ten dollars;" again he said, "I'll give fifteen." At the close of the appeal he was very much moved and thought he would give fifty dollars. Now, the boxes were passed. As they moved along, his charity began to ooze out. He came down from fifty to twenty, to ten, to five, to zero. He concluded he would not give anything. "Yet said he, "this won't do—I am in a bad fix. This covetousness will be my ruin."

"The boxes were getting nearer and nearer. The crisis was now upon him What should he do? The box was now under his chin—all the congregation were looking. He had been holding his pocket-book in his hand during this soliloquy, which was half audible, though in his deafness he did not know that he was heard. In agony of the final moment he took his pocket-book and laid it in the box, saying to himself as he did it,—"*Now squirm old natur!*"

"Singing Lies."

A LITTLE girl gave as her reason for not singing in Sunday school, that she could not *sing lies*. After relating some of her wicked acts to her mother, she asked, "How then could I stand up and sing:—

"Jesus loves me, this I know,"

Is it not as wrong to *sing* as it is to *tell* lies?"

IN a church in London, the hymn commencing,

"When I survey the wondrous cross,"

was sung after a collection had been taken.

When it ended the preacher slowly repeated the last line:—

"Demands my soul, my life, my all."

adding, "Well, I *am* surprised to hear you sing that. Do you know that altogether you only put fifteen shillings into the bag this morning."

A negro woman in Jamaica was very fond of going to missionary meetings, and singing with great fervor,

"Fly abroad, thou mighty gospel.'

But whenever the plates went round for collection she always sang with her eyes fixed on the ceiling. On one occasion, however, a negro touched her with the plate, and said: "Sissy, it's no use for you to sing 'Fly abroad' with your eyes on the ceiling; it's no use to sing 'fly' at all, unless you give something to make it fly,"

A GENTLEMAN in Kentucky worth $100,000 was present at a meeting to solicit aid for some sufferers.

He wept profusely. and when the plate went round he gave *fifty cents;* whereupon a little girl sitting near, said: "That was a heap of crying for a little giving."

A Hymn Illustrated while it was Being Sung.

A SPEAKER, arguing in favor of addressing the eye as well as the ear, said that man was more anxious to *see* than to hear. As evidence he referred to the almost universal tendency, during preaching, for an audience to turn round their heads to *see* when any persons may be entering the church, no matter what is being said.

Commencing the delivery of a course of "Illustrated Sermons" in a section of New Jersey, where the people had become accustomed to swing around their heads whenever the church door swung open, we were considerably impressed with a singular coincidence.

In these sermons, we have the hymns painted on canvass to appear above the pulpit in the same frame-work that supports the Scripture scenes used as illustrations, so that all are enabled to join in the singing. On this occasion the hymn being sung was:—

"Come, Holy Spirit, heavenly dove,
  With all Thy quick'ning power."

But as we got along to the words,

"Look how we grovel here below,
  Fond of these trifling toys,"

they turned their heads around with a groveling look to see what "earthly toys" were appearing at the opening church door. A *few* kept on singing the timely words:—

"In vain we tune our formal songs,
  In vain we strive to rise."

But as a long string of other tardy ones came pressing up the aisles, the sound gradually languished away as only a very few continued truthfully to sing:—

"Hosannas languish on our tongues,
  And our devotion dies,"

until at length the pastor, myself, and the organ sang out:

"Dear Lord, and shall we ever live
  At this poor dying rate."

"Kindle a flame of sacred love."

A SPEAKER, in illustrating the want of religious enthusiasm, said:—

"A Scottish doctor got fidgety because the train was delaying.

"'What's the matter? Isn't there plenty of water?' some one asked.

"'O yes,' was the reply; 'there's plenty o' water; but it isn't a bilin'!'

"There is the trouble with a great many trains of usefulness that ought to be moving. Water enough, but 'it isn't a boiling!'"

"SUPPOSE," says one, "we saw an army of soldiers before a granite fort and they told us they intended to batter it down, we might ask, with what?" They point to a cannon-ball. Well, but there is no power in that. They say, 'No; but look at the cannon.' Well, but there is no power in that. A child may ride upon it; a bird may perch in its mouth. It is a machine, and nothing more. 'But look at the powder.' Well, there is no power in that; a child may spill it, a sparrow may pick it. Yet this powerless powder and powerless ball are put in the powerless cannon; one spark of fire enters it, and then in a twinkling of an eye that powder is a flash of lightning, and that cannon-ball is a thunderbolt, which smites as if it had been sent from heaven. So it is with our church (or school) machinery of this day; we have the instruments necessary for pulling down strong holds, but oh, for the fire from heaven!"

It was the "live coal" from the altar that touched the lips of Isaiah; it was when the Spirit rested upon the disciples as flaming tongues of fire that they were endued with power. John was a *burning* and shining light.

A Hymn that a Church Refused to Sing.

THE late Rev. R. V. Lawrence related the following interesting incident that occurred in New Jersey:

"A minister was called to take charge of a congregation that his predecessor had left in a blessed state of revival, with hearts all aglow with the heavenly fire.

"At the first prayer-meeting service he began to read the hymn:—

> "'Come Holy Spirit heavenly dove
> With all Thy quick'ning powers,'"

As he read the next two lines,

> "'Kindle a flame of sacred love
> In these cold hearts of ours'

a brother called out, 'Dear pastor, that hymn does not suit us. Our hearts are not "cold."' As he still proceeded in reading the next verse,

> "Look how we grovel here below
> Fond of these trifling toys!
> Our souls can neither fly nor go
> To reach eternal joys.'

another responded 'We *can* "fly" and "go" and "reach eternal joys."'

"The confused pastor however persisted in reading the third verse.

> "'In vain we tune our formal songs
> In vain we strive to rise:
> Hosannas languish on our tongues
> And our devotion dies.'

When being told again that their songs were *not* 'formal,' that their 'hosannas' did *not* 'languish,' he closed by saying, 'Well, that is *my* condition if it is not *yours*.' Asking the prayers of the warm hearted brethren on his behalf, he dropped on bended knees."

A Hymn to Wake up the Sleepers.

A PASTOR, preaching in Southern New Jersey, finding a goodly number of his hearers accustomed to take a churchly nap, undertook a plan to break up the habit. He told his chorister that on some occasion when he found his drowsy hearers asleep, he would stop preaching and turn around to drink a glass of water, and when that signal was given he should, without any further notice, burst out in singing the hymn:—

> "My drowsy powers why sleep ye so?
> Awake! my sluggish soul."

One evening as he observed the sleepy heads nodding, he thought he would try his experiment. So coming to a sudden stop in his discourse, he lifted the glass of water to his lips, but the expected sound of singing did not follow. When lo! to his astonishment, he found the chorister himself asleep. A friend near by who was in the secret woke him up, when he saw at a glance what was wanted, and at once commenced singing the appropriate words;

> "My drowsy powers why sleep ye so?
> Awake! my sluggish soul.
> Nothing has half thy work to do
> Yet nothing's half so dull."

This aroused the sleepers, who, thinking that the sermon had closed and that this was the last hymn, at once arose to their feet, as was the custom in singing. But as they stood alone, and saw others laughing, they soon perceived their mistake and one after another sat down again to the great amusement of the wakeful part of the audience.

It was a long while before the pastor had occasion to resort to another expedient to stir up the "drowsy powers" of "sluggish souls."

> "I'll speak the honors of Thy name
> With my last laboring breath."

WHEN Beveridge was on his death-bed a ministerial friend called to see him. When conducted into the bed-room, he said, "Bishop Beveridge, do you know me?" "Who are you?" said the Bishop. Being told, he answered, "I don't know you."

Another friend, equally well-known, asked him the same question; but still his answer was, "I don't know you."

Then his wife asked him if he knew her; still the answer was, "I don't know you." At length, one said, "Do you know the Lord Jesus Christ?" "Jesus Christ?" said he, reviving, as if the name had the influence of a charm; "O yes, I have known him these forty years. Precious Saviour, HE IS MY ONLY HOPE."

VERY similar was the experience of Rev. Dudley A. Tyng, who breathed out towards his last the ever-memorable words, "Stand up for Jesus."

Says his father, Rev. Dr. Stephen H. Tyng,—

"But the power of life was now very rapidly sinking. Soon he seemed no longer conscious of our presence, his eyes were fixed, and the blood settled around them in the dark hue of death.

"At his physician's request, I roused him again, and asked him with a loud voice, 'Do you see me, my dear son?' 'No.' 'Do you know me?' 'No.' 'Do you not know your father's voice?' 'No.' His wife then made the same attempts, with the same result. Then I said, 'Do you know Jesus?' 'Oh! yes,' in a voice of wonderful strength and deliberation, very loud, as if to be able to hear his own voice, and very slow, as if the power of speech was passing away, '*I know Jesus.*'"

"And must this body die?
This mortal frame decay?"

XERXES the Great, was much impressed by this thought while on his way to conquer Greece. Having paused on the banks of the Hellespont, he gathered around him his immense army of some two million soldiers in battle array,—the largest body of men, it is thought, that were ever before or since thus assembled. After causing a marble throne to be erected on an eminence, he seated himself upon it. As he looked down upon such a sea of upturned faces,—of men willing to do or dare anything for their leader,—smiles of approbation wreathed his countenance, but, at length, tears were found to stream down his face, when an astonished friend by his side inquired, "Xerxes the Great, why weepest thou?" He replied, "The thought has just filled my mind, that in one hundred years hence, not one of those millions will be above ground."

"Shall I not weep?"

THIS was the question of Rabbi Jochanan Ben Zachi. When sick his disciples visited him, and as he began to weep, they said unto him, "Rabbi, the light of Israel, the right hand pillar, wherefore dost thou weep?" He answered "Now I am going before the King of kings, the holy God; if he condemn me to death, that death will be eternal; there are before me two ways, the one to hell and the other to paradise, and I know not into which they are carrying me, *shall I not weep?*"

Charles Wesley and his Hymns.

AMONG uninspired men, whom God has raised up to furnish songs for Zion, Watts and Wesley stand pre-eminent. Which of the two was the greater, the light of eternity only can reveal. Neither is it a matter of any great moment for us to know, as both laid their trophies at Jesus' feet and crowned Him Lord of all. "Watts created a people's hymnal; Wesley created a people of hymn singers." Watts wrote in retirement and leisure; Wesley amid a great religious upheaval, and under the inspiration of the moment. The hymns of Watts were begotten in time of general religious dearth; those of Wesley, amid the refreshing showers of a gracious revival. While Wesley wrote seven thousand hymns, and thus excelled in numbers, Watts wrote but six hundred and ninety-seven, and yet far outnumbers Wesley in the quantity of his hymns in actual use.* Isabella L. Bird, an able and prolific writer on the subject of hymnology, says:—

"Judging from the results of an examination of seven hundred and fifty hymn books, it is safe to assign to Watts the authorship of two-fifths of the hymns, which are used in public worship in the English speaking world."

Charles Wesley was born December, 18, 1708. He was the third son of the Rev. Samuel Wesley, Sr., who was rector of the Episcopal church at Epworth, England.

It is not surprising that the Wesleys became so eminently useful, when we look into the heart of their saintly mother, who trained them for service. Writing of her Saviour, says she: "O my dear Charles, when I consider the dignity of his person, the perfectness of his purity, the greatness of his sufferings, but above all, his boundless love, I am astonished and utterly confounded. I am lost

---

* In Methodist circles Wesley's hymns outnumber Watts' more than four-fold.

CWesley

in thought. I fall into nothing before Him." It was a singular coincidence that Wesley wrote the following lines, when he was forty, and died in his eightieth year.

"And have I measured half my days,
And half my journey run?"*

Having been thrown from his horse one day, he made the following record: "My companions thought I had broken my neck; but my leg only was bruised, my hand sprained, and my head stunned, which *spoiled my making hymns* until—next day." From 1738 to 1788, Wesley issued, in connection with his brother, John, thirty-nine different books of hymns and poetry.

The Church of England closed her doors against Wesley while living, but now her most magnificent cathedrals echo with such of his hymns as "Hark, the herald angels sing," "Christ the Lord is risen to-day," and "Hail the day that sees Him rise." The hymns used by the eleven millions of people, which the Methodists are supposed to number, are mainly his, and every year as his merits become better known, and as Christians get nearer each other as they get nearer the cross, the hymns of Charles Wesley become more highly appreciated and more widely used.

Wesley began to write hymns when he was twenty-nine and kept his pen going till in his eightieth year, and when at last it dropped from his hand, in the hour of death, he could not yet keep silent, but dictated his last hymn, just as he was preparing to mount up, and join in the hallelujahs of the skies. How significant therefore his last words in verse:—

"In age and feebleness extreme,
Who shall a helpless worm redeem?
Jesus my only hope thou art,
Strength to my failing flesh and heart;
Oh, could I catch a smile from thee,
Then drop into eternity."

---

* See Creamer's "Methodist Hymnology," page 344.

A Thousand Tongues to Sing.

O Charles Wesley, the Christian world is indebted for many of its most precious hymns. The instrument that led him into the sunlight of God's grace, was a Mrs. Turner, a poor Moravian woman.

During a spell of sickness, he was detained in London, at the house of a pious mechanic, of whom, it is said, "he knew nothing but Christ."

After a night of agony, Wesley awoke, May 21 1738, "full of tossings to and fro," calling aloud, "O Jesus, thou hast said, '*I will come unto you.*' Thou hast said, '*I will send the comforter unto you.*' Thou hast said, '*My Father and I will come unto you and will make our abode with you.*' Thou art God, who can'st not lie. I wholly rely upon thy promise."

As Mrs. Turner heard these plaintive cries, she was constrained to gently say through the slightly opened door, "*In the name of Jesus of Nazareth arise, and believe, and thou shalt be healed of all thy infirmities.*"

It was "a word fitly spoken." Said he, "O that Christ would but thus speak to me," and then added "I believe, I believe." The victory was won. The clouds of unbelief melted away, before the rising sun.

With a heart burning with love to the newly-found Saviour, he took his pen, and wrote the hymn;

> "O for a thousand tongues to sing
> My dear Redeemer's praise;
> The glories of my God and King,
> The triumphs of his grace!"

> "O may it all my powers engage
> To do my Master's will."

CHARLES WESLEY fully exemplified these lines of his hymn, relating to "A charge to keep I have."

Mr. Moore gives this description of his absorption in the work of his life, even when nearly eighty years of age:—"He rode every day—clothed for winter even in summer—a little horse, gray with age. When he mounted, if a subject struck him, he proceeded to expand and put it in order. He would write a hymn thus given him, on a card kept for that purpose, with his pencil, in short hand. Not unfrequently he has come to the house in the City Road, and having left the pony in the garden in front, he would enter, crying out, 'Pen and ink! pen and ink!' These being supplied, he wrote the hymn he had been composing. When this was done, he would look round on those present and salute them with much kindness, and thus put all in mind of eternity. He was fond on these occasions of the lines,—

> "There all the ship's company meet,
> Who sailed with the Saviour beneath;
> With shouting each other they greet,
> And triumph o'er sorrow and death;
> The voyage of life's at an end,
> The mortal affliction is past;
> The age that in heaven they spend
> For ever and ever shall last."

When Newton, whose busy pen produced many of our church hymns, was eighty years of age, he was advised to relax his manifold labors. "I cannot stop," said he, raising his voice. "What! shall the old African blasphemer stop while he can speak?"

John Wesley said in like manner in old age:—

> "My body with my charge lay down,
> And cease at once to work and live."

Origin of "Jesus lover of my soul."

CHARLES and John Wesley, and Richard Pilmore were holding one of their twilight meetings on the common, when the mob assailed them, and they were compelled to flee for their lives.

Being separated for a time, as they were being pelted with stones, they at length in their flight, succeeded in getting beyond a hedge row, where they prostrated themselves on the ground, and placed their hands on the back of their heads for protection from the stones which still came so near that they could feel the current of air made by the missiles as they went whizzing over them.

In the night shades that were gathering, they managed to hide from the fury of the rabble in a spring-house. Here they struck a light with a flint-stone, and after dusting their clothes, and washing, they refreshed themselves with the cooling water that came bubbling up in a spring, and rolling out in a silver streamlet.

Charles Wesley pulled out a lead pencil (made by hammering to a point a piece of lead,) and from the inspiration of these surroundings, composed the precious hymn:—

"Jesus, lover of my soul."

The flight had no doubt suggested the second line:—

"Let me to Thy bosom fly."

The waters gliding at his feet,—

"While the nearer waters roll."

Thus it was originally written. It is now often sung:—

"While the billows near me roll."

The tempest and storm from which they had just found a hiding-place, the figure,—

> "While the tempest still is high;
> Hide me, O my Saviour hide
> Till the storm of life is past."

As each was left alone to seek safety in flight,—

> "Leave, Oh, leave me not alone,
> Still support and comfort me."

Trying to cover their defenceless heads with their hands, the lines,—

> "Cover my defenceless head
> With the shadow of Thy wing."

Having sunk to the ground, faint and weary, the third verse. As this is generally omitted, we give it entire:—

> "Wilt Thou not regard my call?
> Wilt Thou not accept my prayer?
> Lo! I sink, I faint, I fall!
> Lo! on Thee I cast my care.
> Reach me out Thy gracious hand!
> While I of Thy strength receive,
> Hoping against hope I stand,
> Dying, and behold I live."

Washing their wounds and bruises the thoughts of the last verse, which is the fifth in the original,—

> "Let the healing streams abound,
> Make and keep me pure within."

And lastly, the fountain of spring-water from which they drank, and obtained fresh life,—

> "Thou of life the fountain art,
> Freely let me take of Thee.
> Spring Thou up within my heart
> Rise to all eternity."

These interesting facts were given by Mr. Pilmore, who was an eye-witness, to an intimate friend, Mr. Hicks, who stated them to Rev. I. H. Torrence of Phila., from whom I received them.

The same statement was also previously given to me by the aged Rev. Dr. Collier, who received them from an Englishman, who was co-temporary with Wesley.

"Jesus, lover of my soul," on a Sinking Ship.

YEARS ago the following touching incident was published in the *Baptist Reaper* concerning two sisters:

"In the midst of their conversation, at the dusk of the evening, they were alarmed by the stopping of the boat. As the girls and Mr. Percy, who were the only passengers on board, rushed to the deck, they were astonished to see the vessel abandoned by the captain and the whole crew, who had just seated themselves in the only boat which had been on board the steamer, and were pulling for the rocky coast, only about a mile distant. The agitation was fearful when the captain stated that the steamer had sprung a leak, and would sink in a few minutes.

"'Oh, stop, stop, for heaven's sake, and save us, too!' cried Mr. Percy.

"'No,' answered the captain, somewhat confused, 'the boat will hold no more; some one will have to be lost.'

"Mr. Percy examined the steamer, and found that she was fast sinking, and that in a very few moments more there would be no possible way of escape. He looked this way and that, to find some means of fleeing to the shore, but he could see no hope. At length he found a a small hatch which could easily be detached, and which, with great skill of management, and the kind favor of Providence, might save one. He threw it into the water and embarked upon it. It was with great difficulty that he kept afloat, and while he was within a few feet of the steamer, it sunk before his eyes. What passed through the minds of the girls, as they met death so suddenly and so terribly, we can only imagine. The period for Mr. Percy's escape was so short, and so full of the most fearful excitement, that he can tell us but little about them. As the steamer was gradually sinking be-

SINGING ON A SINKING VESSEL.

side his slender raft, he saw them standing on the deck, with their arms around each other, and singing:—

> "Jesus, lover of my soul,
> Let me to thy bosom fly,
> While the raging billows roll,
> While the tempest still is high.

As they were about finishing the verse,—

> "All my trust on Thee is stayed;
> All my help from Thee I bring;
> Cover my defenceless head
> With the shadow of Thy wing."

they sank to rise no more.

"Leave, ah! leave me not alone."

REV. T. L. CUYLER thus refers to these lines in "Jesus, lover of my soul."

"The one central, all-prevailing idea of this matchless hymn is the soul's yearning for its Saviour. The figures of speech vary, but not the thought. In one line we see a storm-tossed voyager crying out for shelter till the tempest is over. In another line we see a timid, tearful child nestling in a mother's arms, with the words faltering on its tongue—

> "Let me to Thy bosom fly,"
> "Hangs my helpless soul on Thee."

Two lines of the hymn have been breathed fervently and often out of bleeding hearts. When we were once in the valley of death-shade, with one beautiful child in the new-made grave, and the others threatened with fatal disease, there was no prayer which we said oftener than this:

> "Leave, ah! leave me not alone,
> Still support and comfort me."

We do not doubt that tens of thousands of other bereaved and wounded hearts have tried this piercing cry, out of the depths, "Still support and comfort me!"

Singing Among the Billows.

A SHIP was on fire at sea. During the alarm and confusion, a mother and babe were crowded overboard. She clung to a piece of the wreck and drifted out upon the ocean billows.

Toward evening a vessel bound to Boston was moving slowly along her course. As the captain was walking on the deck, his attention was called to an object, some distance off, which looked like a person in the water. As no vessel was near, the crew thought no one could have fallen overboard. To satisfy their curiosity, a small boat was sent towards the object.

To the surprise of those who remained on deck, they saw that as the rowers approached the drifting speck, they rested on their oars some minutes, then moved on and took in a person or thing. As the boat's crew returned bringing the woman and child, they explained it all, by saying that as they drew near they heard singing—a female voice sweetly singing. So astonished were they that they ceased rowing to listen, when over the waves came ringing the words of the hymn,—

"Jesus lover of my soul."

What joy thrilled this mother's heart in finding that while singing the words,—

"While the billows near me roll,
While the tempest still is high;
Hide me, Oh my Saviour, hide,
Till the storm of life is past."

Jesus was extending a helping hand, and a hiding-place.

"Other refuge have I none."

DURING the rebellion in Ireland in 1793, the rebels had long meditated an attack on the Moravian settlement at Grace-Hill. At length they put their threat in execution, and a large body of them marched to the town. When they arrived there, they saw no one in the street nor in the houses.

The brethren had long expected this attack, but true to their Christian profession, they would not have recourse to arms for their defence but assembled in their chapel, and in solemn prayer besought Him in whom they trusted, to be their shield in the hour of danger.

The ruffians, hitherto breathing nothing but destruction and slaughter, were struck with astonishment at this novel sight. Where they expected an armed hand, they saw it clasped in prayer. Where they expected weapon to weapon, and a body armed for the fight, they saw the bended knee. They heard the prayer for protection; they heard the intended victims asking mercy for their murderers; they heard the song of praise, and the hymn of confidence in the "sure promise of the Lord." So impressed were they by what they thus saw and heard, that they left the place without doing any harm. Others afterward fled to it as "the city of refuge."

AS a little bird was closely pursued by a hawk, it flew for refuge into a garden, and strove to hide among the bushes, but the hawk followed; the little bird again flew, but again barely escaped. Just, however, as its strength was nearly exhausted, and as it would have been torn to pieces by its pursuer, the garden-gate was opened, and a poor old man entered; the little bird flew towards him and darted into his breast, where it nestled safely from the hawk.

"Jesus lover of my soul" in a Hurricane.

SOME twenty years ago a terrific gale swept along the rock bound coast of the British Channel. The crew in charge of a coasting vessel struggled hard and long to reach some shelter, but in vain. Getting into a small boat, they left the ship. "Then came the last pull for life; the boat was swung off and manned; captain and crew united in one more brave effort, but their toiling at the oar was soon over, their boat was swamped.

"They seemed to have sunk together, 'and in death they were not divided,' for, when the morning dawned, they were found lying all but side by side under the shelter of a weedy rock. The ship was borne in upon a heavy sea close under the cliff, where she was jammed immovably between two rocks, and in the morning the ebb tide left her lying high and dry. There was no sign of life on deck. One token of peace and salvation there was; it was the captain's hymn-book still lying on the locker, closed upon the pencil with which the good man had marked the last passages upon which his eye had rested before he left the ship to meet his fate. A leaf of the page was turned down, and there were pencil lines in the margin at several passages of Charles Wesley's precious hymn:—

"Jesus, lover of my soul,
Let me to thy bosom fly."

The Last Hymn on a Wrecked Vessel.

IN the Maria mail-boat in 1826 five missionaries, three wives of missionaries, with several children and nurses were returning to Antiqua. In sight of land, a storm arose, and before its fury the mail-boat was wrecked. When the storm arose, one of the missionaries' sons, a little boy, gave out the verse commencing,

"Though waves and storms go o'er my head."

After this had been sung, a holy inspiration came over the child, and he astonished the party in the boat by the address he gave on the ship-wreck of Jonah. A strange feeling came over those who heard the child. Mrs. Jones, the wife of one of the missionaries, tried to pray, but could not. At length she cried, "Lord! Lord! help me."

Scarcely had she uttered the words, when she became composed and repeated the verse:—

"Jesus protects; my fears begone."

In that time of trouble and sorrow, she gladdened her own heart and those of her companions, by singing for the last hymn most of them heard on earth:—

"When passing through the watery deep,
I asked in faith His promised aid,
The waves an awful distance keep,
And shrink from my devoted head;
Fearless their violence I dare;
They cannot harm for God is there."

She was the only one who could sing in that distressing hour, and the only one saved in that redeemed company.

Singing as death's "billows near me roll."

UTTERANCES of joy, and singing of hymns have often characterized the departure of God's faithful martyrs.

A touching scene of this kind occurred in Scotland, during the reign of James II.

The king was a Papist, and endeavored to compel his subjects to become Roman Catholics. The "Covenanters were driven to the bleak moors or mountain gorges, where alone they could worship the God of their fathers.

"Spies and informers were sent to the meetings, who gave to the government the names of those whom they saw present on such occasions, and many were thus, for no other offences, dragged to the scaffold, or shot in the open field."

Margaret Wilson of Wigtown, a girl eighteen years of age, with her sister Agnes, a child of thirteen, was in the habit of attending these meetings.

Being informed on by a young man whom they took to be a friend, they were thrown into prison. The terror-stricken father, alarmed for the safety of his children, hastened to Edinburgh, and by paying a heavy sum obtained the liberation of his younger daughter.

But Margaret, they would not release. With an old woman named Mary McLachlin, over seventy years of age, who was charged with the same offence, she was condemned to be drowned.

The two women received their sentence with cheerful composure.

On the morning of May 11th 1665, the day fixed for

the execution of this cruel sentence, they were led down to the shore under a guard of soldiers, commanded by Major Windham.

They were both to be fastened to stakes along the sea-shore, so that when the tide would rise they would be drowned.

The old woman's stake was fixed further in beyond the other, so that Margaret should witness her death struggles and be induced to recant her faith.

Calmly did Margaret watch the water overflowing her fellow-martyr.

As some one asked what she thought of her now, she replied, "What do I see but Christ wrestling there? Think you we are the sufferers? No, it is Christ in us; for he sends none on a warfare upon his own charges."

While the tide was approaching, she mingled her voice with the murmuring waves by singing the 25th Psalm, beginning with the words:—

"Let not the errors of my youth,
Nor sins remembered be,
In mercy, for thy goodness sake,
O Lord, remember me."

She then repeated with a cheerful voice the eighth chapter of Romans, ending with this sublime sentence, "For I am persuaded that neither death, nor life, nor angels, nor principalities, nor powers, nor things present, nor things to come, nor height, nor depth, nor any other creature, shall be able to separate us from the love of God, which is in Christ Jesus our Lord."

She then prayed, and while thus engaged, the water which had been gradually swelling around, covered her head.

A monument was erected in the neighborhood shortly after the Revolution, to commemorate the heroism of the two martyrs.

The Drummer Boy's Last Hymn.

A CHAPLAIN in our army one morning found Tom, the drummer-boy, a great favorite with all the men, and whom, because of his sobriety and religious example, they called "the young deacon," sitting under a tree. At first he thought him asleep, but, as he drew near, the boy lifted up his head, and he saw tears in his eyes.

"Well, Tom, my boy, what is it; for I see your thoughts are sad? What is it?"

"Why, sir, I had a dream last night, which I can't get out of my mind."

"What was it?"

"You know that my little sister Mary is dead—died when ten years old. My mother was a widow, poor, but good. She never seemed like herself afterwards. In a year or so, she died too; and then I, having no home, and no mother, came to the war. But last night I dreamed the war was over, and I went back to my home, and just before I got to the house, my mother and little sister came out to meet me. I didn't seem to remember they were dead! How glad they were! And how my mother, in her smiles, pressed me to her heart! Oh! sir, it was just as real as you are real now!"

"Thank God, Tom, that you have such a mother, not really dead, but in heaven, and that you are hoping, through Christ, to meet her again." The boy wiped his eyes and was comforted.

The next day there was terrible fighting, Tom's drum was heard all day long, here and there. Four times the ground was swept and occupied by the two contending armies. But as the night came on, both paused, and neither dared to go on the field, lest the foe be there.

Tom, "the young deacon," it was known, was wounded

and left on the battle-field. His company encamped near the battle-field. In the evening, when the noise of battle was over, and all was still, they heard a voice singing, away off on the field. They felt sure it was Tom's voice. Softly and beautifully the words floated on the wings of night:—

> "Jesus! lover of my soul,
>   Let me to Thy bosom fly,
> While the billows near me roll,
>   While the tempest still is high.
> Hide me, O my Saviour hide,
>   Till the storm of life is past!
> Safe into the haven guide,
>   Oh, receive my soul at last.
>
> "Other refuge have I none,
>   Hangs my helpless soul on Thee!
> Leave, ah! leave me not alone,
>   Still support and comfort me!"——

The voice stopped here, and there was silence. In the morning the soldiers went out, and found Tom sitting on the ground, and leaning against a stump—dead!

This touching narrative is given by *The Sunday School Times*.

"Can say 'Hallelujah' now."

wo children were very ill in the same room. The elder one was heard attempting to teach the younger one to pronounce the word, "Hallelujah," but without success. The little one died before he could repeat it.

When his brother was told of his death, he was silent for a moment, and then, looking up at his mother, said: "Johnny can say 'Hallelujah,' now mother." In a few hours, the two brothers were united in heaven, singing together "Hallelujah."

Effects of Singing "Jesus lover of my soul."

A CORRESPONDENT of the American Baptist Chronicle furnishes the following interesting narrative:—

"'It is of no use,' said Frank B―― impatiently throwing down a book. 'I have gone through a whole pile of books: have listened to arguments enough to satisfy a whole regiment of lawyers, but it all remains a mystery to me. I wonder whether, after all, there is such a thing in the world as a religion that will satisfy all these restless longings?' As he paused a moment in his walk the sound of singing reached his ear; he opened the door and listened. It was the children's nurse just putting her young charge to bed. Clear and distinct came the tone to Frank's ear,—

"'Jesus! lover of my soul,
Let me to thy bosom fly,
While the raging billows roll,
While the tempest still is high.'

"'Ah!' thought the listener, 'that is just what I need. I would give the world to be able to sing that from my soul.'

"Still the sweet restful music came floating down:—

"'Other refuge have I none,
Hangs my helpless soul on thee!'

"He could stand no more, but going back into the room, he muttered:—'Other refuge, indeed! I have not even that; and none of these books that I have so patiently read have given it to me. All the money that I have given away has brought me no peace. I have tried good works and miserably failed.'

"'Thou, O Christ, art all I want.'

"'I am not so sure of that' murmured he. 'It would be like a beggar in his filthy garments, associating with

A YOUNG MAN SUNG TO CHRIST.

a king in his royal robes.' As though it were the echo of his thought he heard again,—

"'I am all unrighteousness;
Vile and full of sin I am,
Thou art full of truth and grace.'

"'I wonder whether that girl sings those words from her heart,' thought he some time afterwards as he was preparing to go out. As he was passing the kitchen door, it was ajar, and he saw Mary sitting by the table, holding a book so that the dim rays of the candle should fall upon it; and so intently engaged in reading, that, except for a low murmur you might have thought her a statue. 'What can she be reading?' thought he: 'some novel, I suppose, nothing else would so fascinate a young girl like her; then all that singing amounts to nothing after all!' And stealing behind her, he peeped over her shoulder. It was a well used Bible, and she was reading in an undertone,—'This is a faithful saying and worthy of all acceptation, that Christ Jesus came into the world to save sinners; of whom I am the chief.'

"'That's me!' said Frank, unconsciously aloud.
"Mary dropped her book, and started, but Frank said earnestly, 'Do you really think, Mary, that Jesus can love sinners? What a love that must be!'

"Mary's eyes grew moist, as she said,—'The love of Christ, which passeth knowledge.'

"Here at the feet of this humble disciple of her Saviour, did the proud Frank B—— drink in the truth as it is in Jesus. Here was his heart filled with that peace which he had failed to find in his good works; which he had sought for in vain in learned essays. It was not long before, in the fullness of his joy, he could exclaim,—'Unto him that loved us, and washed us from our sins in his own blood,——to him be glory and dominion for ever. Amen!'"

Beecher's Idea of "Jesus, lover of my soul."

AMONG the many forcible remarks that Rev. Henry Ward Beecher has made in relation to hymnology, we give the following; says he, "I would rather have written that hymn of Wesley's—

"Jesus, lover of my soul,
  Let me to Thy bosom fly,"

than to have the fame of all the kings that ever sat on the earth. It is more glorious. It has more power in it. I would rather be the author of that hymn than to hold the wealth of the richest man in New York. He will die. He *is* dead, and does not know it. He will pass, after a little while, out of men's thoughts. What will there be to speak of him? What will he have done that will stop trouble, or encourage hope? His money will go to his heirs, and they will divide it. It is like a stream divided and growing narrower by division. They will die, and it will go to their heirs. Thus in a few generations everything comes to the ground again for redistribution. But that hymn will go on singing until the last trump brings forth the angel band; and then, I think, it will mount up on some lip to the very presence of God. I would rather have written such a hymn than to have all the treasures of the richest man on the globe."

Of the last hours of Dr. Lyman Beecher, the father of Henry Ward Beecher, Mrs. Harriet Beecher Stowe says: "The last indication of life, on the day of his death, was a mute response to his wife, repeating—

'Jesus, lover of my soul,
  Let me to Thy bosom fly.'"

An Accident the Occasion of a Hymn.

IN Charles Wesley's "Hymns and Sacred Poems," is the hymn that commences,—

"Glory, and thanks, to God we give,"

which he says was written "*after deliverance from death by the fall of a house.*"

George J. Stevenson gives the following account:—

"The accident which originated this fine composition is related in Charles Wesley's journal. On his third visit to Leeds he met the society in an old upper room, which was densely packed, and crowds could not gain admission. He removed nearer the door, that those without might hear, and drew the people towards him. Instantly the rafters broke off short, close to the main beam, the floor sank, and more than one hundred people fell, amid dust and ruins, into the room below. One sister had her arm broken, and set immediately; rejoicing with joy unspeakable. Another, strong in faith, was so crushed, that she expected instant death, but she was without fear, and only said, in calm faith, 'Jesus, receive my spirit.' A boy of eighteen, who had come to make a disturbance, who struck several women on entering, was taken up roaring, '*I will be good! I will be good!*' They got his leg set, which was broken in two places. The preacher did not fall, but slid down softly, and lighted on his feet. His hand was bruised, and part of the skin rubbed off his head. He lost his senses, but recovered them in a moment, and was filled with power from above. He writes, 'I lifted up my head and saw the people under me, heaps upon heaps. I cried out, 'Fear not: the Lord is with us; our lives are all safe;' and then gave out to be sung,—

"'Praise God from whom all blessings flow.'"

CROSS BEARING IN SONG.

DECISION for Jesus, was richly rewarded in the case of the daughter of an English nobleman. She was led to visit a Church in London, and became a devoted Christian.

She was the idol of her father and it was with deep regret that he noticed the change that had taken place in her views and conduct.

He placed at her disposal large sums of money, and by threats, temptations to extravagance in dress, by reading works of fiction, and by traveling in foreign countries, yea, by every means, in his power, he tried to divert her mind from things unseen and eternal.

But her heart was fixed. She resolved that, by divine help, nothing should displace her Saviour from the centre of her affections.

At last her father resolved upon one final and desperate expedient. A large company of the nobility were invited to his house. The drawing room was crowded.

It was arranged that all the daughters of the nobility present should entertain the company with a worldly song, accompanied by the piano, and her father determined that if his daughter refused, she should, as far as property was concerned, be ruined! She felt that if she complied, she would grieve away the Holy Spirit, and be again entangled in the world. If she refused, she would lose caste and be disgraced in society. Dreadful was the moment!

With peaceful confidence she awaited the arrival of her turn to occupy the piano and sing. At last her name was called; for a moment all were in silent suspense to see how she would act.

Without hesitation she arose, and with a calm, dignified step, went to the instrument. She spent a moment in silent prayer, and then with a sweetness and solemnity almost supernatural, she sang, accompanying her voice with notes on the instrument, the following hymn:

>No room for mirth or trifling here,
>For worldly hope or worldly fear,
>   If life so soon is gone!
>If now the Judge is at the door,
>And all mankind must stand before
>   The inexorable throne.
>
>No matter which my thoughts employ,
>A moment's misery or joy;
>   But, oh, when both shall end,
>Where shall I find my destined place?
>Shall I my everlasting days,
>   With fiends or angels spend?
>
>Nothing is worth a thought beneath,
>But how I may escape the death
>   That never, never dies.
>How make my own election sure,
>And when I fall on earth, secure
>   A mansion in the skies.
>
>Jesus, vouchsafe a pitying ray,
>Be thou my guide, be thou my stay,
>   To glorious happiness;
>Oh, write thy pardon on my heart,
>And whensoe'r I hence depart,
>   Let me depart in peace!

The minstrel ceased. The solemnity of eternity overshadowed the assembly. They dispersed in silence, the father wept aloud. He sought the instructions and prayers of his dear child. His soul was saved, and after uniting with the church, he contributed to benevolent purposes over half a million of dollars.

The Actress and "Depth of Mercy."

AN actress of an English theatre was one day passing through the streets, when her attention was attracted by the sound of voices in a poor cottage. Curiosity prompted her to look in at the open door, when she saw a few praying people, who were singing:

> "Depth of mercy! can there be
> Mercy still reserved for me?"

Her attention was riveted by these words, and she was invited to enter. After listening to prayer, she left, but the words of the hymn followed her. She became truly penitent, and resolved to leave the stage. Telling the manager, he attempted to overcome her scruples by ridicule, then by the loss he would incur, and then as the last request to appear but once more in a piece in which she was quite popular. She consented to this last request, and in the evening appeared at the theatre.

The play required her first to sing a song: and when the curtain was drawn up, the orchestra began the accompaniment. But she stood as if lost in thought. The music ceased, and, supposing her to be overcome by embarrassment, the band again commenced. A second time they paused for her to begin, and still she did not open her lips. A third time the air was played, and then with clasped hands, and eyes suffused with tears, she sang,

> "Depth of mercy! can there be
> Mercy still reserved for me?
> Can my God His wrath forbear?
> Me, the chief of sinners, spare?"

The performance suddenly ended. Some ridiculed, but others were led "to consider their ways," and cry for mercy too.

She lived a consistent Christian life and at length became the wife of a minister.

Origin of "Come, O Thou all-victorious Lord."

THIS hymn was written by Charles Wesley while preaching at Portland, a peninsular section of England, noted for its stone quarries. Here, on this isolated spot lived many rude and uncared-for quarrymen, whose eternal welfare lay near the heart of Wesley.

Arriving there June 4, 1746, he commenced a series of meetings, of which he says: "I preached to a houseful of staring, loving people, from Jer. i, 20. Some wept, but most looked quite unawakened. At noon and night I preached on the hill in the midst of the island. Most of the inhabitants came to hear, but few as yet feel the burden of sin or the want of a Saviour."

"Sunday, June 8.—After the evening service we had all the islanders that were able to come. I asked, 'Is it nothing to you, all ye that pass by?' About half a dozen answered, 'It is nothing to us,' by turning their backs; but the rest hearkened with greater signs of emotion than I had before observed.

"Monday, June 9.—At Southwell, some very old men attended. I distributed a few books among them, rode round the island, and returned by noon to preach on the hill, and by night at my lodgings. Now the power and blessing came. My mouth and their ears were opened. The rocks were broken in pieces and melted into tears on every side."

With the sound of stone-breaking echoing all around him, and Jeremiah's comparison of "the word . . . like a hammer that breaketh the rock in pieces," he penned the appropriate lines, commencing,—

> "Come, O Thou all victorious Lord,
> Thy power to us make known:
> Strike with the hammer of Thy Word,
> And break these hearts of stone!"

The Song in the Alley.

IN a narrow alley in Boston, noted for its poverty and haunts of vice, a young gas-fitter was sent one winter evening in 1873, to repair a gas pipe. Near by was the North End Mission Chapel, surrounded by dance halls and tippling shops. The alley was very foggy and still, and the music of harps and fiddles seemed to echo in strange contrast with the inspiring strains of "Coronation," and other familiar tunes that issued from the house of God. The young gas-fitter was weary, and paused at times in this extra work to listen to this commingling of musical sounds. At last there was a loud outburst of song in the chapel. Through the crisp evening air echoed the words of Wesley's hymn:—

> "Jesus, the name high over all,
>   In hell, or earth, or sky;
> Angels and men before it fall,
>   And devils fear and fly.
>
> "Jesus, the name to sinners dear,—
>   The name to sinners given;
> It scatters all their guilty fear;
>   It turns their hell to heaven.
>
> "Jesus the prisoner's fetters breaks,
>   And bruises Satan's head;
> Power into strengthless souls He speaks,
>   And life into the dead."

The refrain and chorus to these stanzas were heartily sung, but he could not distinguish the words. The music affected him strangely. There was something in the tinkling sounds, coming out of the beer rooms that told him of the emptiness of earth's follies.

"I wish I was a true Christian," said the young man, as he resumed the work in the basement. As the bell was striking nine he again paused, and went to the basement window and listened. The chapel seemed silent, but there was a mingling of people, and a murmuring of voices out on the street, and the tinkling of instruments in the dance halls still went on. He stood thinking, and the old thoughts returned with greater force, that there was no hope or promise in any pursuits or pleasures which were destitute of God. The music and the sounds of laughter seemed a mockery. He again said, as he was about to resume his work, "I would like to be a Christian." Something detained him a moment more at the window. A low bent form flitted through the misty ring of light at the head of the alley, and approached with a pattering step in the deep shadows. It was an old woman returning from the chapel. She was singing. It was the hymn which he had imperfectly heard. He waited for the refrain:—

> "Jesus, the name high over all,
> In hell, or earth, or sky;
> Angels and men before it fall,
> And devils fear and fly.
> O how I love Jesus,
> O how I love Jesus,
> O how I love Jesus,
> Because He first loved me."

The old woman passed on and disappeared through one of the dark doors at the foot of the alley. She knew not the sermon her song had preached. Then and there the young man saw what he wanted to make him happy, what the world wants to make it happy,—the love of Jesus. On the following day he arose in the Young Men's Christian Association rooms, related substantially the above story, and asked the remembrance of prayers. A great change had come over his feelings. Jesus had been, as it were, revealed to him as both his need and his Saviour, in the song in the alley.

We are indebted to Mr. H. Butterwork for this interesting narrative.

The Death Song of a Murdered Christian.

ABOUT the year 1854 the unusual scene of a court room in tears was witnessed in Exeter Castle, England. It is thus described by Rev. S. W. Christophers:—"A good young woman had been set upon by a villain on her way from the Sunday school, and was left for dead by the roadside. On being discovered, she was restored to consciousness so far as to identify the perpetrator of the crime; and then she died, singing one of Charles Wesley's triumphant anthems of hope:

> "How happy every child of grace,
> Who knows his sins forgiven!
> This earth, he cries, is not my place,
> I seek my place in heaven;
>
> "A country far from mortal sight;—
> Yet, oh! by faith I see
> The land of rest, the saints' delight,
> The heaven prepared for me.
>
> "To that Jerusalem above
> With singing I repair;
> While in the flesh my hope and love,
> My heart and soul are there."

"The counsel for the prosecution at the murderer's trial, in his appeal to the jury, described the death scene, and rehearsed the hymn, a part of which the dying girl sang on her upward flight. The judge, the jury, all but the prisoner, wept. Who could help it? To hear, in that solemn court, the youthful martyr's song of glory! and such a song!"

A Mob Occasioning a Hymn.

ON many occasions, Charles Wesley and his associates, were assaulted by men of the "baser sort." His hymn
"Worship, and thanks, and blessing, etc.,"
was "written after a deliverance in a tumult," and was often sung after similar occurrences. Of the "Mob at Devizes" in 1747, he writes a long account, of which we give a part from Mr. Creamer's "Hymnology."

"I looked back and saw Mr. Merton on the ground, in the midst of the mob, and two bull-dogs upon him. One was first let loose, which leaped at the horse's nose; but the horse with his foot beat him down. The other fastened on his nose, and hung there, till Mr. Merton, with the but end of his whip felled him to the ground. Then the first dog recovering, flew at the horse's breast, and fastened there. The beast reared up, and Mr. Merton slid gently off. The dog kept his hold till the flesh tore off. Then some of the men took off the dogs; others cried, 'Let him alone.' I stopped the horse, and delivered him to my friend. He remounted, with great composure, and we rode on leisurely, as before, till out of sight. Then we mended our pace, and in an hour came to Seend, having rode three miles about, and by seven to Wrexall. The news of our danger was got thither before us, but we brought the welcome tidings of our own deliverance. Now we saw the hand of Providence, in suffering them to turn out our horses; that is to send them to us against we wanted them. Again, how plainly were we overruled to send our horses down the town, which blinded the rioters without our designing it, and drew off their engines and them, leaving us a free passage to the town! We joined in hearty praises to our Deliverer, singing the hymn,—

"'Worship, and thanks, and blessing, etc.'"

"Lo! on a narrow neck of land.

THIS grand hymn was written on the narrow neck of land in England called Land's End, on the coast of Cornwall. It is "between two unbounded seas, the Bristol Channel to the north, and the English Channel to the south; or we may add, the great Atlantic Ocean to the west, and the German Ocean to the east, all uniting at this point."

There is said to be a rock in the water at the dividing point, so pivoted that it is rocked to and fro by the pressure of the two oceans.

What a striking picture of the position of an Eternity bound human being.

Rev. Thomas Taylor, a cotemporary with Wesley, having visited Land's End in 1761, says, "Here, Mr. Charles Wesley wrote,

'Lo! on a narrow neck of land.'"

Dr. Adam Clarke, a personal friend of Wesley, also says, Oct. 11. 1819:—

"I write this on the last projecting point of rock of Land's End, upward of two hundred feet perpendicular above the sea, which is raging and roaring tremendously, threatening destruction to myself and the narrow point of rock on which I am sitting. On my right hand is the Bristol Channel, and before me the vast Atlantic Ocean. There is not one inch of land from the place on which my feet rest to the American continent. This is the place where Charles Wesley composed those fine lines,—

"'Lo! on a narrow neck of land,
'Twixt two unbounded seas I stand,
Yet how insensible!
A point of time—a moment's space—
Removes me to yon heavenly place
Or shuts me up in hell!'"

"Is it true?"

THE inquiry suggested by this hymn had great emphasis given to it by a touching incident, related to the author by an old physician, who kindly entertained me during the delivery of a course of Illustrated Sermons at Mount Joy, Pa.

Having asked him how many of the unconverted he had known, during his life, to leave this world, whose eyes were open to see what was before them, said he, "I can recall but two cases. I hope never to meet with another like the one.

"A lady, taken suddenly ill, sent for me. I saw at once that she could not live twenty-four hours, and told her so. Said she, 'Doctor, it cannot be; you must be mistaken. I'll send for an older physician.' And so she did. I waited till he arrived. As he saw the symptoms he corroborated what I had said. 'Oh! said she, *is it true?* True, that in less than a day, I shall leave this world, I shall be in eternity? Dr. S———, as you have told me the truth, stay with me till I am gone.' From that time on she shrieked out continually, 'E-ter-ni-ty. E-ter-ni-ty. Oh! to think I am so near eternity!' I talked and prayed with her, but my voice could not be heard amid her repeated cries of the word, 'Eternity! O Eternity!'

"The house was on a high hill. There were no shades or shutters to the windows. And to add still further to the impressiveness of the occasion, a thunder shower arose during the night. While her glaring eyes and quivering lips were evincing the agony of soul within, the lightning flashes were intensifying the scene without. While to the thunder's roar, she would respond with the bitter cry of 'Eternity! O Eternity!' and with these words upon her lips, she passed away."

PASSING AWAY.

Words and Music by Rev. E. M. Long.

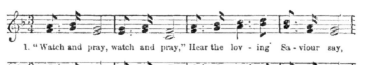

1. "Watch and pray, watch and pray," Hear the loving Saviour say,

Such an hour when all is bright, Death may come with shades of night.

Chorus.

Time is passing, passing quick away, Behold, the Bridegroom cometh,

And the judgment day, And then eternity.

2. Holy One, Holy One,
Through the merits of thy Son,
Grant, that when life's storms are past,
I may dwell with thee at last.

3. Spirit, come! Spirit, come!
Let thy perfect work be come;
Clothe me now, that I may rise,
Robed in white, to yonder skies.

4. Make me pure, pure within,
Cleanse my soul from every sin,
I shall then prepared be,
For a long eternity.

Passing Away.

VERY solemn was the incident that attended the singing of this hymn, and illustrated its sentiments. Soon after its composition I was delivering a course of "Illustrated Sermons" at Newport, Pa.

At the first service my last painting was an illustration of the words, "Time No Longer," by which I sought to impress the audience with our momentary nearness to eternity, and referred to the many persons I had met with, who, in the twinkling of an eye, had passed away. Then to give emphasis to these thoughts, I closed by singing the hymn, "Passing Away."

Three pews from the pulpit sat one whose eyes saw the words, shining in gilt, before him, "Time No Longer," whose ears heard my voice, singing the words,

"Such an hour as ye think not,
Death may come a thief at night."

After walking home from church, a distance of about two squares, he ascended the porch of his house with a firm step. Placing his hand on the door latch, he was heard to exclaim, "Don't let me fall." Caught by the arms of his wife, he was laid down—a corpse.

The next morning I was awakened from my slumbers by the tolling of the church bell, which startled the village by the news, "George Mickey dropped dead on his way home from church last night."

He had eaten a hearty supper, and spoken of his health as being unusually good. Surely, "there is but a step between me and death."

"Eternal Things Impress."

THESE words occur in the second verse of

"Lo! on a narrow neck of land."

To impress eternal things, a lady wrote on a card, and placed it on the top of an hour-glass in her garden-house, the following simple verse from the poems of J. Clare. It was when the flowers were in their highest glory:

"To think of summers yet to come,
That I am not to see!
To think a weed is yet to bloom
From dust that I shall be!"

The next morning she found the following lines, in pencil, on the back of the same card:

"To think when heaven and earth are fled
And times and seasons o'er,
When all that can die shall be dead
That I must die no more!
O where will then my portion be!
Where shall I spend eternity?"

An impressive figure is contained in the following:—

If all the water flowing round this earth,
And with ten thousand times as much, were pent
In a huge cistern, whose unwieldly bulk
The whole contained; but at one leaky pore
At certain periods should one drop dispense;
And at the distance of ten thousand years,
Of intervening time, those periods fix;
—Yet sooner twice ten thousand times the whole,
Thus drop by drop shall draw the ocean dry,
Than the duration of eternity,
One moment of its endless term abridge!
Then what avails it, whether here we taste
Life's transient joys or heart-corroding cares,
If we, in peace and triumph end our race;
A race how like the shuttle's rapid flight,
Or faint illusion of a morning dream!"

"Give me the enlarged desire."

THIS is one of Charles Wesley's hymns, in which he gives expression to those heart-yearnings so characteristic of the growing Christian, who would be "filled with all the fullness of God."

This hymn is also associated with the memory of John Fletcher, who was the Head-Master of Lady Huntingdon's College at Trevecca, for the education of young ministers, of which Mr. Fletcher was the President.

Referring to his devotion, Mr. Benson says: "After speaking a while in the school-room, he used frequently to say, 'As many of you as are athirst for this fullness of the Spirit, follow me into my room.' On this, many of us have instantly followed him, and there continued for two or three hours, wrestling like Jacob for a blessing, praying one after the other till we could bear to kneel no longer. This was not done once or twice, but many times. And I have sometimes seen him on these occasions, once in particular, so filled with the love of God that he could contain no more, but cried out, 'O my God, withhold thy hand, or the vessel will burst.' But he afterward told me he was afraid he had grieved the Spirit of God, and that he ought rather to have prayed that the Lord would have enlarged the vessel, that the soul might have no further interruption to the enjoyment of the Supreme God. For, as Mr. Wesley has observed, the proper prayer on such an occasion would have been:—

> 'Give me the enlarged desire,
>   And open, Lord, my soul,
> Thy own fullness to require
>   And comprehend the whole.
> Stretch my faith's capacity
>   Wider and yet wider still;
> Then with all that is in Thee
>   My ravished spirit fill.'"

An Evening Funeral Song.

AMONG the Cornish miners in England they are accustomed to sing on the way to the church and from the church to the grave at the funeral of a comrade. Rev. S. W. Christophers says:—

"Some few years ago, of a summer's evening, a long crowd was seen passing down the church path from the town, pressing around a bier as if they would guard it in front, flank, and rear, and singing as they moved.

"The strain was measured like their steps, and it was in the minor key, although it seemed at times more like a triumphant shout than a wail of sorrow. They were keeping up the beautiful custom of their fathers, the evening funeral, and the burial hymn from the house of bereavement to the grave. They were singing one of their tunes to one of Charles Wesley's grandest hymns:—

> "Rejoice for a brother deceased,
> Our loss is his infinite gain;
> A soul out of prison released,
> And free from its bodily chain;
> With songs let us follow his flight
> And mount with his spirit above,
> Escaped to the mansions of light,
> And lodged in the Eden of love."

"The bier and the train passed into the ancient sanctuary, by and by again to appear, moving towards the grave. The benediction had scarcely closed the funeral service before the devout multitude once more lifted up its voice—it was a full, a mighty voice—and, pressing around the open grave, they uttered in thrilling tones that glowing and impassioned hymn that seems to melt the earthy and the heavenly into one—

> "Come, let us join our friends above,
> That have obtained the prize."

"Why, I shall Sing Forever!"

THUS spake a young Cornish miner. Shortly before he had heartily joined in singing at the evening burial of a comrade, not thinking, perhaps that his burial song should soon follow. But so it was. On his triumphant death bed he remarked:

"I am going! said he, "I am going! going early; but God has brightened my short life into a full one! Oh, those hymns! they have taught me to live in the light of the future! They have been my 'songs in the house of my pilgrimage'! How often while I have sung them down deep in the mine has the darkness been light about me! Never, since I learnt to praise God from my heart, have I begun to work in the rock for blasting, without stopping a moment to ask myself, Now, if the hole should go off about me, am I ready for heaven? Sometimes, sir, there has been a little shrinking and some doubt, and then I have dropped on my knees, and asked God to bless me before I took one stroke; and never did I pray in vain; my prayer has always passed into praise. And those blessed hymns have come bursting from my heart and lips as I have toiled at the point of death!

"Oh, sir! do you remember our singing at our last funeral?' 'Yes,' it was replied, 'and some thought then, that you would never sing again!' 'Never sing again, sir! why, I shall sing for ever! Oh that glorious hymn, let us sing it now!' And he began—

> "Oh! that we now might grasp our Guide!
> Oh! that the word were given!
> Come, Lord of Hosts! the waves divide,
> And land us—land—me—now in—

"Heaven!" he would have sung, but he was gone! He had joined another choir!

John Wesley and his Hymns.

THE number of hymns composed by Rev. John Wesley is not exactly known, as at first he and his brother "agreed not to distinguish their hymns from each other." Some thirty are ascribed to him in the Methodist hymn-book. Of these the best are his translations from the German, such as

"Jesus, thy blood and righteousness,"
"Commit thou all thy griefs."

In person, Wesley has been described as "rather below the middle size, but beautifully proportioned, with a forehead clear and smooth, a bright penetrating eye, and a lovely face, which retained the freshness of its complexion to the latest period of his life."

Our limits prevent us from going into the many interesting details of his eventful life, neither is it necessary, since his career and great achievements, as the founder of Methodism, have made his history familiar to all.

John Wesley was born June, 17th, 1703, and born again, as he says, May 24, 1738. Although he had entered the ministry, and crossed the ocean to preach to the settlers and Indians in America, yet he himself was ignorant of the way of life. On the failure of his mission, and his return to London, he met with the Moravians, and especially Peter Boehler, and by him, says Wesley, "I was clearly convinced of unbelief, and of the want of that faith whereby alone we are saved." On the evening of the day referred to, when listening to the reading of Luther's preface to the Epistle to the Romans, he says: "While he was describing the change, which God works in the heart, through faith in Christ, I felt my heart strangely warmed; I felt I did trust in Christ, Christ alone, for salvation; and an assurance was given me that he had taken away *my* sins, even *mine.*"

As in his childhood, every possible avenue and means were made use of to save him from his father's burning house, so he thought it but proper, that in saving souls from eternal burnings, every available instrumentality should be employed. Hence his frequent use of song. A church at New Castle grew out of a revival, that started among the crowd that were drawn together by his singing a Psalm in the street, on a Sunday morning.

The familiar hymn, entitled "The Pilgrim," is considered an epitome of his autobiography. It commences,

> "How happy is the pilgrim's lot!
> How free from every anxious thought,
> From worldly hope and fear!
> Confined to neither court not cell,
> His soul disdains on earth to dwell,
> He only sojourns here."

Mr. Creamer says: "This hymn was published about five years before his unhappy union with his wife, at a period when he had probably no intention of ever entering the marriage state, and breathes only the language of one, who had devoted to God, as he had done, his ease, his time, his life, and his reputation." This fact gives a clue to a verse now generally omitted, that says,

> "I have no sharer of my heart,
> To rob my Saviour of a part,
> And desecrate the whole:
> Only betrothed to Christ am I,
> And wait his coming from the sky,
> To wed my happy soul."

Wesley's busy life closed on the 2nd of March, 1791, he being then in the eighty-eight year of his age, and the sixty-fifth of his ministry. After the spirit had left its clay tenement, his friends gathered around his cold remains and sang:—

> "Waiting to receive thy spirit,
> Lo! the Saviour stands above;
> Shows the purchase of his merit,
> Reaches out the crown of love."

"I'll praise my Maker while I've breath."

JOHN Wesley improved the first line of this expressive hymn of Watts, and illustrated its sentiments at last. It is associated with the tender scenes of his death-bed.

Stevenson states that on Monday, February 28, 1791, he was exceedingly weak, slept much, and spoke but little. On Tuesday morning he sang two verses of a hymn, then, lying still, as if to recover strength, he called for pen and ink, but could not write. Miss Ritchie proposed to write for him, and asked what to say. He replied, "Nothing, but that God is with us." In the forenoon he said, "I will get up." While they were preparing his clothes, he broke out in a manner that astonished all who were about him in singing:—

> "I'll praise my Maker while I've breath;
> And when my voice is lost in death,
>   Praise shall employ my nobler powers;
> My days of praise shall ne'er be past,
> While life, and thought, and being last,
>   Or immortality endures."

Having finished the verse, and sitting upon a chair, they observed him change for death. But he, regardless of his body, said with a weak voice, "Lord, Thou givest strength." He then sang his brother's doxology:—

> "To Father, Son, and Holy Ghost,
> Who sweetly all agree."

Here his voice failed. After gasping for breath he said, "Now we have done all." He was then laid on the bed, from which he rose no more. After a while he exclaimed, "The best of all is, God is with us," and until his last breath he kept trying to repeat the hymn of Watts, but could only get out the words:—

> "I'll praise, I'll praise."

Wesleys Hymn and Foolish Dick.

WESLEY'S "Pilgrim's Hymn" seemed just suited to one who has been widely known as "Foolish Dick." Though but half-witted in early life, he became "wise unto salvation." While Dick was going for water, one morning, an old Christian, leaning over his garden gate, remarked: "So you are going to the well for water, Dick?" "Yes, sir." "Well, Dick, the woman of Samaria found Jesus at the well." "Did she, sir?" "Yes, Dick." This conversation suggested this thought, as he went on his way: "Why may I not find Him there too!" While at the well, his heart ascended in ejaculations, "Oh! that I could find Him! Will He come to me?" He, who will not break the bruised reed, nor quench the smoking flax, heard these soul breathings; the fountain of eternal life began to well up within, and his heart soon became so full of peace and joy, that he could not refrain from telling others what the Lord had done for him. His conversion seemed to add strength to his faculties of memory and speech. When a portion of Scripture, or a hymn was read in his hearing, it would imprint itself upon his mind in such a way that he could retain and reproduce it. Constrained by love to Christ and perishing souls, he commenced to itinerate as an Evangelist. Though he went without purse or scrip, yet he never lacked food or clothing, and many were the seals to his ministry. Wesley's hymn was his favorite, and in the dwellings that gave him a welcome, he would sit, and waving to and fro, would sing the favorite lines:—

> "No foot of land do I possess,
> No cottage in this wilderness;
> A poor wayfaring man,
> I lodge awhile in tents below;
> Or gladly wander to and fro,
> Till I my Canaan gain."

Singing at the Table.

OPENING the lips in songs of praise to God is but "a reasonable service" after those lips have been fed by his hand.

After participating in the feast of the passover, we are told that Jesus and his diciples "sung a hymn." This consisted, doubtless, of the six Psalms 113—118, that were usually sung at their tables on such occasions.

In many of the German hymn books, we find "Table Hymns." They are used at each meal.

A writer, speaking of the relics of Mr. Wesley, remaining in his parsonage, such as the old chair and book case, says, "Among the rest an old tea pot, that holds a gallon. We were told that this was made to order for him. On one side is inscribed, burnt in the material by the potter,

> 'Be present at our table, Lord
> Be here and everywhere adored,
> Thy creatures bless, and grant that we
> May feast in Paradise with Thee.'

These lines were always sung before sitting down to tea with his helpers. On the other side of this ancient teapot, were the words sung on rising from the table, and read thus,

> 'We thank thee, Lord, for this our food,
> Much more because of Jesus' blood;
> Let manna to our souls be given,
> The bread of life sent down from heaven.'

These words are still used at the Methodist Public Tea meetings, and often in private families."

Singing a Hymn the Moment after Death.

MR. D. E. McNab gives an account of a friend of his, a young minister, who, while lying on his deathbed, would let no one weep for him. He bade the friend who waited on him to be sure the moment he died to sing a hymn, and he told her the hymn to sing. She kept her promise: as the gentle hand was shutting the cold eyelids on the eyes from which all light had at last gone out, she sang, though with a choked voice and the tears streaming down her cheeks:—

> "Farewell mortality—
>   Jesus is mine;
> Welcome eternity—
>   Jesus is mine;
> He my redemption is,
> Wisdom and righteousness,
> Life, light and holiness—
>   Jesus is mine."

SUSANNAH WESLEY was the mother of nineteen children, among whom where John and Charles the founders of Methodism. When on her deathbed, she said among her last utterances, "Children, as soon as I am released, sing a song of praise to God."

As the spirit was bursting its clay tenement, they encircled her bed in prayer, and as soon as her last breath was drawn, they complied with her last request, and sung a song of praise:—

> "Hosannah to Jesus on high!
>   Another has entered her rest:
> Another has 'scaped to the sky
>   And lodged in Immanuel's breast.
> The soul of our mother is gone
>   To heighten the triumph above;
> Exalted to Jesus' throne
>   And clasped in the arms of his love."

Henry Kirk White and his Hymns.

HENRY KIRK WHITE was born in 1785, at Nottingham. His father was a butcher, and wished Henry to follow the same occupation, but he, being a "book-worm," soon lost all relish for carrying around the butcher's basket. At fourteen he was placed at a stocking-loom; but his thirst for knowledge rendered him so unhappy that the mother induced the father to give his consent to the study of law.

With such great avidity he pursued this, as well as the study of Greek, Latin, Italian, Spanish and Portugese, that at the age of fifteen he became so distinguished for his studies that he received from his preceptor a silver medal and other prizes.

At seventeen he was already prominent as a writer for the periodicals of the day, and issued a volume of poems.

Although he had made such rapid advances in the field of literature, he was a stranger to grace, and even pretended to disbelieve the Bible and its Author. During this period, an intimate companion, Almond, was led by Providence to witness a death-bed scene that opened his eyes to his danger, and caused him to flee to Christ for refuge.

As Almond now seemed to shrink from his former friend because of his infidel scoffings, White wished to ascertain the cause, and when it was stated, he felt much mortified, became penitent, and was assisted in finding the way to the cross by reading "Scott's Force of Truth," which his friend had introduced to him.

After realizing the blessing of pardon and peace, he felt anxious to make his Saviour known to others. To this end he discontinued the study of law and prepared for the gospel ministry. About this time he also wrote the well-known hymn commencing,—

> "When marshaled on the nightly train,
> The glittering host bestud the sky,
> One star alone of all the train
> Can fix the sinner's wandering eye."

This hymn vividly describes the author's conversion. His experience on the sea of skepticism he portrays in the third verse:—

> "Once on the raging seas I rode,
> The storm was loud, the night was dark."

In the hymn commencing—

> "The Lord our God is clothed with might,"

is found a much admired verse.

> "Howl, winds of night! your force combine;
> Without His high behest,
> Ye shall not, in the mountain-pine,
> Disturb the sparrow's nest."

His hymn for evening family worship is oft repeated in England and America:—

> "O Lord! another day has flown;
> And we, a lowly band,
> Are met once more before Thy throne
> To bless Thy fostering hand."

Through his intense application to study, without rest or intermission by day or night, his bodily strength gave way, and he sank into an untimely grave in 1806, when but twenty-one years of age.

> "Pale o'er his lamp, and in his cell retired
> The martyr-student faded and expired."

In one of his poems he seems to lament his own early departure in the line:—

> "Fifty years hence, and who shall hear of Henry?"

The fifty years have gone, and yet Henry is not forgotten, and will not be as long as the church loves to repeat the ten precious hymns he bequeathed her as his legacy.

> "Oh, what a noble heart was here undone,
> When science self-destroyed her favorite son!"

William Williams.

"Let the fiery, cloudy pillar,
Lead me all my journey through."

DEPENDENT upon heavenly guidance for every step taken in life's journey, how natural to God's Israel is the prayer, that heads these lines, taken from the grand old hymn:—

"Guide me, O thou Great Jehovah."

As this hymn is so often repeated, our readers will gladly welcome some acquaintance with its author, the Rev. William Williams, a celebrated Welsh poet.

He was born at Cefncyoed, Carmarthenshire, Wales, in 1717. He commenced the study of medicine, after securing a good education. But after hearing the gospel from the lips of Howell Harris in Talgarth churchyard, he was led to Christ, and induced to prepare for the work of the ministry. Of his conversion his biographer says: "His convictions of sin were deep and alarming; but his subsequent joy proportionably high." He was ordained deacon in the English church in his twenty-third year, but being encouraged by Whitefield and Lady Huntingdon to become an itinerant minister, he was refused "full orders," and so united with the Calvinistic Methodists. His labors were ardent and incessant, continuing without abatement for half a century. It is said that he "travelled on an average two thousand two hundred and thirty miles a year, for forty-three years, when there were no railroads and but few stage coaches."

He issued a number of books, containing his hymns, entitled as follows: "Alleluia," "The Sea of Glass," ",Visible Farewell; Welcome to Invisible Things," "Alleluia again;" and in English, "Hosannah to the Son of David," and "Gloria in Excelsis." The latter was prepared by Lady Huntingdon's suggestion, for use in Whitefield's Orphan House in America. In this book appeared that universally popular hymn:—

"O'er the gloomy hills of darkness."

He died in 1791, being seventy-four years of age. Though his speech failed him before his departure, he gave signs of his happy state of mind, and that the prayer of his hymn "Guide me," etc., was being realized:—

"When I tread the verge of Jordan
Bid my anxious fears subside."

The last verse of this hymn, generally omitted, reads:—

"Musing on my habitation,
Musing on my heavenly home,
Fills my soul with holy longings:
Come, my Jesus, quickly come;
Vanity is all I see;
Lord, I long to be with thee!

"Let the fiery, cloudy pillar
Lead me all my journey through."

THAT Israel's God still leads the way with a pillar of cloud was literally shown in the experience of a Baptist minister in the mountains of Virginia, who related the following facts to the author:—

During the late war he was exposed to many perils because of his loyalty to the Union.

One evening as he left the door of his house, an unaccountable presentiment of danger impressed him so much that he told his wife he must flee to the woods for shelter. After night she conveyed to him the intelligence of his Providential escape, saying that soon after he left a party of guerrillas arrived, and while some of them searched for him, others were erecting a gallows at the barn for his execution.

During the night he was enabled to conceal himself, but he apprehended great difficulty the next day in getting across a wide plain that lay between two mountains, while on his way to the Union lines.

The valley had no shelter and he would necessarily be exposed to sight and to the quick pursuit of his enemies, who were on horse-back. This extremity was God's opportunity. As he approached the plain next day there arose from it a fog high enough to cover him as he walked through it, and yet low enough to enable him to see above it some trees on the mountain top to guide his feet to the place of safety on the other side.

Well could he sing as his feet rested on the Mount of Deliverance, and his eyes looked down upon the cloudy pillar that enabled him to get there:—

"Strong Deliverer, Strong Deliverer,
Be thou still my strength and shield."

We will also add an illustration of the "fiery pillar."

During our late war, a prisoner in Andersonville, managed one night to surmount his prison, and get beyond the picket line, but it was so dark that he could not tell which was North or South. He was afraid to move, for fear of moving still further southward into the ranks of the enemy. He had a compass with him, that pointed northward to the land of freedom, to his home and friends, but it was useless to him without light. A candle or even a match would have been of priceless value to him in this time of need, for his very life seemed to hang upon the needed light. In his extremity, a kind providence directed a little fire-fly to wing its way to his relief. He eagerly and gladly seized it, and its wings gave out light enough to let him see the finger on his compass, and thus his feet were directed, and he was led at length to his home in safety. A beautiful illustration of that Spirit that lightens up the sacred page, and shows us the way that leads to our heavenly home.

The following is Keble's new version of "Guide me, O Thou great Jehovah:"—

"Guide us, thou, whose name is Saviour,
  Pilgrims in the barren land;
We are weak, and thou Almighty;
  Hold us with thy strong right hand,
    As in Egypt,
  As upon the Red Sea strand.

"Let the cloud and fire supernal
  Day and night before us go;
Lead us to the Rock and Fountain
  Whence the living waters flow;
    Bread of heaven,
  Feed us, till no want we know.

"When we touch the cold dark river,
  Cleave for us the swelling tide;
Through the flood and through the whirlpool
  Let thine ark our footsteps guide;
    Jesus lead us;
  Land us safe on Canaan's side."

Singing Satan away.

SOME one says "A hymn is a singing Angel that goes walking through the earth, scattering the devils before it. Therefore, he who creates hymns imitates the most excellent and lovely works of God, who made the Angels."

Christmas Evans, so celebrated in Welsh revivals, vividly pictures this "Scattering of the devils by God's Angel of song" in his sermon on "the dry places" where Satan "is seeking rest and findeth none." Says he:—

"I see the unclean spirit rising like a winged dragon, circling in the air, and seeking for a resting place. Casting his fiery glances toward a certain neighborhood, he spies a young man in the bloom of life, and rejoicing in his strength, seated on the front of his cart, going for lime. 'There he is!' said the old dragon; 'his veins are full of blood, and his bones of marrow; I will throw into his bosom sparks from hell; I will set all his passions on fire; I will lead him from bad to worse, until he shall perpetrate every sin. I will make him a murderer, and his soul shall sink, never again to arise, in the lake of fire.' By this time, I see it descend, with a full swoop toward the earth; but nearing the youth, the dragon heard him sing,

> "'Guide me, O Thou Great Jehovah!
> Pilgrim through this barren land,
>   I am weak, but thou art mighty;
> Hold me with thy powerful hand.
>   Strong Deliverer,
>   Be thou still my strength and shield.'

'A dry, dry place, this,' says the old dragon; and away he goes, But I see him again hovering about in the air, and casting about for a suitable resting-place. Beneath his eye there is a flowery meadow, watered by a crystal stream; and he descries among the kine a maiden, about eighteen years of age, picking up here and there a beautiful flower. 'There she is!' says Apollyon, intent upon her soul; 'I will poison her thoughts; she shall think evil thoughts, and become impure; she shall become a lost creature in the great city, and, at last, I will cast her down from the precipice into everlasting burnings.' Again he took his downward flight, but he no sooner came near the maiden, than he heard her sing the following words, with a voice that might have melted the rocks:—

> "'Other refuge have I none;
> Hangs my helpless soul on thee;
> Leave, ah! leave me not alone;
> Still support and comfort me.'

And so again he fled away defeated."

The Name that makes "Devils fear and fly."

THE following is the first verse of one of Charles Wesley's popular hymns:—

> "Jesus, the Name high over all,
> In hell, or earth, or sky;
> Angels and men before it fall,
> And devils fear and fly."

This hymn is said to have been suggested by the following circumstances, which are referred to in his Journal, August 6, 1744.

While preaching in Cornwall, and condemning the drunken revels of the people, he was urging them to "repent and be converted," when one of the congregation contradicted and blasphemed. "Who is he that pleads for the devil?" asked Wesley. As the reviler stood boldly forward, the preacher so fearlessly exposed his iniquity that the man fled from the church, as if driven by an irresistible power.

"Sweet hour of prayer, sweet hour of prayer."

THIS much-loved hymn appeared in an English hymn-book of 1849. It was written by Rev. Mr. Walford, a blind preacher, who was supposed to have first composed it about 1846. The tune, "Sweet hour," to which it has become closely wedded, was written for it by William Bradbury. As originally printed, it had four verses, of which the following was the second. As it is generally omitted we insert it herewith:—

> "Sweet hour of prayer, sweet hour of prayer,
> The joy I feel, the bliss I share,
> Of those whose anxious spirits burn
> With strong desire for thy return,
> With such I hasten to the place
> Where God, my Saviour, shows his face,
> And gladly take my station there,
> To wait for thee, sweet hour of prayer."

IN the memoir of Caroline Hyde it is stated that, though compelled to earn a livelihood by going from house to house as a seamstress, whenever her "Sweet hour of prayer" arrived, however employed, she would beg to be excused, saying that a dear friend was waiting to see her.

OF Xavier it is said, that one day he told his servant to call him at the end of his usual two hours of devotion. When the time arrived, as he did not respond to the call, the servant opened the door, and found his face shining with such a sweet expression of delight, and his soul so enraptured with heavenly intercourse, that he felt reluctant to break the charm, and so waited and called again and again, until four hours had passed, and then, when he laid his hand on his shoulders, the saint exclaimed, "Are the *two* hours gone *already*?" He was utterly amazed when told that even *four* hours had elapsed.

Xavier's Hymn.

XAVIER (Francis) was a celebrated Roman Catholic missionary who was born at Navarre, in 1506.

He wrote a hymn in 1550, that has been echoing for over three hundred years, and is still highly prized by Christians of different denominations.

In some books the first verse is omitted. It commences:—

"My God, I love Thee, not because
I hope for heaven thereby."

Some books commence the hymn with this verse:—

"Thou, O my Jesus, Thou didst me
Upon the cross embrace;
For me didst bear the nails and spear,
And manifold disgrace."

King John III. sent him out as a missionary to the Portuguese Colonies in the East. At Goa he baptized ten thousand natives in a single month. Having been the means of the conversion of a Japanese of high rank at Malacca, and having such great success in various parts of heathendom, he turned his attention to Japan.

In less than three years, he established a mission here, that continued to flourish for above one hundred years, until the final expulsion of Christianity from the Empire.

While preaching in one of the cities of Japan, a man drew near as if he had something to communicate. Xavier leaned his head to hear what he had to say, when the man spit freely upon his face. Xavier simply wiped his face with his handkerchief, and continued his sermon. By this meekness many were won to Christ.

Author of "Jesus, thy blood and righteousness."

ZINZENDORF wrote this hymn in 1739, while on a voyage to visit the missionaries who had gone forth from Herrnhut to the West Indies.

In 1740, it was translated by John Wesley. The original contained thirty-three verses.

Zinzendorf was born at Dresden, May 1700. He was blessed with a mother and grandmother, who were conspicuous for their piety and talents. The latter also having been a writer of hymns, and religious works.

Early in life he was remarkable for his piety, and while a child would gather other children together to pray with him. Referring in 1740 to his childhood, he says, "It is more than thirty years since I received a deep impression of Divine grace through the preaching of the cross. The desire to bring souls to Christ took possession of me, and my heart became fixed on the Lamb."

While still a youth he began to write hymns. In this he continued till in old age, having composed in all about two thousand.

In 1722, some poor persecuted Christians, followers of John Huss of Moravia and Bohemia, obtained leave to settle on his estate, where they built a church. Converts began to multiply. Zinzendorf joined them.

This was the origin of the village of Herrnhut, and of the church known as the Moravian or United Brethren.

COUNT ZINZENDORF.

The three eras in the Moravian church comprise the "Ancient Church," from 1457 to 1627; the "Hidden Seed," from 1627 to 1722; the "Renewed Church," from 1722 to the present time.

In 1732, Zinzendorf, with his little band of brethren of Herrnhut, started the mission work, that has been so vigorously and extensively carried on ever since. In a few years four thousand natives were baptized in the West Indies, and the converts in Greenland numbered seven hundred and eighty-four.

In 1741, he extended his travels to America, and preached at Germantown and Bethlehem, Pennsylvania. At Oly, Pennsylvania, he ordained the missionaries Rauch and Buettner, and after visiting various tribes of Indians, established at Shekomeco, the first Indian Moravian congregation.

Zinzendorf was a prolific writer. His published works amounted to one hundred and eight in number. Many of his hymns were produced in an impromptu manner. "After the discourse," says he, "I generally announce another hymn, appropriate to the subject. When I cannot find one, I compose one; I say, in the Saviour's name, what comes into my heart. I am, as ever, a poor sinner, a captive of love, running by the side of His triumphal chariot, and have no desire to be anything else as long as I live."

In 1721, he issued the hymn "Jesu, geh voran," that is highly prized. It was translated into English by Miss Jane Borthwick, and is still found in English hymn-books. The first verse is

"Jesus, still lead on,
Till our rest be won;
And although the way be cheerless,
We will follow, calm and fearless,
Guide us by thy hand,
To our father-land."

Zinzendorf is described as "a noble, grand-looking person, with high forehead, and blue eyes; manly in his bearing, and above the middle height in stature." Even up to the last, this servant of God did with his might whatsoever his hands found to do. He worked like a man who felt deeply impressed with the thought that he had much to do, and little time in which to do it. His biographer says that in the last year of his life, "he determined to seek the personal acquaintance of every member of the church, that he might ascertain the spiritual state of each one. This was a vast undertaking; and, considering the large number of inhabitants at Herrnhut, it might well have appeared a simple impossibility. But Zinzendorf, instead of recoiling before the difficulty, resolutely set to work, and in four months from that time, there was scarcely an individual in the colony that he had not conversed with privately, as he proposed."

The ninth of May, 1760, was his last day on earth. Before closing his eyes in the sleep of death, he said: "I am going to the Saviour, I am ready. If he is no longer willing to make use of me here, I am ready to go to him."

For several days, while he lay in his coffin, clothed in the white gown he was wont to wear in the discharge of his ministerial functions, groups of friends would gather and sing around his endeared remains, those hymns, with which he had so often led them in their songs of praise.

His coffin was borne to the tomb by thirty-two preachers and missionaries, who happened to be in Herrnhut at the time. They were men whom he had trained for the Lord's work; they had come from their field of labor in Holland, England, Ireland, North America, and Greenland. The funeral procession was composed of over two thousand individuals. Well may one ask, "What monarch was ever honored by a funeral like this?"

"Praise Him with stringed instruments and organs." Ps. 150

DEPARTMENT

OF

Hymn Singing and Church Music.

"Lord, how delightful 'tis to see
A whole assembly worship Thee!
At once they sing, at once they pray;
They hear of heaven and learn the way."

Watts.

Churches Opposed to Singing.

AS the singing of God's praise is so often referred to in the Scriptures, and forms such a prominent and delightful part of the service of the sanctuary, it seems to us incredible that there should ever have been evangelical churches bitterly opposed to it.

The following statements are taken from authentic and original documents, kindly furnished by Mr. Francis Jennings.

The Second Baptist Church of Newport, Rhode Island, of which Rev. C. H. Malcolm is now the pastor, was constituted in 1656, when it is said they rejected singing as a part of religious service, and omitted it for over one hundred years.

In 1765 singing was introduced. After very great agitation, numerous church meetings, and much opposition, permission was given to sing one hymn or psalm during service.

Out of regard to tender consciences, those who could not endure the sound were allowed to remain out in the cold until it was concluded. A merciful permission! A generous provis'on!

On the arrival of Rev. James Manning in Providence R. I. a part of the church withdrew with the pastor, Rev. Samuel Winsor, because the church introduced singing. Afterwards, in 1771, they formed a Baptist church, where singing was not tolerated.

June 5th, 1771, according to *Allen's Register*, a division took place in the Baptist Church in New York city, because a part adopted singing. Those who seceded said, "Singing in public worship was an innovation which the withdrawing party never could tolerate."

It seems that the same spirit prevailed in England. The practice of singing in public worship was by no means general among the churches in 1689. So odious had been the pompous and theatrical music in the papal churches, that many Protestants went to the opposite extreme, and so dispensed with singing altogether, except after the Lord's supper.

The church which grew into the one that Spurgeon is now pastor of was originally opposed to singing. It was known at the start as the Horselydown Baptist Church. While under the charge of Rev. Benjamin Keach, he published a treatise on singing in 1691, entitled, "The Breach in God's Worship Repaired." This led to much commotion. Those opposed to singing withdrew, and formed themselves into the church at Maze Pond, London, electing one of their number, Mr. Edward Wallen, as pastor.

For nearly forty years they omitted singing, except when partaking of the Lord's supper, until their pastor died. As they found it difficult to get another to suit them, they elected his son, Mr. Benjamin Wallen. But to their astonishment, he would only accept the call on condition that they would introduce singing.

At length they yielded to this requirement, and, in 1741, the meeting-house again became vocal with praise.

Dr. Watts says of his day: "There are some churches that utterly disallow singing, and I am persuaded that the poor performance of it in the best societies, with the mistaken rules to which it is confined, is one great reason of their entire neglect."

Dr. Cuyler says: "God made us to sing as truly as he made us to smile and weep.

"One thing is incontestable, and that is, that we shall *sing in heaven.* Even our beloved brethren, the Quakers, had better take a few lessons by way of rehearsal on this side of the pearly gates."

Singing in America two Centuries Ago.

THE first printing press in America was "put up" at Cambridge, in 1639, by Stephen Day, and the first book printed upon it was "*The Psalms in Metre,* faithfully translated, for the use, edification, and comfort of the saints, in public and private, especially in New England, printed at Cambridge in 1640."

The Pilgrim Fathers entered on their records, "Stephen Day, being the first that set up printing, is granted three hundred acres of land, where it may be convenient without prejudice to any town."

We give below a forest relic of these early days, composed by a converted savage, who spent his days in teaching salvation to his tribe.

    1. In de dark wood, no Injin nigh,
       Den me look heben, send up cry
          Upon my knees so low.
    God hear poor Injin in de wood,
    Den me lub God and dat be good,
       Me heart, he tell me so.

    2. Den God, He say Poor Injun, come
       Me goin to take poor Injun home
          Where he may lib in Heben.
    Den Injun he wing up an fly,
    An tell de angels bove de sky
       How he hab been forgiben.

    3. When me be old, me head be gray,
       He neber lebe me,—so He say—
          He wid me till me die,
    Den take me up to shiny place;
    See red man, white man, black man face
       All happy den on high.

We give below a verse of one of the Psalms in the Indian tongue as printed for their use by Eliot in 1663.

    "Kesuk Kukootumushteaumoo
      God wussohsumoonk
    Mamahehekesuk wumahtuhkon
      Wutanakausnonk."

Old Style Hymnology.

WE give herewith some specimens of the hymns sung before the days of Watts and Wesley. They were "deaconed off and sung one line at a time."

> "'Tis like the precious ointment
> Down Aaron's beard did go;
> Down Aaron's beard it downward went,
> His garment skirts unto."

In 1562 a version of the Psalms known as Sternhold and Hopkins', was issued, in which the 10th and 11th verses of the 74th Psalm are put into verse.

The Psalmist says, "O God, how long shall the adversary reproach? Why withdrawest thou thy hand, even thy right hand? pluck it out of thy bosom." The poet renders it for singing thus;—

> "Why dost withdraw thy hand aback
> And hide it in thy lappe?
> O pluck it out and be not slack
> To give thy foes a rappe."

The Scripture language, "The race is not to the swift nor the battle to the strong," was thus arranged for singing, one says, "It contains truth, whatever may be said of its poetry,

> "The race is not forever got
> By him who fastest runs;
> Nor the battle by those people
> Who shoot the longest guns."

Of the following specimen, Dr. Belcher says, "though our readers may smile at it, their fathers did not,"

> "Ye monsters of the bubbling deep,
> Your Maker's praises spout:
> Up from the sands, ye codlings, peep,
> And wag your tails about."

Church Singing in Olden Times.

WE will give a few extracts from the early history of our country, that our readers may take a glance at the manner in which our forefathers sang their notes of praise.

September 16, 1723. *The New England Courant* gave this item of news: "A council of churches was held at Baintree, to regulate disorders, occasioned by regular singing in that place, Mr. Niles, the minister, having suspended seven or eight of the church, for persisting in singing by rule." The council declared the suspension unjust, and the church was "ordered to sing by note and by rule, *alternately* for the satisfaction of both parties."

A choir in Massachusetts, having commenced singing without waiting for the Psalm to be lined out, the pastor waited till they were finished, when he gravely put on his spectacles, and said: "Now let the *people of God* sing," when the congregation joined with him in singing according to the old form.

It is said of Dr. Joseph Bellamy, that after his choir had sung in sad style, he gave out another Psalm, saying: "You must try again; for it is impossible to preach after such singing."

The servant of the Rev. S. Moody, having led the singing one day, the dominie remarked at the close of the meeting: "John, you shall never set the Psalm again, for you are ready to burst with pride."

But few tunes were known in those days, and the use of notes little understood, so that the melody was "tortured, and twisted as every unskillful throat saw fit." The Rev. Mr. Walker says, it sounded "like five hundred different tunes roared out at the same time, so hideously and disorderly as is bad beyond expression. I myself have twice in one note paused to take breath."

CHURCH SINGING IN OLDEN TIMES.

"The Dearest Idol I have Known."

THIS line is from Cowper's well known hymn,
"O for a closer walk with God."

A volume of illustrations could be made of the "dearest idol known" to those who make music in the christian sanctuary.

While preaching in a country German church, not forty miles from Philadelphia, I was elevated above my fellow mortals by the old fashioned "wine glass pulpit." Being thus brought on a level with the choir gallery I was enabled, from this high point of observation, to solve mysteries that my less privileged auditors below could not unravel.

After giving out the second hymn, according to custom, I lined it, but the music did not follow. The audience waited and wondered, but it was in vain. Many faces were now upturned to ascertain the cause, when lo! the leader had taken out his little black idol—not very "little" indeed for it was a *big* plug of tobacco, to which he had first to pay his respects, before he sent up his song of praise to the God of Heaven.

Unfortuately, as he took a bite, he could not *tear* it off; so he had to pull, and pull, and pull, to the great consternation of his fellow singers; until at length he was rewarded for his devotion, by a mouth full larger than he anticipated, so that the music not having room to escape through the mouth had to get out with a "nasal twang," that was not very "harmonious to our ear."

It was a sad comment of the poet's prayer, which was surely appropriate for him.

> "The dearest idol I have known.
> Whate'er that idol be,
> Help me to tear it from thy throne,
> And worship only thee."

Expressive Epitaph of a Chorister.

A CHOIR leader, familiarly known as "Stephen," had been accustomed to stand at a conspicuous position and beat time at full arms length. So much emphasis did he seem to give to the music that many supposed that good church singing was dependent on the motion of that long arm.

In the midst of his usefulness death succeeded at length in stopping this musical pendulum from swinging. On a plain marble slab at the head of his grave were placed the lines:—

> "Stephen and Time at length are even,
> Stephen beat Time and Time beat Stephen."

An Unexpected Coincidence.

A CORRESPONDENT of *The Cincinnatti Gazette* is responsible for the following:—

"A clergyman in Pittsburg, Pa. married a lady with whom he received the substantial dowry of ten thousand dollars, and a fair prospect for more. Shortly afterward, while occupying the pulpit, he gave out the hymn, read the first four verses, and was proceeding to read the fifth, commencing,

> "'Forever let my grateful heart,'

when he hesitated, baulked and exclaimed: 'Ahem! the choir will omit the fifth verse,' and sat down. The congregation, attracted by his apparent confusion, read the verse for themselves, and smiled almost audibly as they read:

> "'Forever let my grateful heart
> His boundless grace adore,
> Who gives ten thousand blessings now,
> And bids me hope for more.'"

A Hymn Illustrated by a Thunder-Storm.

WHILE George Whitefield was delivering a sermon in Boston on the wonders of creation, providence and redemption, a terrific storm of thunder and lightning arose. Dr. Belcher says it "so alarmed the congregation that they sat in breathless awe. The preacher closed his note-book, and, stepping into one of the wings of the desk, fell on his knees, and, with much feeling and fine taste, repeated from Dr. Watts:—

> "Hark! the Eternal rends the sky!
> A mighty voice before him goes,—
> A voice of music to his friends,
> But threatening thunder to his foes.
>
> "Come, children, to your Father's arms!
> Hide in the chambers of my grace
> Till the fierce storm is overblown
> And my revenging fury cease!"

'Let us devotedly sing to the praise and glory of God this hymn: Old Hundred.'

"The whole congregation instantly rose and poured forth the sacred song. By the time the hymn was finished, the storm was hushed, and the sun, bursting forth, showed the magnificent arch of peace. Resuming the desk, the preacher quoted, with admirable tact, 'Look upon the rainbow: praise him that made it. Very beautiful is it in the brightness thereof! It compasseth the heaven about with a glorious circle; and the hands of the Most High have bended it.' The episode added intense interest to the service."

Incidents of the Tune of Old Hundred.

THE name given to the tune of "Old Hundred" is derived from the hundreth Psalm, to which it was originally sung.

It was composed by William Franc, for the Calvinistic Psalm-book in 1553, and afterwards "transferred by Ainsworth to his book compiled for the exiled Puritans in Holland, who," at length, "brought it to America, where it has become the National Te Deum."

It was very much changed and improved by Luther, so much so, that some have supposed it was his composition.

Maria P. Woolridge, in the *Ladies' Repository*, says: "A friend of the writer was not long since visiting a Catholic Cathedral, and innocently inquired why such a magnificent composition as *Old Hundred* was never sung by the Catholics. The priest's face contracted with a look of deadly hate, as he replied, 'The heretic Luther wrote that, madam.'"

"A remarkable incident is that of a Scottish youth, who learned from a pious mother to sing the old psalms, that were as household words to them in the kirk and by the fireside. When he grew up, he wandered away from his native country, was taken captive by the Turks, and made a slave in one of the Barbary states. But he never forgot the songs of Zion, although he sung them in a strange land and to heathen ears. One night he was solacing himself in this manner, when the attention of some sailors on board of an English man-of-war was directed to the familiar tune of 'Old Hundred,' as it came floating over the moon-lit waves. At once they surmised the truth, that one of their countrymen was languishing away his life as a captive. Quickly arming themselves, they manned a boat, and lost no time in effecting his release. What a joy to him after eighteen long years passed in slavery! Should not you think he would ever after love the glorious tune of "Old Hundred?"

The following incident is related of Deacon Hunt, who was naturally a man of high temper, and often made it manifest in beating his oxen severely. When he became a new creature in Christ Jesus, his cattle seemed to be more docile. A friend inquired into the secret. "Why," said the deacon, "formerly, when my oxen were a little contrary, I flew into a passion, and beat them unmercifully. This made the matter worse. Now, when they do not behave well, I go behind the load, sit down, and sing Old Hundred. I don't know how it is, but the psalm-tune has a surprising effect upon my oxen."

Music does not always have such a soothing effect, as would appear from the following amusing incident:—

A young man being surrounded in the parlor by a party of several friends was urgently besought to favor them with some singing. He replied that he would first tell them a story, and then if they still insisted on it, he would gratify their wishes.

When a boy, he said, he took lessons in singing; and one Sunday morning went up into his father's garret to practice by himself. While under full headway, he was suddenly sent for by the old gentleman.

"This is pretty conduct," said the father, "pretty employment for the son of pious parents, to be sawing boards in the garret on a Sunday morning, loud enough to be heard by all the neighbors. Sit down and take your book."

We scarcely need add that, after this revelation of his musical powers, the young man was excused from singing.

Hymns Disjointed by Fugue Tunes.

SAD and often amusing have been the consequences of singing hymns in fugue style. The following verse of the one hundred and thirty-third Psalm,

> "True love is like that precious oil
> Which poured on Aaron's head,
> Ran down his beard, and o'er his robes
> Its costly moisture shed,"

has been wedded to a tune of this kind. In order to get the "precious oil" to "run down his beard," the following prodigious effort is made in the music:—

> "Ran down his beard and o'er his robes—
> Ran down his beard———
> ——————————his robes,
> And o'er his robes—
> Ran down his beard—ran down his
> ——————————o'er his robes—
> His robes, his robes, ran down his beard,
> Ran down his———
> ——————————o'er his robes
> Ran down his beard
> ——————————h-i-s b-e-a-r-d
> Its costly moist———
> Ran down his beard———
> ———ure—beard—his—beard—his— shed
> Ran down his beard—his—down his robes—
> ——its costly moist—his beard—ure shed
> his—cost—his robes—his robes—ure shed
> I-t-s c-o-s-t-l-y moist—ure———s-h-e-d."

Bishop Seabury, being present at one time when a choir was going through this performance, he was asked what he thought of it. His reply was that "he had paid no attention to the music, in that his sympathies were so much excited for poor Aaron that he was afraid he would not have a hair left."

Some pastors have kindly furnished us, in our travels, with various other specimens, that we give herewith.

One related an instance where the tune required the first three words of a line to be repeated, so that when the words,

"Send down salvation"

occurred, the choir sang aloud:—

"Send down sal——
Send down sal——
Send down sal——"

At another time, the tune sundered the line,

"And take the poor pilgrim home,"

so that it was repeated thus:—

"And take the poor pil——
And take the poor pil——"

Another hymn and tune thus "unequally yoked" together, caused an unfortunate rupture in the words,

"And chase the fleeting hour,"

so that the choir sang:—

"And chase the flee——
And chase the flee——."

No less amusing was the following occurrence of the singing of a tune that disjointed the line,

"O, for a mansion in the skies,"

so that it was sung:—

"O, for a man——
O, for a man——
O, for a man——"

The effect of a half dozen young ladies in the choir gallery singing aloud,

"O, for a man——,"

can be better imagined than described.

The Massacre of Church Music.

UNDER this heading Rev. T. DeWitt Talmage gives the following description of an illustrative incident:—

"The minister read the hymn beautifully. The organ began, and the choir sang, as near as I could understand, as follows:—

> " 'Oo—aw—gee—bah
> Ah—me—la—he
> O—pah—sah—dah
> Wo---haw---gee-e-e-e.'

"My wife, seated beside me, did not like the music. But I said: "What beautiful sentiment! My dear, it is a pastoral. You might have known that from ' *Wo-haw-gee!*' You have had your taste ruined by attending the Brooklyn Tabernacle.

"The choir repeated the last line of the hymn four times. Then the prima donna leaped on to the first line, and slipped, and fell on to the second, and that broke and let her through into the third. The other voices came in to pick her up and got into a grand wrangle."

A GENTLEMAN from the country attended one of our city churches, where he found four persons employed to do the singing for the congregation.

The music was scientific, and the language of the hymn, he says, sounded as follows:—

> "Waw-kaw, swaw daw aw raw,
> Thaw saw thaw law aw waw;
> Waw-kaw taw thaw raw vaw yaw braw
> Aw thaw raw-jaw saw aws."

Which, rendered into English, reads as follows:—

> "Welcome, sweet day of rest,
> That saw the Lord arise;
> Welcome to this reviving breast
> And these rejoicing eyes."

Choir Difficulties.

A CHOIR in a New England church took offence at a stranger who officiated in the absence of the pastor, because he had unwittingly disregarded some of their rules.

After several vain attempts to induce them to sing, he gave out the verse:—

> "Let those refuse to sing
> Who never knew our God;
> But children of the heavenly King
> May speak their joys abroad."

This it seems had the desired effect, for as the whole congregation joined in with the minister, the choir could not keep silent and admit that, like the heathen, they

> "—never knew our God."

AT another time the common metre hymn

> "I love to steal a while away,"

was announced. The chorister tried a tune, but when he got as far as

> "I love to steal,"

found out that the metre would not suit.

Then he tried another, but stuck when he got on as far again as

> "I love to steal."

Being well supplied with the grace of perseverance, he resolved to "try, try again;" but always unfortunately stopped after saying,

> "I love to steal,"

When, with a smile, the pastor remarked, "It is very much to be regretted. Let us pray."

It is strange to add, that this little circumstance led to the dismission of the pastor.

Solemn Mockery in Singing.

WHAT is more painful to behold than that wicked trifling that is sometimes shown by those who lead the singing in God's Sanctuary. Very many pastors speak of the bitter pangs experienced when compelled to see the irreverent conduct in the choir gallery.

One remarked to me, that he had received so many "cold shocks" by witnessing the talking, laughing, leaf-turning, and note writing of members of the choir, that to avoid a "chill," he had so trained his eyes that, when looking over the congregation in his sermon, he kept his singers out of sight.

At one of our meetings a lady leader retired to the rear of the gallery, took two chairs, on the one she spread out her feet and leaned back on the other in true loafer's style. She kept reading in what looked like a red covered novel, till the close of the sermon, when she advanced to the front, and led again the song of the Sanctuary.

I was present at a funeral service, in which the whole audience seemed bathed in tears.

The deceased was a mother in Israel, whose body was placed in front of the pulpit. The elevated position of the choir brought the pale face of death in view, and yet with these impressive surroundings, they could not sing the funeral hymns without their accustomed whispering, and "tittering." While singing the solemn words,

> "Why do ye mourn departed friends,
> Or shake at death's alarm,"

they could even "shake" with laughter, as the organ played the interludes.

If God consumed Nadab and Abihu for trifling in his presence, fearful to such will be the coming judgment day.

Old Adam Manifested.

THE Rev. John Adams was ordained in 1748. After preaching thirty years at Durham, N. H., some difficulties brought about his dismission. At the close of his farewell sermon, he asked his people to "sing to the praise of God, and to their *own edification*," the first three verses of the one hundred and twentieth psalm of Dr. Watts:—

> "Thou God of love thou ever blest,
> Pity my suffering state:
> When wilt thou set my soul at rest
> From lips which love deceit?"

> "Hard lot of mine! my days are cast
> Among the sons of strife,
> Whose never-ceasing brawlings waste
> My golden hours of life.

> "Oh, might I fly to change my place,
> How would I choose to dwell
> In some wild, lonesome wilderness,
> And leave these gates of hell!"

DR. BELCHER also gives the following crook in one of the Lord's earthen vessels:—

"Not many years since, a minister in New Hampshire fell, as will sometimes happen, into a difficulty with his choir, which for some time prevented their accustomed services. At length the choir relented, and appeared, as heretofore, at the usual time of service. The minister most unexpectedly saw them in their places, and in due time, looking very significantly, rose and read the hymn,—

> "'And are ye wretches yet alive,
> And do ye yet rebel?'"

A New Way to Blow the Organ.

IN an Episcopal church the person who blew the bellows of the organ was also accustomed to attend to the furnance, and, finding it necessary to look after the fire, told a man, lately imported, to blow the bellows if it was required during his absence. Soon the *Gloria in Excelsis* came in the order of exercises, to be chanted, and Patrick was directed to furnish the organic element. After waiting some time for the instrument to respond to the touch, the lady performer whispered, "*blow*." "Blow" repeated the leader. "Blow," echoed the entire choir.

An investigation now took place, when Patrick was found behind the organ with both hands tightly clinched around the bellows-handle, and he, with inflated cheeks and distended eyes, was trying his utmost to blow his own breath into the bellows so as to fill the instrument.

A Big Tuning Fork.

TO give a correct pitch to church tunes, musical pitchforks were formerly much in use. When they were first introduced into the British realms, the precentor of Carnock parish ordered the Edinburgh Carrier to bring him one. As the carrier had never heard of any other pitchfork but that used by the farmers, he purchased one that was about eight feet long. It was late on Saturday night when he came home, and, as a message had been left to bring it up when he came to church next day, he marched into the church yard before the bell rung, and, to the no little astonishment and amusement of the leader of song, who was standing amid a group of villagers, he exclaimed "Aweel, John, here's the pitchfork you wanted; but I can tell you, I ne'er thought much o' your singing before, and I'm sair mistaken if ye'll sing ony better now!"

A Clergyman in a Fix.

YEARS ago, an aged minister was officiating for the first time in a Methodist church in Georgia, where they kept up the old custom of having the hymns "lined," that the whole congregation may, according to the wise discipline of that Church, join in the singing, whether they have hymn-books or not. The venerable man could not see distinctly, and intended to omit singing during that service. To announce his purpose, he arose and said,

"My eyes are dim: I cannot see"—

and immediately the chorister commenced singing it to the tune of "Old Hundred." Surprise and mortification made the clergyman almost speechless; but he stammered out,

"I meant but an apology."

This line was immediately sung by the congregation, and the minister, now quite excited, exclaimed,

"Forbear, I pray; my sight is dim"—

but the singing proceeded, and the couplet was finished by his beseeching explanation,

"I do not mean to read a hymn."

Strange as it may seem, this was also sung with much energy, while the worthy old gentleman sat down in actual despair of accomplishing his purpose to do without singing.

Inappropriate Hymns.

SHEER thoughtlessness is sometimes manifested in the announcement of unsuitable hymns.

On a bright Sabbath *morning* a pastor gave out, to a large and intelligent audience, the expressive evening hymn composed by James Edmeston, in 1820:—

"Saviour breathe an evening blessing,
Ere repose our spirits seal."

DURING the preaching of a farewell sermon, the people were so melted down with emotion, that the speaker was scarcely able to proceed. Calling upon a ministerial brother to close the service, he announced the hymn,

"Jesus, we lift our souls to thee;
Thy Holy Spirit breathe,
And let this little infant be
Baptised into thy death."

The effect may easily be imagined.

IN some churches, choirs are permitted to select their own voluntaries with which to close a service.

At the funeral of a distinguished gentleman in Massachusetts, the singers sang of their own accord,

"Believing we rejoice
To see the curse remove."

Surely this sentiment could not have been very much in accord with the weeping friends of the departed.

On another funeral occasion, in the presence of the deceased body of one who had been noted for her irritability and propensity to scold, the officiating clergyman gave out the hymn:—

> "Sister, thou wast mild and lovely,
> Gentle as the summer breeze,
> Pleasant as the air of evening,
> When it floats among the trees."

 A PRESBYTERIAN clergyman, who had been in his pastorate near a half century, in the State of New York, was called upon to preach the funeral sermon of one of his most devoted female members. On this occasion his tender feelings would now and then so overcome him, that he would pause in the midst of a sentence and repeat a part several times before he could control his emotions so as to complete it.

In describing the prayerfulness of the deceased he was adapting the verse of the hymn,

> "I love to steal awhile away,"

when his feelings so overpowered him, that he had to stop after saying, "She *loved to steal;*" and after a tearful pause, that rendered it more emphatic, he said again, "She *loved to steal;*" and not till a third trial could he go on to say:—

> "She loved to steal awhile away,
> From every cumbering care,
> And spend the hours of closing day
> In humble, grateful prayer."

A ministerial brother, a resident of the same place, in narrating to the author the above, said that his brother was an eye-witness of the scene, and of the many futile attempts to repress untimely laughter at each repetition of the assertion, "She *loved to steal.*"

Roman Catholic Hymns.

To give an idea of what the young are taught to sing in the Papal communion, we append some of their songs, from "The Catholic Youth's Hymn-Book." To Saint Mary, who is entitled, "The Queen of the Heavens, Mistress of Earth," is addressed the following:—

> "These praises and prayers
> I lay at thy feet!
> O virgin of virgins!
> O Mary most sweet!
> Be thou my true guide through this pilgrimage here,
> And stand by my side when death draweth near."

Saint Joseph is honored with the following supplication:—

> "O father of Jesus! be father to me,
> Sweet spouse of our Lady! and I will love thee."

And thus again:—

> "There's no saint in heaven, Saint Joseph, like thee,
> Sweet spouse of our Lady! O deign to love me."

Of purgatory, they sing as follows:—

> "The holy sacrifice of Mass
> Assists the souls in purgatory;
> Through this most holy sacrifice,
> O God of mercy, hear their cry.
> May they receive eternal rest,
> And with the light of heaven be blest."

In the last verse of a hymn entitled, "The Church of the Saints:"—

> "Then we'll cling to the priest, and we'll cling to the Pope:
> We'll cling to Christ's vicar, for Christ is our hope;
> We'll fight a good battle, and Mary the while
> From her throne in the skies, on her children will smile."

The Braying of an Ass Imitated in Church Song.

REV. DR. DOWLING, in his *History of Romanism*, while showing the midnight darkness of the dark ages, and the senseless superstition of the Roman Catholic Church during that period, refers, as an illustration, to a festival called, *The Feast of the Ass*.

On the 14th of January it was celebrated at Beauvais and other places.

A young lady, with an infant in her arms, was chosen to represent the Virgin Mary and the infant Jesus. Seated upon an ass, richly caparisoned, she was followed in procession by the bishop and clergy, from the cathedral to the church of St. Stephen, where she was placed near the altar, and then commenced the "high mass." The people, instead of the usual responses, were taught to imitate the braying of the ass, or to imitate the sounds *hinham, hinham, hinham.*

The learned Edgar refers to the close of this religious mummury on this wise: "The worship concluded with a BRAYING-MATCH between the clergy and laity, in *honor of the ass*. The officiating priest turned to the people, and in a fine treble voice, and with great devotion, *brayed three times like an ass, whose representative he was*; while the people, imitating his example in thanking God, brayed three times in concert." We give one of the nine verses, sung with great vociferation in praise of the ass on this occasion:—

"Gold, from Araby the blest,
Seba myrrh, of myrrh the best,
To the church this ass did bring;
We his sturdy labors sing.
  Now, Signior Ass, a noble bray;
  That beauteous mouth at large display,
  Abundant food our hay-lofts yield,
  And oats abundant load the field."

A Maniac Subdued by the Singing of a Hymn.

WHILE Mr. T. E. Perkins was sitting in the room of the Howard Mission, New York, conversing with Rev. Mr. Van Meter, they were interrupted by the entrance of a wild looking man, who exclaimed, "Is Awful Gardner here?" "No," replied Mr. Van Meter. "Then I am lost," said the man in accents of despair. "If awful Gardner was here *he* could save me; he would know how, because he's been the same road; but now I am lost;" and drawing a bowie-knife from under his vest, he was about to plunge it into his bosom, when Mr. Van Meter sprang forward and caught his arm.

Seeing that it would be useless to attempt to wrest the knife from his grasp, Mr. Van Meter sought to distract the man's attention from his suicidal purpose, but the unfortunate creature was seized with a fit of delirium tremens, and became unmanageable.

Mr. Perkins, not knowing what else to do, sat down at the melodeon, and began to play and sing:—

"Come, ye disconsolate, where'er ye languish;
 Come to the mercy-seat, fervently kneel;
Here bring your wounded hearts, here tell your anguish;
 Earth has no sorrow that heaven cannot heal."

The effect was magical. The man became sufficiently calm for Mr. Van Meter to march him up and down the room, while Mr. Perkins continued to play and sing. After finishing "Come, ye disconsolate," he sang:—

> "Jesus, to thy dear arms I flee,
> I have no other hope but thee."

The effect was still more marked.

After singing that beautiful hymn Mr. Perkins commenced:—

> "Flee as a bird to your mountain."

As the strains of this exquisite composition filled the room, the maniac paused, sat down, covered his face with his hands, and sobbed like a child, or rather like a broken-hearted, remorseful man.

By this time Mrs. Van Meter, who was present when the man first burst into the room, came in with a bowl of strong coffee, which she had thoughtfully made, and as soon as the weeping stranger became sufficiently composed, she gave it to him. That quieted his nerves and renewed his strength, and in a little while he became completely restored to the possession of his faculties.

"Who is this man?" was the question which rose spontaneously to the lips of his deliverer, but all efforts to ascertain seemed to prove fruitless. He persistently refused to give his name, or to furnish any clue to his residence or identity.

Mr. Perkins accompanied him to the St. Nicholas Hotel, where he took a room under an assumed name. As in his conversation he had chanced to mention a clergyman in Newport, R. I., whom Mr. Van Meter knew, the latter immediately wrote to the clergyman, stating the case. The clergyman came by the first boat, and at once recognized the unfortunate man, took him back again to his home in Hartford, where, before the period of his dissipation, he had been a man of wealth and responsibility. He threw off the thralldom of rum, and is now a respected Christian man.

A Life Saved by Singing.

THE editor of the "Musical Journal" narrates the following account, given him by a retired sea-captain, whom he describes as "a gentleman of high and honorable character, whose truthfulness we have no reason to doubt."

Being at sea, the cook had the sad misfortune one day, on attempting to draw a bucket of water over the side of the ship, to lose his balance, and fall overboard.

One of the sailors, who was addicted to stuttering, but who was a good singer, came running to the captain, who happened to be in the cabin, and cried out at the head of the stairs: "Captain, the co-co-co-co-co-co-."

"What's the matter?" asked the captain, "*sing* it," when the sailor lustily struck up:—

The cook is o-ver-board, buck-et and all!

upon which "the captain ran up on deck, caused the boat to be lowered, and thus saved the life of the poor 'cook, bucket and all.'"

AMONG the relics of hymnology, of the days of the revolution, is the following, "issued in 1770, in the *New England Psalm-Singer or American Chorister*, by William Billings, a native of Boston, in New England:"—

> "O, praise the Lord with one consent,
> And, in this grand design,
> Let Britain and the colonies
> Unanimously join."

To which a historian adds: "This opened a new era for the history of psalmody in the colonies."

Saved by the Attraction of Music.

AN old Inn keeper in England, who had often swore that he would never attend church, heard of the choice music, and of the crowds attracted by it, and so resolved, one Sabbath afternoon, to go and hear the singing, but not to hear one word of the sermon.

The church was six miles distant, and as it was a hot summer day, and he a corpulent man, he came in with the sweat pouring down on every side, and with difficulty crowded into a narrow pew.

He listened with rapt attention to the singing of the first hymns, but then leaned his elbows on the back of the next pew, and put his two fore-fingers in his ears, so as not to hear one word of the sermon that followed.

He seemed well fortified from the darts of truth, until a little tricky fly came flying along, and lit on his red carbuncled nose, and stung it so that in self defence, he was compelled to take one of his hands to knock off the naughty fly, when to his surprise the words of the preacher came ringing in the unstopped ear. "*He that hath ears to hear, let him hear.*"

They sounded like a clap of thunder in the clear sky. He opened both ears, and was very much impressed by the words that followed.

That day was the beginning of days to him: a change was produced upon him which could not but be noticed by all his former companions. He never from that day returned to any of his former practices, nor ever afterwards was he seen in liquor, nor heard to swear. He became truly serious, and for many years went, all weathers, six miles to church where he first received the knowledge of Divine things.

After about eighteen years faithful and close walk with God, he died rejoicing in the hope of the glory of God.

Solomon's Song.

A RICH young gentleman in New York, hearing a minister, in a Fifth Avenue church, highly applaud Solomon's Song, thought it would make a nice present for one of his musical female friends. So calling at Messrs. Brown and Perkin's music store he inquired:

"Have you Solomon's Song? I—aw—want to get a cawpy."

"N-o-oo," thougthfully replied the senior member, "I th-ink not."

"Aw!" said the young amateur drawing on his kid, "perhaps it isn't out yet. Our rector spoke of it last Sunday as a work of great genius and beauty, and I want Miss——aw—a certain young lady to learn it."

THE chorister of a choir in Vermont wrote to a publisher in Boston for a copy of the popular singing book, "*The Ancient Lyre.*" His communication ran, "Please send me the *Ancient Liar, well bound.*"

The publisher replied: "My dear sir:—I do not doubt that the devil has been and still is in Boston, but it will be difficult to comply with your request, for the reason that Boston's influence is so strong in his favor, it will be impossible to *bind* him."

AT an evening service, Deacon H—— was reading the lines of Watts' hymn:—

"The fondness of a creature's love,
How strong it strikes the sense!"

when, his eye-sight being poor and his education no better, he brought out the two lines with a full voice as follows:—

"The fatness of a critter's love,
How strange it strikes the sense."

A Ruffian Charmed.

DURING the persecutions of Christians at Wexford, Ireland, by the Catholics, they met in a closed barn.

"One violent opposer agreed to conceal himself in the barn before the worship began, that at a suitable time he might open the door to his comrades; and for that purpose he crept into a sack near the door.

When the singing commenced, the Hibernian was so impressed with the music that he thought he would hear it through before he began the disturbance. The singing so much gratified him that he thought he would also hear the prayer; and such was the effect of the prayer that he was seized with remorse and trembling, so that he roared with fright,—which led the people to remove the sack, whereupon the Irishman was disclosed, praying with all his might as a penitent. Southey says, "This is the most comical case of instantaneous conversion that ever was recorded: and yet the man is said to have been thoroughly converted."

Provoking a Smile.

A chorister in Connecticut finding the words of the ninety-second Psalm as arranged by Watts:—

"Oh may my heart in tune be found
Like David's harp of solemn sound!"

not adapted to some new music, came to his pastor with this proposed change,

"Oh may my heart be tuned within,
Like David's sacred violin!"

Checking his "risibles," the pastor proposed to change it to read thus:—

"Oh may my heart go diddle, diddle,
Like Uncle David's sacred fiddle!"

The abashed critic meekly retired.

Hymn books.

List of Hymn Books.

The 800 hymn-writers, referred to in this book, include the authors of nearly all the hymns contained in the following standard hymn-books:—

THE PRESBYTERIAN HYMNAL, Joseph Duryea D. D. Pres Board of Pub.
THE CHURCH HYMN BOOK, Edwin F. Hatfield D D
        ·   Ivison, Blakeman, Taylor and Co, New York.
PSALMS AND HYMNS AND SPIRITUAL SONGS, Charles Robinson D. D.
        A S Barnes and Co. 111 William St, N. Y.
HYMNS AND SONGS OF PRAISE, Rev. Drs Hitchcock, Eddy, and Schaff
        A D F Randolph and Co , New York
BAPTIST HYMN AND TUNE BOOK, Baptist Board of Publication, Philadelphia.
THE BAPTIST PRAISE BOOK, Rev. Messrs. Fuller, Levy, Phelps, Fisk, etc.
        A S Barnes and Co , New York
HYMNS FOR THE METHODIST E. CHURCH. Nelson and Phillips, N. Y.
THE VOICE OF PRAISE Rev Messrs Alex Clark, McKeever, etc.
        James Robison, Pittsburg, Pa.
THE SERVICE OF SONG, S L. Caldwell and A. J Gordon.
        Gould and Lincoln, Boston, Mass.
THE PSALMIST, Rev. Messrs Baron Stow and S F Smith
        Gould and Lincoln, Boston, Mass.
HYMNS OF THE CHURCH, Rev. Dr J B Thompson, A G Vermilye, etc.
        A S Barnes and Co, New York.
HYMNS FOR THE REFORMED CHURCH IN THE U. S.
        Reformed Church Publication Board, Phila.
THE BOOK OF PRAISE, Rev Messrs. Eustis, Jr., Parker, Dana, Dunning, etc.
        Hamersley and Co.. Hartford, Conn.
THE NEW SABBATH HYMN AND TUNE BOOK, Rev Messrs Lowell Mason, Edward A. Park, and Austin Phelps
        Hamersley and Co , Hartford, Conn.
HYMNAL WITH TUNES OF THE PROTESTANT EPISCOPAL CHURCH.
        A. S Barnes and Co , New York.
PLYMOUTH COLLECTION, Rev. Henry Ward Beecher. A S Barnes and Co
HYMNS FOR THE SANCTUARY, Rev. Messrs. Lanthurn, Shuey, Kumler, etc.
        United Brethren Pub. House, Dayton, O.
CHURCH BOOK FOR THE USE OF EVANGELICAL LUTHERAN CONGREGATIONS.
        Lutheran Book Store Philadelphia.
BOOK OF WORSHIP, General Synod of the Lutheran church.
        Lutheran Board of Publication. Phila.
EVANGELICAL HYMN BOOK, Evangelical Association, Cleveland, Ohio.

"In Psalms and Hymns and Spiritual Songs, Singing to the Lord."

Synopsis of Hymn Writers.

EXPLANATIONS.—The letter *N* attached to the figures preceding a name refers to a note in the *Appendix*. (See page 552.) The asterisk (*) indicates a clergyman. Ch. Eng. stands for the Church of England. Cath. for Roman Catholic, ordinarily. Numbers in parentheses refer to the date of the hymn. While all the hymns are found in English, some are translations from the languages in which they were first written.

PAGE.	NAME.	HOME.	Birth...Death.	CHURCH.	FIRST LINE OF ONE OF THEIR HYMNS.
	Abelard, Peter......	Eng...	1079...1142	Cath......	He sends to the virgin.
N. 1	Adam, S. Victor...	Eng...	1086	Cath......	The church on earth, with
	Adams, John........	Eng...	1751...1835	Bapt......	Jesus is our great salvation.
	Adams, John Q...	U. S...	1767...1848	Unit'n....	How swift, alas! our moments
29	Adams, S. F........	Eng...	1805...1849	Unit'n....	Nearer, my God, to thee.
	Addiscott, H.......	Eng...	1806...1860	Cong	And is there, Lord, a cross for
25	Addison, J..........	Eng...	1672...1719	Ch. Eng.	When all thy mercies, O my
	Alber, Erasmus...	Ger ...	1553	Luth.*...	O children of your God, rejoice
	Alberti, Henry.....	Prus...	1604...1668	Luth	God, who made the earth and
	Albertini, J. B.....	Ger ...	1769...1831	Mora	Long in the spirit-world my
	Albernus, J. G.....	Sax ...	1624...1679	Luth......	Not in anger smite us, Lord.
N. 2	Alexander, C. F...	Ire...	1823.........	Ch. Eng.	The roseate hues of early dawn.
	Alexander, J. A...	U.S...	1809...1860	Pres*.....	There is a time we know not
	Alexander, W. L..	Scot...	1808.........	Cong*...	Spirit of power and truth and
40	Alfred the Great...	Eng...	871... 900	Cath......	As the sun doth daily rise.
34	Alford, Henry......	Eng...	1810...1871	C. Eng.*	Come, ye thankful people, come
N. 3	Allen, James.	Eng...	1734...1804	Meth.*...	Sweet the moments, rich in
	Allen, Oswald......	....	1816.........	....	To-day thy mercy calls me.
	Allendorf, J. L. C.	Ger ...	1693...1773	Ref.*.....	Now rest my soul in Jesus' arm.
	Altenberg, J. M...	Prus...	1583...1640	Luth......	Fear not, O little one, the foe.
	Ambrose, St.......	Fran..	340... 397	Cath.*...	O God of truth, O Lord of might.
	Anatolius, St.......	Turk..	 458	....	The day is past and over.
	Anderson, G. W...	U. S...	1816.........	Bapt.*...	Onward, herald of the Gospel.
	Anderson, Mrs.....	Fran..	1819.........	Bapt......	Our country's voice is pleading.
	Andrew, St........	Crete.	660... 731	Greek....	O the mystery, passing wonder.
	Angelus, S..........	Siles..	1624...1677	Ref.*.....	Most high and holy Trinity.
	Anselm, St..........	Italy..	1086	Cath.*....	Jesus, solace of my soul.
	Anstice, Joseph...	Eng...	1818...1836	C. Eng.*	In all things like thy brethren.
	Apelles, Matth......	Prus ..	1594...1648	Luth	O Christ, the leader of that war-

Page	Name	Home	Birth..Death	Church	First Link of one of their Hymns
	Aquinas, St. Thos.	Italy.	1227..1274	Cath...	Now my tongue the mystery
	Arndt, Ernest M.	Ger...	1769...1860	Luth.....	Go, and dig my grave to-day!
	Arnold, Gottfried.	Ger...	1666 1714	Ref..	Well for him, who all things
N 4	Auber, Harriet .	Eng .	1773 1862	Ch Eng	Our blest Redeemer, ere we
	Austin, John	Eng	 1669	Cath.	Blest be thy love, dear Lord
	Aveling, T. W .	Eng .	1815	Cong *...	Hail ! thou God of grace and
	Bache, Mrs S .	Eng..	1744 1808	Unit'n..	"See how He loved!" exclaimed
	Bacon, Leonard...	U. S .	1802...... .	Cong.*..	Wake the song of jubilee.
	Bahnmaier, J. F.	Ger ...	1774 .1841	Luth.*..	Spread, oh spread, thou mighty
N 5	Baker, H W ...	Eng .	1821.........	C Eng.*	Oh ! what if we are Christ's
N 6	Bakewell, John .	Eng...	1721...1819	Meth.*...	Hail ! thou once despised Jesus !
N 7	Baldwin, Thomas	U S.	1753...1825	Bapt.*....	Come, happy souls, adore the
	Balfour, Alex	Scot .	1767. 1829	Pres ...	Go, messengers of peace and love
	Ball, William ...	Eng...	....(1864)..	Quaker.	Hallelujah! praise to God
	Balthaser, S P..	Ger ...	1657. 1742	Ref.. ..	If Thou, True Life, wilt in me
	Bancroft, J H	U.S ..	1819...1844	. . . *	Brother, though from yonder
	Bancroft, C L ...	Ire ...	... .	Ch Eng	Oh for the robes of whiteness!
N. 8	Barbauld, A L.	Eng...	1744 1825	Unit'n...	Praise to God, immortal praise
	Baring-Gould, S	Eng	.. ..	. .... *	Onward, Christian soldiers.
	Barlow, Joel .	U S	1757 1812	Pres ..	Awake, my soul, to sound his
	Bartholomew, W	Eng .	1793.....	. ...	Praise Jehovah, bow before him.
N 9	Barton, Bernard.	Eng .	1784 1849	Quaker.	Lamp of our feet ! whereby we
	Bateman, C H .	.... ..	1813 (1848)	. . ....	Blessed Jesus, ere we part
	Bateman, Henry.	....	1800.......	. .... *	Jesus ! Jesus ! come and save.
N 10	Bathurst, W H...	Eng ..	1796... . .	C. Eng.*	Oh ! for a faith that will not
	Batty, Chris.. ...	Eng ..	1715 . 1797	Meth *.	Captain of thine enlisted host.
	Baxter, Lydia ..	U S	1809 1874	Bapt..	There is a gate that stands ajar.
42	Baxter, Richard.	Eng ..	1615...1691	Pres *.	Lord, it belongs not to my care
	Beadon, H W .	Eng	.. ...	C Eng *	All praise to thee, O Lord !
	Beaumont, John	....	1810. ...	. ..... *	Many times since days of youth
259	Bede, Venerable.	Eng...	672 .. 735	Cath *..	A hymn for martyrs, sweetly
54	Beddome, B .	Eng...	1717 1795	Bapt *..	Did Christ o'er sinners weep.
	Beecher, Charles	U S .	1819.........	Cong *.	We are on our journey home.
	Behemb, M	Ger ..	1537 1622	Luth* ..	Lord Jesus Christ, my life, my
	Beman, N S .	U.S	1786 1871	Pres. *	Hark ! the judgment trumpet
	Benedictis, J De	Umb	. . 1306	Cath	At the cross her station keeping.
	Bengel, J A ..	Ger ..	1687...1782	Luth* ...	I'll think upon the woes.
	Bennett, Henry	....	1813 1868	.... *	I have a home above
	Benson, R. W...	Eng .	..(1861)..	C. Eng *	Praise to God who reigns above.
56	Bernard, St	Eng	1150.........	Cath *..	Brief life is here our portion
	Bernard of Cluny.	Fran.	1091.. 1153	Cath.*...	Jesus, thou joy of loving hearts
58	Berridge, John	Eng	1716 1793	C. Eng *	Oh, happy saints who dwell in
N. 11	Bethune, Geo W	U.S	1805 1862	Ref *	O Thou who in Jordan didst
	Bianco da Siena...	Italy..	1434	Cath......	Come down, O Love Divine.
	Biarowsky, W E	Ger .	1814. ...	Luth *	Remember me
	Bickersteth, Edw	Eng .	1786 . 1850	C. Eng.*	With thankful hearts our songs
	Bickersteth, E. H.	Eng...	1825.........	C Eng *	Father of heaven above
	Bickersteth, John	Eng...	1781...1855	C. Eng *	Hast Thou, Holy Lord, Redeemer
	Bienemann, C. .	Ger ..	1540 1591	Luth*	Come, O my soul, in sacred lays
N 12	Bilby, Thomas	Eng	1794 .*...	. .	Here we suffer grief and pain.
	Binney, Thomas.	Eng..	1798 .	Cong.*.	Eternal light ! eternal light !
	Birken, S ...	Bohe	1626...1681	Luth ..	*Wrote many hymns, 2 tr in Eng*
	Birks, T R ..	Eng	1810 .	C. Eng.*	Oh ! when from all the ends of

Synopsis of Hymn Writers. 537

Page	Name	Home	Birth..Death	Church	First Line of one of their Hymns
	Blackall, C R	U.S.	1830........	Bapt...	Follow the paths of Jesus.
N. 13	Blacklock, T.	Scot..	1721..1791	Pres *.	Come, oh my soul in sacred lays
	Blackie, J S.	Scot.	1809	Pres	Angels, holy, high and lowly
	Blair, Robert	Scot...	1699..1746	Pres.*	What though no flowers the fig-
	Blew, W. J	Eng...	1808........	C. Eng.*	The day is past and gone, Great
	Bliss, Philip P..	U S	1838 ...	Cong	Almost persuaded, now to believe
	Blunt, R. W	Eng	(1841)..	Ch Eng	Jesus, thy blessed brow is torn
	Bode, J E	Eng	1816........	C. Eng.*	All wandering on the blessed
	Boden, James	Eng	1757..1841	Cong *.	Ye dying sons of men
	Bogatzky, C H.	Prus	1690 1774	Ref..	Awake, thou Spirit, who of old
	Bohme, D	Prus	1605.1657	Ref.*	Lord, now let thy servant
	Bohmer, J H	Ger.	1674.1749	Ref.*	O risen Lord, O conquering King.
	Bohnmaier, J	Ger.	1774.1841	....*	Spread, O spread, thou mighty
66	Bonar, H.	Scot.	1808........	Pres.*	I lay my sins on Jesus.
	Bonaventura, St	Italy	1221 1274	. . *	In the Lord's atoning grief.
N. 14	Borthwick, J.	Scot.	. (1858)	. ..	My Jesus, as thou wilt
	Boschenstein, J...	Ger	1472...1536	Luth .	When on the cross the Saviour
	Bourignon, A	Hol ..	1616..1680	....	Come, Saviour Jesus, from above
	Bourne, H	Eng.	1772..1852	Meth.*.	O Saviour, welcome to my heart
	Bowdler, John	Eng	1783..1815	Ch Eng	As panting in the sultry beam
N. 15	Bowring, John	Eng...	1792..1872	Unit'n ..	In the cross of Christ I glory.
	Brackenbury,R C	Eng	1752.1818	Meth.*.	My son, know thou the Lord.
	Brady, Nicholas .	Ire.	1659 1726	C. Eng *	With Tate wrote a version of Ps
	Brooks, C. T.	U.S...	1813	Unit'n *.	God bless our native land (tr)
	Brewer, J	Eng	1752. 1817	Cong *..	Hail, sovereign Love, that first
	Bridges, M.	Eng	. (1860)..	Cath .	My God, accept my heart this day
	Bronte, Anne	Eng.	1820.1849	Ch. Eng.	Oppressed with sin and woe
	Brown, J N	U S.	1803..1868	Bapt	Go, spirit of the sainted dead
77	Brown, Mrs P H	U.S.	1783...1861	Cong.	O Lord, thy work revive
N. 16	Browne, Simon	Eng	1680 1732	Cong *...	Come, Holy Spirit heavenly
	Brown, William	.....	.. (1822)...	...	Welcome, sacred day of rest
	Browne, Thos	Eng.	1605 1682	Ch. Eng	The night is come, like to the
N. 17	Bruce, M.	Scot	1746 1767	Pres .	O happy is the man who hears.
	Brumgk, H........	Ger ...	.1785	Morav *.	Thou source of my salvation
	Bryant, J H.	U.S.	1807.....	....	O Lord, our eyes have waited
	Bryant, W.C..	U.S.	1797. ...	Unit'n ...	Deem not that they are blest alone
	Bubier, G. B	Eng..	1823 ..	Cong.*	I would commune with thee, my
	Buckoll, H J.	Eng.	...(1840)	C Eng *	Word of Him whose sovereign
	Bulfinch, S G	U S.	1809.1870	Unit'n *	Hail to the Sabbath day
	Bullock, Wm	U S ..	1798 ..	C Eng *	We love the place, O God
	Bulmer, A.	Eng ..	1775...1837	Meth ..	Lord, if the vast creation
	Bulmer, J	Eng	1784 1857	Cong *.	Thou who hast in Zion laid
	Bunting, W. M.	Eng.	1805.1866	Meth .. .	My Sabbath suns may all have
	Burde, S G........	Prus.	1753.1831	Luth ...	When the Lord wields the
N. 18	Burder, G	Eng...	1752. 1832	Cong.*..	Come ye that know and fear the
	Burdsall, R.	Eng.	1735.. 1824	Meth ...	The voice of free grace
	Burgess, G .	U.S.	1809.1866	Epis.* ..	When forth from Egypt's
	Burleigh, W..	U.S.	1812..1871	Unit'n ..	Father, beneath thy sheltering
	Burmeister, F...	Ger	1688	Ref. ...	Thou virgin soul, O thou
	Burnham, R	Eng..	1749..1810	Bapt.*..	Holy Spirit, now descend
	Burns, J. D	Scot..	1823.1864	Pres.* ...	Still with thee, O my God.
	Burton, John...	Eng.	1773..1822	Bapt .	Time is winging us away.
	Burton, John .	Eng.	1803	Cong	O thou that hearest prayer
	Butcher, E......	Eng..	1757...1822	Unit'n.*	Hosannah! let us join to sing

Synopsis of Hymn Writers.

Page	Name	Home	Birth..Death	Church	First Link of one of their Hymns
	Butterworth, J ..	Eng ..	...(1846)..	C Eng.*	Spirit of wisdom, guide thine
	Byles, ...	U.S ..	.. ..	Cong.. .	When wild confusion wrecks the
	Byrom, J	Eng ..	1691...1763	Ch. Eng.	My spirit longs for thee
	Calvin, John... .	Switz.	1500 ..1564	Pres *. .	I greet thee, who my sure Redeem
	Cambridge, Ada...	Eng	1844..... ..	Ch. Eng.	Humbly now, with deep contrition
	Cameron, Wm .	Scot..	1751 . 1811	Pres.. .	How bright these glorious spirits
	Campbell, Robert.	Sco'.	1868	Cath . .	At the Lamb's high feast we sing.
	Campbell, Thos...	Scot .	1777.. 1844	Pres.... ..	When Jordan hushed his waters
	Canitz, F. R. L.	Ger ..	1654.. 1699	Luth . ..	Come, my soul, awake ! 'tis
	Carlyle, Jos D	Eng...	1759...1804	C. Eng.*	Lord, when we bow before thy
	Carpenter, Jos E.	Eng ..	1813.........	Ch. Eng.	Lord and Father of creation.
	Cary, Alice	U S .	1820 . 1870	Univ . ..	I cannot plainly see the way
84	Cary, Phœbe .	U S .	1824 . 1871	Univ	One sweetly solemn thought.
N. 19	Caswall, Edward .	Eng ..	1814.........	Cath π ..	Jesus, the very thought of thee.
	Cawood, John	Eng...	1775...1852	C Eng.*	Hark ! what mean those holy
	Cecil, Richard ...	Eng ..	1748...1810	Ch Eng	Cease here longer to detain me
	Celano, Thomas .	... .	1255	Cath	The day of wrath, that dreadful
90	Cennick, John	Eng ..	1717 . 1755	Morav *	Children of the heavenly King.
	Chambers, J. D ..	Eng ..	. . . . . .	Ch. Eng	Let every heart exulting sing
N. 20	Chandler, John ..	Eng	1806..	C. Eng.*	Christ is our corner stone
	Chapin, Edwin H.	U.S ..	1814...	Univ *	Now, host with host assembling.
	Chapman, R. C. .	Eng	1837..	..	My soul, amid this stormy world.
	Charles, Mrs. E .	Eng	. ....	Ch Eng.	A hymn of glory let us sing.
	Churton, Edward	Eng ..	1800)	C Eng.*	God of grace, O let thy light
	Clark, Wm G ..	U S .	1810. 1843	.....	We have met in peace together
	Clarke, J. F ..	U S	1810. . . .	Unit'n.*	Hast thou wasted all thy powers?
	Claudius, Matth .	Ger ..	1743 ..1815	Luth	The moon hath risen on high.
	Clausnitzer, T...	Ger ..	1619.. 1684	Luth * .	Gracious Jesu ' in thy name.
	Clayton, George..	Eng ..	1783 . 1862	Cong *.	From yon delusive scene.
	Cleaveland, B	U S..	1717.....	Bapt ...	Oh ! could I find from day to day
N 21	Clemens, A. St ...	Egypt ..	 217	... ...*	Shepherd of tender youth.
	Cobbin, Ingram .	Eng ..	1777. 1851	Cong.*.	If 'tis sweet to mingle where
N. 22	Codner, Elizabeth	Eng ..	(1860)	Ch Eng	Lord, I hear of showers of bless-
	Coffin, Charles ..	Fran.	1676...1749	Cath.*....	Once more the solemn season
	Collins, Charles .	U S ..	1823.. ..	Pres.*...	Far beyond this world of sorrow
	Collins, Henry	Eng .	(1852)	Cath * .	Jesus, my Lord, my God, my all
N 23	Collyer, Wm B .	Eng ..	1782...1854	Cong.*.	Return, O wanderer, return.
	Colver, Nathaniel	U.S ..	1794	Bapt .	Weep for the lost, thy Saviour
	Conder, Joan E	Eng ..	1796. ..	Cong ..	The hours of evening close.
N 24	Conder, Josiah.	Eng ..	1789 .1855	Cong *.	Bread of heaven, on thee we feed
N 25	Cook, Russell S.	U S ..	1811 . 1864	Cong *.	Just as thou art, without one
	Cooper, John . .	Eng .	(1810)	Ch. Eng.	Father of heaven, whose love
	Copeland, Wm. J.	Eng .	(1848)	C. Eng.*	Jesus, the world's redeeming
	Cosin, John........	Eng...	1594...1672	C. Eng.*	Come, Holy Ghost, our souls
	Cosmas, S	Syria..	 760	Gr. Ch *	Christ is born, exalt his name
N. 26	Cotterill, Thomas	Eng...	1779 . 1823	C. Eng *	O'er the realms of pagan darkness
	Cotton, Nathan'l	Eng ..	1707...1788	Ch Eng.	Why, O my soul, O why
	Coverdale, Myles	Eng ..	1488 .1569	C Eng *	O Holy Spirit our Comforter
92	Cowper, Wm ..	Eng .	1731 . 1800	C Eng *	There is a fountain filled with
	Coxe, Arthur C	U S .	1818 . . .	Epis *	We are living, we are dwelling.
	Crabbe, George....	Eng	1754 .1832	C. Eng.*	Pilgrim, burdened with thy sin.
	Crasselius, Barth.	Prus ..	1677...1724	Luth * .	Awake, O man, and from thee
	Crewdson Jane	Eng .	1809...1863	Ch. Eng.	I've found a joy in sorrow.

Page	Name	Home	Birth	Death	Church	First Line of one of their Hymns
	Croly, George	Ire.	1780	1860	C Eng *	Lift up your eyes, ye sons of
	Crosby, Mrs F. J.	U.S.	1823	. .	Meth	Pass me not, O gentle Saviour.
	Crossman, Sam'l	Eng	1628	1683	C. Eng.*	Jerusalem on high.
	Crosswell, Wm	U.S.	1804	1854	Epis.*	Lord, lead the way the Saviour
	Creutziger, E	Ger	.	1558	Luth	O Thou, of God the Father.
	Cruttenden, R.	Eng	1690	1763	Cong.	Lord, didst thou die, but not for
	Cummins, J. J.	Eng	.	1867	C. Eng.	Shall hymns of grateful love?
	Cunningham, J. W.	Eng	1780	1861	Ch. Eng.	From Calvary a cry was heard.
	Cutting, S S	U S	1816	. . .	Bapt.*	Father, we bless thy gentle care
	Dach, Simon	Ger	1605	1659	Luth	Wouldst thou inherit life with
	Dale, Thomas	Eng	1797	1870	C Eng.*	When the spark of life is waning.
	Damiani, Peter	Italy	988	1072	Cath.	For the fount of life eternal
122	Davies, Samuel	U.S.	1724	1761	Pres.*	Lord, I am thine, entirely thine.
	Davis, Eliel	Eng	1803	1849	Bapt.*	From every earthly pleasure.
	Davis, Thomas	Eng	1810	.	C. Eng *	O Paradise eternal!
	Dayman, Edw. A	Eng	(1868)		C Eng *	Who is this with garments dyed?
	D'Aubigné, J H M	Switz.	1794	187–	Ref *.	Jesus, I thy triumphs sing.
	Deacon, Samuel	Eng	1746	1816	Bapt *.	To Jordan's stream the Saviour
	Decius, Nicholas	Ger	.	1529	Luth *	All glory be to God on high.
	Deck, James G.	Eng	1802	.	Plym. B.	Lord Jesus, are we one with thee?
364	De Courcy, Rich'd	Ire	1743	1803	C. Eng *	Jesus, at thy command
N 27	De Fleury, Maria	Eng	(1791)		Bapt	Ye angels, who stand round the
	De la M Fouqué, F H	Ger	1777	1843	Ref	My Saviour, what thou didst of
	Denham, David	Eng	1791	1848	Bapt.*	'Mid scenes of confusion and
	Denicke, David	Ger	1603	1680	Luth.*	My God, I call upon thy name.
N. 28	Denny, Sir Edw.	Ire	1796	. . .	Plym. B.	Light of the lonely pilgrim's
	Dent, Caroline	Eng	(1855)			Jesus, Saviour! Thou dost know.
	Dessler, Wolf C	Ger	1660	1722	Luth	Jesus, whose glory's streaming
	Dickinson, Wm	Eng	1816	1868	C Eng *	Hallelujah! who shall part?
	Dickson, David	Scot	1583	1662	Pres *.	O Mother dear, Jerusalem.
	Dillon, Wentw'th	Ire	1633	1684	Epis	The last loud trumpet's wondrous
	Dix, Wm C	Eng	1837	.	Ch Eng	As with gladness, men of old
N. 29	Doane, Geo W.	U.S	1799	1859	Epis.*	Thou art the way, to thee alone.
	Dobell, John	Eng	1757	1840	Cong	Now is the accepted time
	Dober, Anna	Ger	1713	1739	Morav.	Holy Lamb, who thee receive.
128	Doddridge, Philip	Eng	1702	1751	Cong.*	Grace, 'tis a charming sound.
	Downton, Henry.	Eng	1818		C Eng.*	For thy mercy and thy grace.
	Dracup, John	Eng	.	1795	Bapt *	Thanks to thy name, O Lord,
	Drennan, Wm	Ire	1754	1820	Unit'n	The heaven of heavens cannot
	Drewes, John F.	Ger	1762	.	Ref.*	My God; lo, here before thy face.
	Drummond, W. H	Ire	1772	1856	Pres.*.	Is this the feast for me?
	Dryden, John.	Eng	1632	1700	Cath	Creator Spirit! by whose aid.
	Duffield, George	U S	1818	. .	Pres.*.	Stand up! stand up for Jesus
N. 30	Duncan, Mary L.	Scot.	1814	1840	Pres.	Jesus, tender Shepherd, hear me.
	Dunn, R P	. .	1825	1867	. . .*	Jesus, Jesus, visit me
	Dyer, Sidney	U S	1814	. .	Bapt.*	Go preach the blest salvation.
N. 31	Dwight, John S	U S	1812	. .	Cong *	God bless our native land! (alt.)
150	Dwight, Timothy.	U. S.	1752	1817	Cong *	I love thy kingdom, Lord
	Eastburn, J. W.	U S	1798	1819	Epis	O Holy, holy, holy Lord!
	East, John	Eng	(1836)		C Eng.*	There is a fold whence none can
	Eber, Paul.	Ger	1511	1569	Ger.*.	In anger, Lord, rebuke me not
N 32	Ebert, Jacob	Ger	1549	1614	Luth *.	Lord Jesus Christ, the Prince of

PAGE	NAME	HOME	Birth	Death	CHURCH	FIRST LINE OF ONE OF THEIR HYMNS
	Edeling, Chr. L.	Ger	1751	1812	Luth.*	My Saviour, make me cleave to
N. 33	Edmeston, James	Eng	1791	1867	Ch. Eng.	Saviour! breathe an evening
	Elliot, Robert	Eng		..1788	Cong *..	Prepare me, gracious God.
156	Elliott, Charlotte	Eng	1789	1871	Ch. Eng.	Just as I am, without one plea.
	Ellıott, Julıa A	Eng		..1841	Ch Eng.	Great Creator, who this day.
	Elven, Cornelius	Eng	1797		Bapt *	With broken heart and contrite
	Enfield, William	Eng	1741	1797	Unit'n *	Behold where in a mortal form.
	England, Sam'l S.	Eng	1810		Cong* ...	In anger, Lord, rebuke me not.
	Ephrem, Syrus	Turk	...	381	...*	To thee, O Lord, loud praise
	Evans, James H.	Eng	1785	1849	Bapt.¶.	Faint not, Christian, though the
	Evans, John M	U. S.	1825		Bapt...	Amid the joyous scenes of earth.
	Evans, Jonathan	Eng	1749	1809	Cong. *...	Hark! the voice of love and
N. 34	Faber, Fred. W	Eng	1815	1863	Cath *.	Sweet Saviour, bless us ere we go.
	Fanch, James	Eng	1704	1767	Bapt ? .	Beyond the glittering starry
166	Fawcett, John.	Eng	1739	1817	Bapt *..	Blest be the tie that binds
	Fellows, John.	Eng		..1785	Bapt	Jesus, mighty king in Zion.
	Feneberg, J M.	Ger	1751	1812	Cath.*..	The moon hath risen on high.
	Fitch, Eleazer T.		1790	1871	.. ..*	Lord, at this closing hour.
	Flemming, Paul.	Ger	1606	1640	Luth	Where'er I go, whate'er my task.
	Fletcher, Samuel	Eng	1785	1863	Cong	Father of life and light.
	Flittner, John	Ger	1618	1678	Luth *	What shall I, a sinner, do?
	Flowerdew, Alice.	Eng	1759	1830	Bapt ..	Fountain of mercy, God of love.
	Follen, E L.	U.S	1787		Unit'n .	How sweet upon the Sabbath
	Ford, Charles L	Eng ..			Ch. Eng	Earthly joys no longer please us.
	Ford, David E .	...	(1828)		.. ..*	How vain is all beneath the skies.
	Ford, James.	Eng			Ch Eng	Awake, my soul, awake to pray.
	Fortunatus, V H C	Italy	550	609	Cath *..	The God, whom earth and sky
	Fortzsch, Basil	Ger		..1619	Luth †	O Christ, thou bright and morn
	Fountain, John	Eng	1723	1800	Bapt *..	Sinners, you are now addressed
	Fouqué, De la M	Ger	1777	1843	Ref ..	My Saviour, what thou didst of
N. 35	Francis, Benj	Wales	1734	1799	Bapt * .	My gracious Redeemer I love.
	Frank, John.	Ger	1618	1677	Luth ...	Let who will in thee rejoice.
	Frank, Solomon	Ger	1659	1725	Luth ...	Rest of the weary, Thou!
	Franke, Aug. H.	Ger	1663	1727	Luth *	What within me and without.
	Freudentheil, W N	Ger.	1771	1853	Luth *	The Father knows thee.
	Freylinghausen, J A	Ger.	1670	1739	Luth *...	Pure essence! Spotless Fount of
	Freystein, J. B..	Ger....		1720	Luth ...	Rise my soul, to watch and pray,
	Frothingham, N L	U.S	1793		Unit'n *	Our Christ has reached his
	Fugger, Casper.	Ger....		1617	Luth *.	We Christians may rejoice to-day
	Fulbert, St.	Fran		1029	...*	Ye choirs of new Jerusalem.
	Furness, Wm	U.S	1802		Unit'n *	Feeble, helpless, how shall I
	Gabb, James	Eng	(1854)		C. Eng.*	Jesus, thou wast once a child.
	Gadsby, William	Eng	1773	1844	Bapt *.	Holy Ghost, we look to thee.
	Gambold, John	Wales		..1771	Morav *.	O tell me no more
	Gandy, Sam'l W	Eng...		..1858	C. Eng *	His be the victor's name.
	Ganse, H D	Ger	1822		.. ..*	Thou, who like the wind dost
	Garve, Charles B	Ger	1763	1841	Morav *	Thy Word, O Lord, like gentle
	Gascoigne, Geo	Eng		1577	Ch Eng	We that have passed in slumbers
	Gaskell, Mrs.E C	U S	1810	1865	....	Mighty God, the First, the Last.
	Gates, Mrs. E H	U S		.1863		I will sing you a song
	Gauldett, T H .	U S	1807	1851	Epis .	Jesus, in sickness and in pain.
	Gellert, Chr. F ..	Ger	1717	1769	Luth	Jesus lives no longer now.

Synopsis of Hymn Writers.

Page	Name	Home	Birth	Death	Church	First Line of one of their Hymns
172	Gerhardt, Paul	Ger	1606	1676	Luth *	Commit thou all thy griefs
	Gesenius, Justus	Ger	1601	1671	Luth *	When sorrow and remorse.
	Geste, Guillaume	Fran	...	1702	Cath.*	The Shepherd now was smitten.
N. 36	Gibbons, Thomas	Eng	1720	1785	Cong.*	Great God, is not thy promise?
	Gilbert, Ann	Eng	1782	1866	Cong	Hark! the sounds of joy and
	Giles, Charles		1783	1867	. *	This world is poor from shore to
	Giles, John E	Eng	1805	...	Bapt.*	Hast thou said, exalted Jesus?
	Gill, Thomas H	Eng	1819	...	Ch. Eng.	Holy, delightful day!
N. 37	Gilmore, J. H	U. S.	..(1870)..		Bapt. *	He leadeth me, O blessed thought
	Gisborne, Thos.	Eng	1758	1846	Ch. Eng.	A soldier's course from battles.
	Good, John M	Eng	1764	1827	...	Not worlds on worlds in phalanx
N. 38	Goode, William	Eng	1762	1816	C Eng *	Praise ye Jehovah's name
	Gotter, Louis A	Ger	1661	1735	Luth	O Cross, we hail thy bitter reign.
	Gough, Benjamin	Eng	1805		Meth	Blessed are the dead who die
	Gould, Hannah F.	U. S	.	.	...	O thou, who hast spread out the
	Gould, Sabine B	...	1834	...	... *	Onward, Christian soldiers.
	Gramlich, J. A	Ger	1689	1728	Luth *	When the last agony draws nigh.
	Granade, John A	U S	1763	1807	Meth *.	Sweet rivers of redeeming love.
	Grant, James	Scot	.	1785	Pres	O Zion, afflicted with wave upon
N. 39	Grant, Robert	Scot	1785	1838	Ch Eng.	When gathering clouds around
	Graumann, John	Ger	1487	1541	Luth*	My soul, now praise thy Maker.
	Gray, Jane L	Eng	1796	1871	Pres	Hark to the solemn bell!
	Greding, John L.	Ger	1676	1748	Luth *	Him on yonder cross I love.
	Greene, Thomas	Eng	1753	...	Cong	It is the Lord enthroned in light.
	Gregor, Christ'n	Ger	1723	1801	Morav	Man of sorrows and acquainted
	Gregory the Great	Italy	550	604	Cath *	O Christ, our King, Creator,
	Greville, R K	Eng	1794	1866	Ch. Eng.	O God, from thee alone
180	Grigg, Joseph	Eng	1728	1768	Pres *	Jesus, and shall it ever be?
	Groser, William	Eng	1791	1856	Bapt *	Praise the Redeemer, almighty
	Grunbeck, Esther	Ger.	1717	.	Morav.	Grace, grace, oh! that's a joyful
	Guest, Benjamin	Eng	1790	1869	C. Eng *	Heavenly Father, may thy love.
	Guiet, Charles	Fran	.	1684	Cath	O Word of God above.
	Gunn, H. Mayo	Eng	1818	.	Cong *	To realms beyond the sounding
	Günther, C	Ger	1649	1704	Luth	With joyful heart your praises
	Gurney, A T	Eng	1820	...	C Eng.*	Come, ye lofty, come, ye lowly
	Gurney, John H	Eng	1802	1862	C. Eng *	Lord, as to thy dear cross we flee.
	Gurney, Joseph J.	Eng	1788	1747	Quak *.	Let deepest silence all around.
184	Guyon, Madame	Fran	1648	1717	Cath.	I would love thee, God and Fath
	Hall, Mrs. E. M	U S	.(1870).		.	I hear the voice of Jesus say,
N. 40	Hall, C Newman	Eng	1816	.	Cong *	Hallelujah! joyful raise.
	Hamilton, R W.	Eng	1794	1848	Cong.*	Though poor in lot and scorned
N. 41	Hammond, Wm	Eng		1783	Morav *.	Awake and sing the song.
	Hankey, Kate	Eng	..(1865).		...	I love to tell the story.
190	Harbaugh, Henry	U S	1818	1867	Ref.*	Jesus, I live to thee
	Harbottle, Joseph	Eng	1798	1864	Bapt	See how the fruitless fig-tree.
	Hardenberg, F.	Ger	1772	1801	Morav.	What had I been, if thou wert not
	Harland, Edward	Eng	1809	...	C. Eng.*	Lord, when earthly comforts flee
	Harmer, Sam'l Y.	Eng	1809	...	*	In the Christian's home in glory.
	Hartsough, L	U. S.	18—	1872	Meth.*.	I hear thy welcome voice
	Harris, John	Eng	1802	1856	Cong *	Light up this house with glory,
	Harrison, Susan	Eng	1757	1784	Cong	I languish for a sight.
196	Hart, Joseph	Eng	1712	1768	Cong.*	Come, ye sinners, poor and
N. 42	Hastings, Thomas	U. S.	1784	1872	Pres	To-day the Saviour calls. (alt.)

Page	Name.	Home.	Birth	Death	Church	First Line of one of their Hymns
	Hatfield, Edw. F.	U S...	1807	. . .	Pres * .	My Shepherd's name is love.
201	Havergal, W H.	Eng .	1793	. 1870	C Eng.*	Hosannah ! raise the pealing
200	Havergal, F R. ...	Eng...		. ..	Ch. Eng	I gave my life for thee
N. 43	Haweis, Thomas.	Eng...	1732..	1820	C. Eng *	From the cross uplifted high.
	Hawks, Mrs. A S	U. S.	1835	....	.. .	I need thee every hour
	Hawkins, Ernest	Eng .	1802...	1868	C. Eng *	Lord, a Saviour's love displaying
	Hawksworth, J ..	Eng...	1715...	1773	Ch. Eng.	In sleep's serene oblivion laid.
	Hayn, Henriet L	Ger	1724...	1782	Morav...	Seeing I am Jesus' lamb.
205	Heber, Reginald.	Eng .	1783...	1826	C. Eng *	From Greenland's icy mountains
	Heermann, John..	Ger ...	1585...	1647	Luth *...	Thou weepest o'er Jerusalem
	Heginbotham, O.	Eng .	1744	. 1768	Cong.*.	God of our life, thy various praise
	Held, Henry .	Ger ...		 1643	Luth . ..	Let the earth now praise the
	Helmbold, Lewis	Ger.	1532	. 1598	Luth* .	From God shall nought divide
	Hemans, Felicia D	Wales	1794...	1835	Ch. Eng.	The Saviour knelt and prayed
	Hensel, Louisa		1798.	..	Cath ..	Ever would I fain be reading.
	Herberger, V .	Pol	1562	. 1627	Luth	Farewell ! I gladly bid thee
	Herbert, Daniel...	Eng	1751	1833	Cong *.	Come, dear Lord, thyself reveal
	Herbert, George ..	Eng	1593	1632	C Eng *.	Teach me, my God and King.
	Hermann, N	Ger ..		1561	Luth	Mine hour appointed is at hand
	Herman, J G	Ger....	1707...	1791	Luth *...	On wings of faith, ye thoughts,
	Herrick, Robert..	Eng ..	1591	....	C. Eng *	In the hour of my distress
	Hervey, James	Eng .	1714	. 1758	C Eng *	Since all the downward tracts
	Herzog, John F .	Ger .	1647..	1699	Luth ..	Now that the sun doth shine no
	Hesse, John .	Ger ..	1490	1547	Luth *...	O world, I now must leave thee
	Hessenthaler, M .	Ger	1623 ..	..	Luth ...	True Shepherd, who in love
	Heusser, Meta . ..	Switz	1797	...	Ret .	Long hast thou wept and sorrow
	Hewett, John W..	Eng..	..(1859)..		C. Eng.*	In the name of God the Father
	Hey, William	Ger .	1789	1854	Luth * ..	Whene'er thou sinkest
	Hildegarde, St .	Ger	1098	. 1179	Cath	O Fire of God, the Comforter
	Hildebert, Bish ...	Fran..	....	1133	Cath.*. ...	O pious Paraclete
212	Hill, Rowland.	Eng...	1744	. 1833	Ind.* .	Ye that in his courts are found
	Hill, L S .	U. S..	1806	....	Bapt ...	When floating on life's troubled
	Hiller, Fred C	Ger..	1662	. 1726	Luth	O Jerusalem, the golden
	Hiller, Ph F . ..	Ger.	1699...	1769	Luth *...	My God, to thee I now commend
	Hillhouse, A L.	U. S	1792	1859	... .	Trembling before thine awful
	Hinds, Samuel . .	Eng .	1793	..18—	C. Eng *	Lord, shall thy children come
	Hinton, J. H	Eng ..	1791	.1872	Bapt.*.....	Once I was estranged from God
	Hofel, John . . .	Ger...	1600	. 1683	Luth	O sweetest words
	Hoffmann, G .	Ger .	1658	. 1712	Luth *...	Depart, my child,
	Hogg, James	Scot.	1773..	1835	Pres	O thou that dwellest in the heav
	Hojer, Conrad ...	Ger ..	. (1560).		Luth ...	Ah God, my days are dark
	Holmes, O W .	U S..	1809	....	Unit'n	Lord of all being, throned afar.
	Homburg, E. C.....	Ger ...	1605...	1681	Luth.. ...	Of my life the Life, O Jesus
	Hope Henry........	Ire.	1809	. 1872	Pres ..	Now I have found a friend
	Hopkins, John .	Eng ..	(1551)	..	C Eng.*	Edited a book of Psalms in 1551
	Hopkins, Josiah.	... ..	1786	. 1862	. ..... *	Oh turn ye, Oh turn ye, for why
	Hopper, E.		1818	. ...	.........*	Wrecked and struggling in mid
	Horne, George	Eng..	1730	1792	C. Eng *	See the leaves around us falling
	Hoskins, Joseph	Eng ..	1745	. 1788	Cong * .	The time is short
	How, Wm. W	Eng...	1823	(1854)	C. Eng *	Jesus, Name of wondrous love.
	Huie, Richard . .	Scot	1795	.	Pres . ..	O ye with silent tear.
	Hull Amelia M..	Eng .	.	.	..	There is life for a look at the
	Humphreys, Jos.	Eng .	1720		C Eng *	Blessed are the sons of God
	Hunter, Wm	U S..	1811	(1842)	Meth.*...	My heavenly home is bright and

Synopsis of Hymn Writers.

Page.	Name.	Home.	Birth...Death.	Church.	First Line of one of their Hymns.
220	Huntingdon, Lady	Eng...	1707...1791	Ch. Eng.	When thou, my righteous Judge,
	Huntington, F. D.	U. S...	1819... ...	Epis.*	Come, sinner, to the gospel feast.
	Hupton, Job...	Eng...	1762...1849	Bapt.*...	Come, ye saints, and raise an
	Hurn, William...	Eng...	1754...1829	Cong.*...	Angels rejoiced and sweetly
	Hutton, James...	Eng...	1715...1795	Morav...	O teach us more of thy blest ways
	Huss, John	Austr.	1373...1415	Ref.*...	Jesus Christ, our true salvation.
	Hyde, Mrs. A. B.	U. S...	1872	Cong.....	And canst thou, sinner, slight.
	Ide, George B......	U. S...	1805...1872	Bapt.*...	Son of God, our glorious head
	Ingemann, B. S....	Den...	1789...1862	Luth.....	Through the night of doubt and
	Irons, Joseph	Eng...	1785...1852	Cong.*...	Plead my cause, O Lord of hosts.
	Irons, Wm. J......	Eng...	1812 (1848)	C. Eng.*	Day of wrath, O day of mourning
	Jacobi, John C.....	Eng...	....(1722)....	Luth.....	Holy Ghost! dispel our darkness
	Jacobus, de Bene..	Italy..	1306	Cath......	At the cross her station keeping.
	James, R. S.........	U. S...	1824.........	Bapt. *...	Hastening on to death's dark
	Jervis, Thomas.....	Eng...	1748...1833	Unit'n*..	With joy we lift our eyes.
	Jesse, Henry......	Eng...	1601...1663	Bapt.*...	Unclean! unclean and full of
	John, St. D.........	Syr....	 780	Greek.*..	'Tis the day of resurrection
	Johns, Henry D...	U. S...	....(1865)....	............*	Come, Kingdom of our God.
	Johnson, Samuel..	U. S...	1822 (1846)	Unit'n*..	Father! in thy mysterious pres-
233	Jones, Edmund....	Eng...	1722...1765	Bapt.*...	Come, humble sinner, in whose
	Joseph, St..	Gree ..	...9th cent..	............*	Jesus, Lord of life eternal
	Josephson, Lewis.	Ger....	1809.........	Ref.*......	Now darkness over all is spread
	Jowett, William...	Eng...	....(1806)....	............*	While conscious sinners tremble
	Joyce, James.......	Eng..	1781...1850	C. Eng.*	Disowned of heaven, by man
	Judkin, Thos. J...	Eng...	....(1837)....	Ch. Eng.	Enthroned is Jesus now.
234	Judson, Adonir....	Burm	1788...1850	Bapt.*...	Our Father God, who art in
	Judson, Sarah B..	U. S...	1803...1845	Bapt......	Proclaim the lofty praise
	Jukes, Richard....	Eng...	....	Meth......	What is this that steals upon my
240	Keble, John........	Eng...	1792...1866	C. Eng.*	Sun of my soul, thou Saviour
	Keith, George......	Eng...	17—...17—	Bapt......	How firm a foundation, ye saints
243	Kelly, Thomas.....	Ire.....	1769...1855	Indep.*..	Hark, ten thousand harps and
	Kempenfelt, R.....	Eng...	1718...1782	Ch. Eng.	Burst, ye emerald gates! and
	Kempf, John.......	Ger....	1604...1625	Luth.*...	When in the pains of death my
	Kempthorn, J......	Eng...	1775...1838	C. Eng.*	Praise the Lord, ye heavens.
244	Ken, Thomas......	Eng...	1637...1711	C. Eng.*	Praise God, from whom all
	Kennedy, B. Hall	Eng...	1804.........	C. Eng.*	Come, Lord Jesus, take thy rest.
	Kent, John.........	Eng...	1766...1843	Cong......	Where two or three together
	Kenyon, A..........	U. S...	18—.........	Bapt.*...	Go, work while you may.
	Kern, Chris. G.....	Ger....	1792...1835	Luth.*...	Oh how could I forget Him!
	Kethe, William....	Eng...	1561.........	C. Eng.*	All people, that on earth do
291	Key, Francis S....	U S...	1779...1843	Epis......	Lord, with glowing heart I praise
	Keymann, Chris...	Ger....	1607...1656	Luth.*...	Jesus, will I never leave.
	Kidder, Mrs. M. A	U. S...	1825.........	Meth	Look on me, Saviour mine.
	Kill, Tobiah.......	Ger....	1584...1627	Luth.*...	Lord God, now open wide thy
	Killinghall, John	Eng...	1740	Cong.*...	In all my troubles sharp and
	King, Joshua......	Eng...	....(1840)....	....	When his salvation bringing.
	Kingo, Bishop.....	Den ...	....	Luth.*...	Over Kedron Jesus treadeth
	Kingsbury, Wm...	Eng...	1744...1818	Cong.*...	Great, Lord of all, thy churches
	Kingsbury, H......	U. S...	18—(1850)	Pres.*...	Once was heard the song of
	Kippis, Andrew...	Eng...	1725...1795	Unit'n*..	Great God, in vain man's narrow
	Klopstock, F. G...	Ger....	1724...1803	Luth......	Lord, remove the veil away.

Page	Name	Home	Birth	Death	Church	First line of one of their Hymns
	Knapp, Albert	Ger..	1798	1864	Luth.*	O Father, Thou, who hast created
	Knollis, F. M	....	18---	(1860)	..*	There is no night in heaven.
	Knorr, Christian	Ger ..	1636	1689	Luth...	Dayspring of Eternity.
	Knowles, Jas. D	U. S.	1798	1838	Bapt..	O God, through countless worlds
	Kortsch, C. J ..	Ger...	....	1735	Luth .	O Fountain eternal of life and
	Krummacher, F A	Ger ...	1768	1845	Ref.*.	Though love may weep with
	Kunth, John S	Ger .	1700	1779	Luth * .	Yes, there remaineth yet a rest.
	Kynaston, Herb.	Eng ..	1809	.. ....	C. Eng.*	Jesus, solace of my soul
	Lagniel, John	Eng ..	.	.1728	.. ...	Doth He who came the lost to
	Landon, Letitia E	.. ..	1802	. ..	. .	While yet the youthful spirit.
	Langbecker, E C G	Ger ...	1792	1843	Luth	What shall I be, my Lord, when
	Lange, Ernest	Ger ...	1650	1727	Luth....	O God, Thou bottomless abyss.
	Lange, Joachim	Ger ..	1670	1744	Luth *..	O God, what offering shall I
	Lange, J. C	Ger ..	1669	1756	Luth *..	Jesus, thou art my heart's delight
	Lange, John P.....	Ger ..	1802.	...	Evang.*.	My Father is the mighty Lord
	Langford, John .	Eng .	. .	1790	Bapt * .	Now begin the heavenly theme
	Langford, G W	.. .	(1847).		.. ..	Speak gently, it is better far
	Latrobe, John A.	Eng..	....(1841)	. .	C. Eng *	O bring to Jehovah your tribute
	Laurenti, Laur .	Ger....	1660	1722	Luth ..	Rejoice, rejoice, believers.
	Layritz, Fred ...	Ger...	. (1844)		Luth *-.	Ah, Jesus, the merit
	Lee, Fred. G	Eng ..	.	1868	C. Eng *	Laud the grace of God victorious
	Lee, Richard.	.. ...	....(1794)		....	When I view my Saviour bleed-
	Leeson, Jane E	Eng	. ..1853		.	Loving Shepherd of thy sheep
	Lehr, L F. F	Ger .	1709..	1744	Luth *	Why halt thus, O deluded heart?
	Leland, John. ..	U. S..	1754	1841	Bapt *.	The day is past and gone. The
	Liebich, Ehrenfr	Ger .	1713	1780	Luth * .	Come, Christians, praise your
	Liguori, St. Alpon	Italy.	1696..	1787	Cath.*...	My Jesus, say what wretch has
	Lindemann, J.....	Ger..	1550	1630	Luth	In Thee is gladness.
	Lingley, James. ...	Eng ..	. (1829)	.	Bapt. ..	Once more we leave the busy
	Littledale, R. F...	Eng ..	..(1867)		C Eng *	*Wrote hymns for "The People's Hymnal"*
	Lloyde, Wm F....	Eng...	1791	1853	Ch. Eng	Wait, my soul, upon the Lord.
472	Long, Edwin M .	U. S..	1827	.... ..	Pres *...	Draw me, Saviour, nearer.
	Longfellow, H W	U S	1807	. ...	Unit'n.	Tell me not in mournful numbers
	Louisa, Henrietta	Ger	1627	1667	Ref..	Jesus, my Redeemer lives
	Lowrie, John M	U. S .	18---	....	.... *	Jesus, Author of Salvation.
	Lowry, Robert	U. S..	1826	.... ..	Bapt *.	Shall we gather at the river
	Ludaemilia, Eliz .	Ger .	1640	1672	Luth . .	Draw me to thee, Lord Jesus.
N. 44	Luke, Jemima ..	Eng .	1813..	.... ..	Cong.. .	I think, when I read that sweet
262	Luther, Martin, ..	Ger ..	1483	1546	Luth *	Out of the deep, O Lord, we call.
	Lynch, Thos. T...	Eng .	1818..	1871	Cong *.	Gracious Spirit, dwell with me.
274	Lyte, H Francis.	Eng	1793	1847	C. Eng *	Abide with me, fast falls the
	Macduff, John R .	Scot	... (1853)	.	Pres *...	Oh do not, blessed Lord, depart
	Mackay, Margaret	Scot.	... (1832)	.	.	Asleep in Jesus! blessed sleep.
	Madan, Judith	Eng .	... (1763)	.	Ch Eng	In this world of sin and sorrow.
	Madan, Martin .	Eng..	1726	1790	C. Eng *	Now begin the heavenly theme.
	Maitland, Fanny F	Eng .	(1827)		....	Much in sorrow, oft in woe.
	Malan, C H. A .	Switz.	1787	1864	Ref.*.....	No, no, it is not dying.
	Manley, Basil.......	U. S...	1825	....	Bapt * ..	Holy, holy, holy Lord.
	Mant, Richard ..	Eng .	1776	1848	C Eng *	Come, Holy Ghost, my soul
	March, Henry .	Eng .	1790	..	Cong *	No more, my God, I boast no
	Mardley, John ..	Eng...	.	1562	Ch. Eng.	O Lord, turn not thy face from
	Maria, Q of Hun	Hung	1505	1558	Luth.	Can I my fate no more withstand

Synopsis of Hymn Writers.

PAGE.	NAME.	Home	Birth . Death	Church.	First Line of one of their Hymns
	Marot, Samuel	Ger ...	1770 ..18—	Evang *.	From thy heavenly throne.
	Marperger, B W.	Ger ...	1681 ..1746	Luth.* .	Who seeks in weakness an excuse
	Marriott, John . .	Eng .	1780 . 1825	C Eng *	Thou, whose Almighty word.
	Marsden, Joshua	Eng	1777.. 1837	Meth "	Go, ye messengers of God.
N. 45	Mason, John	Eng .	...1694	C. Eng *	Blest day of God, most calm, most
	Mason, William...	Eng ..	1725 . 1791	C Eng.*	Again returns the day of holy
	Masters, Mary...	Eng ..	1702 (1755)	....	'Tis religion that can give.
	Matthew, Julia A.	U. S .	18—..........	Epis. ...	"Peace upon earth!" the angels
	Matthesius, J. E.	Ger ...	1504 ..1565	Luth *	My inmost heart now raises
	Maude, Mary F.	Eng ..	(1848) .	Ch. Eng	Thine forever, God of love.
	Maxwell, James...	Scot..	....	Meth	Didst thou, dear Saviour, suffer
	McAll, Robert S.	Scot..	1792..1838	.. .	Hark ! how the choral song of
	McCheyne, R M	Scot..	1813.. 1843	Pres * ...	I once was a stranger to grace
	McDonald, W . .	U. S .	18— (1858)	Meth *...	I am coming to the cross.
280	Medley, Samuel...	Eng ..	1738...1799	Bapt.*...	Awake, my soul, in joyful lays
	Meinhold, J W	Ger ..	1797. 1851	Luth.*..	Gentle Shepherd, thou hast
	Mentzer, John .. .	Ger	1658. 1734	Luth.*..	Oh that I had a thousand tongues
	Merrick, James.	Eng ..	1720 ..1769	C. Eng	The festal morn, my God, is come
	Metrophanes of Smyr	Turk	 910	Gr. Ch *	O Unity of threefold Light.
	Meyfart, J M ..	Ger .	1590...1642	Luth *	Jerusalem, thou city fair and
	Middleton, T F .	Eng	1769...1822	C Eng.*	As o'er the past my memory
	Midlane, Albert...	Eng ..	1825	....	Onward, upward, homeward.
	Miles, Sarah E	U. S	(1840) .	. .	Thou who didst stoop below
	Millard, James E	Eng..	1821 (1848)	C Eng *	God eternal ! Lord of all !
N. 46	Mills, Elizabeth...	Eng..	1805 .1829	Ch. Eng.	We speak of the realms of the
	Mills, Henry .	. .....	1786 .1867	... . *	The trumpet sounds ! the day
	Miller, W. E . ..	.. ..	1766 .1839	.... *	Our souls, by love together knit
	Milman, H. H .	Eng..	1791 .1868	C. Eng.*	Ride on, ride on in majesty.
N. 47	Milton, John	Eng...	1608...1674	Bapt ..	Let us with a gladsome mind.
	Mitchel, William.	.. ..	...(1831) ..	. . *	Jesus, thy love shall we forget
	Mogridge, George.	Eng .	1787..1854	Ch Eng.	The Son of God, the Lord of life.
	Moir, David M .	Scot...	1798 . 1851	Pres....	Oh ! who is like the mighty one
	Monod, Adolphe. .	Fran.	1800. . ..	.. .. *	God of my health, I would thy
	Monsell, J S B ..	Ire	1811 . 1875	C. Eng.*	Birds have their quiet nest
290	Montgomery, Jas.	Scot...	1771 ..1854	Morav...	Prayer is the soul's sincere
	Moore, Hannah ..	Eng	1743 ..1833	Ch. Eng.	Oh how wondrous is the story !
	Moore, Henry ..	Eng .	1732 . 1802	Unit'n*..	My God, thy boundless love.
N. 48	Moore, Thomas. ..	Ire ...	1779 . 1852	Cath......	Come, ye disconsolate, where'er
	Moraht, Adolph ..	Ger ..	1805..........	Luth."...	From Thy heavenly throne.
	More, Henry	Eng	1614...1687	C Eng *	On all the earth, Thy Spirit.
	Morell, Thomas ..	Eng ..	1781. 1840	Cong.*..	Go, and the Saviour's grace
	Morris, Eliza F ...	Eng.	1821 (1858)	... ..	God of pity, God of grace.
	Morris, George P	U. S.	18— (1858)	. .	Searcher of hearts ! from mine
	Morrison, John.	Scot	1749. 1798	Pres *..	The race that long in darkness.
	Mote, Edward .	Eng..	1797.... ..	Bapt *..	My hope is built on nothing less
	Moultrie, G ..	Eng .	.(1867)...	C. Eng *	Brother, now thy toils are over
	Moultrie, Mary D	Eng ..	(1860) ..	Ch Eng.	Agnes, fair martyr
	Mowes, Henry..	Ger....	1793 1834	Luth *...	Thus said the Lord, thy days of
288	Muhlenberg, W.A	U. S .	1796	Epis.* ...	I would not live always, I ask
	Muhlmann, John.	Ger ..	1543.. 1613	Luth *..	Who putts his trust in God most
	Muller, Michael.	Ger....	1673 1704	Luth * .	Good and pleasant 'tis to see
	Nachtenhöfer,C.F	Ger. ..	1624...1685	Luth "...	So, Lord, thou goest forth to die.
	Nason, Elias	U. S .	... (1857)...	... .	Jesus only, when the morning

Synopsis of Hymn Writers.

Page	Name.	Home	Birth. Death	Church	First Line of one of their Hymns
	Naur, Elias E......	Den...	1728	Luth......	When my tongue can no more
N. 49	Neale, John M.	Eng ..	1818...1866	C. Eng.*	Jerusalem, the golden
	Neander, Joachim	Ger. ..	1640...1680	Ref.*. ..	Holy Spirit, once again.
	Needham, John...	Eng ..	1710...1768	Bapt.*....	Holy and reverend is the name.
	Nelson, David	U. S...	1793...1844	Pres.*.....	My days are gliding swiftly by.
	Nelson, Earl	Eng .	1823 (1864)	Ch. Eng.	At thy birth, Incarnate Lord.
	Nettleton, As ..	U S	1783 . 1844	Cong.*..	Amazing sight! the Saviour
303	Neumark, George	Ger. .	1621.. 1681	Luth	Leave God to order all thy ways.
	Neumeister, E .	Ger	1671.. 1756	Luth *...	Jesus sinners doth receive
	Neumann, Casper	Ger... .	1648 . 1715	Luth *..	Lord, on earth I dwell in pain.
	Neumann, G. .	Ger ..	..(1736)...	Morav ..	At length released from many
	Neunherz, John..	Ger....	1653...1737	Luth.*.	Sad with longing, sick with fears.
	Neuss, H. G ..	Ger....	1654 1716	Luth.*...	A new and contrite heart create.
	Nevin, Edwin H	U. S..	1814(1857)	Ref.*. ..	Always with us, always with
	Newman, John H	Eng ..	1801 (1833)	Cath. ?....	Lead, kindly light, amid the
	Newton, James ..	Eng .	1733...1790	Bapt ˝ .	Let plenteous grace descend on
306	Newton, John ...	Eng .	1725. 1807	C. Eng.*	Glorious things of Thee are spok
	Nicholas, T. G. ..	Eng...	1823...1860	C. Eng *	Lord, when before thy throne we
	Nicholson, James.	U.S ..	18—.	Meth	Dear Jesus, I long to be perfectly
	Nicolai, Dr Phil	Ger.	1556 . 1608	Luth * ..	Awake, awake, for night is flying
	Noel, Baptist W..	Eng ..	1799...1873	Bapt.*..	There's not a bird without
	Noel, Gerard T .	Eng ..	1782 . 1851	C. Eng.*	If human kindness meets return.
	Norton, Andrew.	U. S.	1786 ..1853	Unit'n ..	My God, I thank thee.
	Notker, Balbulus	...	. . . 912	Cath.* .	In the midst of life, behold.
	Nunn, Marianne .	Eng ..	1779 1847	. . .	There is a Friend above all others
	Nyberg, L T.. .	..	1720 1792	... ...	Father, throned on high
	Oakeley, Fred.....	Eng .	....(1841) .	Cath.*,...	O come, all ye faithful
	Oberlin, John F	Ger...	1740. 1826	Luth *..	O Lord, thy heavenly grace
324	Occom, Samson ..	U. S ..	1723. .1792	Pres *..	Awaked by Sinai's awful sound
	Odo, St.(of Cluny)	Fran..	879 . 942	Cath.*..	O Church, our Mother, speak his
	Ogilvie, John . .	Scot .	1733 1814	Pres * ..	Begin my soul, the exalted lay
	Olearius, John	Ger ...	1611 ..1684	Luth *	See Cox's Sacred Hymns
N. 50	Olivers, Thomas,	Wales	1725 ..1799	Meth *...	The God of Abra'm praise.
	Onderdonk, H. U.	U S..	1788.. 1858	Ep*.. ...	The Spirit in our hearts.
	Onslow, Phipps ..	Eng...	....(1860)	C. Eng *	Hark! a glad exulting (Transl.)
	Opie, Amelia.	. Eng .	1769...1853	Quak .	There seems a voice in every
	Osler, Edward ...	Eng...	1798...1863	Ch. Eng.	O God unseen, yet ever near.
	Oswald, Henry	Ger ...	1751...1837	Ref . .	O let him whose sorrow
330	Pal, Krishna	Ind .	1764...1822	Bapt.*....	O thou, my soul, forget no more.
	Palgrave, Fr. T ...	Eng .	1824.	Ch. Eng	Star of morn and even.
	Palmer, Phœbe .	U. S	1807 . 1874	Meth...	Blessed Bible! how I love thee!
331	Palmer, Ray	U S...	1808.........	Cong.*..	My faith looks up to thee.
	Pappus, John	Ger	1549 1610	Luth.*.	My cause is God's, and I am still
	Park, Roswell	U S ..	1807 . 1869	Epis * .	Jesus spreads his banner o'er us
	Park, Thomas .	Eng ..	1760...1835	Ch. Eng.	My soul, praise the Lord, seek
	Parker, John	. U S..	18—.. .. .	Meth.*..	The blood, the blood is all my
	Parr, Harriet.	Eng .	..(1856).	. ...	Hear my prayer, O heavenly
	Parson, Eliz ...	Eng ..	1812 (1836)	. . ...	Jesus, we love to meet
	Patrick, John..	Eng...	...(1679)...	Ch Eng	O God, we praise thee and
	Paulus, Diaconus	Italy..	 799	Cath *...	Greatest of prophets, messenger
	Peabody, W B O	U. S ..	1799 . 1847	Unit'n*.	Behold the western evening light
	Pearce, John.	....	...(1766)..	. ...	All hail, the glorious morn!

Synopsis of Hymn Writers.

PAGE.	NAME.	HOME.	Birth...Death.	CHURCH.	FIRST LINE OF ONE OF THEIR HYMNS.
	Pearce, Samuel....	Eng...	1766...1799	Bapt.*....	In the floods of tribulation.
	Peck, George B....	U. S...	18—.........	Meth.*...	Come, come to Jesus.
338	Perronet, Edward.	Eng...	17—...1792	Indep.*..	All hail the power of Jesus' name
	Peters, Mary B. ...	Eng...	1856	Ch. Eng.	Jesus, how much thy name
	Pfefferkorn, G. M.	Ger....	1646...1732	Luth.*...	Who knows how near my end
	Pfeil, C. C. L. von	Ger....	1712...1784	Luth......	Oh, blest the house, whate'r
	Phelps, S. D.......	U. S...	1816.........	Bapt.*....	Christ who came my soul to save
	Phillips, Philip....	U. S...	1834.........	Meth......	I will sing the story
	Phillimore, G......	Eng...	....(1863)...	C. Eng.*	O Lord of health and life.
	Philpot, Charles...	....	....(1831)...	....	Again from calm and sweet
	Pierpont, John....	U. S...	1785...1866	Unit'n*..	O Thou, to whom in ancient
	Pierson, A. T.......	U. S...	1836(1873)	Pres.*....	To thee, O God, we raise.
	Pirie, Alexander..	....	1804	.........*..	Come, let us join in songs of
	Pitt, Christopher..	Eng...	1699...1748	Ch. Eng.	On God we build our sure defense
	Plumptre, E. H...	....	1821(186)	.........*..	Hark! the hosts of heaven are
	Pollard, Josephine	U. S...	18—.........	Epis	I stood outside the gate
	Pope, Alexander..	Eng...	1688...1744	Cath......	Vital spark of heavenly flame!
	Porter, Elbert S...	U. S...	18—.........	.........*	In the far better land of glory
	Pott, Francis......	Eng...	....(1861)...	C. Eng.*	Lift up your heads, eternal gates.
	Potter, Tho. J......	....	....(1860)...	Cath.*....	Brightly gleams our banner.
	Pratt, Josiah.......	Eng...	1768...1844	C. Eng.*	Why should our tears in sorrow
	Preiswerk, S........	Switz.	1799.........	Ref.*......	Hark, the church proclaims her
	Prentiss, Mrs. E.P	....	1819(1869)	....	More love to Thee, O Christ!
	Procter, James.....	Eng...	....(1858)...	Cong.*...	Nothing either great or small.
	Prudentius, A. C..	Spain	348... 413	Cath......	Of the Father's love begotten.
	Prynne, G. R.......	Eng...	....(1860)...	C. Eng.*	Jesu, meek and gentle.
	Puchta, C. R. H...	Ger....	1808...1858	Luth.*...	Lord, a whole long day of pain.
	Pyer, John..........	Eng...	1790...1859	Cong.*...	Met again in Jesus' name.
	Quarles, Francis...	Eng...	1592...1644	Ch. Eng.	Fountain of light and living
	Quarles, John.......	Eng...	1624...1665	Ch. Eng.	O mother, dear Jerusalem.
	Rabanus, St. M.....	Ger....	776... 856	Cath.*....	Christ, the Father's mirrored
N. 51	Raffles, Thomas...	Eng...	1788...1863	Cong.*...	Blest hour when mortal man
	Ramback, J. J......	Ger....	1693...1735	Luth.*...	I am baptized into thy name.
	Rawson, George...	Eng...	1807.........	Bapt......	Praise ye the Lord, immortal
N. 52	Reed, Andrew......	Eng...	1787...1862	Cong.*...	Holy Ghost with light divine.
	Reed, Elizabeth...	Eng...	1794...1867	Cong......	My longing spirit faints to see.
	Reese, Eli Yates...	U. S...	1816...1861	Meth.*...	Do this and remember the blood.
	Reisner, Adam.....	Ger....	1471...1563	Luth......	In thee, Lord, have I put my
	Reusner, Chris.....	Swed.	....(1678)...	Luth......	Am I a stranger here, on earth
	Rhodes, Benj.......	Eng...	1743...1815	Meth.*...	My heart and voice I raise.
	Richstein, Wm. F.	U. S...	18—.........	Luth......	Come, sinner, turn thy feet.
	Riehter, C. F.......	Ger....	1676...1711	Luth......	O watchman, will the night of
	Riehter, Greg......	Ger....	1645	Luth.*...	Now from earth retire, my heart.
	Ringwaldt, B.......	Ger....	1530...1598	Luth.*...	Great God, what do I see and
	Rinkart, M..........	Ger....	1586...1649	Luth.*...	Now thank we all our God
N. 53	Rippon, John......	Eng...	1751...1836	Bapt.*....	Great God, where'r we pitch our
	Rist, John...........	Ger....	1607...1667	Luth.*...	How shall I meet Thee?
	Ritter, Jacob.......	Ger....	1627...1669	Luth......	Oh, ye your Saviour's name who
	Robert II. of Fran	Fran..	972...1031	Cath......	Come, thou Holy Spirit, come.
	Robertson, Wm....	Scot...	1743	Pres.*....	A little child the Saviour came.
	Robins, Gurdon...	U. S...	18—.........	Bapt......	There is a land mine eye hath
	Robinson, Ch. S...	U. S...	1829.........	Pres.*...	Saviour, I follow on

Synopsis of Hymn Writers.

Page	Name	Home	Birth . Death	Church	First Line of One of their Hymns
	Robinson, Geo	Eng	. (1842) .	Cong	One sole baptismal sign.
344	Robinson, Rob. ...	Eng .	1735 1790	Bapt *...	Come, thou Fount of every bless-
	Rodigast, Sam. .	Ger ..	1649. 1708	Luth. ...	Whate'er my God ordains is right
	Ronson, Gilb ..	Scot.	1821 1869	C Eng.*	Three in One, and One in Three.
	Roscommon, E of	Eng .	1684	Ch Eng	My God, my Father, and my
	Rossetti, Chris. G.	Eng .	1830.... .	. ..	What are these that glow from
	Rouse, Louisa M.	U. S..	18— (1873)	Meth ...	Precious Saviour, thou hast saved
	Rothe, John A .	Ger...	1688 . 1758	Luth.*	Now I have found the ground.
	Rowe, Elizabeth .	Eng .	1674.. 1736	Cong .	Begin the high celestial strain
	Rowland, A J.	U S .	18—........	Bapt *...	There's rest in the shadow of
	Rowe, John . .	Eng ..	1764 ..1832	Bapt * ..	From the table now returning
	Russell, A T	Eng	1806	C. Eng.*	O'er the dark sea of Galilee.
	Russell, Wm .	....	..(1861) ..	....	More married than any man's
	Rutilius, Martin.	Ger..	1550 ..1618	Luth *..	Alas! my Lord and God!
350	Ryland, John ...	Eng	1753 ..1825	Bapt *.	Sovereign Ruler of the skies.
	Sacer, Gottfried W	Ger..	1635...1699	Luth	Then I have conquered.
354	Sachs, Hans	Ger..	1494...1576	Luth .	Why art thou thus cast down,
	Sachse, C F. H....	Ger.	1785 1860	Luth.*	See "Hymns from Land of Luther"
	Saffery, Maria G	Eng	1773 1858	Bapt. ...	'Tis the great Father we adore.
	Sample, R. F.	U. S	18— (1868)	Pres.*..	I hear a voice, 'tis soft and sweet
	Sandys, George. .	Eng .	1577 .1643	C Eng *	Thou, who art enthroned above.
	Santolius, M..	Fran .	1628...1684	Cath *..	Now, my soul, thy voice upris-
	Santolius, Vict	Fran	1630 ..1697	Cath.*	O Lord, how joyful 'tis to see !
	Scales, Thomas	Eng	1786 ..1860	Cong *..	Amazing was the grace!
	Schade, John C....	Ger...	1666 1698	Luth.*..	Up! yes, upward to thy gladness
	Schalling, Martin	Ger ..	1532 ..1608	Luth *.	Lord, all my heart is fixed on
N 54	Scheffler, John	Ger .	1624 .1677	Cath.. .	Jesus, Jesus! visit me.
	Schenk, H Theod	Ger..		... 1727	Luth.*..	Who are these like stars appear,
	Schiebelei, D	Ger	1741. 1771	Luth .	How oft have I the covenant
	Schirmer, Mich'l	Ger .	1606 1673	Luth '	O Holy Spirit, enter in
	Schlegel, John A	Ger....	1721. .1793	Luth **	See his hymns in "Chorale Book"
	Schmidt, John E	Ger ..	1669 ..1745	Luth * .	All is fulfilled, my heart, record
	Schmolke, Benj. ..	Ger	1672 ..1737	Luth.*.	Hosannah to the Son of David
	Schmucker, S S	U S	1799 1873	Luth * .	From Calvary's sacred mountain
	Schneegass, Cyr...	Ger. .	... .1597	Luth.*..	The holy Son, the new-born child.
	Schneesing, John	Ger..	1567	Luth *	Lord Jesus Christ, in Thee alone
	Scholefield, Jas . .	Eng .	1789 1853	Ch Eng.	Draw me, O draw me, my gracious
	Schroder, J. H ..	Ger....	1666...1699	Luth *..	Wisdom's unexhausted treasure
	Schubart, C F. ...	Ger...	1739 ..1791	Luth ...	All things are yours
	Schutz, John J ...	Ger...	1640 1690	Ref ...	All praise and thanks to God
	Schweinitz, H. C..	Ger...	1645 ..1722	Luth..	Will not that joyful be?
	Scott, Elizabeth .	Eng .	(1764) .	Pres	All hail, incarnate God.
	Scott, Jacob R . .	U. S	1815 1861	Bapt *...	To Thee, this temple we devote.
	Scott, Robert A	Eng	..(1839) .	C Eng *	All glory be to Thee.
	Scott, Thomas... .	Eng..	...1776	Pres.* ...	Hasten, sinner, to be wise.
	Scott, Sir Walter .	Scot .	1771 1832	Ch Eng	The day of wrath, that dreadful
	Scriver, Chris... ..	Ger....	1629 1693	Luth *	See No 6, Russell's Psalms and Hymns
	Seagrave, Robert.	Eng...	1693.. . ..	C Eng *.	Rise, my soul, and stretch thy
	Sears, Edmund H	U. S .	1810....	Cong *.	Calm on the listening ear of
	Sedulius, Coelius..	. ...	.5th Cent	. .	Why doth that impious Herod
	Selnecker, Nich .	Ger....	1530 1592	Luth *..	O Lord, my God, I cry to Thee.
	Serle, Ambrose	Eng...	1742 . 1812	Ch Eng	Thy way, O Lord, with wise
	Seward, Theo F. .	U S ..	1835.	Pres .	Go and tell Jesus, weary, sin-sick

Synopsis of Hymn Writers. 549

Page.	Name.	Home.	Birth...Death	Church.	First Line of one of their Hymns.
	Seymour, A. C. H.	Ire....	1789........	Ch. Eng.	Awake, All-conquering Arm,
	Shepherd, Anne...	Eng...	1809...1857	Ch. Eng.	Around the throne of God in
	Shepherd, Thos....	Eng...	1809...1857	Cong.*...	When wilt thou come unto me,
	Sherwin, W. F.....	U. S...	18—......	Bapt.....	Wake the song of joy and glad-
220	Shirley, Selina.....	Eng...	1707...1791	Ch. Eng.	Generally known as Lady Huntingdon.
358	Shirley, Walter....	Eng...	1725...1786	C. Eng.*	Lord, dismiss us with thy bless-
	Shrubsole, Wm...	Eng...	1759...1829	Cong.*...	Arm of the Lord! awake, awake
N. 61	Sigourney, Lydia H..	U. S...	1791...1865	Cong......	Laborers of Christ, arise
	Smith, Car. S......	U. S...	18— (1855)	Cong.....	Tarry with me, O my Saviour.
	Smith, George.....	Eng...	1803...1870	Cong.*...	Thou art, O Christ, the way.
	Smith, J. Wheaton	U. S...	1826........	Bapt.*...	'Tis sweet, in trials of conflicts
	Smith, Sir J. E.....	Eng...	1759...1828	Unit'n....	Praise waits in Zion, Lord, for
	Smith, Joseph D..	Eng...	1816........	Cong.*...	Just as thou art, how wondrous
	Smith, Samuel F..	U. S...	1809........	Bapt.*...	My country, 'tis of thee.
	Smith, Samuel J..	U. S...	1771...1835	Quak.....	Arise, my soul, with rapture
	Smyltan, Geo. H..	Eng...	182-........	C. Eng.*	Forty days and forty nights
	Spurgeon, C. H....	Eng...	1834........	Bapt.*....	The Holy Ghost is here
	Stammers, Jos.....	Eng...	1801........	Ch. Eng.	Breast the wave, Christian
	Stanley, Arth. P...	Eng...	1815........	C. Eng.*	He is gone beyond the skies.
360	Steele, Anne........	Eng...	1716...1778	Bapt......	Father, whate'er of earthly bliss
366	Stennett, Joseph..	Eng...	1663...1713	Bapt.*....	Another six days' work is done
366	Stennett, Samuel..	Eng...	1727...1795	Bapt.*....	On Jordan's stormy banks I
	Sterling, John.....	Eng...	1806...1844	C. Eng.*	O Source divine, and Life of all
	Sternhold, Thos....	Eng...	1549	Ch. Eng.	The Lord descends from heaven
	Stevenson, Wm....	U. S...	18—........	Meth......	Shall we meet in heaven, shall
	Stockton, T. H.....	U. S...	18— (1871)	Meth.*...	The cross! the cross! the blood-
	Stowe, Harriet B..	U. S...	1814........	Epis......	Still, still with thee, when purple
	Stowell, Hugh.....	Eng...	1799...1865	C. Eng.*	From every stormy wind that
	Straphan, Joseph	Eng...	1757........	Ch. Eng.	Blest is the man whose heart
	Summers, Thos....	U. S...	1812........	Meth.*...	We are joyously voyaging over
	Sutton, Amos......	Eng...	1804...1854	Bapt.*...	Hail, sweetest, dearest tie that
N. 55	Swain, Joseph......	Eng...	1761...1796	Bapt.*....	Come, ye souls by sin afflicted.
	Swaine, Edward...	Eng...	1795...1862	Cong.*...	Lord Jesus, let thy watchful care
N. 56	Tappan, Wm.......	U. S...	1795...1849	Cong.*...	'Tis midnight and on Olive's
N. 57	Tate, Nahum.......	Ire.....	1652...1715	Ch. Eng.	To bless thy chosen race.
	Tauler, John.......	Ger....	1294...1361	Cath.*....	There comes a galley sailing.
	Taylor, Anne.......	Eng...	1782...1866	Cong.....	There is a dear and hallowed spot
	Taylor, Clara.......	Eng...	1778	Ch. Eng.	What wondrous course could
	Taylor, Jane........	Eng...	1783...1824	Cong.....	Come, my fond fluttering heart!
	Taylor, Jeremy....	Eng...	1613...1667	C. Eng.*	Draw nigh to Thy Jerusalem, O
	Taylor, John.......	Eng...	1694...1761	Unit'n*..	God of mercy, God of love.
	Taylor, Thos. R....	Eng...	1807...1835	Cong.*...	I'm but a stranger here.
	Taylor, Vergil......	U. S...	1817........	............*	Nothing but leaves—the Spirit
N. 58	Tersteegen, Ger...	Ger....	1697...1769	Ref......	Lo, God is here; let us adore.
	Thrupp, D. A......	Eng...	1779...1847	Ch. Eng.	Saviour, like a Shepherd lead us
	Toke, Emma.......	Eng...	....(1851)...	Ch. Eng.	Thou art gone up on high
	Tonna, Charl. E...	Eng...	1790...1846	Ch. Eng.	Sinner, what has earth to show?
380	Toplady, Aug. M..	Eng...	1740...1778	C. Eng.*	Rock of ages, cleft for me.
	Tourneaux, N. C...	Fran..	1640...1686	Cath.*...	Angels, to our jubilee.
	Trench, Rich. C...	Eng...	1807........	C. Eng.*	Pour forth the oil, pour boldly
	Trend, Henry......	Eng...	1804........	C. Eng.*	Praise, O praise our Heavenly
	Tritton, G...........	Eng...	....(1861)...	Ch. Eng.	Sing to the Lord with heart and
	Tucker, William..	Eng...	1731...1816	Bapt......	Amidst ten thousand anxious

Page.	Name.	Home.	Birth....Death.	Church.	First Line of one of their Hymns.
	Turner, Daniel.....	Eng..	1710...1798	Bapt.*....	Jesus, full of all compassion.
	Turney, Edward...	U. S...	1817...1872	Bapt.*....	Oh love divine! oh matchless
	Tuttiett, Lawr.......	Eng...	1825.........	C. Eng.*	Go forward, Christian soldier.
	Twells, H............		1823 (1868)	.............*	At even whene'er the sun was
	Upham, R. T. C...	U. S...	1799...1872	.............*	Fear not, poor weary one
	Upton, James......	Eng...	1760...1831	Bapt.*....	Come, ye who bow to sovereign
	Urwick, William..		1791...1868	Cong.*....	How sweet to bless the Lord.
	Vaughan, Chas. J.	Eng...	1817.........	C. Eng.*	Lord, whose temple once did
	Vaughan, Henry..	Wales	1621...1695	Ch. Eng.	My soul, there is a country
	Venn, Henry.	Eng...	1724...1797	C. Eng.*	Thy miracles of love
	Vinet, Alexander.	Fran..	1797...1847		Beneath thy veil of shame and
	Voke, Mrs..........	Eng...	17—...18—	Cong......	Thy people, Lord! who trust
496	Walford, W. W....	Eng...	....(1849)....	.............*	Sweet hour of prayer, sweet hour
	Wallin, Benj.......	Eng...	1711...1782	Bapt.*....	Hail, mighty Jesus! how divine!
	Wardlaw, Ralph..	Scot...	1779...1855	Cong.*....	Lift up to God the voice of praise
	Watts, Alaric A...	Eng...	1797...1884	Ch. Eng.	When shall we meet again?
396	Watts, Isaac.......	Eng...	1674...1748	Indep.....	Salvation! O, the joyful sound.
434	Wesley, Charles...	Eng...	1708...1788	C. Eng.*	Jesus, lover of my soul.
478	Wesley, John......	Eng...	1703...1791	C. Eng.*	How happy is the pilgrim's lot!
N. 59	Wesley, Sam'l, Sr.	Eng...	1662...1735	C. Eng.*	Behold the Saviour of mankind!
N. 60	Wesley, Sam'l, Jr.	Eng...	1690...1739	C. Eng.*	From whence these dire portents
	Whitfield, Fred....	Eng...	1829.........	C. Eng.*	I need Thee, precious Jesus
486	White, Henry K..	Eng...	1785...1806	Ch. Eng.	When marshalled on the mighty
	Whiting, William	Eng...	1825.........	C. Eng.*	Eternal Father, strong to save
	Whittemore, Miss H.	Eng...	....(1860)....	Ch. Eng.	How sweet to think that all who
	Whittier, John G.	U. S...	1808.........	Quak......	Another hand is beckoning on.
	Whytehead, Thos.	Eng...	1815...1843	C. Eng.*	Resting from His work to-day.
	Williams, Benj....	Eng...	....(1778)....	Unit'n*..	Lord! what our ears have heard!
	Williams, Helen M	Eng...	1762...1827	Unit'n....	While Thee I seek, protecting
	Williams, Isaac...	Eng...	1802...1865	C. Eng.*	O heavenly Jerusalem.
490	Williams, Wm.....	Wales	1717...1791	Meth.*...	Guide me, O thou great Jehovah
	Willis, N. P.........	U. S...	1807...1867		The perfect world by Adam trod.
	Windgrove, John.	Eng...	1720...1793	Meth......	Hail! my ever blessed Jesus.
	Winkler, Edwin T	U. S...	....(1871)....	Bapt.*....	Our land with mercies crowned.
	Winkworth, Cath.	Eng...	1829 (1855)	Ch. Eng.	If Jesus be my friend.
	Wither, George....	Eng...	1588...1667	Ch. Eng.	Come, O come, with sacred lay.
	Wittemeyer, Mrs. A..	U. S...	18—(1868)	Meth......	I have entered the valley of
	Wolcot, Samuel...		1813 (1869)	.............*	Christ for the world we sing.
	Wolf, Aaron R....		1821...1852	.............*	Draw near, O Holy Dove, draw
	Wood, Basil........	Eng...	1760...1831	C. Eng.*	Blest be Jehovah, mighty Lord.
	Woodford, Jas. R.	Eng...	....(1852)....	C. Eng.*	Lamb of God, for sinners slain.
	Wordsworth, Chr.	Eng...	1807.........	C. Eng.*	O day of rest and gladness.
	Wordsworth, Wm	Eng...	1770...1850	Ch. Eng.	Not seldom clad in radiant vest.
	Wreford, John R.	Eng...	....(1837)....	Pres.*....	Lord, while for all mankind we
	Wright, Philip J.	Eng...	1810...1863	Meth.*...	The Lord of Glory left his throne
	Wyatt, Henry H..	Eng...	....(1859)....	C. Eng.*	God, the Lord, has heard our
497	Xavier, Francis...	Spain	1506...1552	Cath.*....	My God, I love Thee, not because
	Young, Andrew...	Scot...	1810.........	Pres......	There is a happy land.
498	Zinzendorf, N. L.	Ger....	1700...1760	Morav.*.	Jesus, thy blood and righteous-

APPENDIX.

BRIEF NOTES REFERRED TO IN THE SYNOPSIS.

1. ADAM, ST. VICTOR.—Trench styles him "The foremost amongst the sacred Latin poets of the Middle Ages" Out of one hundred pieces at least fifty are of the highest excellence."
2. ALEXANDER, MRS C. F.—Wife of the Rev. W. Alexander. Author of "Hymns for Little Children," of which a quarter of a million have been sold.
3. ALLEN, JAMES.—Editor of "The Kendal Hymn Book," for which he wrote seventy hymns. The precious hymn, "Sweet the moments, rich in blessing," was written by him, but much altered and improved by Shirley.
4. AUBER, MISS HARRIET.—Her hymns are taken from her work, entitled, "The Spirit of the Psalms, or a Compressed Version of the Psalms of David," (1829). She lived a retired life, and reached her eighty-ninth year.
5. BAKER, REV. HENRY—His hymns are found in "Hymns Ancient and Modern," (1861), of which he was the principal compiler
6. BAKEWELL, JOHN.—Lived to his 98th year On his tomb it is said, "He adorned the doctrine of God, our Saviour eighty years, and preached his glorious gospel about seventy years" He wrote for the press after he was ninety He was author of a number of hymns.
7. BALDWIN, THOMAS D D.—He was in early life a member of the Legislature in Connecticut In 1790, became pastor of the 2nd Baptist Church, Boston. While in this charge, his labors were greatly blessed. He died suddenly while on a journey from home, in 1825.
8. BARBAULD, MRS. ANNA.—She was the daughter of Dr. John Aikin, and wife of Rev. R. Barbauld, a student of Dr. Doddridge Four editions of her hymns were sold in the year 1773 In 1775, she issued "Devotional Pieces compiled from the Psalms of David" A fine specimen of her poetic powers is given in her much-admired hymn, "How blest the righteous when he dies" Her peaceful death occurred in her eighty-second year.
9. BARTON, BERNARD —He is known as the "Quaker poet" His hymns are taken from his "Half dozen volumes of verse," which were composed during his forty-years' clerkship in a bank.
10. BATHURST, WILLIAM H.—He issued in 1831, "Psalms and Hymns for Public and Private use.' The two hundred and six hymns were all his own, as well as most of the psalms.
11. BETHUNE, G W., D. D —His hymn, "Oh, for the happy hour," was written in church, while waiting for the arrival of his audience, and while his heart was burdened with a "Longing for a Revival"
12. BILBY, THOMAS.—His well-known hymn, "Oh, that will be joyful,' was issued in 1832 He died in 1872, aged seventy-eight
13. BLACKLOCK, THOMAS, D. D.—Was blind during the seventy years of his life, yet became quite learned, and was the author of several works in prose and one in poetry.
14. BORTHWICK, MISS JANE.—One of the authoresses of "Hymns from the Land of Luther."

15. BOWRING, SIR JOHN.—A voluminous writer. Author of "Matins and Vespers, with Hymns and Devotional Pieces," (1823), and of "Hymns as a Sequel to the Matins," (1825)
16. BROWNE, SIMON.—He was a cotemporary with Watts. Among the twenty-three works, from his pen, was a hymn-book entitled, "Hymns and Spiritual Songs" During the last years of his life, he had s malady that led him to imagine that he could not think, and yet, at the same time, as Toplady says, "Instead of having no soul, he wrote, and reasoned, and prayed as if he had two"
17. BRUCE, MICHAEL.—This promising young poet was found dead in bed, one morning He died at twenty-one, the same age as Henry Kirk White, whom he resembled in many respects. After his death, the poet Logan plagerized some of his productions
18. BURDER, GEORGE.—Widely known as the author of eight volumes of "Village Sermons" In 1784, he published "A Collection of Hymns from Various Authors," in which were several of his own His busy and useful life reached its eightieth year.
19. CASWALL, EDWARD.—Transferred his relation from the Church of England to the Roman Catholic Church, in 1847.
20. CHANDLER, JOHN.—Author of "Hymns of the Primitive Church," issued in 1837. He has translated many hymns from the Latin
21. CLEMENS, ST.—His hymn is supposed to be the oldest extant.
22. CODNER, ELIZABETH.—Author of "The Missionary Ship,' and "The Bible in the Kitchen,' etc.
23. COLLYER, WILLIAM B.—Mr. Miller says "For half a century Dr. Collyer was one of the most popular Dissenting ministers in London." In 1812, he issued a collection of hymns, of which fifty-seven were by himself, and in 1837, another work, in which were eighty-nine hymns of his own composition. His last sermon, delivered shortly before his death in his seventy second year, was from the text: "How wilt thou do in the swellings of Jordan"
24. CONDER, JOSIAH.—Produced in 1836 the first "Congregational Hymn Book," in which were fifty-six hymns from his own pen
25. COOK, R. S.—He was highly esteemed as one of the Secretaries of the American Tract Society. His hymn was prepared for the American Messenger, March, 1850.
26. COTTRILL, THOMAS.—Author of "A Selection of Psalms and Hymns for Public and Private Use," in which twenty-two hymns and a few Psalms are attributed to him
27. DE FLEURY, MARIA.—Author of "Divine Poems and Essays on Various Subjects" (1791)
28. DENNY, SIR EDWARD.—His "Hymns and Poems" appeared in 1839.
29. DOANE, GEO. W., D. D.—In 1832, he was consecrated Bishop of the Protestant Episcopal Church of New Jersey
30. DUNCAN, MARY L.—Wife of Rev. W W Duncan, and author of "Rhymes for My Children."
31. DWIGHT, JOHN S.—Son of Dr. Timothy Dwight
33. EDMESTON, JAMES.—A London architect. Author of "Sacred Lyrics," 1820; "The Cottage Minstrel," 1821, "Closet Hymns and Poems," 1843; ' Hymns for the Young," 1846, and over 100 hymns for Sabbath Schools

Appendix. 553

34. FABER, F W., D D.—Author of one hundred and fifty hymns In a preface, he says, "It is an immense mercy of God to allow any one to do the least thing which brings souls nearer to Him." He became a Roman Catholic in 1846. His hymns are of high repute among Protestants.
35. FRANCIS, BENJAMIN—A Welshman. Began to preach when nineteen years of age. Was ordained at Shortwood, England, where he preached for forty-one years. His success occasioned the enlargement of his church three times. He composed two volumes of Welsh hymns.
36. GIBBONS, THOMAS, D D—An intimate friend of Whitefield. Was pastor of an Independent church for forty-two years Wrote the "Memoir of Dr. Watts." His first collections of hymns appeared in 1769, the second in 1784.
37. GILMORE, J. H—Professor in Rochester University, New York. His hymn, "He leadeth me," etc., was written at the close of a lecture on the 23rd Psalm, in the 1st Baptist Church, Philadelphia
38. GOODE, WILLIAM.—Author of "New Version of the Psalms." Noted for early and earnest piety. Was successor to the celebrated Romaine.
39. GRANT, SIR ROBERT.—English Governor of Bombay, and author of "Sacred Poems."
40. HALL, C. NEWMAN.—Author of the well-known work, "Come to Jesus." He is one of the successors of Rowland Hill.
41. HAMMOND, WILLIAM—Author of "Psalms, Hymns and Spiritual Songs" issued in 1745.
42. HASTINGS, T.—Widely known as a musician. Issued the "Union Minstrel" for Sunday Schools, in 1830; "Spiritual Songs," in 1832; "Christian Psalmist," in 1836, "Devotional Hymns and Religious Poems," in 1850; and "Church Melodies," in 1864.
43. HAWEIS, THOMAS.—Author of "Carmina Christo, or Hymns to the Saviour," 1792. The enlarged edition of 1808 has 256 hymns by the author.
44. LUKE, JEMIMA.—Wife of Rev. Samuel Luke. Wrote her popular hymn, "I think when I read that sweet story of old," in a stage coach in 1841.
45. MASON, JOHN.—Author of "Spiritual Songs," etc., issued in 1683 He was one of the few who wrote good hymns before the time when "Watts made an era in the history of the hymn-writing art."
46. MILLS, ELIZABETH.—Her hymn, "We speak of the realms of the blest," was written a few weeks before her death, and was suggested by the remark: "We speak of heaven but oh! to be there"
47. MILTON, JOHN—Author of "Nine Psalms done in Metre." Wrote the psalm, "Let us with a gladsome mind," when but fifteen years of age
48. MOORE, THOMAS—The gifted Irish poet His hymns are taken from his "Sacred Songs," 33 in number, issued in 1816
49. NEALE, JOHN M—Author of "Mediæval Hymns," 1851; "Hymns for Children," 1854, and numerous other works
50. OLIVERS, THOMAS.—A convert through Whitfield's preaching. Of him it is said, "He spent so many hours on his knees in prayer, as to make him limp a little in walking" Though previous to his conversion an illiterate shoemaker, yet of his hymn, "The God of Abraham praise," Montgomery says "There is not in our language, a lyric of more majestic style, more elevated thought, or more glorious imagery."

51. RAFFLES, DR. THO's.—A popular and eloquent preacher. Wrote many hymns for the use of his congregation in Liverpool, Eng., of which he continued the pastor for over fifteen years.
52. REED, ANDREW, D D —Compiled "The Hymn Book," for which he and his wife wrote forty hymns. When near the end of life, his hymn, "There is an hour when I must part," was read in his hearing "That hymn," said he, "I wrote at Geneva; it has brought comfort to many, and now it brings comfort to me."
53. RIPPON, JOHN —Commenced, in 1778, the issue of his "Selection of Hymns from the best Authors, with a great number of Originals." Over thirty editions have been published. He was pastor for 63 years of a Baptist church in London.
54. SCHEFFLER, JOHN —Was the founder of tha Silesian or Mystical school. Is sometimes known as Angelus Silesius, an adopted name.
55. SWAIN, JOSEPH —Author of the "Walworth Hymns." After his conversion he wrote hymns to give utterance to his new joy. It is said. "A friend, having overheard him singing these Christian hymns, took him to hear Gospel preaching,—a privilege he had not enjoyed before." He afterwards became a popular preacher
56 TAPPAN, W. B —A voluminous religious poet. Author of "Poems and Lyrics," 1842, "Sacred and Miscellaneous Poems," 1858. His life was spent mainly in the service of the American Sunday School Union
57. TATE, NAHUM —This psalm-writer was associated with Dr. Nicholas Brady in rendering a metrical version of the Psalms, issued in 1696, which took the place of the "Psalter," by Sternhold and Hopkins, published in the year 1562
58 TERSTEEGEN, GERARD —Author of one hundred and eleven hymns. When sixteen, he became the subject of divine grace, and would spend "whole nights in prayer, reading and meditation." After finding rest in the atoning blood of Christ, he wrote a dedication of himself to Christ with his own blood. Having gained great celebrity, through his writings and soul-saving efforts, the sick in soul and body flocked, from all countries, to his "Pilgrim's Cottage." His time became thus so much absorbed, that he relinquished his business,—the manufacture of silk ribbons.
59 WESLEY, SAMUEL SR.—The father of nineteen children, of which Charles, John, and Samuel became distinguished. His hymn, "Behold the Saviour of mankind," was rescued from the flames, with some marks of the fire upon it, at the same time that his son, John, was snatched as a brand from the burning. While engaged in his old age in writing a comment on Job his right arm became paralized He afterward seized the pen with his left hand, and wrote to a friend saying, that he was sending his left hand to school to learn to write for Jesus
60 WESLEY, SAMUEL JR.—Brother of John and Charles. His "Poems on Several Occasions," 1736, together with his hymns, evince considerable poetic talent.
61 SIGOURNEY, L. H —Of her, it is said "At three years of age she might be seen reading her Bible." and at "eight years she knew how to express her thoughts in writing with ease and beauty." In her 23rd year she issued the first of her numerous works, entitled, "Moral Pieces."

First Lines of Hymns Referred to or Illustrated.

Abide with me, fast falls the eventide..................................Page 276
A charge to keep I have...439
A guilty, weak and helpless worm..423
Alas! and did my Saviour bleed...420-423
All hail the power of Jesus' name.....................................338-342
Alone, yet not alone, am I..83
Amazing grace, how sweet the sound....................................306
A mighty fortress is our God...270
And must I part with all I have...55
And must this body die..433
Another six days' work is done..366
As the sun doth daily rise..40
Awaked by Sinai's awful sound..324
Awake, my soul, and with the sun..244
Awake, my soul, in joyful lays..280
Awake, my soul, stretch every nerve.....................................144
Awake, my soul, to meet the day..135
Before Jehovah's awful throne..417
Behold the glories of the Lamb...408
Be present at our table, Lord..484
Beyond the parting and the meeting..28
Blest be the tie that binds...170
Children of the heavenly King...260
Come, every pious heart..369
Come, Holy Spirit, heavenly Dove....................................419, 426
Come, Holy Spirit, come..196, 55
Come, humble sinner in whose breast....................................253
Come, let us join our friends above..476
Commit thou all thy griefs...478, 175
Come on, my partners in distress...370
Come, O thou all victorious Lord..465
Come, thou Fount of every blessing..................................344-349
Come to Jesus, come to Jesus..329
Come, we that love the Lord..260, 519
Come, ye disconsolate...528, 289
Come, ye sinners, poor and needy..156
Daughter of Zion from the dust...
Dear Christian people, now rejoice...265
Dear Jesus, let an infant claim...216
Depth of mercy, can there be..464
Did Christ o'er sinners weep..54
Draw me, Saviour, nearer..32

First lines of hymns.

Fade each earthly joy	485
Far from the world, O Lord, I flee	99
Forever let my grateful heart	512
Forever with the Lord	299
Forth to the land of promise bound	37
From every stormy wind that blows	376
From Greenland's icy mountains	205
From the cross uplifted high	199
Gentle Jesus, meek and mild	285
Gently, my Saviour, let me down	219
Give me the enlarged desire	475
Give me the wings of faith to rise	409
Give to the winds thy fears	172
Glory and thanks to God we give	461
Glory to thee, my God, this night	244, 255, 247, 256
God moves in a mysterious way	283, 336, 120
Grace 'tis a charming sound	128
Guide me, O thou great Jehovah	490-495
Hark! my soul, it is the Lord	121
Hark! ten thousand harps and voices	243
Hark! the eternal rends the sky	513
Hear, gracious Saviour, from thy throne	146
Heavenly Father, we thy children meet	258
Here at thy table, Lord, we meet	369
Hosannah to Jesus on high	485
How are thy servants blessed, O Lord	27
How blest the creature is, O God	96
How charming is the place	369
How happy every child of grace	468
How sweet the melting lay	80
How sweet the name of Jesus sounds	316
How tedious and tasteless the hours	183, 256
How vain are all things here below	407
I am weary of my sin	279
If life's pleasures charm thee	261
I gave my life for thee	201
I heard the voice of Jesus say	70
I lay my sins on Jesus	73
I'll praise my Maker while I've breath	248
I love thy kingdom, Lord	150
I love to steal a while away	74, 525
I'm a poor sinner	343
In age and feebleness extreme	437
In all my Lord's appointed ways	350
In evil long I took delight	306
In peace let me resign my breath	322
I send the joys of earth away	278
I was a wandering sheep	66, 172
I would love thee, God and Father	189
I would not live alway	288

First lines of hymns.

Jesus, and shall it ever be	333, 180
Jesus, at thy command	364
Jesus, I live to thee	194
Jesus, I love thy charming name	138, 432
Jesus, I my cross have taken	274, 277, 183
Jesus, lover of my soul	440-460
Jesus loves me, this I know	199
Jesus, my all to heaven is gone	91
Jesus, the name high over all	466, 495
Jesus, the very thought of thee	56
Jesus, this midday hour	80
Jesus, thy blood and righteousness	478, 498, 230
Jesus, we lift our souls to thee	524
Jesus, where'er thy children meet	101
Jesus, who knows full well	310
Joyfully on earth adore him	169
Just as I am, without one plea	156-162, 375
Leave God to order all thy ways	305
Let not the errors of my youth	453
Like the sea that cannot rest	450
Lo! on a narrow neck of land	470-474
Lord, I am thine, entirely thine	122-123
Lord, in the morning thou shalt hear	418
Lord, it belongs not to my care	45
Majestic sweetness sits enthroned	369
'Mid scenes of confusion and creature complaints	124
Mighty God! while angels bless thee	348
My country, 'tis of thee	359
My faith looks up to thee	334-337
My drowsy powers, why sleep ye so	431
My God, I love thee, not because	497
My Lord, how full of sweet content	188
Nearer, my God, to thee	29-31
No room for mirth and trifling here	463
Not all the blood of beasts	414-416
O could I speak the matchless worth	280, 283
O do not be discouraged	321
O happy saints who dwell in light	58
O for a closer walk with God	97, 511
O for a thousand tongues to sing	438
O glorious hope of perfect love	370
O happy day that fixed my choice	142
O Lord, another day is flown	489
O Lord, I would delight in thee	353
O Lord, thy work revive	79
One sweetly solemn thought	84
One there is above all others	317-320
O thou, my soul, forget no more	330
O turn ye, O turn ye	324-328
Our Father, God, who art in heaven	239

O what amazing words of grace	286
O where shall rest be found	298
Peace, troubled soul, whose plaintive moan	358
People of the living God	299
Praise God, from whom all blessings flow	257-260
Praise the Lord ye Gentiles all	251
Prayer was appointed to convey	299, 196
Prostrate, dear Jesus, at thy feet	369
Religion is the chief concern	169
Rock of ages, cleft for me	380-395
Saviour, breathe an evening blessing	524
Servants of God, in joyful lays	293
Since Jesus freely did appear	65
Sister, thou wast mild and lovely	525
Show pity, Lord, O Lord, forgive	277, 411
Stop, poor sinner, stop and think	323
Sun of my soul, thou Saviour dear	240
Sweet hour of prayer, sweet hour of prayer	490
Sweet is the work, my God, my King	155
Sweet the moments, rich in blessing	551
Ten thousand times ten thousand	38
The birds more happier far than I	419
The Lord himself my Shepherd is	42
The Lord my pasture shall prepare	26
The Lord our God is clothed with might	489
There all the ship's company meet	439
There is a fountain filled with blood	102
There is a happy land	372
There is a land of pure delight	372, 403, 408
The Saviour, O what endless charms	360
The spacious firmament on high	26
Thine earthly Sabbaths, Lord, we love	138
Thou art gone to the grave	211
Though waves and storms go over my head	419
Thou God of love, thou ever blest	521
Thou, O my Jesus, didst me embrace	497
"'Tis finished," so the Saviour cried	369
"Watch and pray, watch and pray"	472
When all thy mercies, O my God	26
When I can read my title clear	412
When I survey the wondrous cross	385, 424-425
When marshaled on the nightly plain	489
When rising from the bed of death	27
When thou, my righteous judge shalt come	220-228
Where two or three, together meet	106
While life prolongs its precious light	150
While on the verge of life I stand	136
Who knows how near my life's expended	52
Why vail thyself in gloom my heart	357
Worship and thanks and blessing	469

ILLUSTRATED HISTORY

of

Sunday School Song.

The Singing of Children.

EVER since "the morning stars sang together, and all the sons of God shouted for joy," the fresh music of childhood's early morn has risen as sweet incense to the Lord of Host. During the great revival in Jerusalem, in the times of Nehemiah, not only were streets made wet with the tears of penitence, as "all the people wept when they heard the words of the law," but they were also made to resound with "gladness, both with thanksgiving, and with singing, with cymbals, psalteries, and with harps." Among the sounds of joy were blended the sweet echoes of children's praise, for, while the "singers sang loud with Jezrahiah, the overseer, the wives also and the *children* rejoiced, so that the joy of Jerusalem was heard even afar off."

Neither were the children silent, when, in after years the same streets became vocal with the Pentecostal revival. Peter made it prominent that the promise was to the children as well as to those afar off. This was but right, for did they not shout "Hosanna to the Son of David" in the temple, and when some were sore displeased, the Saviour replied, "Have ye never read, 'Out of the mouth of babes and sucklings thou hast perfected praise?'"

During the revival of modern hymnology, Dr. Watts was led by heavenly wisdom to provide hymns and songs for children. And no sentence, carved in the granite monument, lately erected to his memory, has greater significance than that

"He gave to lisping infancy its earliest and purest lessons."

As showing some of the happy results of his hymns for children we give the following from the address of a pastor, furnished by the Rev. S. W. Christophers:—

"A good man in declining life told me that the first book in which, as a child, he took an interest, was a small edition of Watts' 'Hymns and Divine Songs' for children. Each hymn was headed by a woodcut, and one especially was his favorite. It represented a little boy, something like himself, as he thought, leaning at an open window, looking at a calm happy face on the setting sun, which was throwing his parting light upon a quiet country scene. Many of the hymns, and that one in particular, had been read often, until they lived in his soul. But as he grew up, the impressions were worn off by more exciting and less pure thoughts and pursuits. He fell into a course of dissipation and vice, and seemed for a time to be given up to sin, and devoted to ruin. Worn down at last and threatened with consumption, he was ordered into the country for change of air; and after some time spent in quietness and retirement, far away from the scenes of old temptations, he wandered out one evening about sunset, and hanging pensively over a gate, he watched the sun as it sunk behind the copse, and was throwing its last beams upon the silent and peaceful hill-side. There was a hush upon his spirits, and suddenly, as if sketched by an unseen hand before his inward eye, the little picture which used to interest his boyish mind lived again, and the hymn which it illustrated seemed to be spoken sweetly to his heart:—

"And now another day is gone,
I'll sing my Maker's praise." Etc.

The tear started. He had seen many of his days go, but as yet his Maker had never heard an even-song from his lips or from his heart. What an ungrateful life his had been! The 'remembrance was grevious,' But his heart was broken, and there and then the softened man made his vows of return to God, and offered the prayer which was answered in blessings which filled both the mornings and evenings of his mature life with hymns and songs of thanksgiving and praise."

No instrumentality has been so efficient in calling forth and stimulating the hosannas of children as Sunday schools. The start and perpetuity of this institution as a system is generally accredited to Robert Raikes, of Gloucester, England. Says he: "The beginning of this scheme was entirely owing to accident. Some business leading me one morning into the suburbs of the city, where the lowest of the people reside, I was struck with concern at seeing a group of children, wretched and ragged, at play in the street.

"Speaking to a woman, said she: 'Ah! sir, could you take a view of this part of the town on a Sunday, you would be shocked indeed, for then the street is filled with multitudes of these wretches, who, released that day from employment, spend their time in noise and riot, playing at chuck, and cursing and swearing, as to convey to any serious mind an idea of hell rather than of any other place.'"

This led to the employment of four Sunday school teachers, whom he engaged to pay each a shilling (twenty-four cents) for their day's work.

Mr. Raikes once remarked, "When I was revolving the subject of Sunday schools in my thoughts, the word TRY was so powerfully impressed upon my mind that it impelled me to action." He then added, "I can never pass by the spot where the word TRY came so powerfully into my mind, without lifting up my heart and hands to Heaven, in gratitude to God, for having put such a thought into my heart." At another time he writes: "My eldest boy was born the very day that I made public to the world the scheme of Sunday schools, in my paper of Nov. 3, 1783. In four years' time it has extended so rapidly, as now to include two hundred and fifty thousand children. It is increasing more and more; it reminds me of the grain of mustard seed."

How Mr. Raikes would now be enraptured could he but listen to the entire world echoing with Sunday school songs, and behold the millions simultaneously engaged in the study of the same lessons.

The Rev. Dr. Belcher states the singular fact that "Mr. Raikes's first thorough conviction of sin, and his first approach to the cross of Christ for mercy, was the

result of reading the fifty-third chapter of Isaiah to a little girl, one of his own Sunday school scholars. So marvelously does the blessed God work in the accomplishment of his greatest designs."

While seeking that which was lost, our Saviour was wont at times to take new and untrodden paths, when, it is said, his followers "murmured." The introduction of Sunday schools was saluted with similar murmurs.

At a conference of ministers held in London the opponents argued that it was a desecration of the Lord's day. One wrote in 1794, that "no single instance of moral improvement has occurred to distinguish any of the Sunday school children from others;" and then closes by asking, "How can the Divine Being give a blessing to an institution which appears contrary to his revealed will?"

Even in our own day the novelty of the Sabbath school has awakened singular opposition.

About the year 1854, a young evangelical minister proposed to introduce a Sunday school in a section of Pennsylvania, not fifty miles from Philadelphia, when, some of his members regarding it as an innovation upon the good old customs of their fathers, not only bitterly opposed it, but went so far as to threaten their pastor with personal violence while he was addressing the children from the church altar. At length they drove the children from the church and scattered the books upon the road. A law-suit ensued, in which the opponents of the school took the ground that the charter stated that there should be nothing in the church but *preaching*. For this reason the jury decided in their favor. After gaining the suit they dragged a cannon a distance of ten miles, and placing it aside of the church, fired it off a whole half day, as a jubilee of their victory in having tumbled the Sunday school out of church.

In 1829, James Montgomery, the Christian poet, wrote: "It has occurred to me that a Sunday school Jubilee in the year 1831, fifty years from the origin of Sunday schools might be the means of extraordinary and happy excitement to the public mind in favor of these institutions."

This proposal met with general approval, and the Jubilee was arranged for September 14th, 1831, the anniversary of Raikes's birth. This proved to be one of the most interesting epochs connected with the history of Sunday schools.

We give herewith one of the hymns written for this occasion by Mr. Montgomery. It was not only sung by the tens of thousands on the day of Jubilee, but has mingled with the glad hosannas of children ever since.

"Hosanna be the children's song,
To Christ the children's king
His praise to whom our souls belong,
Let all the children sing.

"From little ones to Jesus brought
Hosanna now be heard;
Let infants at the breast be taught,
To lisp that lovely word.

"Hosanna here, in joyful bands,
Maidens and youths proclaim,
And hail with voices, hearts, and hands
The Son of David's name.

"Hosanna sound from hill to hill,
And spread from plain to plain,
While louder, sweeter, clearer still,
Woods echo to the strain.

"Hosanna, on the wings of light,
O'er earth and ocean fly,
Till morn to eve, and noon to night,
And heaven to earth reply.

"The city to the country call,
Let realm with realm accord;
And this their watchword, one and all—
Hosanna, praise the Lord.

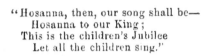

"Hosanna, then, our song shall be—
Hosanna to our King;
This is the children's Jubilee
Let all the children sing."

JUBILEE GATHERING AT EXETER HALL.

The grand Jubilee meeting was held in Exeter Hall, London. This vast building, so widely known on account of the many religious anniversaries held within its walls, was never more crowded, or the scene of greater enthusiasm than on this memorable occasion.

The Right Honorable Lord Henley, who officiated as chairman, said: "This meeting exceeds, in point of numbers, any that I have ever seen,—exceeds, as I am sure it does, in knowledge and intelligence and in Christian spirit, every meeting which I have ever beheld before collected within the walls of an assembly."

William B. Bradbury.

THE extensive interest and warm enthusiasm now manifested in Sunday schools is largely to be attributed to the prominent place given to song—lively song, adapted to the quick motion and sprightly expression so natural to the young. Children live and move in a world of thought, peculiarly their own. "When I was a child," says the Apostle, "I spake as a child, I understood as a child, I thought as a child." Hymns suited to the "thought" of children were provided by Watts, Charles Wesley, Hill, Montgomery and others, but they had no musical tongue given them, so as to speak with the voice of childhood, till the days of William B. Bradbury. The memory of his name will be endeared to millions of the present generation as the pioneer in Sunday school song.

He was born in York, York county, Maine, October 6, 1816. Although from early life he was specially fond of music, yet until the age of seventeen he was unable to devote much time to its study. After many struggles, owing to his straitened circumstances, he was enabled at length, through the assistance of some kind friends, to attend the Academy of Music at Boston, in charge of Dr. Lowell Mason and his coadjutor, George J. Webb, who at that time stood at the head of the musical celebrities of New England.

"About this time," says Mr. T. F. Seward, "an incident occurred which was a source of great mortification to the young enthusiast. His parents, both of them old fashioned singers, were, of course, greatly interested in his progress. He went home from the school one night, full of ardor and excitement, and undertook to give them an example of the new method of singing and beating time. His gestures were so extravagant, swinging his

WILLIAM B. BRADBURY.

arm nearly its whole length, that his parents were far more amused than edified. However, they restrained their mirth, not wishing to check their son's enthusiasm, but at last the scene became too much for them, and they burst into a peal of unresistible laughter. This was too much for the eager performer. His rapture was turned into fiery indignation, and slamming his book shut in a rage, he declared that they knew nothing at all about music, and marched out of the room.

Another mental shower-bath occurred in connection with his first appointment for a singing-school. After the issue of many circulars and stirring advertisements, he anticipated a great crowd, when, at the appointed time, not a single soul was there to greet his arrival. After a while a young man made his appearance, and still later five others came to witness the mortification of the ambitious young teacher, who sat on the platform in a clammy perspiration, "inwardly longing for some blessed knot-hole through which he might disappear." This magnificent fizzle is spoken of as of great value to him in bringing him down from the clouds and of more real service than a grand success would have been. Through the influence of Dr. Mason, his former teacher, he secured a position as teacher of singing-schools at Machias, in Maine, and afterwards in St. Johns, New Brunswick.

At length a position was given him as music teacher, in the 1st Baptist Church of Brooklyn, N. Y., and later in the Baptist Tabernacle in New York City.

In 1841, he turned his attention to the children, and first held his free singing classes which became so very popular. It was a thrilling scene at his annual "Juvenile Musical Festivals," to behold a thousand children on a gradually rising platform,—the girls clad in white with a white wreath and blue sash, and the boys in jackets, with collars turned over in Byron style.

These efforts among the young gave him great celebrity, a host of warm friends, and led him eventually into his life work of providing Sunday school song for the countless millions. And if, as it is said, he who makes the ballads of a nation has mightier power than he who makes its laws, how far reaching must be the sweep of his undying influence. Some estimate may be formed from the fact that over three million copies of his "*Golden Trio:*"—"*Golden Chain,*" "*Golden Shower,*" and "*Golden Censer,*" have been issued, and yet these form but a small part of the number of his publications as will appear from the subjoined list:

1841	Young Choir.*	1856	Sabbath School Choir.
1843	School Singer, or Young Choir's Companion.*	1856	Cantata of Esther.
		1856	Musical Bouquet.§
1844	Psalmodist.†	1857	Jubilee.
1844	Social Singing Book.	1859	Cottage Melodies.**
1845	Young Melodist.	1859	Oriola.
1847	Flora's Festival.	1860	Eclectic Tune Book.
1847	New York Choralist.‡	1860	Bradbury's Anthem Book
1849	Musical Gems.	1861	The Golden Chain.
1849	Mendelssohn Collection.†	1861	The Carol.
1850	Alpine Glee Singer.	1862	The Golden Shower.
1850	S. S. Melodies.	1863	Key Note.
1851	Psalmista.†	1863	Pilgrims' Songs.**
1852	The Seasons.	1864	Devotional Hymn and Tune Book.**
1852	Singing Bird.		
1852	Metropolitan Glee Book.	1865	Plymouth Collection.**
1853	Shawm.‡	1866	Golden Hymns.**
1854	Book for Boys' and Girls' Meetings.	1867	Clariona.**
		1867	Songs of Praise.**
1855	Young Shawm.	1864	The Golden Censer.**
1855	New York Glee and Chorus Book.	1867	Fresh Laurels.**
		1867	The Temple Choir.‖

Thus it will appear that in twenty-six years he was instrumental, with the assistance of others, in bringing

* In connection with Mr. C. W. Sanders.
† In connection with Dr. Thomas Hastings.
‡ In connection with Dr. Hastings, Mr. G. F. Root and Mr. T, B, Mason,
§ In connection with Mr. C, C, Converse,
** In connection with Mr Sylvester Main.
‖ In connection with Dr, Lowell Mason and Mr. Theodore F, Seward,

out no less than forty different publications. It was regretted by many that some of his earlier works did not contain a higher standard of poetry. But then it must be remembered that this was a transition period in the musical history of our country. "The mind of the public," says Mr. Seward, "had just undergone a complete reaction. From the almost exclusive use of plain church tunes in the exercise of the Sunday school, there began to be a general adoption of street melodies of every description, from 'Co-co-che-lunk' to 'We wont go home till morning;' and there is no doubt but that Mr. Bradbury's music was the barrier by which the fearful tide was stopped. He expressly states that the 'Golden Chain' was compiled with that special object in view."

In 1847, Mr. Bradbury went to Europe to perfect his knowledge of music under the tuition of the best German masters. While crossing the Alps, he relates this incident: Having met a German, who was so enraptured, as he beheld the Alpine peaks bathed with the golden glories of the rising sun, that he sang aloud for joy. "Not wishing," says Mr. Bradbury, "to be outdone by a 'foreigner,' especially in my own profession, *I* commenced singing." This captivated the 'foreigner' so that he would not rest till he was taught the same pieces. "This," Mr. Bradbury quaintly adds, "was the only music-lesson I gave on the top of the Alps."

When about fifteen years of age he became a member of the Charles St. Baptist Church, Boston, Mass., under the pastorate of the Rev. Dr. Sharp. While settled in New York he united with the Baptist Tabernacle. For many years, in the latter part of his life, he stood in connection with the Presbyterian Church of Bloomfield, N. J. His widow, in furnishing the writer with these facts, adds: "He was not strictly sectarian in his views, often saying he belonged to the 'children's church,' meaning that wherever he could meet with the children and do them good he felt at home."

The following is a specimen of one of his many acts of generosity: A theological student once wrote to Mr. Bradbury for a loan of five dollars, that he might buy himself a pair of boots. By return of mail he received Mr. Bradbury's check for twenty-five dollars, and a note saying that he did not feel able to spare him the five dollars, but that he might manage to get along with the twenty-five for the present, and until he could accommodate him with the five dollars.

The strain of music that he composed to "Sweet hour of prayer," was but the sweet echo of his own experience.

In the rear of his ware-rooms in New York, was a small office, where he was wont to "renew his strength" and "mount up with wings as eagles." Whenever, with the cars, he had to leave his home without having had sufficient time for his closet duties, it is said, he never failed to repair at once to this little private sanctuary and spend some time in his devotions. Nor would he permit any pressure of business to break in upon this habit. His much-loved Bible occupied a prominent place on the table, and was well worn and filled with marked passages that had become luminous in his own experience. In his private journal he wrote, "The 37th Psalm has been to me a never-failing source of comfort and consolation. My little Bible frequently opens to it of its own accord. The 27th is also a favorite when the enemy comes in like a flood."

Mr. Bradbury ended his fifty-two years of a busy life on the 7th of January, 1868. For two years previous he suffered from the lingering torments of consumption. A few weeks before his death he said to Mr. Seward, in accents of touching pathos, "I long to be free from this evil body, which does so much to drag me down. I feel that I *want* to do right, that I *want* to love my Saviour, and act to please Him, but this busy brain and hasty nature lead me oftentimes to things that are contrary to the real feelings of my heart."

He need no longer express such desires or sing to his much loved song, "Sweet hour of prayer," the words:—

> "This robe of flesh I'll drop, and rise
> To seize the everlasting prize."

His longing desires have ended in joyful fruitions.

Some of the sweet melodies that Mr. Bradbury set afloat in his life accompanied him in his descent to the dark valley, and followed him in his ascent to the skies.

The night he passed away some of the brethren, who had convened for a prayer-meeting, sang with much feeling the appropriate lines from the "Golden Censer:"—

> "We are going, we are going,
> To a home beyond the skies,
> Where the fields are robed in beauty,
> And the sunlight never dies."

These words were sung again by the dear children as they stood around his cold remains at the funeral.

A week before his death the children of Montclair paid him a visit and each brought him an oak leaf, which was woven into a beautiful wreath. At his funeral it was laid on his coffin and buried with him in his grave.

Well has a friend said, "His triumphs began and ended with the children of whom he was passionately fond." Among Mr. Bradbury's earliest and best pieces was the one so often sung on funeral occasions, and so well fitted to give expression to the words:—

> "Asleep in Jesus; blessed sleep,
> From which none ever wakes to weep,
> A calm and undisturbed repose,
> Unbroken by the last of foes."

This was sung while the cold body of his mother lay

"asleep in Jesus," and now also, as by his own request, his clay was being buried by her side. The Saturday before his death he remarked to a friend, "My soul seems to have gained the victory. I am so happy now. I rest wholly upon Christ. May God give me grace to die. I am going to *see mother*." Now, while he and his sainted mother were blending their voices with the ransomed host above, the funeral attendants below were singing with plaintive voices and tear-bathed cheeks:—

> "Asleep in Jesus; O how sweet
> To be for such a slumber meet;
> With holy confidence to sing,
> That death has lost its venomed sting.

After the singing of these words, the Rev. Dr. Hastings of New York, son of the eminent composer, Dr. Thomas Hastings, paid a beautiful tribute to Mr. Bradbury's memory, and said that he well remembered the first manuscript of the hymn just sung, as he saw it in his father's household, while Mr. Bradbury was associated with his father in musical composition. The music was inspired by the hymn. They were married together, so that they could never be divorced in the Christian's heart and memory during coming generations. Mr. Bradbury shall cause hearts to live and sing when stars and worlds are no more. No friend can desire a nobler monument than is raised for him in Sabbath schools, homes and church, where the gospel is preached and sung."

After these remarks the children sang another of Mr. Bradbury's pieces from the "Fresh Laurels:"—

> "Above the waves of earthly strife,
> Above the ills and cares of life
> Where all is peaceful, bright and fair,
> My home is there, my home is there."

Before the last look upon the pale face was taken, the choir sung a voluntary of Mr. Bradbury's composition:—

> "Let me go where saints are going,
> To the mansions of the blest,"

after which the remains were removed to the hillside in the Bloomfield Cemetery, beside his much-loved mother, there to rest till "time shall be no longer."

While passing under the rod of affliction in his last days, he prepared some of his best pieces that were "like crushed flowers, fragrant with the odors of heaven."

The "Fresh Laurels," his last Sunday school book, he prepared, while, as he expressed it, he was gathering about him his robes for his upward flight.

How appropriate the words of one of his last songs:—

> "I am waiting by the river,
> And my heart has waited long;
> Now I think I hear the chorus
> Of the angels' welcome song;
> Oh, I see the dawn is breaking
> On the hill-tops of the blest,
> "Where the wicked cease from troubling,
> And the weary are at rest."

In the preface to the "Fresh Laurels," he says: "Though the voice of the author of these songs of praise is silent, he has the satisfaction of knowing that multitudes of other and sweeter voices will take them up and echo them throughout the land." As one million and three hundred thousand copies of this book have been sold, surely this wish has been fully realized.

Five days before his departure he was in an ecstacy of delight, which continued till consciousness was gone. Again and again he wished to have repeated the beautiful descriptions of heaven, given in the last two chapters of Revelation, when he would exclaim: "What have I done that I should have such delightful assurance and comfort." As he was going up to be robed in white, he did not wish his friends to attire themselves in black for him, or to mourn his departure.

Origin of "I want to be an angel."

IT is a singular coincidence that the similar utterances of two children should occasion two hymns about the same time on the same subject.

Dr. Prime wrote for the *New York Observer*, of which he is senior editor, the incident given below, April 5. 1845. This was turned into verse by Park Benjamin.

A child sat in the door of a cottage at the close of a summer Sabbath. The twilight was fading, and as the shades of evening darkened, one after another of the stars stood in the sky, and looked down on the child in his thoughtful mood. He was looking up at the stars and counting them as they came, till they were too many to be counted, and his eyes wandered all over the heavens, watching the bright worlds above. They seemed just like "holes in the floor of heaven to let the glory through," but he knew better. Yet he loved to look up there, and was so absorbed, that his mother called to him:

"My son, what are you thinking of?"

He started as if aroused from sleep, and answered: "I was thinking———"

"Yes," said his mother, "I know you were thinking, but what were you thinking about?"

"Oh," said he, and his little eyes sparkled with the thought, "I want to be an angel."

"And why, my son, would you be an angel?"

"Heaven is up there, is it not, mother? and there the angels live and love God, and are happy; I do wish I was good, and God would take me there, and let me *wait on him forever.*"

The mother called him to her knee, and he leaned on her bosom and wept. She wept too, and smoothed the soft hair of his head as he stood there, and kissed his forehead, and then told him that if he would give his heart to God, now while he was young, that the Saviour would forgive all his sins and take him up to heaven when he died, and he would then be with God forever.

His young heart was comforted. He knelt at his mother's side and said:—

> "Jesus, Saviour, Son of God,
> Wash me in thy precious blood;
> I thy little lamb would be,
> Help me, Lord, to look to thee."

The mother took the young child to his chamber and soon he was asleep, dreaming perhaps of angels and heaven. A few months afterwards sickness was on him, and the light of that cottage, the joy of that mother's heart, went out. He breathed his last in her arms, and as he took her parting kiss, he whispered in her ear:—

> "I want to be an angel."

Just two weeks after the publication of the above, Miss Sidney P. Gill wrote the hymn which, for nearly thirty years, has been so popular in Europe and America. It took its rise in the infant school of the Clinton Street Presbyterian Sabbath-School of Philadelphia, which was taught by Miss Gill.

On the Sabbath, previous to its composition, she was speaking to her little infants about heaven picturing its beauties and glories, the blessedness of being there with "a crown upon the forehead, a harp within the hand," when a little dark-eyed girl, about five years of age, became so enraptured that she unconsciously clasped her hands together, and looking wistfully into her teacher's face, exclaimed aloud, "O, I want to be an angel."

That week this little scholar, Annie Louisa Farrand, took sick and died. Miss Gill at once wrote the hymn, on the next Sunday taught it to her scholars, and millions of infant voices have since been singing,—

> "I want to be an angel."

Mrs. Lydia Baxter.

ASSOCIATED with some of our most popular Sunday school hymns is the name of Mrs. Lydia Baxter. The many, who for years have been singing her words:—

> "Take the name of Jesus with you,
> Child of sorrow and of woe,"

> "There is a gate that stands ajar,
> And through its portals gleaming,"

will be pleased to read the following sketch of her life, prepared for this volume by her former pastor, the Rev. Thomas Armitage, D. D.

This saintly woman was born in the town of Petersburgh, Rensselaer Co., N. Y., Sept. 2nd, 1809. She became a disciple of Christ while very young, under the labors of the Rev. Eber Tucker, a Baptist home missionary, and soon evinced her healthful influence in her native town, by the fact that her conversion, in connection with that of her younger sister, led to the organization of a Baptist Church in that place. There she was educated, and became a successful Sabbath school teacher.

After her marriage to Col. John C. Baxter, the rest of her life was spent in the city of New York, where she died, June 22, 1874. Principally through her holy influence her husband was brought to Christ, not many years after their marriage, and for more than a generation, she was known in her home, and in all the Christian circles of the city, as a refined, tender and hallowed lady. In person, she was slightly built, but compact and comely, and her manners were very sprightly and winning, so that her society was much appreciated by all classes. For nearly thirty years she was an invalid, much of the time a prisoner at home, and often the victim of excruciating pain. Yet, in the midst of so much

LYDIA BAXTER.

to render her life pensive, and even sombre, seldom did a shade of sadness pass over her heart or house. On the contrary, her quaint humor, a sharp eye for the ludicrous, with the quiet power of story and repartee, were constant sources of light-heartedness to all around her. Hence, pastors, missionaries, Sunday school laborers, and persons of literary tastes, loved to spend a cheerful hour in her company. She was a close student of nature and the Bible. A clear, ringing, gospel truth ever found a joyful welcome to her heart, and the simple, the beautiful, the sublime in nature, ever created a feast to her eye. The delicious scenery of her country home had educated her to a love of birds and flowers, in all their refining persuasiveness. One of her chief joys was the culture of rare and delicate plants, and she acquired the happy art of so arranging the petals and leaves of flowers, in the making of artificial birds and other objects, as to leave the impression that all the hues of light and shade in their delicate blendings were real, and that you had the fascinating reality before your eyes. Her rooms were hung with such specimens of her own handiwork, and many such precious mementoes still adorn the homes of her friends. With a body as weak as a bruised reed, and constantly suffering, her soul was as blithe, her heart as young, and her fingers as active, as if she spent her days in the flush of vigor and youth. This winsome buoyency evinced itself in the fact that the young were constantly attached to her, and in return for their love she lavished upon them her wonderfully pure, sensitive, and pathetic poetic inspirations.

For many years it was her custom to present the Sunday schools of New York with one or more anniversary hymns, in May, which were generally sung in the various churches with great zest. Usually, she kept her room or bed while they were making our metropolitan sanctuaries ring with the praises which she had framed for their lips. But once the writer saw her on such an occasion, steal quietly into a church, pale and weary, to hear the children sing one of her own hymns. And it was touching in the extreme to see the tears follow each other, in great round drops down her cheek, her very heart weeping for joy, while her voice was unable to join them in a single note. Her productions show that she was endowed with a high degree of poetic ability, and she sanctified all its revelations, at the Saviour's feet to the salvation of the young. Hence, there are few Sunday schools in our land where her ennobling verses are not sung every Lord's day, and they are quite as well known in Great Britain as in America. A caged songster herself, she sung for the outside world.

A volume of her chaste poems, entitled "Gems by the Wayside," was published in 1855, and had a large sale, while recently, many of her productions have had an immense circulation in connection with the labors of Messrs Moody and Sankey. Some of those which are the best known are these:—

> "We are coming, blessed Saviour,"
> "On the banks beyond the river,"
> "The angel boatman,"
> "The Precious Name,"
> "The Gate Ajar,"
> "O! shall I wear a starless crown,"
> "By the gate they'll meet us,"
> "The bright hills of glory."

When Messrs Moody and Sankey were in Scotland, her hymn "Gate Ajar," contributed largely to the power of the revival scenes, and was sung to the comfort of many thousands, both in the highlands and in the lowlands. Millions of hearts have been touched by the story of poor Maggie Lindsay of Aberdeen, in association with this hymn, given on the following pages. The knowledge of these facts gave Mrs. Baxter great consolation in the last struggles of her own life, and probably moved her to write her last hymn, entitled, "One more song for Jesus:"—

"One more song I'll sing for Jesus,
　Once again his love repeat;
Though my earthly harp is broken
　Love still makes its numbers sweet.

CHORUS.

"Oh! 'tis sweet to love my Master,
　Sweet His precious love to tell;
But I hear the angels whisper
　I must bid farewell, farewell!

"Oh! improve life's precious moment
　To secure the heavenly prize;
Jesus made a full atonement,—
　'Twas a costly sacrifice.

"Standing on the verge of Jordan
　I can hear its waters roll;
But beyond, the light is golden,
　And it beems upon my soul.

"Faith beholds a sea of glory,
　And the pearly gates appear;
Gentle breezes float around me,
　Oh! the portals must be near."

She made no mention of this sweet hymn until the day before her death, when she presented it to the family, asking that it might be read before them all.

Mrs. Baxter had been chastened by many afflictions in her family as well as in her person, not the least of which was the sudden death of a married son, whom she dearly loved, and who was worthy of her in his devotion to Christ, and his whole household, as well as to his mother. She was a remarkable woman, and her memory with her works is blessed indeed.

"For me! For me! For me!"

THESE were the dying words sung by Maggie Lindsay of Aberdeen, Scotland. An account furnished *The Sunday School Times* gives the following interesting particulars: She was brought to Christ on the last night of 1873, during the great revival in Edinburgh. Meeting her pastor some days afterwards, she told him the secret of her joyful looks.

At parting they knelt together, and when the man of God asked, "For what shall we pray?" she replied, "That I may have more faith, and remain steadfast." When her governess returned after several days' absence, Maggie was impatient to tell of her new-found joy, and came to her room with the message that she had good news to tell her. "Ah, I know what it is, Maggie, before you tell me, you have found Jesus, is not that it?" "Yes, my feet are on the rock," said she, as she went on to tell the joyous story of Jesus' love to her. She seemed powerfully impressed by the oft-repeated hymn:—

> "There is a gate that stands ajar,
> And through its portal gleaming
> A radiance from the Cross afar,
> The Saviour's love revealing.
> Oh depth of mercy! can it be
> That gate was left ajar for me?"

January 27, 1874, she spent her last evening in Edinburgh with her governess and sister, and on returning from the meeting, the latter said to her, "Maggie, I am to give you a text on leaving us; it is one of the words of Jesus, 'Lo, I am with you alway.'" The next morning she took the train for Aberdeen. A fearful railroad collision took place. Maggie was left for several hours lying on the bank. She was at last taken up on a stretcher, and removed to a cottage near by. It was supposed she was reading her much-loved hymn, as the leaf was turned down to the words, "The gate ajar for me," and the pages of the book were stained with her own heart's blood. Lying on that stretcher, with both limbs broken, a fractured skull, and other internal injuries, she could yet *sing with bleeding lips* the hymn:—

> "Nothing either great or small,
> Remains for me to do;
> Jesus died and paid it all,
> Yes, all the debt I owe."

And then after that,

> "Oh depth of mercy! can it be
> That gate stands open wide for me?"

"For *me*! for *me*! for *me*!" she sang plaintively, to the uncontrollable emotion of those who were beside her.

Amid all her sufferings she never murmured. Her chief concern was for the effect which the sight of her poor scarred face would have on her mother, who could not reach her before seven in the evening. She was twelve hours alone among strangers; "alone—yet not alone," she said, "for Jesus is here! He has been with me *alway*. He has kept his word."

At last, unable to utter another word whenever a hymn was sung, there was a gurgling sound in her throat, as if she was trying to join in the song of praise.

Mr. Sankey, writing of her says: "I am persuaded that already the story of her patient suffering and triumphant death has been the means under God of bringing some to the feet of Jesus; and that the sweet testimony which she bore, even while her feet were passing through the cold waters of Jordan, 'Jesus has kept his word' will cheer many a pilgrim on the way to that city which hath foundations, whose builder and maker is God.

> "'Faith a golden vision brings us
> Of that pure transcendent shore,
> Where the blest shall walk with Jesus
> Robed in white forevermore,'"

One Who Could not Sing "Jesus is mine."

> "Now I have found a Friend,
>   Jesus is mine;
> His love shall never end,
>   Jesus is mine.
> Though earthly joys decrease,
> Though human friendships cease,
> Now I have lasting peace,
>   Jesus is mine!"

THIS hymn was issued in 1852 by Henry Hope of Belfast, Ireland. After the singing of it in Dublin, Rev. Denham Smith, while speaking on the value of hymns gave in substance the following touching incident:

A little boy, about four years old, came one day where a group of young converts were singing this hymn. Immediately the little fellow stood still, with closed lips, a very unusual thing with him, and when asked why he did not sing, he said he could not sing, for Jesus was not his; but he said, "Will you pray for me, for I want to know Jesus as mine."

When he went home his mother said to his sisters, "Let us sing two or three other hymns, and then 'Jesus is mine,' and then perhaps he will sing it too;" so they sang several others, and the little fellow caroled away at the top of his voice, until they commenced:—

> "Now I have found a friend,
>   Jesus is mine."

His lips again closed, and in a voice of craving sorrow, turning to his mamma, he said, "Ah, mamma, why do you ask me to sing that? I cannot sing that, for Jesus is not mine."

When his father came home in the evening and heard it, he said: "Oh, it must be fancy in the child; a good night's sleep will wear it away; he is too young to know much of the reality of such things." So he went to bed, and next morning when the father opened the door, what do you think he saw? There was the little one standing in his night-clothes, looking a perfect picture of anxiety and inquiry. He said, "Dear papa, is not the day after to-morrow Friday?" "Yes, my child." "And papa, will there not be a prayer-meeting on Friday?" "Yes, my child." "Then, papa, will you not ask them to pray for me, that I may be able to sing, 'Jesus is Mine,' for I have been looking for Jesus, but I cannot find him; Jesus is not mine." His papa promised that he would have him prayed for.

Wednesday came, and Thursday, and at last Friday; but he could not say, "Jesus is mine;" and mid the engagements of the day, the father actually forgot his own child. Toward the end of the meeting, the congregation rose and sung:—

"Now I have found a Friend,
Jesus is mine."

It happened that the father was in one part of the church and his little boy in another; and as they sung, the little fellow wended his way through the crowded aisles and groups of young converts, till he reached the father, and resting his hands upon his knees, he burst into tears, saying, "Dear papa, I have found Jesus! Jesus is mine!"

Sweet is the young love of that child. It is twelve months ago since he found Jesus, and he can still, with many other happy ones of his circle, joyfully sing:

"I'm a pilgrim bound for glory;
I'm a pilgrim going home;
Come and hear me tell the story
All that love the Saviour, come.

"When first I commenced my journey,
Many said, 'He'll turn again;'
But they all have been deceived;
In the way I still remain.'"

Philip P. Bliss.

BUT few hymns of late years have been more effective in deciding the destiny of souls, or more frequently sung in times of religious awakening than the one commencing:—

> "'Almost persuaded,' now to believe:
> 'Almost persuaded,' Christ to receive."

Many, we are sure, will be glad to form a more intimate acquaintance with the author of these words and music. On the opposite page will be seen his friendly countenance, which speaks for itself and bears the impress of a soul consecrated to the joyous work of the Lord.

Mr. Philip P. Bliss was born in Clearfield county, Pennsylvania, July 9th, 1838. His religious experience illustrates the power of home influence, in that he was "born again" before he was five years old. In fact, he says he cannot remember when he was not a child of God, a believer in Jesus Christ. At the age of twelve he was baptized, and united with the Baptist Church of Cherry Flatts, Tioga county, Pa., the only church organization convenient to his home at that time. His parents were Methodists; and at family worship, prayer-meeting, and camp-meeting revivals, he first imbibed the love of song, and received his first musical impressions.

Since 1865, Mr. Bliss has been a resident of Chicago, and for a number of years an active member of the First Congregational Church, under the pastorate of the Rev. Dr. Goodwin.

One of his first published songs was a tribute to the memory of his teacher, Wm. B. Bradbury, entitled, "He's Gone." His first Sunday school singing-book was "*The Charm*," which had just gotten into market when the great Chicago fire destroyed the plates and dimmed its lustre, at least in the eyes of the author. Mr. Bliss,

PHILIP P. BLISS.

immediately after the fire, in company with Mr. Moody, started on a trip to Boston and other eastern cities, and held "Fire meetings," in aid of the suffering ones of the stricken city. While on this tour he missed the train of cars at Albany, and then wrote the "Fire Song," "Roll on, O Billow of Fire."

Mr. Bliss is the author of the following works:—

"The Charm"	published in 1871.
"Song Tree," for concerts, etc.	" 1872.
"Joy," for choirs and classes	" 1873.
"Sunshine for Sunday schools"	" 1873.
"Gospel Songs for Gospel Meetings"	" 1874.
"Gospel Hymns and Sacred Songs"	" 1875.

This last book was issued in conjunction with Mr. Ira D. Sankey, and as it is used in connection with the "Moody and Sankey meetings," it has met with an immense circulation.

Mr. Bliss has united with Major D. W. Whittle in evangelistic labors in the same way as Mr. Sankey with Mr. Moody. In their first united efforts at Louisville, Kentucky, the seal of the divine approval was set upon their labors. The effective singing of Mr. Bliss and the earnest gospel utterances of Mr. Whittle drew out immense crowds. The whole city was swept by a wave of salvation. The twenty-four pastors who had extended an invitation to the evangelists found their hands full of work. The large hall where they met was marked off into twenty-four sections, each of which was put into charge of a pastor, who, with the assistance of active laymen, devoted his attention to the inquirers, who came into his division. Similar success has since crowned their labors in other sections of the United States.

Among the many incidents illustrative of the hymns of Mr. Bliss we give the following:—

> "Seems now some soul to say,
> 'Go, Spirit, go Thy way,
> Some more convenient day
> On Thee I'll call.'"

In closing a series of extra sermons in Canada, I took for my text the prayer of the perishing disciples on the Sea of Galilee, "*Lord save; we perish.*" Mention was made of this prayer as being a timely one; because the disciples upon finding all efforts to save themselves fail, did not settle down in despair, but at once applied to Christ as the only source of help.

The congregation was then urged upon to make immediate application to the same Saviour for mercy. Many responded to the call, and rose for prayer. It was a precious meeting.

There was present that night a youth for whom many prayers had ascended. Night after night he had promised to yield himself to Christ, but as yet he had not done so. This was the last meeting of the course, and the village people being absorbed in the morrow's fair, we trembled lest John should be tempted, while with ungodly companions, to stifle his convictions. He seemed now anxious about his soul and, humanly speaking, he might never feel thus again. Prayer was offered for him especially, and before it his strong frame was convulsed with feeling.

For a time he seemed on the point of yielding himself to the claims of Christ, but suddenly becoming more calmed, he remarked with an air of indifference, that while he purposed sometime calling to Christ for aid he would not do so that night.

Three months had hardly elapsed from that time when the writer, returning home from a distant engagement, was informed that John A—— was dangerously ill, that his life was despaired of, and that he had repeatedly during our absence sent over for us. Soon we stood at his bedside, and although burning with fever and greatly exhausted, we found him with bitter tenacity clinging to life. Being informed of our presence, he turned his deathly eyes and looked pitifully at us. O, we shall never forget that look! "John," we inquired, "how is it with you now?" Burying his face in his pillow, he made no reply. "Can you not trust your soul with a merciful Saviour?" we further inquired. After a painful pause, he groaned heavily but still did not reply. "Why, John," we again inquired with feelings of pain, "do you doubt Christ's willingness to save the chief of sinners?" He made an effort to answer but was at first choked with grief; we waited, however, and he dispairingly exclaimed, "Mr. C— my day is past, my vessel is sinking, yes sinking, *almost gone.*"

How bitterly he uttered the concluding words, "*almost gone.*" Giving him a moment to recover himself we exhorted him to do at once as did the disciples, and call upon Christ for help. Making no reply, we were about to continue our remarks, when he suddenly exclaimed with a voice that sent a thrill through every heart present, "O sir, call upon Christ, do you say? *Christ has left the vessel. I am sinking all alone.*" Pausing to recover strength, he continued, "It is no use trying now, it is too late, I could have been saved, but now I have no hope, Christ has left the ship." Thus he sank hopelessly in the waters of death.

In this touching incident, furnished by the Rev. W. Codville, rings out the solemn truth in the last verse of the hymn of Mr. Bliss:—

"'Almost persuaded,' harvest is past!
'Almost persuaded,' doom comes at last!
'Almost' can not avail;
'Almost' is but to fail!
Sad, sad, that bitter wail—
'Almost—but lost!'

Fanny J. Crosby.

THE world is indebted to four blind poets for some of the sweetest songs of the sanctuary. One of the grandest hymns of praise that has ever ascended to the skies is the following, which was written by the Rev. Thomas Blacklock, D. D., who lived his three score years and ten in total blindness. The hymn is now over a century old, and will doubtless find a place in the hymnody of the church until the last trump shall sound the end of time. It reads:—

> "Come, O my soul! in sacred lays,
> Attempt thy great Creator's praise;
> But Oh! what tongue can speak his fame?
> What mortal verse can reach the theme!
>
> "Enthroned amidst the radiant spheres,
> He glory, like a garment, wears;
> To form a robe of light divine,
> Ten thousand suns around him shine.
>
> "In all our Maker's grand designs,
> Omnipotence with wisdom shines;
> His works, through all this wondrous frame,
> Bear the great impress of his name.
>
> "Raised on devotion's lofty wing,
> Do thou, my soul! his glories sing;
> And let his praise employ thy tongue,
> Till listening words applaud the song."

John Milton, the world-renowned poet, a part of whose life was spent in blindness, wrote, when a boy of fifteen years of age, the Psalm that has been so oft repeated during the past two hundred and fifty years commencing,

> "Let us, with a gladsome mind,
> Praise the Lord, for He is kind."

The well-known hymn, "Sweet hour of prayer," was penned by the blind preacher, Rev. W. W. Walford who, sitting in darkness, could say from blest experience,

FANNY J. CROSBY.

> "In seasons of distress and grief,
> My soul has often found relief,
> And oft escaped the tempter's snare,
> By thy return, sweet hour of prayer."

No one in our day is doing more by means of her poetic pen to remove the scales from the blind eyes of sinners than the one whose likeness is given on a preceding page. No name is more familiar, or associated with more precious Sunday school hymns, than that of "Fanny Crosby." Although unable to see a line of one of her many hymns she has written; yet by and by she will surely behold a bright array of starry gems that they have gathered for the Saviour's crown.

What pen can number the millions whose voices have risen in song while singing her hymns which begin:—

> "Safe in the arms of Jesus,
> Safe on his gentle breast,
> There by his love o'ershadowed,
> Sweetly my soul shall rest."

> "Pass me not, O gentle Saviour,
> Hear my humble cry;
> While on others thou art smiling,
> Do not pass me by."

Fanny J. Crosby was born at South East, Putman Co., New York, in 1823. When about six weeks old she lost her sight through cold and improper treatment. "A warm poultice," says she, "laid on my eyes did the mischief and caused the loss of sight in a moment." Early in life she seemed to have a keen sense of right and wrong, and also evinced that poetic talent by which she has gained so much celebrity in later years. Her first piece was written when only about eight years of age, and was entitled, "Elegy to a little Robin." When about twelve years old she came to New York City to be educated in the "Institution for the Blind." After pursuing her studies for seven years, she became a teacher in the same Institution, and was thus employed for eleven years. Here in 1844, she issued a volume, entitled: "The Blind Girl and other Poems;" in 1849, another work: "Monterey and other poems."

In the fall of 1851, she united with the 30th Street Methodist E. Church, in charge of the Rev. John D. Black. Shortly previous, she was awakened from the death-sleep of sin, in an unusual manner, which she thus describes:—

"My conversion was owing to a dream. I had a dear friend who was a devoted Christian man. After saying one night the Lord's prayer, I was thinking, while going asleep, how hard it was to say and feel, 'Thy will be done.' During my sleep, I dreamed that I was summoned to the death chamber of my friend. He looked up to me and said: 'Fanny, can you give me up?' I said: 'No, I cannot, I'm afraid I cannot.' 'Why,' said he, 'would you chain a spirit to earth that longs to fly away and be at rest.' I replied, 'I cannot do it with my own strength, but by the grace of God assisting me, I will try.' He said: 'I want you to make me one promise. Think well before you make it, and remember you are making it to a dying man. Will you promise to meet me in heaven?' I paused for a moment, and looking in his face I said: 'I do promise to meet you in heaven.' A calm, unearthly radiance spread over his face, his eyes closed and he passed away. I woke from my dream, and never rested till I found peace, and could say from the heart, 'Thy will be done.' This was in Oct. 1851."

The experience of this "echo of the pure and holy throng" is well expressed in her sweet hymn, "The Bright Forever:"—

"Breaking through the clouds that gather
O'er the christian's natal skies,

> Distant beams, like floods of glory,
> Fill our soul with glad surprise;
> And we almost hear the echo
> Of the pure and holy throng,
> In the bright, the bright forever,
> In the summer-land of song.
>
> CHORUS:—
> On the banks beyond the river,
> We shall meet no more to sever;
> In the bright, the bright forever,
> In the summer-land of song."

In 1858, she was married to Mr. Alexander Van Alstyne, who is the author of some choice pieces of music, and possessed quite a musical talent. Mrs. Van Alstyne, having been so widely known by her maiden name, Fanny J. Crosby, it is still retained in connection with her hymns, though of late years some few of her productions are accredited to Mrs. Van Alstyne, or Mrs. F. J. Van Alstyne.

Her husband can enter into hearty sympathy with her sightless condition, as he also is blind, and was formerly a teacher in an Institution for the Blind. Both of their mental visions are, however, clear, and the sky above beams with brightness around. He is enabled by his sweet strains of music to guild the passing moments, and she with her flowers of poesy to make their feet ever pass through the pleasant summer-land of song. During the last four years of Mr. Bradbury's life, Mrs. Van Alstyne was in his employ. The first hymn she wrote for him was the one sung by his friends in his dying moments, and the first one sung by the children at his funeral.

> "We are going, we are going
> To a home beyond the skies."

While seated together, in his office, one bright autumn day, Mr. Bradbury spake of his anticipated death, and said: "Fanny, take up the work where I leave it. It will not be long till you will come to that beautiful region too. I'll wait for you on the bank of the river." It was a touching scene when, in after days, she was led to the coffin of her departed friend, and lifted the cold hand of clay, to bid a painful adieu. Faithfully has she complied with the dying request of her sainted friend to carry on the work. Through the liberal support granted her for her productions, by Messrs Biglow and Main, she has ever since been enabled to devote her whole time to the composition of hymns.

Fanny Crosby has a wonderful faculty for impromptu composition. Many of her best pieces have flowed out of her soul like sparkling water from a fountain. One day Mr. Doane came into her room hurriedly, saying, "Fanny, I want you to write a hymn on 'Safe in the arms of Jesus.'" At the same time, he sat down and played the melody. "I wrote it," said Fanny, "in twenty minutes. My heart was in it."

This, she says, has proven to be one of the most popular hymns she ever wrote. When it first welled up from the warm hearts of thousands, in Spurgeon's Tabernacle, in London, the effect was so grand, that he with streaming eyes, cried out at the close: "That is *so* good. Let us have it over again."

At another time, Mr. Doane came in, saying: "Fanny, I want you to write," and as he struck the keys of the instrument, there flowed from the lips of the blind poetess, the words of the popular hymn, beginning:—

"There's a gentle voice within, calls away."

Under the same inspiration and at the same time, she composed another hymn that is often sung:—

"Jesus, keep me near the cross,
    There a precious fountain,
Free to all—a healing stream,
    Flows from Calvary's mountain,"

with the familiar chorus words:—

> "In the cross, in the cross
> Be my glory ever;
> Till my raptured soul shall find
> Rest beyond the river."

A touching incident occurred in New York in connection with the singing of the last hymn.

A small boy was run over by a Third Avenue railroad car and taken to a hospital. A few moments before his death he said: "May I sing?" After clasping his little hands and saying the Lord's prayer, he broke out in singing the hymn,

> "Jesus, keep me near the cross."

His voice gradually grew weaker as he sang:—

> "Near the cross I'll watch and wait,
> Hoping, trusting ever,
> Till I reach the golden strand,
> Just beyond the river."

and with these words upon his lips he crossed the river.

One summer evening, Fanny Crosby was present at a meeting in the Water Street Mission in New York, when a number of sailors were present. One of their number arose and said that for many years he had lived far from God—a reckless life—until strolling along the streets the first Sunday after his vessel had landed, he happened to hear music proceeding from that building. He stopped and listened, and was induced to enter while they were singing:—

> "Safe in the arms of Jesus."

It so stirred his soul, that he rested not till he was "Safe in the arms of Jesus."

Fanny has been a busy writer. About six hundred of her Sunday school hymns have been printed, and three hundred miscellaneous poems. Mr. H. P. Main says: "We have also about one thousand of her unpublished hymns which will appear in due season."

Mrs. Elvina M. Hall.

IN central Pennsylvania is a spring of water that rushes forth from under an immense rock, in force sufficient to make vocal at once some adjacent flour-mills, and to make green the meadows through which it spreads its life-giving waters. So there are some hymns that have gushed spontaneously from some overflowing heart, and instantly have been like the "river, the streams whereof make glad the city of our God."

Beside the organ in a choir gallery of the Monument Street Methodist E. Church, in Baltimore, Md., there started such a stream of soul-saving influence in 1865.

On a Sabbath morning, one of the singers had knelt in prayer at the opening service, led by the pastor, the Rev. S. Barnes. Feeling her own weakness and unworthiness, she says, she inwardly exclaimed: "O Lord, I am *so* poor and helpless, what have I to bring to Thee," when there seemed to flow into my soul a sweet echo of the words of my hymn:—

"I hear the Saviour say, Thy strength indeed is small;
Child of weakness, watch and pray, Find in me thine all in all."

"That these heaven-born thoughts might not escape, I took my pencil and commenced writing them down on the fly-leaf of the 'Lute of Zion,' and so rapidly did the words pour into the heart, that before the prayer was ended, I had completed the hymn, and, as I rose from my knees, the chorus words rose jubilantly to my lips:—

"Jesus paid it all, All to him I owe,
Sin had left a crimson stain, He washed it white as snow."

The author of these divinely inspired words was Mrs. Elvina M. Hall, who was born in Alexandria, Va., in 1818, but for many years past has been a resident of Baltimore City. When but ten years of age she found her Saviour, and has ever since been a useful member of the Church.

Mrs. Annie S. Hawks.

AMID the trials and temptations that beset the path of the Christian pilgrim, how natural the language of the hymn:—

> "I need Thee every hour,
> Most gracious Lord."

Doubtless many happy greetings await the author of these lines as she enters the bright mansions above.

Mrs. Annie S. Hawks was born in Hoosick, New York, May 28, 1835. For the several past years she has been a resident of Brooklyn, New York. Although from early life she has given much attention to educational and literary pursuits, yet there was not much publicity given to her effusions till about 1868, when her pastor, the Rev. R. Lowry, discovering her talent, encouraged her to write for the good of others. Among the first and tenderest of her hymns was, "Why weepest thou?" in "Bright Jewels." Her songs have also appeared in "Pure Gold," "Royal Diadem," "Brightest and Best," "Temple Anthems," and "Tidal Wave," and have been copied in numerous other works. Among her songs best known are:—

> "Who'll be the next?"
> "In the valley."
> "Here am I."
> "Yield, O yield."
> "Wholly Thine."
> "Living for Christ."
> 'I need Thee every hour."

The last hymn was the outgrowth of her own experience. Having sent it to the Rev. Mr. Lowry, he caught the spirit of the hymn and gave it musical expression.

It was first sung in the National Baptist Sunday School Convention in Cincinnati, Nov. 20, 1872, by three thousand people. Its popularity began from that hour.

Rev. Robert Lowry, D. D.

ON a very hot summer day, in 1864, a pastor was seated in his parlor in Brooklyn, N. Y. It was a time when an epidemic was sweeping through the city, and draping many persons and dwellings in mourning. All around friends and acquaintances were passing away to the spirit-land in large numbers. The question began to arise in the heart, with unusual emphasis, "Shall we meet again? We are parting at the river of death, shall we meet at the river of life?" "Seating myself at the organ," says he, "simply to give vent to the pent up emotions of the heart, the words and music of the hymn began to flow out, as if by inspiration:—

> "Shall we gather at the river,
> Where bright angel feet have trod."

That pastor was the Rev. Mr. Lowry, who has since become so widely known in connection with Sunday school song. He was born in Philadelphia, March 12, 1826. In early boyhood he began to throw off scraps of songs and composed melodies before he knew anything of harmony, yet publishers picked up his airs and issued them, as he says, "with all their harmonic crudeness." As he came into the circle of musical men, he detected his own deficiencies and gave himself to the thorough study of harmony.

In early life he learned to love his Saviour, and in 1854, graduated in the Lewisburg University, and began the work of the gospel ministry. His first charge was the Baptist church at West Chester, Pa. His subsequent pastorates were in New York City and Brooklyn, N. Y. In 1869, he was elected professor of Belles Lettres in the University, and pastor of the Baptist Church at Lewisburg, Pa. After continuing this double duty for six years, the pressure of the work, together with the

ROBERT LOWRY.

composition of music books, was so great that he was compelled to withdraw for rest, and is at the present a resident of Plainfield, N. J.

The books with which his name has been connected have been the most successful of all that have been prepared for Sunday schools. The "Bright Jewels," issued in 1869, attained a circulation of half a million copies in four years; "Pure Gold" has reached a sale of a million copies; "Royal Diadem" and "Brightest and Best" are following in the same successful career.

Among his best known pieces we may mention the following:—

"Shall we gather at the river,"
"Shall we know each other there,"
"Who'll be the next,"
"Weeping will not save me,"
"One more day's work for Jesus,"
"Rifted rock."

"We are going down the valley" was written under peculiar circumstances. Says he, "I was sick in bed, propped up with pillows. At the same time three persons, who had been members of my congregation, two of them Sunday school scholars, were lying dead within a stone's throw of my house. It distressed me that I could not attend any of these funerals. This extraordinary mortality impressed me deeply. My feeling was so oppressive that I could relieve it only in song. On the back of an envelope I wrote the refrain, and the music came with it. The hymn followed in close connection, and the whole song took shape the same afternoon. This also was born, not made.

W. Howard Doane.

THE names of Messrs. Doane and Lowry are as familiar as household words, being so prominently associated as authors of some of our most popular singing books, such as "Pure Gold," "Royal Diadem," and "Brightest and Best."

Mr. W. Howard Doane was born in Preston, Conn., February 3, 1831. In early life he gave evidences of that musical talent that has given him in later years so much celebrity. When but fourteen years of age he composed a long metre tune. At sixteen he was the leader of a choir, and at seventeen both conductor and organist. About this time he commenced the study of harmony and thorough bass under the most eminent teachers of the day, and also to compose songs with piano accompaniment. Music with him is a sort of second nature, a constant source of enjoyment and delight. So that many of his pieces have spontaneously bubbled up from the musical depths within. Thus the music of "Safe in the arms of Jesus" swept over the cords of his soul, while the cars were sweeping through the land on a journey to New York. At another time, while riding through the White Mountains on the old style of stage coach, the music of the "Old, old story" began to float through the inner man.

Among his best pieces which have taken a warm hold on the Christian heart, and which will never be forgotten we may mention those entitled:—

'Pass me not, O gentle Saviour,"

"Jesus, keep me near the cross,"

"More love to thee, O Christ,"

"Take the name of Jesus with you.'

Praise from a Boat Cabin.

A HIBERNIAN asking a minister to come and see his child, the following conversation ensued:—

"'What is your name, sir, and where do you live?'

"'My name is Pater M———: I live on an ould canal-boat at the fut of Harrison Street. I wint there whin I was burnt out; and nobody at all has driv me out of it.'

"'And what is the matter with your child?'

"'Och! and is it Kitty, my own little darling Kitty. The only child I've lift of the six that has been born til me? Och! Kitty! she was playing about on a ship where I was til wark, and she fell down the hatchway and broke her leg, and poor Kitty's leg is not set right, your riverence, for I have no money til pay a docther. Och! poor Kitty! and I've nothing to give her to ate, your riverence.'

"'Well, Peter, I will come down and see your Kitty, and see what can be done for you.'

"I did so, and found a wretched state of things. The poor little suffering child was overjoyed to see me. I remembered her countenance,—a sweet, mild little girl, not yet five years of age. She lay upon the side seat of an old canal-boat which had been laid up for the winter. There was no fire, though it was a bitter cold day,—no chair, no bed, no food, scarcely an article of furniture or any comfort whatever. I did what I could to relieve the wants of the little sufferer. I asked her if she could read. No, she could not read a word; 'but I can sing,' said she. 'What can you sing?' 'Something I learned at Sabbath-School.' 'Well, what is it you can sing, Kitty?' In a moment her sweet little voice broke out,

"'There is a happy land,
Far, far away,
Where saints in glory stand
Bright, bright as day.'"

Philip Phillips.

MR. PHILIP PHILLIPS is widely known as the "Singing Pilgrim," and of late has extended his pilgrimage around the world, making the entire circuit vocal with song. Like Mr. Sankey, he has been privileged to reach and sway great multitudes with the eloquence of musical speech, and to preach effective song sermons. Mr. Phillips was born in Chatauqua County, New York, August 13, 1834. In early life he lost his mother. His father, having a large family to care for, little Philip was apprenticed to a farmer until he should attain to the age of twenty-one. Amid his daily toil his soul was full of song, and in his spare moments he began the study of music. Availing himself of every opportunity of attending upon musical schools and conventions, under Dr. Lowell Mason and other eminent teachers, he was enabled by the time he was seventeen, to begin his life work of "Singing for Jesus." When nineteen years of age his employer released him from service, and he was permitted to give his undivided attention to the teaching and study of music. While singing at musical and other conventions, and large Sunday school gatherings, he became extensively known as a sweet singer in Israel, and so extensive has been his sphere of labor that he has held his "Evenings of Sacred Song" in every State of the Union, and in all sections of Canada and Great Britain, as well as in India, Australia, and other remote parts of the globe.

Having given his heart to the Lord when but a boy of thirteen, he early blossomed in the vineyard of the Lord, and in after years gave to his first publication the expressive title: "Early Blossom." These blossom leaves ended in abundant fruit, as twenty thousand copies of the book were sold. Soon after there followed his

PHILIP PHILLIPS.

Philip Phillips continued.

"Musical Leaves," that spread over the land like the leaves of the tree of life, fragrant with that odor which is "for the healing of the nations." Soon after there came treading through the land his "Singing Pilgrim," which made many homes vocal with the name of Jesus.

The singing of Mr. Phillips' song, "I will sing for Jesus," has been attended with happy results. One evening a great throng had gathered in the Effingham Theater, London, in connection with William Booth's mission, to hear Mr. Phillips "sing for Jesus." The song was wafted to the ears of a dispairing man, while on his way to the London docks to commit suicide. It arrested his attention. As he listened the inquiry was made to echo through his soul,

> "Can there overtake me
> Any dark disaster,
> While I sing for Jesus,
> My blessed, blessed Master?"

His purpose was thwarted. It brought home to his heart the memory of a mother's prayers and praises in his early days, and brought him broken-hearted to the feet of his Saviour. So that afterwards he could say:—

> "I will sing for Jesus;
> His name alone revealing,
> Shall be my sweetest music,
> When heart and flesh are failing."

In the early part of Mr. Phillips' career he was filling an engagement in the West. While singing the words,

> "Can there overtake me," etc.

his store with all its contents was burned, throwing him out of business capital, and thereby forcing him to the writing and singing of sacred songs. While this seemed like dark disaster it proved to be but the dark cloud that brought a blessing in disguise. On the following page we give an illustration of the sentiment contained in one of Mr. Phillips' hymn, the "Home of the Soul."

Echo of the Heavenly Choir.

> "Till I fancy but thinly the vail intervenes
> Between the fair city and me."

SOPHIE Rubeti, eighteen years of age, died at Highland, Kansas Jan. 25, 1861.

Not long before her death, she said to one supporting her, "*Is not the village band playing this evening?*" On being told it was not, she said, "*I hear delightful music*, I thought the band was playing. Oh! it is delightful, *listen*, and *I think you can hear it*," and added, "I have now lost the use of one of my hands, (it was cold in death,) but if I could use it, I would raise it and *clap both my hands for joy in the beautiful prospect.*" She continued, as she had strength, to exhort and to praise, until just before her departure she exclaimed, "Jesus is coming—*they are coming*—raise me up," and in a few seconds, without a struggle or a moan, she ceased to breathe.

The following verses were written in her own hand, on the inner lid of her Bible:—

> "Worlds should not bribe me back to tread
> Again life's weary waste,
> To see again my days o'erspread
> With all the gloomy past.
> My home henceforth is in heaven,
> Earth, sea, and sun adieu,
> All heaven unfolded to mine eyes,
> I have no sight for you."

AS a mother bent over a death bed, her daughter Margaret said, "Kiss me dearest Mamma, and fold your arms about me, that I may die in them."

When this was done, a heavenly lustre lit up her countenance as she exclaimed, "*I hear the songs of angels*, and go to join them, and to be forever with Jesus." She then bade adieu to earth.

"Jesus Is Right Here."

HOW expressive these words, as uttered by a little one, in the valley of the shadow of death.

He had sent for his Sunday school teacher.

As he drew near the death bed, Johnny exclaimed, "I am not afraid to die now, dear teacher, *Jesus is right here*, and *he* makes it *very light*." "Sing, father," said he, "Sing,—

"There is a fountain filled with blood,
Drawn from Immanuel's veins."

The father tried to sing, but his strong voice failed him. Then the mother with faltering voice, commenced the hymn. And amid the echoes of this sweet hymn he passed up to the hallelujahs of the heavenly world.

Truthfully the marble grave stone says of him,

"NOT LOST,
BUT GONE BEFORE."

A little girl, who had a sweet realization of the nearness of the Saviour, whispered, with her dying breath, "Father, take me."

Her father, who sat weeping by her bedside, thought she meant him, and so lifted her up into his lap. She smiled and thanked him, and said, "*I spoke to my heavenly Father*," and then died.

Ira D. Sankey.

A FEW years ago nearly every one thought that we had reached the culmination in the Sunday school world, that its utmost capacity for good was comprehended, but the clearer light of each new year's experience reveals our mistake. So it has been in the sphere of music. The wonderful effects that have been lately developed in the soul-saving power of sanctified music, and of singing *only for Jesus*, have shown to the church great undeveloped resources in that direction. And if the sweet ring of a few consecrated "bells," has produced such a deep impression, as the chariot of the Lord passes through the land, what may we not expect, when we shall live in the full meridian of that day, when "there shall be upon *all* the bells of the horses, Holiness unto the Lord."

Hitherto the world has had some idea of the reading and singing of hymns, but not the full meaning of "Speaking, and teaching and admonishing one another in Psalms and hymns and spiritual songs." New beauty has appeared in this portion of the holy writ since Mr. Sankey and other sweet singers have been speaking to and teaching and admonishing the great multitudes in the melodious strains of the gospel in song.

Mr. Ira D. Sankey was born in Edinburg, Pennsylvania, in 1840. With four brothers and sisters, he grew up, under the soul saving influences of godly parents, in connection with the Methodist Episcopal church. His conversion took place in his sixteenth year, during a series of revival meetings held in King's Chapel. At the commencement of these extra services, he seemed quite indifferent, but night after night an old steward in the church was wont to urge him to lay hold on eternal life, and persisted in his exhortations, until he at length yielded to the claims of the gospel and united his destiny

IRA D. SANKEY.

with the people of God. His parents shortly afterwards removing to New Castle, Pennsylvania, he was there received into full membership with the Methodist E. Church. When about twenty years of age he became the superintendent of a large Sabbath school, and in this capacity commenced his career of singing the gospel into the hearts of the people. Mr. Moody, having heard him at the International Convention of the Young Men's Christian Association, at Indianapolis, said to him, after an introduction: "I want you?" "What for?" was the reply. "To help me in my work at Chicago." "I cannot leave my business." "You must," said Mr. Moody, "I have been looking for you for the last eight years."

After looking up to heaven for direction, Mr. Sankey yielded to the request, and the two united their tact and talents in winning souls to Christ.

Solo-singing had been in vogue before, but it had been looked upon rather as a "method of pious enjoyment," than as a "means of grace and salvation." After some two or three years of labor together in Chicago and other cities, they set sail for England on June 7, 1872, as Mr. Moody said: "To win ten thousand souls to Christ." On landing at Liverpool they discovered that the two friends, by whom they had been invited to England, had recently died.

Their first meeting was held at York, in a small room of the Young Men's Christian Association, and was attended by only eight persons. But from that small beginning there started a work that spread like a mighty wave of salvation over Great Britain.

At York an interesting conversion took place in connection with the singing of Mr. Sankey. While engaged in singing at his private lodgings, the people would gather in the streets, in great crowds to hear him.

Among the number was a woman who was so deeply convicted of her sins, by one of the hymns sung, that she sought an interview with Mr. Sankey, and was at once led by him to Christ.

This was the first of that long series of song-trophies which became so characteristic of the great English revival. One secret of Mr. Sankey's success was the prominence he gave to hymns having a Scriptural basis, such as "Jesus of Nazareth passeth by," Almost persuaded," and "The Ninety-and-nine." This helped to open the way to the hearts of the psalm-singers of Scotland, who had so long been averse to instrumental music in the sanctuary. One writer says, "His singing has swept away our prejudices; no one has thought of arguing whether or not it is suited to public worship, because every one feels that it is. What Mr. Sankey does is to preach by song. He is no performer. We think when we hear him of *what* he is singing, not of *how* he sings. That a man should stand up at the music stool and pray that the song he is about to sing may carry a message to many hearts, or that he should, in a short speech, ask Christians to pray while he is singing, that God will bless his song, is a thing that none of us ever heard of before."

A Scotchman came to his pastor one day, saying, "I cannot do with the hymns. They are all the time in my head and I cannot get them out. The psalms never trouble me that way." "Very well," said the pastor, "then I think you should keep to the hymns."

In connection with Mr. Sankey's singing have been many illustrations of Herbert's couplet:—

> "A verse may win him who the gospel flies,
> And turn delight into sacrifice."

A young lady who had been led to Christ was anxious to know what to do in relation to a wild young man to whom she was engaged to be married.

While paying her a visit one evening he noticed a great change in her mind, and asked her what it meant. After telling him of her conversion and her fears that she would not be happy in living with one who had no regard for religion, he relieved her mind by saying, "Don't be troubled, Mary, I have been to the meetings too. I went down there the other night just to see what the fun was, and before I had been there long Mr. Sankey sang something that went straight to my heart. So now I am a Christian too and we will go to heaven together."

A comic singer was going upon the stage to sing a comic song, in England, when suddenly a verse of a Sunday school hymn so filled his mind as to crowd out the song, and he was unable to perform his part, when the manager at once dismissed him from his service. To recover from his failure he thought he would write a comedy ending with a burlesque on Moody and Sankey. In order to sharpen the edge of his satire he went to hear them for himself. At the meeting while waiting to gather material for his comedy he was so wrought upon by what he heard that he confessed his sin, and sent up the Bartimeus cry for mercy. After peace was obtained he began at once to sing the new song of redeeming love.

While riding in the cars in Scotland, Mr. Sankey met with the words of the hymn, "Ninety and nine," in the corner of a newspaper. A few days later the subject of of the "Shepherd" was under consideration at one of their meetings, when the hymn seemed so appropriate to the remarks made that he was led as if by inspiration at once to give musical expression to the words by singing the tune to which they have become wedded ever since. The unwritten melody surprised Mr. Moody who asked, "Where did you get it? It is the best piece you ever sung,"

Plan of Illustrated Sermons.

In the preparation of these sermons Mr. Long has employed eminent artists to paint on canvas, (making a roll for each discourse) first the text in letters large enough to be seen over the largest building, then underneath a painting of the occasion of the text, after this as many other verses of Scripture with illustrations below as there are points in the sermons or links in the chain of thought. By means of a frame twelve feet high, placed in the rear, the illustrations appear above the top of the pulpit. Suspended on three rollers they revolve silently and as quickly as the turning of a leaf of a written sermon.

The frame is made of tin-ware, so narrow that it occupies but a handbreadth of space behind the pulpit sofa, in telescopic form, so that the parts drop one into the other, and can be put up or taken down in five minutes. It is all concealed with becoming drapery, so as to form a neat back ground to any pulpit, and the audience see nothing but the Scripture text and its illustration underneath.

For example, one sermon is on the text *"Thy heart is not right in the sight of God."* Below the text is seen the occasion of the words, to wit: Simon Magus disclosing the state of his heart by offering money to the Apostles with which to buy the Holy Ghost. Then follow various Scripture illustrations of the heart as it appears in God's sight. A miniature view of one of these illustrations is given on the opposite page, showing Solomon's vain endeavor to satisfy his heart with earthly good. In the scene is seen all the objects he found to be "vanity."

Department of Sunday School Song.

Portrait of Robert Raikes..21
Jubilee Gathering at Exeter Hall........................25
Portrait of Wm. B. Bradbury...27
Portrait of Mrs. Lydia Baxter...38
      Author of "There is a gate that stands ajar."
Portrait of P. P. Bliss..49
      Author of "'Almost persuaded' now to believe."
Portrait of Fanny J. Crosby...55
      Author of "Pass me not, O gentle Saviour."
Portrait of Rev. Robert Lowry, D. D..........................66
      Author of "Shall we gather at the river."
Portrait of Philip Phillips...71
      Author of "Still I am singing, Jesus is mine."
Portrait of Ira D. Sankey...77

Department of Sunday School Song.

Children's hosannas in Jerusalem 17
Watts' hymns for children 18
Raikes and the origin of Sunday Schools 20
Firing off a cannon at the overthrow of a Sunday School 23
Hymns for the grand Sunday School Jubilee 24
Wm. B. Bradbury's life and songs 26-35
Origin of "I want to be an angel." 36-37
Mrs. Lydia Baxter's life and hymns 38-45
A child who could not sing "Jesus is mine." 46-47
P. P. Bliss and his hymns 48-53
Fanny J. Crosby's life and hymns 54-61
Mrs. E. M. Hall and origin of "I hear the Saviour say" 62
Mrs. Annie S. Hawks, author of "I need Thee every hour." ... 63
Rev. R. Lowry's life and hymns 64-67
W. Howard Doane and his songs 68
Philip Phillips' life and songs 70-73
Echoes of the heavenly choir 74
Jesus is right here 75
Ira. D. Sankey's life and songs 76-81
Illustrated Sermons 82-83

AGENTS WANTED
FOR THE
GRAND NEW BOOK,

PRESENT CONFLICT

OF

SCIENCE WITH RELIGION,

OR

MODERN SKEPTICISM MET ON ITS OWN GROUND.

The grandest theme and most vital question of the day. By the author of "SCIENCE AND THE BIBLE." Every man, woman and child wants to read it. It gives the Christian a reason for his **Faith**, proves the **wonderful discoveries of Science in harmony with God's Word**, disproves the **Tyndall assertions**, and destroys the **Darwin Theory**. It sells beyond all expectation. First agent sold 33, second 17, third 25, first week. First agent, 31 second week. Everybody buys it.

"The volume before us is not only ably written, but opportune, meeting modern skepticism on its own chosen ground. The reader is furnished with irrefutable arguments in support of the claims of the Christian religion against the sophistry of those who would exalt science above Divine Revelation. At the same time the author fully appreciates the influence of science, but repudiates what modern skepticism claims as science, as wholly destitute of its essential elements. The harmony of Science and Religion he admits, but rejects as science what Tyndall, Darwin and others claim it to be. The work meets a state of things long felt as dangerous to the best interests of every Christian community, and puts a check upon the pretentious claims of the learned skeptics of this age. We have rarely seen a work better adapted to the present state of the public mind, and more fully to have answered the pretended arguments and sophistry of the learned infidels of the day, than this most valuable work.

"The book is destined to occupy a high position in the literary world. We hope and believe in its general circulation it will meet favor commensurate with its great merits. A careful study cannot fail to accomplish the glorious object intended by its learned author."—*Rev. W. H. Babcock, in St. Louis Christian Advocate.*

Send for circular and terms to agents.

P. W. ZIEGLER & CO., Publishers,

518 Arch Street, Philadelphia, Pa., or
201 South Clark Street, Chicago, Ill.

Lightning Source UK Ltd.
Milton Keynes UK
UKHW022011030521
383075UK00003B/225